Praise for *Law, War and the Penumbra of Uncertainty*

In this innovative, inter-disciplinary and imaginative study, Sam Selvadurai asks how much the prior strategic and ethical views of international lawyers, as well as their general approach to law, influence their views on the use of force. He offers suggestions drawn from risk management and strategic assessment to help them to navigate their way through hard cases.

Sir Lawrence Freedman, Emeritus Professor of War Studies, King's College London

Selvadurai's seminal book on the law of force navigates skilfully and elegantly between empirical, theoretical and doctrinal arguments to produce an informed and original analysis of decision-making cultures on the use of force. Drawing on interviews and surveys, this book makes important claims about what ought to be required in decisions about resort to force, claims that will no doubt advance discourse in international law, foreign policy and legal philosophy alike.

Professor Guglielmo Verdirame, King's College London

The book takes a unique approach, subjecting doctrinal legal questions to a forensic examination of how they are interpreted and applied in practice. It provides a bridge between law and policy, uncovering the reality of how States formulate their legal position on use of force. As such, it will be of much interest to scholars of law as well as those seeking to understand policy and decision-making in this area.

Professor Noam Lubell, University of Essex

At a time when the *jus ad bellum* is under strain and having to demonstrate its relevance to new challenges, Selvadurai's book provides an insightful and compelling inter-disciplinary investigation into the particularly problematic issues of legal and factual uncertainty that perennially plague assessments regarding the decision to resort to war.

Professor Christian Henderson, University of Sussex

'Hard cases make bad law' as they say, but Sam Selvadurai analyses precisely these 'hard cases' to show that the law on the use of force, the *jus ad bellum*, is necessarily indeterminate, what he terms the 'penumbra of uncertainty'. This is an interdisciplinary work that is impressive in its breadth and scope, but also in its depth of analysis, which is supported by a number of structured interviews with practitioners.

Dr Natasha Kuhrt, Department of War Studies, King's College London

Dr Selvadurai's book offers an insightful and skilful analysis and explanation of how legal decisions about the use of force are made in situations of legal and factual uncertainty by using innovative methods of inquiry, combining legal risk management and strategic intelligence analysis. The proposed risk management framework provides a systematic guide for assessing the merits of alternative choices and possible outcomes. This is very much a book about the law and politics underpinning use of force decisions and, for this reason, it is a 'must-read' for government lawyers, judges and scholars.

Professor Nicholas Tsagourias, University of Sheffield

This is a monumental, interdisciplinary volume that confirms how law cannot be separated from politics in international affairs and how black letter law, despite the naive expectations of some, is impossible in matters of war and peace. Strategy and the legitimacy of international law are deeply intertwined in a hazy twilight of interpretative and factual uncertainty. But, crucially, as this brilliant analysis uniquely shows, lawyers' contrasting interpretations on the use of force are politically, ethically and culturally embedded; to echo the great Bradley F. Smith on the Nuremberg judges, international lawyers cannot escape their prejudices and these both shape their legal opinions and fuel continuing uncertainty. This rich study blends law, politics, ethics and strategy to chart the way forward.

Professor James Gow, Professor of International Peace and Security, King's College London

In a masterly manner, this book, by examining the decision-making processes actually used, seeks to answer how decisions are taken on the use of force, amidst the uncertainty of facts and law, and recommends best practice. A 'must read' for those involved in such decisions.

Professor Charles Garraway, Fellow, Human Rights Centre, University of Essex

His curiosity aroused by service in the UK's FCO, Dr Selvadurai has written a brilliant and startlingly original text on *jus ad bellum*, the law of war. He draws on analytical philosophy on 'vagueness', and on close analysis of 15 scholarly texts, and interviews with 31 scholars and practitioners, to develop a framework with which to challenge the claim that international law is fatally undermined by indeterminacy. Essential reading.

Professor Bill Bowring, Birkbeck College, University of London

Dr Selvadurai's book deserves praise because it does what other studies of the *jus ad bellum* have not done yet: it explores how legal reasoning works in this area of law by also using concepts and methods from other disciplines, including interviews and surveys with UK-based international lawyers. The result is a fascinating inside look into the uncertainties and subjectivities of the law governing the use of force and its 'specifically indeterminate' nature. Not to be missed.

Professor Marco Roscini, University of Westminster

LAW, WAR AND THE PENUMBRA OF UNCERTAINTY

This book argues that lawyers must often rely on contestable ethical and strategic intuitions when dealing with legal and factual uncertainties in 'hard cases' of resort to force. This area of international law relies on multiple tests which can be interpreted in different ways, do not yield binary 'yes/no' answers, and together define 'paradigms' of lawful and unlawful force. Controversial cases of force differ from these paradigms, requiring lawyers to assess complex, incomplete factual evidence, and to forecast the immediate and long-term consequences of using and not using force. Legal rules cannot resolve such uncertainties; instead, techniques from legal risk management, strategic intelligence assessment and political forecasting may help. This study develops these arguments using the philosophy of knowledge, socio-legal, politico-strategic and ethical theory, structured interviews and a survey with thirty-one UK-based international lawyers, and systematic analysis of key International Court of Justice cases and scholarly assessments of US-led interventions.

Sam Selvadurai is Visiting Senior Research Fellow at the Department of War Studies in King's College London. He has worked in the Foreign, Commonwealth and Development Office since 1993.

Law, War and the Penumbra of Uncertainty

LEGAL CULTURES, EXTRA-LEGAL REASONING AND THE USE OF FORCE

SAM SELVADURAI
King's College, University of London

CAMBRIDGE
UNIVERSITY PRESS

CAMBRIDGE
UNIVERSITY PRESS

Shaftesbury Road, Cambridge CB2 8EA, United Kingdom

One Liberty Plaza, 20th Floor, New York, NY 10006, USA

477 Williamstown Road, Port Melbourne, VIC 3207, Australia

314–321, 3rd Floor, Plot 3, Splendor Forum, Jasola District Centre, New Delhi – 110025, India

103 Penang Road, #05–06/07, Visioncrest Commercial, Singapore 238467

Cambridge University Press is part of Cambridge University Press & Assessment, a department of the University of Cambridge.

We share the University's mission to contribute to society through the pursuit of education, learning and research at the highest international levels of excellence.

www.cambridge.org
Information on this title: www.cambridge.org/9781009054874

DOI: 10.1017/9781009051934

First published 2022
First paperback edition 2026

A catalogue record for this publication is available from the British Library

Library of Congress Cataloging-in-Publication data
NAMES: Selvadurai, Sam, author.
TITLE: Law, war and the penumbra of uncertainty : legal cultures, extra-legal reasoning and the use of force / Sam Selvadurai, King's College University of London.
DESCRIPTION: Cambridge, United Kingdom ; New York, NY : Cambridge University Press, 2021. | Based on author's thesis (doctoral – King's College London, 2020) issued under title: Law, war and the penumbra of uncertainty : legal and factual uncertainty and extra-legal reasoning in the jus ad bellum. | Includes bibliographical references and index.
IDENTIFIERS: LCCN 2021045498 (print) | LCCN 2021045499 (ebook) | ISBN 9781316511985 (hardback) | ISBN 9781009051934 (ebook)
SUBJECTS: LCSH: War (International law) | Legal certainty.
CLASSIFICATION: LCC KZ6385 .S45 2021 (print) | LCC KZ6385 (ebook) | DDC 341.6–dc23/eng/20220131
LC record available at https://lccn.loc.gov/2021045498
LC ebook record available at https://lccn.loc.gov/2021045499

ISBN 978-1-316-51198-5 Hardback
ISBN 978-1-009-05487-4 Paperback

Contents

Figures

Acknowledgements

I could not have written this book without the support and encouragement of many academic and professional colleagues, and of my family and friends.

Professor Guglielmo Verdirame QC was my wise, erudite and patient PhD supervisor at the Department of War Studies in King's College London, whose advice profoundly shaped my thesis. Professor Sir Lawrence Freedman and Professor Dapo Akande were forensic PhD examiners whose suggestions helped significantly in turning my thesis into a book. Dr Natasha Kuhrt was a consistently supportive second supervisor, and teacher of a course that foreshadowed my PhD. Conversations and lessons with Professor James Gow in his MA in International Peace and Security played a key role in developing my ideas. The late Dr David Fisher's inspirational course was the basis of my understanding of ethics and military conflict. Professor Marco Roscini expertly taught the *jus ad bellum* and *jus in bello* courses that underpinned my knowledge of these areas of international law. Professor Michael Rainsborough's course and our joint work on a journal article greatly enhanced my appreciation of strategic theory.

Fellow students and others actively participated in seminars where I shared and developed my ideas. Thirty-one international lawyers generously took part in the online survey and/or interviews that are crucial for this book's empirical research. King's granted me a doctoral studentship, which provided essential financial support for my research.

I am indebted to many colleagues at the Foreign, Commonwealth and Development Office. Supportive and understanding managers, colleagues and two patient job-share partners enabled me to continue working part-time for nine years while undertaking my research and writing. Informal conversations with several insightful colleagues greatly helped my thinking, and kept my research grounded in reality.

I thank Tom Randall and the team at Cambridge University Press for their support in the publication process. I am grateful to the anonymous readers, whose advice and suggestions greatly improved the book.

I thank my friends for sometimes heated, always intellectually stimulating conversations. Particular thanks go to Dr Robin Munro, for impromptu statistics tutorials and for finding the striking image for the book cover.

Most of all, I thank my whole family for their support and understanding over the past decade. In that time, my son Callum and daughter Hannah have grown from adorable children into wonderful young adults, while enduring the often distracted care of a parent writing a PhD. And my wife Louise has been an inspiration to me as she has made her own academic and professional journey, a source of steadfast and patient support, care and love, without whom I could not have completed this work.

1

Introduction

Investigating Law, War and the Penumbra of Uncertainty

Between these two points, indeed, the *is*, and the *ought to be*, so opposite as they frequently are in the eyes of other men, that spirit of obsequious *quietism* that seems constitutional in our Author, will scarce ever let him recognize a difference.

Jeremy Bentham, 'A Fragment on Government'[1]

INTRODUCTION

The law governing the resort to military force, the *jus ad bellum*, is the area of international law perhaps most critical to the very survival of states. It is also the field of international law that seeks to regulate how states initiate the kinds of military campaigns that have caused untold death and suffering throughout history. It is therefore unsurprising that this part of international law remains the subject of sharp controversy. Military interventions routinely provoke claims and counter-claims about their justification in law, as can be seen by the arguments about the legality of US-led military interventions in Iraq, Kosovo, Afghanistan and Syria, as well as around the lawfulness of Russia's interventions in Georgia and Ukraine. Such controversies persist in spite of the apparently clear rules in the UN Charter, and in the detailed further supplementary means of determining law provided by UN General Assembly declarations and International Court of Justice (ICJ) cases. This book examines such uncertainty and contestation, and specifically considers the effects of international lawyers' extra-legal political, strategic and ethical intuitions on their legal assessments of controversial cases engaging the *jus ad bellum*.

1 Jeremy Bentham, 'A Fragment on Government', in James H. Burns and H. L. A. Hart, eds., A *Comment on the Commentaries and* A *Fragment on Government* (Oxford: Clarendon Press, 2008), 498.

I was motivated to write this book by my own perhaps naïve surprise, as an official in the United Kingdom's Foreign, Commonwealth and Development Office (FCDO), that even respected international lawyers had fundamental disagreements about the legality of the US-led military interventions in Kosovo in 1999, Afghanistan in 2001 and of course Iraq in 2003. Like many FCDO officials, I had a basic understanding of international law and experience of working with the FCDO's international lawyers. So I had some sense that international law had 'grey areas', and that plausible legal arguments could often be advanced for opposing positions. However, I assumed even difficult legal questions ultimately always had a single correct answer, which the FCDO's lawyers could be relied upon to discover after sufficient study of doctrine, precedent and the relevant legal materials. Underpinning this assumption was a sense that such legal questions would ultimately be decided by some authoritative tribunal or other dispute resolution mechanism. It was the sharp and ultimately formally unresolved debates between respected international lawyers around the legality of use of force in Kosovo, Afghanistan and Iraq that led me to realise the naivety of this assumption, and to seek to deepen my knowledge of international law.

My studies showed me that many respected scholars had already examined such controversies in the *jus ad bellum*, through analysis of legal doctrine in treaties and other textual legal materials, in more or less formal expressions of state practice and *opinio juris*, in the decisions of the ICJ and other tribunals and in the writings of other legal scholars. But these analyses seemed to fail to take sufficient account of important aspects of the controversies they examined. A key point that such studies identified was that many wars fought today are different to the wars that many believe the drafters of the UN Charter envisaged when they framed the key provisions of their foundational treaty. Overt invasion of one state by another state for straightforward acquisition of territory or economic resources is rare. Instead, those who use military force internationally today advance other justifications: to defend themselves against terrorists, to avert an imminent attack, to protect their own citizens or other civilians from slaughter, or to enforce UN Security Council (UNSC) resolutions. Many of the scholarly works I studied noted that such controversial justifications for resort to force pointed to intrinsic features of uncertainty in the law, the operation of competing rules of legal interpretation, the potential for partisan politicisation of legal assessment, and lawyers' own beliefs about politics, strategy and ethics to skew their legal assessments. But the legal studies I read devoted relatively little effort to investigating these aspects of controversy in the *jus ad bellum*.

I found explanations advanced by critical legal theorists and legal realists of the political and power-based nature of international law also incomplete. Self-interest, the struggle for power and the dominance of and resistance to hegemonic discourses did not seem sufficient explanation for what appeared to be sincere, deeply held disagreements between highly regarded international lawyers about what the law permitted and prohibited in general and in specific cases. And none of these studies said much about how uncertainty and contestation might be shaped by the *factual* uncertainty around military crises, and by the law's apparent requirement for lawyers to make *forecasts* or counter-factual conjectures of the consequences of using and not using force.

I found potential new ways of thinking about these controversies in other fields within and outside law. Legal philosophers and philosophers of knowledge have investigated vagueness in law. Socio-legal scholars have examined competing legal cultures in legal systems. Scholars of international politics, ethics, strategic culture and political psychology have considered how actors' competing underlying beliefs about the world can determine behaviour in international relations. And the literature around legal risk management, strategic intelligence analysis and political forecasting has considered techniques for dealing with similar dilemmas.

This book is the first that seeks to synthesise approaches from these different disciplines to offer new ways of understanding and dealing with uncertainty, controversy and the role of extra-legal intuitions in hard cases engaging international law governing resort to military force. Unlike other studies of the *jus ad bellum*, this book does not try to identify what the law is, nor to prescribe *the* 'correct' method for framing and assessing legal arguments. Rather, this book explores how legal reasoning works in this area of law, using concepts from the philosophy of knowledge to explain what it is about the *jus ad bellum* that enables uncertainty and disagreement. This book casts light on why and how lawyers' political, ethical and strategic intuitions about how the world works and how it *ought* to work shape their legal assessments of hard cases engaging this law. The book considers how uncertainty about current and *future* facts feeds into legal uncertainty – how hard cases of force often require complex factual assessments, and *forecasting* of the immediate and long-term consequences of both using and not using force. This is the first book to investigate the *jus ad bellum* using interviews and a survey with UK-based international lawyers, alongside systematic textual analysis of ICJ judgments and scholarly writings. And this book is the first to draw on insights from legal risk management, strategic intelligence assessment and political forecasting to suggest techniques lawyers might use to help tackle such analytical dilemmas.

LEGAL AND EXTRA-LEGAL CONTROVERSY IN THE *JUS AD BELLUM*

International law governing the resort to military force has long been and remains the subject of sharp controversy. The Cold War is often seen as having restrained the major powers' willingness to use force for fear of catastrophic escalation, leaving 'international law looking like a frightened rabbit staring into the headlights of an approaching car, obsessed by the fear of an oncoming disaster which it was almost entirely powerless to prevent'.[2] Yet even then, lawyers and states often disagreed, perhaps not always sincerely, about the legality of specific instances of use of force, including by the United Kingdom and France in Suez, by the USSR in Czechoslovakia, by India in East Pakistan, and by the United States in Vietnam and Latin America, prompting one scholar to ask 'Who Killed Article 2(4)?'[3] Lauterpacht's famous description of the *jus in bello* might also be applied to the *jus ad bellum*: 'If international law is, in some ways, at the vanishing point of law, the law of war is, perhaps even more conspicuously, at the vanishing point of international law.'[4]

Such disagreements surprise some non-lawyers, because the *jus ad bellum* appears succinct and unambiguous. Three brief paragraphs in Articles 2(4), 42 and 51 of the UN Charter appear to prohibit all use of force by states internationally, except when authorised by the UNSC or in individual or collective self-defence against armed attack. Yet when assessing specific controversial instances – 'hard cases' – of force, even expert international lawyers often draw 'opposing conclusions regarding the state of the law'.[5] Such contestation can contribute to what Koskenniemi describes as 'the common feeling that international law is somehow "weak" or manipulable', that indeterminacy is a 'structural property' of international law, which is thus 'useless' for 'justifying or criticizing international behaviour'.[6] It can create suspicion that, since lawyers can 'plausibly take a number of different positions' when assessing the lawfulness of hard cases of force, their legal opinions tend to align

[2] Christopher Greenwood, 'Humanitarian Intervention: The Case of Kosovo', in 2002 *Finnish Yearbook of International Law* (Helsinki: Kluwer, 2002), 141–2.

[3] Thomas M. Franck, 'Who Killed Article 2(4)? Or: Changing Norms Governing the Use of Force by States', *American Journal of International Law*, 64 (1970), 809–37.

[4] Hersch Lauterpacht, 'The Problem of the Revision of the Law of War', *British Year Book of International Law*, 29 (1952), 360–82, 382.

[5] Christian Marxsen, 'A Note on Indeterminacy of the Law on Self-Defence Against Non-State Actors', in *Self-Defence Against Non-State Actors: Impulses from the Max Planck Trialogues on the Law of Peace and War*, MPIL Research Paper Series No. 2017–07 (Heidelberg: Max Planck Institute, 2017), 79.

[6] Martti Koskenniemi, *From Apology to Utopia* (Cambridge: Cambridge University Press, 2005), 66, 62, 67.

with, and are 'in fact motivated by', their 'policy preferences' and 'political choices'.[7] Such contestation can even lead some to conclude that, since war is the ultimate contest of politico-military power and blind chance, it is exempt from legal reasoning, vulnerable to Cicero's claim about law and personal self-defence: 'Silent enim leges inter arma.'[8]

This book examines such debates by considering several interconnected, long-established, but still contentious propositions about international law governing resort to force, seeking to describe how far they are valid, with what limitations and under what conditions. This book seeks to develop these propositions using concepts from the philosophy of knowledge, from socio-legal theory and from international strategy, politics and ethics to describe the structure and sources of legal and factual uncertainty in this area of law. The book particularly examines how far this uncertainty is rooted in lawyers' underlying extra-legal intuitions – political, ethical and strategic presuppositions and beliefs about how the world works and how it ought to work.

The collapse in August 2021 of the Afghan Government led by Ashraf Ghani in the face of the Taleban's military campaign came after this book had entered production, so is not discussed in the main text. However, those developments arguably support the relevance of this book's discussion of uncertainty, forecasting and the role of intuitions and biases in decisions about the resort to force.

First, this book argues that the *jus ad bellum*, like many areas of international and domestic law, is 'specifically indeterminate'. In at least some cases, what the law prescribes is vague, and displays specific forms of vagueness described by the philosophy of knowledge. The law relies on 'paradigms' – authoritative examples or 'plain cases' of lawful and unlawful behaviour.[9] These paradigms are vulnerable to 'supervaluationism', when lawfulness is determined by multiple tests that are overlapping, but not entirely co-incident, and may be evaluated using different values.[10] And the law operates not

7 Marxsen, 'Indeterminacy', 80; Marko Milanovic, 'Accounting for the Complexity of the Law Applicable to Modern Armed Conflicts', in Michael N. Schmitt, Shane R. Reeves, Christopher M. Ford and Winston S. Williams, eds., *Complex Battlespaces: The Law of Armed Conflict and the Dynamics of Modern Warfare* (Oxford: Oxford University Press, 2019), 41.

8 Marcus Tullius Cicero, 'Pro Milone', in Albert Curtis Clark, ed., *Oxford Classical Texts: M. Tulli Ciceronis: Orationes*, vol. 2, *Pro Milone; Pro Marcello; Pro Ligario; Pro Rege Deiotaro; Philippicae I–XIV* (Oxford: Oxford University Press, 1918), 5.

9 H. L. A. Hart, *The Concept of Law*, 3rd ed. (Oxford: Oxford University Press, 2012), 127.

10 Timothy Williamson, 'Vagueness in Reality', in Michael J. Loux and Dean W. Zimmermann, eds., *The Oxford Handbook of Metaphysics* (Oxford: Oxford University Press, 2009), 690, 692.

according to 'bivalent logic' but 'fuzzy logic' – lawful and unlawful behaviour is separated, not by a sharp boundary, but a fuzzy 'penumbra of uncertainty'.[11] These forms of vagueness facilitate uncertainty and contestation about the lawfulness of many wars fought today because these wars are different in multiple important ways to the overt invasion by one state to deprive another of its territorial integrity or political independence, which the UN Charter most clearly prohibits.

Second, this book argues that uncertainty about the law in specific cases is exacerbated by uncertainty about current and in particular *future* facts in such cases. Assessing the lawfulness of a potential decision to use force requires both assessment of the current facts of the military crisis that may justify force, and also *forecasts* of the future consequences of either using or not using force in that crisis. But there are usually multiple possible interpretations of the current facts in such cases, and there are always multiple possible forecasts of the future consequences of using or not using force. Different assessments of the present and future flow from different assessors' assumptions and implicit theories 'about how the world works', and 'how events would have unfolded' under different conditions.[12] Uncertainty about the future both in specific cases of force, and in the evolution of force more generally may even mean that vagueness in the *jus ad bellum*, like other law, is both necessary and inevitable.

Third, the *jus ad bellum*, like other law, might be described as 'partially autonomous'. Uncertainty and competing interpretations of law, fact and forecasting in specific hard cases of resort to force and the absence of authoritative legal rules for tackling such uncertainties, encourage lawyers to apply consistent, mutually reinforcing 'extra-legal' 'political and ideological viewpoints' and intuitions, including about strategy and ethics, to choose between competing interpretations of law and fact, and to reach conflicting legal conclusions.[13] Politico-strategic and ethical intuitions can act as forms of cognitive biases that shape choices about the interpretation of facts, expectations of consequences, methods of legal interpretation and thus about what the *jus ad bellum* requires. Uncertainty about the *jus ad bellum* as a system of prescriptive rules and principles may even encourage lawyers to practise 'strategic behaviour in interpretation', to use the *jus ad bellum* in its mode of

[11] Hart, *Concept of Law*, 127; Williamson, 'Vagueness in Reality', 690, 692.

[12] Philip Tetlock, *Expert Political Judgement* (Princeton: Princeton University Press, 2005), 145, 146.

[13] James Green, *The International Court of Justice and Self-Defence in International Law* (Oxford and Portland: Hart Publishing, 2009), 184.

a system of argumentative practices to justify or criticise the lawfulness of specific behaviour in accordance with their extra-legal beliefs and interests.[14]

Fourth, this book argues that lawyers tend to conform to varying degrees to competing 'interpretive' and 'strategic cultures' concerning the *jus ad bellum*. Different 'interpretive–strategic cultures' consist of lawyers who share similar, mutually reinforcing intuitions, assumptions and beliefs about legal interpretation and about extra-legal factors, such as politico-strategic causation and ethical justification.[15] Lawyers in such cultures thus reach similar conclusions about the law and facts in specific cases. These competing cultures vary along a continuum from 'restrictivists', likely to see few legal, politico-strategic and ethical justifications for force, to 'expansionists', likely to see more such justifications.[16]

This book argues that 'restrictivists' adopt approaches to legal interpretation that might be grouped under the heading of 'formalist'. In assessing the lawfulness of resort to force, formalists emphasise the ordinary meaning of the words of the UN Charter and other formal sources of the *jus ad bellum*, hold that the law has evolved little since 1945, accept only explicitly legal statements as evidence of *opinio juris*, require clarity and overwhelming quantity of state practice for new custom, and regard only the UNSC as permitted to authorise force in situations where the law is unclear. 'Expansionists' prefer legal interpretation techniques that this book groups under the heading of 'dynamist'. In assessing the lawfulness of resort to force, dynamists take account of the UN Charter's wider purposes and other law, arguing the law has evolved significantly since 1945, accepting a wider variety and smaller quantity of *opinio juris* and state practice for new custom, and seeing more discretion for states and bodies outside the UNSC to authorise force when the law is unclear.

In terms of extra-legal strategic, political and ethical reasoning, this book argues that 'restrictivists' adopt approaches that might be grouped under the

14 Koskenniemi, *From Apology to Utopia*, 67–9; Duncan Kennedy, *Legal Reasoning: Collected Essays* (Aurora, CO: The Davies Group Publishers, 2008), 159.

15 Michael Waibel, 'Interpretive Communities in International Law', in Andrea Bianchi, Daniel Peat, Matthew Windsor, eds., *Interpretation in International Law* (Oxford: Oxford University Press, 2015), 148; Peter Haas, 'Introduction: Epistemic Communities and International Policy Coordination', *International Organization*, 46 (1992), 1, 3; Theo Farrell, 'World Culture and Military Power', *Security Studies*, 14:3 (2005), 450; Colin Gray, 'National Style in Strategy: The American Example', *International Security*, 6:2 (1981), 22; Alastair Iain Johnston, 'Thinking About Strategic Culture', *International Security*, 19:4 (1995), 46.

16 Anne Peters and Christian Marxsen, 'Editors' Introduction: Self-Defence in Times of Transition', in *Self-Defence Against Non-State Actors: Impulses from the Max Planck Trialogues on the Law of Peace and War*, MPIL Research Paper Series No. 2017–07 (Heidelberg: Max Planck Institute, 2017), 7.

heading of 'pacificist' – effectively viewing the *jus ad bellum* as a *jus contra bellum*.[17] They tend to choose the interpretation of law that they assess minimises potential for future legal uncertainty and abuse, best protects the interests of less powerful states while distrusting more powerful states, and treating the prohibition on force as always the most important decision-making principle. When assessing different interpretations of uncertain facts, and constructing forecasts of potential consequences of using or not using force, pacificists tend to proceed on the basis that unilateral force almost always causes more harm than it prevents for the state using force and for the international system, that only self-interested states use force unilaterally, and only a narrow range of interests and ethical values are sufficiently widely shared to guide decisions about unilateral force. 'Expansionists' adopt approaches to politics, strategy and ethics that this book groups under the heading of 'interventionist'. They tend to choose the interpretation of law that fits with changes in conflict since 1945, and hold that principles such as human rights, preventing genocide, stopping terrorism or the proliferation of weapons of mass destruction (WMDs), can be more important than the prohibition on force. When assessing different interpretations of uncertain facts, 'interventionists' tend to proceed on the basis that unilateral force can often prevent more harm than it causes for the state using force and the international system, states using force unilaterally can advance common interests as well as self-interest, and a range of interests and ethical values can be sufficiently shared internationally to guide decisions about unilateral force.

It is important to note that theorists of interpretive culture and strategic culture do not claim that individuals necessarily conform to cultures consciously, or deliberately coordinate or act collectively. A lawyer's alignment with an interpretive or strategic culture may reflect deeply internalised, unconsciously held intuitions and preferences, the product of both an individual's socialisation and inherent cognitive characteristics. Interpretive and strategic cultures may reflect coherent patterns of what psychologists term 'cognitive biases', 'motivated biases' and 'heuristics' – intuitions, presuppositions and rules of thumb that simplify 'the complex tasks of assessing probabilities and predicting values', and are usually economical and effective, but sometimes 'lead to severe and systematic errors'.[18]

17 Olivier Corten, *The Law against War: The Prohibition on the Use of Force in Contemporary International Law* (London: Hart Publishing, 2010), 2.

18 Amos Tversky and Daniel Kahneman, 'Judgment under Uncertainty: Heuristics and Biases', *Science*, 185:4157 (1974), 1124–31, 1124.

Fifth, this book argues that fields outside the *jus ad bellum* offer insights that might help lawyers manage these uncertainties and subjectivities. Legal risk management, international humanitarian law, strategic intelligence analysis and political forecasting suggest techniques to manage uncertainties and assumptions, and systematically develop and evaluate multiple alternative interpretations and forecasts of fact and law. International lawyers can use such techniques to enhance their assessment of hard cases engaging the *jus ad bellum*.

INVESTIGATING LEGAL AND FACTUAL UNCERTAINTY ABOUT RESORT TO WAR

This book is the first to examine controversies in the *jus ad bellum* using an innovative combination of theoretical concepts and qualitative and quantitative methods.[19] For analytical focus, this book examines the *jus ad bellum* as it applies to states, not considerations for resort to force by non-state actors, nor the *jus in bello* – the law governing military behaviour within armed conflict. This book uses the term '*jus ad bellum*' to describe international law governing resort to force by one state in or against another state. It takes as the main sources of the *jus ad bellum* the UN Charter, the *Caroline* criteria or Webster formulation, which is widely accepted as describing customary international law governing self-defence, and other interpretations of the law that are widely accepted as authoritative, such as UN General Assembly (UNGA) declarations and ICJ jurisprudence. Although states and non-legal commentators still often use the term 'war' to describe international military conflict, this book generally uses the terms 'resort to force', 'use of force' or 'armed attack' – the UN Charter includes the latter two terms.[20] The term 'unilateral use of force' is used to mean resort to force that does not have unambiguous UNSC authorisation.

This book seeks to analyse how international lawyers use competing theoretical frameworks when they apply the *jus ad bellum*, while not intending to endorse any of those frameworks, to the extent that any analysis can exclude theoretical presuppositions. Nevertheless, to provide an intelligible narrative, this book uses terms associated with specific theoretical approaches, although

19 Denis J. Galligan, 'Legal Theory and Empirical Research', in Peter Cane and Herbert Kritzer, eds., *The Oxford Handbook of Empirical Legal Research* (Oxford: Oxford University Press, 2010), 966–1001; Gregory Shaffer and Tom Ginsburg, 'The Empirical Turn in International Legal Scholarship', in *American Journal of International Law*, 106:1 (2012), 1–47.

20 Christine Gray, *International Law and the Use of Force* (Oxford: Oxford University Press, 2008), 9.

that does not mean the book endorses those approaches. For example, many legal scholars see a distinction between what Dworkin described as 'hard cases', which may have 'a unique answer that is either not obvious or is subject to disagreement', and situations where the law is indeterminate – 'it fails to justify a unique answer to an intelligible legal question'.[21] However, this book uses the term 'hard case' to describe any case that provokes significant disagreement between international lawyers and states about what the *jus ad bellum* requires, both 'when no settled rule dictates a decision either way', and also where knowledgeable lawyers cannot readily 'discriminate between two or more interpretations' of the relevant legal materials, since the two kinds of case usually appear identical to an external observer.[22]

Similarly, some scholars argue 'there is no neat distinction between the political factors inherent in law and the political views (conscious or unconscious)' of legal decision-makers.[23] Dworkinian and other contemporary natural law approaches may integrate such factors into legal reasoning, seeking the interpretation of law that best advances those 'principles and policies' providing 'the best political justification for the statute at the time it was passed'.[24] Nevertheless, this book uses the term 'extra-legal' to denote forms of reasoning widely accepted as separate from law, '(in the sense of not-doctrine based) background assumptions'.[25] Even Dworkinian jurists usually seek some legal anchoring – for example, a UNSC resolution, another existing body of international law, a UNGA declaration or other authoritative expression of collective international will – for political and other principles that can be legitimately invoked when interpreting the *jus ad bellum*.[26]

This book regards such extra-legal reasoning as including politics and strategy, concerning the ways and means states and other actors use to pursue their interests, involving 'bargaining and persuasion', 'threats and pressure, psychological as well as physical', 'words as well as deeds' and 'the art of creating power'.[27] It also includes ethical or normative theories about when force might be considered right or wrong, when it might ultimately help 'enable us to live together well in communities and so flourish as human

21 Leslie Green, 'Notes to the Third Edition', in Hart, *Concept of Law*, 319.

22 Ronald Dworkin, 'Hard Cases', *Harvard Law Review*, 88:6 (1975), 1057–109, 1060; Ronald Dworkin, *Law's Empire* (Oxford: Hart Publishing, 1998), 255–6.

23 Green, *Self-Defence*, 176.

24 Ronald Dworkin, *A Matter of Principle* (Oxford: Oxford University Press, 1985), 145, 129.

25 Marxsen, 'Indeterminacy', 80.

26 Sean D Murphy, 'Protean *Jus Ad Bellum*', *Berkeley Journal of International Law*, 27 (2009), 36, 26.

27 Lawrence Freedman, *Strategy: A History*, Kindle ed. (Oxford: Oxford University Press, 2013), xii.

beings'.[28] And extra-legal reasoning also includes notions of legitimacy, ideas about whether law is created and applied according to processes acceptable to a political community, and conforming with substantive moral and political rationales.[29] Other extra-legal factors such as economics may also shape *jus ad bellum* decisions. However, this book concentrates on the effects of politics, strategy and ethics to retain analytical focus and manageability, and because law's autonomy from politics and ethics has consistently been a key concern for jurists such as Hart and Kelsen.[30]

This book examines scholarly writings about the law governing resort to force, about different legal theories and forms of legal interpretation, and theories of international politics and ethics in conflict. It identifies from these sources pivotal contested principles about the legal, factual and ethical analysis and justification of resort to force, which may function as legal and extra-legal intuitions underpinning competing approaches to the *jus ad bellum*. The book uses three methods to consider how these competing principles may be observable in legal reasoning about the *jus ad bellum*.

First, this book reports systematic textual analysis of scholarly writings and UK government statements concerning the legality of military interventions in Kosovo in 1999, Afghanistan in 2001 and Iraq in 2003. Fifteen scholarly writings were analysed, written or co-written by a total of eight influential UK legal scholars: Ian Brownlie and Brian Apperley, Christine Chinkin, Christine Gray, Christopher Greenwood, Vaughan Lowe, Lindsay Moir and Nigel White (writing with Eric Myjer).[31]

28 David Fisher, *Morality and War* (Oxford: Oxford University Press, 2011), 60.

29 Thomas M. Franck, *Fairness in International Law and Institutions* (Oxford: Oxford University Press, 1998), 27; Christine Chinkin, 'Rethinking Legality/Legitimacy after the Iraq War', in Richard Falk, Mark Juergensmeyer and Vessellin Popovski, eds., *Legality and Legitimacy in Global Affairs* (Oxford: Oxford University Press, 2012), 220–39, 221–2; Richard Falk, 'Introduction: Legality and Legitimacy', in Falk, Juergensmeyer and Popovski, *Legality and Legitimacy*, 4–39, 9.

30 Hans Kelsen, *Introduction to the Problems of Legal Theory* (Oxford: Clarendon Press, 1992), 2, 3; H. L. A. Hart, 'Positivism and the Separation of Law and Morals', *Harvard Law Review*, 71 (1958), 615.

31 Christopher Greenwood, 'International Law and the NATO Intervention in Kosovo', *The International and Comparative Law Quarterly*, 49 (2000), 926; Vaughan Lowe, 'International Legal Issues Arising in the Kosovo Crisis', *The International and Comparative Law Quarterly*, 49 (2000), 934; Christine Chinkin, 'The Legality of NATO's action in the FRY', *The International and Comparative Law Quarterly*, 49 (2000), 910; Gray, *International Law*, 132–40, 156–60, 216–22, 354–69; Ian Brownlie and Brian Apperley, 'Kosovo Crisis Inquiry: Memorandum on the International Law Aspects', *The International and Comparative Law Quarterly*, 49 (2000) 878; Christopher Greenwood, 'International Law and the "War against Terrorism"', *International Affairs*, 78 (2002), 301; Chinkin, 'Rethinking Legality/Legitimacy', 220; Lindsay Moir, *Reappraising the Resort to Force: International law,* Jus ad Bellum *and the*

Second, the book reports systematic textual analysis of majority ICJ judgments and twenty-eight separate or dissenting opinions written by a total of twenty-two ICJ judges on three key cases: *Military and Paramilitary Activities in and against Nicaragua* (1986), *Legal Consequences of the Construction of a Wall in the Occupied Palestinian Territory* (2004) and *Armed Activities on the Territory of the Congo* (2005).[32] These cases dealt significantly with the *jus ad bellum* – alleged violations of this law were central to the *Nicaragua* and *Congo* cases. The cases also provide evidence of different national legal cultures, since the judges in these cases came from nineteen countries, including Brazil, Egypt, Germany, India, Nigeria, the United Kingdom and the United States.[33] These

War on Terror (London: Bloomsbury Publishing, 2010), 40; Eric Myjer and Nigel White, 'The Twin Towers Attack: An Unlimited Right to Self-Defence?', *Journal of Conflict and Security Law*, 7 (2002), 5; Christopher Greenwood, 'International Law and the Pre-emptive Use of Force: Afghanistan, Al-Qaida, and Iraq', *San Diego International Law Journal*, 4 (2003), 7–38; Vaughan Lowe 'The Iraq Crisis: What Now', *The International and Comparative Law Quarterly*, 52:4 (2003), 859–71; Ian Brownlie, 'Memorandum from Professor Ian Brownlie QC', Minutes of Evidence Taken Before the Foreign Affairs Committee, 24 October 2002, in Foreign Affairs Committee, *Foreign Policy Aspects of the War on Terrorism*, HC196, Session 2002–2003 (19 Dec. 2002); Nigel D. White and Eric P. J. Myjer, 'Editorial: The Use of Force against Iraq', *Journal of Conflict and Security Law*, 8:1 (2003), 1–14.

32 *Military and Paramilitary Activities in and against Nicaragua (Nicaragua* v. *United States of America)*, Merits, Judgment, International Court of Justice (ICJ) Reports 1986, 14; *Nicaragua*, Separate Opinion of Judge Ago, ICJ Reports 1986, 181; *Nicaragua*, Separate Opinion of Judge Elias, ICJ Reports 1986, 178; *Nicaragua*, Dissenting Opinion of Judge Sir Robert Jennings, ICJ Reports 1986, 528; *Nicaragua*, Separate Opinion of Judge Lachs, ICJ Reports 1986, 158; *Nicaragua*, Separate Opinion of Judge Ni, ICJ Reports 1986, 201; *Nicaragua*, Dissenting Opinion of Judge Oda, ICJ Reports 1986, 212; *Nicaragua*, Separate Opinion of Judge Ruda, ICJ Reports 1986, 174; *Nicaragua*, Dissenting Opinion of Judge Schwebel, ICJ Reports 1986, 259; *Nicaragua*, Separate Opinion of Judge Sette-Camara, ICJ Reports 1986, 192; *Nicaragua*, Separate Opinion of President Nagendra Singh, ICJ Reports 1986, 151; *Legal Consequences of the Construction of a Wall in the Occupied Palestinian Territory*, Advisory Opinion, ICJ Reports 2004, 136; *Wall*, Separate Opinion of Judge Al-Khasawneh, ICJ Reports 2004, 235; *Wall*, Declaration of Judge Buergenthal, ICJ Reports 2004, 240; *Wall*, Separate Opinion of Judge Elaraby, ICJ Reports 2004, 246; *Wall*, Separate Opinion of Judge Higgins, ICJ Reports 2004, 207; *Wall*, Separate Opinion of Judge Kooijmans, ICJ Reports 2004, 219; *Wall*, Separate Opinion of Judge Koroma, ICJ Reports 2004, 204; *Wall*, Separate Opinion of Judge Owada, ICJ Reports 2004, 260; *Armed Activities on the Territory of the Congo (Democratic Republic of the Congo* v. *Uganda)*, Judgment, ICJ Reports 2005, 168; *Congo*, Separate Opinion of Judge Elaraby, ICJ Reports 2005, 327; *Congo*, Dissenting Opinion of Judge *Ad Hoc* Kateka, ICJ Reports 2005, 361; *Congo*, Dissenting Opinion of Judge Kooijmans, ICJ Reports 2005, 306; *Congo*, Declaration of Judge Koroma, ICJ Reports 2005, 284; *Congo*, Separate Opinion of Judge Parra-Aranguren, ICJ Reports 2005, 292; *Congo*, Separate Opinion of Judge Simma, ICJ Reports 2005, 334; *Congo*, Declaration of Judge Tomka, ICJ Reports 2005, 351; *Congo*, Declaration of Judge *Ad Hoc* Verhoeven, ICJ Reports 2005, 355.

33 Argentina, Belgium, Brazil, Egypt, Germany, India, Italy, Japan, Jordan, Netherlands, Nigeria, Poland, People's Republic of China, Sierra Leone, Slovakia, Tanzania, United Kingdom, United States and Venezuela.

cases are key sources of jurisprudence for the *jus ad bellum*, since the ICJ is the only court that at present approximates an authoritative final adjudicator in international disputes about this area of international law. And the cases collectively map the evolving jurisprudence around a contentious question in the *jus ad bellum*: whether armed attacks by non-state actors trigger the right of self-defence.

Both these sets of systematic textual analyses considered how far the legal assessments in the scholarly writings, government legal statements, and ICJ opinions expressed the contested legal and extra-legal principles identified earlier. In other words, this research assessed how far these different sets of lawyers were making 'legal' assessments, and how far they advanced extra-legal opinions.

Third, unlike previous studies of the *jus ad bellum*, this book draws on structured interviews and an online survey with a total of thirty-one UK-based international lawyers with experience and/or knowledge of the *jus ad bellum*. The views of such lawyers, often regarded as impartial experts, can significantly influence perceptions of the lawfulness of force in the wider legal community and society, particularly since the ICJ rarely considers such cases. Such lawyers may provide an indicator of what society agrees the law actually is, since, as D'Amato has noted, lawyers with high standing as academics or practitioners have 'some right to claim, on the basis of professional training and experience', an ability to predict 'what a judge would decide'.[34] Such international lawyers can directly shape states' legal positions through advice to governments, including in international tribunals, and because government legal advisers often draw on scholarly writings in developing national legal positions.[35] And practically, it is more straightforward to interview and survey such lawyers than those currently serving with governments.

The bibliography includes an anonymised list of the thirty-one interview and survey participants. Sixteen were legal scholars, eight, practising international lawyers and seven, former government lawyers. Six of the participants were Queen's Counsel. Although all based in the United Kingdom, they represented ten nationalities: Australia, Canada, Federal Republic of Yugoslavia, Germany, Greece, Israel, Italy, New Zealand, Ireland and the United Kingdom. This book does not claim to provide a statistically accurate assessment of British lawyers' legal and extra-legal views about the *jus ad*

34 Anthony D'Amato, 'Legal Uncertainty', *California Law Review*, 71 (1983), 1.

35 Sir Franklin Berman, KCMG, QC, 'The Role of the International Lawyer in the Making of Foreign Policy', in Chanaka Wickremasinghe, ed., *The International Lawyer as Practitioner* (London: British Institute of International and Comparative Law, 2000), 15; Professor Sir Robert Jennings, 'Introduction', in Wickremasinghe, *International Lawyer*, xxiii.

bellum. Instead this book uses a case study method to investigate the detailed features and range of variation of legal and extra-legal opinions about resort to force within the UK legal community. In the United Kingdom, the population of lawyers being surveyed is too specialised, and the process being investigated – legal advice and commentary about the *jus ad bellum* – too specific and actor-dependent, for random sampling to be reliable. Participants were therefore selected using 'purposive sampling', guided by 'the study's purpose and the researcher's knowledge of the population'.[36] Participants were identified for 'reputational', 'decisional' and 'positional' reasons – they were assessed to have influence on wider expert opinion and official decisions about resort to force, and/or represent a range of opinions across the UK legal profession.[37]

Participants were identified by examining websites of international law departments of all Russell Group universities, and approaching all professors of public international law and other faculty members in those institutions whose research or teaching interests suggested they might have *jus ad bellum* expertise, and UK-based members of the editorial boards of two relevant academic journals.[38] Practising international lawyers were chosen by searching for 'public international law' in the Chambers and Partners website, consulting the attorney general's public international law panel list, and inviting to participate lawyers whose webpages suggested expertise in the *jus ad bellum* or wider international law in armed conflict.[39] All living UK-based authors of legal writings analysed in this research for whom contact details could be found were also approached. Former government lawyers were identified through published works, consultation with colleagues and the author's own knowledge. Finally, some participants were identified by 'snowball' or 'chain referral' – suggested by participants who had already taken part.[40]

Using these methods, the author contacted by email a total of seventy-nine international lawyers between June 2017 and July 2018. Thirty-one individuals eventually participated in the research in some form. Twenty-three completed

36 Oisín Tansey, 'Process Tracing and Elite Interviewing: A Case for Non-probability Sampling', *PS: Political Science and Politics*, 40:3 (2007), 765–72, 770.

37 Ursula Hoffmann-Lange, 'Methods of Elite Research', in Russell J. Dalton and Hans Dieter Klingemann, eds., *The Oxford Handbook of Political Behavior* (Oxford: Oxford University Press, 2007), 910–29.

38 Russell Group Universities, http://russellgroup.ac.uk/about/our-universities/; *Journal on the Use of Force and International Law*, www.tandfonline.com/action/journalInformation?show=editorialBoard&journalCode=rjuf20; *Journal of Conflict and Security Law*, https://academic.oup.com/jcsl/pages/Editorial_Board.

39 Chambers and Partners, www.chambersandpartners.com/11814/96/editorial/1/1.

40 Tansey, 'Process Tracing', 770.

the survey in some form, while thirty participants were interviewed. The author holds copies of all interview transcripts and completed survey questionnaires. Twenty-two of the seventy-nine individuals invited to participate were male, while seven of the thirty-one eventual participants were female. There are various possible explanations for this. These figures may broadly represent the gender distribution of UK-based international lawyers with expertise in the *jus ad bellum* and conflict and security law. The information sources used may not adequately represent female international lawyers with such expertise. Or the methods used to search these information sources may be inadequate to identify those female international lawyers.

The participants referred to several actual UK instances of the use of force, but did not mention the United Kingdom's air strikes on Syria in April 2018, as all interviews were completed by March 2018. In designing the questionnaire and interview, the author drew on training and advice from a professional opinion research specialist and from a scholar specialising in expert survey and interview methodology, published sources on interview and expert/elite survey methods, and the survey conducted in developing the *Chatham House Principles on Self-Defence*.[41]

To maintain anonymity for those who requested it, all participants were assigned an identifying number to which all their inputs are attributed, identifying each individual's profession, such as 'legal scholar', 'former government lawyer' or 'practising international lawyer'. The following interviewees agreed to have their participation noted here, although specific quotes are not attributed to them:

- Professor Dapo Akande, Professor of Public International Law, Co-Director, Oxford Institute for Ethics, Law & Armed Conflict, University of Oxford
- Professor Susan C. Breau, Dean of Law, University of Victoria (when interviewed: Head of School of Law, University of Reading)
- Professor Bill Bowring, School of Law, Birkbeck College, University of London

[41] Ursula Hoffmann-Lange, 'Studying Elite versus Mass Opinion', in Wolfgang Donsbach and Michael W. Traugott, eds., *The SAGE Handbook of Public Opinion Research* (London: SAGE Publications Ltd, 2008), 3–63; Marco R. Steenbergen and Gary Marks, 'Evaluating Expert Judgments', *European Journal of Political Research*, 46 (2007), 347–66; Jon A. Krosnick and Stanley Presser, 'Question and Questionnaire Design', in *Handbook of Survey Research*, 2nd ed. (Bingley: Emerald Group, 2010), 63–313; Alan Bryman and James J. Teevan, *Social Research Methods* (Oxford: Oxford University Press, 2005), 80–4; Dr Kai Opperman, Scholar of Political Science; Dr Hayk Gyuzalyan, Survey Design Specialist, IPSOS-MORI; Elizabeth Wilmshurst, 'The Chatham House Principles of International Law on the Use of Force in Self-Defence', *International and Comparative Law Quarterly*, 55 (2006), 963.

- Professor Charles Garraway, formerly Colonel, Army Legal Services, Fellow, Human Rights Centre, University of Essex
- Professor Christian Henderson, Chair of International Law, University of Sussex
- Professor Noam Lubell, Professor of International Law, Director of the Essex Armed Conflict and Crisis Hub, University of Essex
- Professor Marko Milanovic, Professor of Public International Law, University of Nottingham
- Jasmin Nessa, Postgraduate Research Student and Graduate Teaching Assistant, Liverpool Law School
- Professor Christian J. Tams, Chair of International Law, University of Glasgow
- Professor Nicholas Tsagourias, School of Law, University of Sheffield

Since much of the research conducted for this book focused on UK-based lawyers and UK actions in Kosovo, Afghanistan, and Iraq, this study reveals patterns of opinion and reasoning which can most confidently be applied to the cultural and historic specificities of UK-based international lawyers in the late twentieth and early twenty-first centuries. The book's focus on English language sources and practitioners also potentially limits the generalisability of its conclusions. At the same time, the UK-based focus of the interviews, survey and scholarly analysis made it less likely that disagreements identified by those methods were caused by national differences in legal systems and media discourse, and more likely that those differences were due to individual intuitions and preferences. And the legal and factual arguments discussed with the lawyers interviewed and in the analysis of scholarly writings were not specific to the United Kingdom or to any one country, but instead relate to the justification of resort to military force under international law in general, including in the UNSC and ICJ. The range of nationalities of the lawyers interviewed and of the ICJ judges whose opinions this book analyses, also make it more likely that this book's arguments may be applicable beyond the United Kingdom.

OUTLINE OF THE BOOK

This book is divided into three parts, setting out the conceptual basis for its claims about uncertainty in the *jus ad bellum*, assessing what the empirical research conducted for this book suggests about those claims, and finally considering potential responses to the dilemmas identified. The first part consists of two chapters considering the nature and sources of uncertainty in the *jus ad bellum*. Chapter 2, the book's first substantive chapter, considers legal uncertainty in the *jus ad bellum* as set out in the UN Charter and other sources of law. It describes the four key concepts from the philosophy of vagueness and legal sociology already described in this chapter, which underpin this book's analysis: paradigms, supervaluationism, fuzzy logic and the 'penumbra of uncertainty', and competing interpretive cultures. The chapter outlines 'hard cases' which these sources of uncertainty appear to enable: anticipatory self-defence, pre-emptive self-defence, self-defence against non-state actors, humanitarian intervention, and use of force to prevent WMD proliferation. The chapter describes how interviewees and survey participants evaluated such potential justifications for force, the results displaying the forms of vagueness already identified. The chapter then outlines one possible explanation for this contestation, which the second part of the book will assess: that lawyers with different opinions about the lawfulness of resort to force also align with different 'interpretive cultures', holding different opinions about principles of legal interpretation. 'Restrictivists' espouse in effect a *jus contra bellum*, tending to prefer interpretation techniques that this book groups under the broad heading of 'formalist', while 'expansionists' tend to prefer interpretation techniques which this book groups as 'dynamist' when applying the *jus ad bellum*.

Chapter 3 considers factual uncertainty in the *jus ad bellum*. The chapter describes how the forms of vagueness introduced in Chapter 2 can affect the factual evidence necessary to assess military crises which engage the *jus ad bellum*. The chapter argues that the key *jus ad bellum* tests of necessity, imminence and proportionality also require decision-makers to compare multiple *forecasts* of the harms caused or permitted if force is or is not used. The chapter describes how survey participants evaluated the lawfulness of force in four fictional scenarios, demonstrating how even hypothetical 'facts' elicited varying opinions. The chapter describes rules of evidence the ICJ has developed, which reduce but do not resolve factual uncertainty, and offer no advice for conducting the forecasts required by the *jus ad bellum*. The chapter outlines the second potential explanation for contestation in the *jus ad bellum* which the second part of this book assesses: that lawyers resolve such factual and forecasting uncertainties by applying their own extra-legal politico-strategic and ethical intuitions, forming competing strategic cultures that disagree about the legality of specific instances of force and about the *jus ad bellum* more generally as well. Restrictivists tend to align with what this book describes as a 'pacificist' strategic culture, which sees little political, strategic and ethical justification for force, while expansionists tend to align with an 'interventionist' strategic culture, generally seeing more such extra-legal justifications for force.

The second part of the book consists of two chapters assessing the plausibility of the competing 'interpretive cultures' and 'strategic cultures' proposed in the first part, using systematic textual analysis of writings of legal scholars, UK government legal statements, and ICJ judgments, and interviews and a survey with UK-based international lawyers. Chapter 4 considers the evidence for the explanation advanced in Chapter 2, that contestation in the *jus ad bellum* is associated with differences between competing formalist and dynamist interpretive cultures, in which lawyers apply competing legal interpretation techniques. The chapter describes different legal interpretation techniques identified through textual analysis of UK government legal statements and writings by eight legal scholars assessing the lawfulness of US-led military interventions in Kosovo in 1999, in Afghanistan in 2001 and Iraq in 2003, and in the judgments and separate opinions in three ICJ cases engaging the *jus ad bellum*: *Nicaragua* (1986), *Wall* (2004) and *Congo* (2005). The chapter reports views of interviewees and survey respondents around key principles of legal interpretation, and how these views correlate with participants' assessment of the lawfulness of different justifications for force.

The chapter concludes that these analyses support the general argument that the *jus ad bellum* displays various forms of vagueness: paradigms, supervaluationism and fuzzy logic. There also appear to be associations between lawyers' choices about legal interpretation and their disagreements about the lawfulness of different justifications for force. Lawyers' preferred interpretation techniques appear to display social supervaluationism, ranging on a continuum between interpretive cultures of 'formalism', broadly aligning with a restrictive approach to the *jus ad bellum*, and a 'dynamist' interpretive culture, broadly aligning with a more expansionist approach. But the correlation has caveats. Lawyers did not always display all interpretive preferences under the headings 'formalism' and 'dynamism'. Expansionist lawyers sometimes deployed formalist arguments to support lawfulness of force in Afghanistan, Congo and Iraq, while restrictivist lawyers sometimes used dynamist arguments to argue the law did not permit such use of force. Furthermore, such competing interpretation techniques provide no guidance for the factual assessments and forecasts the *jus ad bellum* requires. Thus the chapter suggests disagreements about legal interpretation do not explain *all* the uncertainty and disagreement that can be observed in the *jus ad bellum*.

Chapter 5 considers evidence for extra-legal intuitions as sources of uncertainty, assessing the explanation advanced in Chapter 3, that uncertainty and contestation in the *jus ad bellum* is associated with competing pacificist and interventionist strategic cultures, in which lawyers hold different views about political, strategic and ethical evaluation of force. The chapter describes differences in extra-legal reasoning identified by textual analysis of the UK Government legal statements, scholarly writings, and ICJ judgments analysed in Chapter 4. The chapter reports interviewees' and survey respondents' views about key extra-legal propositions concerning the *jus ad bellum*, both in the abstract and in fictional scenarios, describing how these views correlate with participants' assessment of the lawfulness of different justifications for force. The chapter concludes that there appears to be a correlation between lawyers' choices about extra-legal reasoning and their disagreements about the lawfulness of different justifications for force. 'Pacificist' lawyers who view unilateral force as politico-strategically and ethically problematic tend to prefer a more restrictive *jus contra bellum*, while 'interventionist' lawyers who see unilateral force as more often politico-strategically and ethically the least bad option tend to favour a more expansionist *jus ad bellum*.

But, as with Chapter 4, these conclusions have caveats. Many 'interventionist' lawyers accept legal prohibitions on for example humanitarian intervention, even where they believe such actions are politico-strategically and/or ethically justifiable. 'Pacificist' lawyers accept the lawfulness of, for example, anticipatory self-defence, despite their politico-strategic and ethical misgivings. Lawyers did not always display all the interpretive preferences grouped under the 'formalism' and 'dynamism' headings, and these preferences did not always align with the extra-legal preferences of the 'pacificist' and 'interventionist' strategic cultures, or with opinions about the *jus ad bellum* proposed in the explanations advanced in part one of the book. This suggests lawyers' extra-legal intuitions and choices about legal interpretation combine to create contestation and uncertainty only in cases where law is most unclear, facts and forecasts of consequences are particularly contestable, or where the most obvious reading of the law creates apparently extremely politico-strategically or ethically unacceptable results. Extra-legal intuitions shape, but do not entirely determine, opinions about legal interpretation and the *jus ad bellum*.

The third part of the book consists of two chapters examining potential responses to uncertainty and extra-legal reasoning in the *jus ad bellum*. Chapter 6 considers how insights from legal risk management, international humanitarian law (IHL) and strategic intelligence analysis and political forecasting might help manage uncertainty and extra-legal biases in the *jus ad bellum*. This chapter describes a potential framework for dealing with legal and factual uncertainty in the *jus ad bellum*, drawing on key principles which the three fields have evolved to manage factual and legal uncertainty, by assessing multiple interpretations of current facts, and multiple forecasts of possible consequences of different policy choices – including risks of legal challenge, that information justifying force is shown to be incorrect, that force does not achieve its goals, or does so only by causing unacceptable harms. The proposed framework suggests a systematic approach to *jus ad bellum* assessments, integrating inter-disciplinary legal and extra-legal expertise to consider the factual and legal context, to assess risks of any legal justification for force being challenged or disproven, and recommending whether to accept these risks and use force, take steps to reduce the risks, or if risks are so severe that force should not be used. The chapter applies this framework to the Kosovo and Afghanistan interventions, and considers how such a framework might have affected UK legal advice on the 2003 intervention in Iraq, which included a section on legal risks. The chapter concludes that the proposed framework provides a way of attempting to address the vagueness, uncertainty and extra-legal intuitions identified in this book, but does not eliminate uncertainty – and raises significant normative questions.

Chapter 7 considers such normative concerns. The chapter first considers different approaches to dealing with legal uncertainty and extra-legal factors in different countries and professional contexts. The chapter then examines legal advisers' professional responsibilities when dealing with politically difficult cases, and reports interviewees' views of lawyers' responsibilities when dealing with difficult *jus ad bellum* cases and about risk management techniques. By focusing on managing risks of legal challenge to a decision to use force, the framework potentially encourages lawyers to act only as 'counsellor', enabling their governments to do whatever they want, rather than fulfilling their normative role of 'conscience', encouraging governments to adjust their behaviour to abide by law. At worst, such a framework might advise decision-makers to proceed with clearly unlawful military action if political and other circumstances meant there was little risk of that action facing legal challenges. The chapter nevertheless argues the framework developed in Chapter 6 can help deal with legal and factual uncertainty and extra-legal intuitions, and suggests how lawyers could use the framework alongside their own professional judgement to achieve a form of Rawlsian 'reflective equilibrium' when evaluating hard cases in the *jus ad bellum*.

Chapter 8 concludes the book by reviewing its arguments, identifying weaknesses in the methods used and proposing ways in which these might be addressed, for example by involving participants in other countries. The chapter importantly notes that uncertainty and contestation remain marginal problems in the *jus ad bellum*, as in other areas of international law. In most cases, the requirements of international law governing resort to force are clear and uncontested. There are many reasons to believe the contemporary international law governing resort to force has contributed to global peace and stability. This book's examination of legal and factual uncertainty and extra-legal intuitions in the *jus ad bellum* seeks to support and assist lawyers and states in their mission to uphold and apply this crucial area of international law, not to encourage lawyers or states to undermine or abandon it.

PART I

VARIETIES OF UNCERTAINTY IN THE JUS AD BELLUM

Here then are three sources of vague and incorrect definitions; indistinctness of the object, imperfection of the organ of perception, inadequateness of the vehicle of ideas. … To the difficulties already mentioned, may be added the interfering pretensions of the larger and smaller states.

James Madison, *The Federalist Papers*[1]

1 James Madison, 'Concerning the Difficulties of the Convention in Devising a Proper Form of Government', in *The Federalist*, ed. George W. Carey and James McClellan (Indianapolis: Liberty Fund, 2001), 179, 183–4.

2

Uncertainty about Law in the *Jus Ad Bellum*

INTRODUCTION

Since this book seeks to understand and identify ways of addressing uncertainty in the *jus ad bellum*, it first needs to make some sense of the various forms and sources of uncertainty in this area of law. That uncertainty can find its roots either in uncertainty about the law itself or in uncertainty about the facts of a case to which that law must be applied. Philosophers of knowledge and legal philosophers have developed the concept of 'vagueness' and its specific manifestations as potentially useful ways of understanding such uncertainties.[2]

Vagueness in law can be ontological: when the law differentiates unlawful from lawful behaviour by evaluating a factual quality that is in some respect vague. Vagueness can be epistemological: when law is framed using vague language, or when a set of relevant facts can only be described using vague language, leaving the lawyer uncertain as to what the law requires in a particular case. And it can be sociological: when competing groups of lawyers disagree either about what the law requires in specific cases or about what the facts are in any specific case.[3] This first part of the book argues that these ways of examining uncertainty and vagueness are useful for understanding the specific features of the *jus ad bellum*, and of factual assessment and forecasting in cases engaging this law, which enable the uncertainty and contestation that generate hard cases.

The next chapter considers various aspects of uncertainty about the facts required to apply the tests that the *jus ad bellum* specifies. Before that, this chapter examines uncertainty and disagreement about identifying applicable law governing resort to force and interpreting this law in specific cases. This chapter uses concepts from the philosophy of vagueness to describe how the most widely accepted features of the *jus ad bellum* can display vagueness and provoke disagreement, particularly in controversial 'hard cases' of resort to force,

2 Timothy A. O. Endicott, *Vagueness in Law* (Oxford: Oxford University Press, 2000), 1–2.

3 D'Amato, 'Legal Uncertainty', 1, 2.

such as self-defence against non-state actors, anticipatory or pre-emptive self-defence, forceful humanitarian intervention, or to counter WMDs. The chapter also proposes one potential explanation for how lawyers attempt to make sense of this vagueness: by applying different, contestable rules of interpretation to resolve legal uncertainties, lawyers inhabit competing interpretive cultures, in turn contributing to uncertainty and disagreement in the law.

VAGUENESS AND DISAGREEMENT IN LAW

Investigating uncertainty in the *jus ad bellum* engages fundamental philosophical disagreements about law. These disagreements affect law both when conceptualised as a system of rules and principles prescribing, permitting or prohibiting certain behaviour in specific circumstances, and in its mode as a system of argumentative practices enabling individuals to justify or criticise behaviour as lawful or unlawful.[4] Many who either deny international law is ever determinate, or who insist it always is, argue that true law always provides a single, 'correct' answer to disputes.[5] Many international lawyers argue that 'while there may not always be an immediate and obvious rule applicable to every international situation, "every international situation is capable of being determined *as a matter of law*"'.[6] However, others share what Koskenniemi has described as 'the common feeling that international law is somehow "weak" or manipulable', that indeterminacy is a 'structural property' of international law, which is thus 'useless' for 'justifying or criticizing international behaviour'.[7] John Bolton goes further, arguing 'international law is not law', but merely 'a series of political and moral arrangements', 'an untried system of authority based so much on assumptions and so little on reality' that it must be considered to be 'theology and superstition masquerading as law'.[8]

Yet the determinacy of *any* law is contestable. Adapting categories proposed by Lawrence Solum, jurists can be described as adopting one of three approaches to indeterminacy in law:[9]

1 *systemic determinacy*: genuine law *always* provides determinate solutions to disputes.

4 Hart, *Concept of Law*, 3; Koskenniemi, *From Apology to Utopia*, 67–8.
5 Endicott, *Vagueness in Law*, 1–2.
6 Malcolm Shaw, *International Law*, 6th ed. (Cambridge: Cambridge University Press, 2008), 99.
7 Koskenniemi, *From Apology to Utopia*, 66, 62, 67.
8 John R. Bolton, 'Is There Really "Law" in International Affairs?', *Transnational Law and Contemporary Problems*, 10:1 (2000), 1–48, 7, 48.
9 Lawrence B. Solum, 'On the Indeterminacy Crisis: Critiquing Critical Dogma', *The University of Chicago Law Review*, 54:2 (1987), 462–503, 473.

2 *systemic indeterminacy*: law *never* provides truly determinate solutions to disputes.
3 *specific indeterminacy*: law *usually* provides determinate solutions to disputes, but in specific circumstances law can be weakly or even radically indeterminate.

One source of indeterminacy in law is the regulation of complex activity using a 'paradigm': 'an authoritative example' or 'plain case' of lawful or unlawful behaviour.[10] Laws based on paradigms can be vague because, instead of specifying a straightforward test, they require lawyers to assess whether cases display sufficient 'family resemblances' to the paradigm 'plain case' of lawful or unlawful behaviour – features shared by cases of one category, and not cases of other categories.[11] And because paradigms are identified by multiple features, they enable a second source of vagueness, described as 'supervaluationism': when law prescribes not a single test of lawfulness, but multiple evaluation tests and standards that are overlapping but not entirely co-extensive – actions may meet all tests or just some.[12] Such laws often use 'multi-part tests', deriving from, explaining or supplementing a 'primary rule', listing 'necessary elements' that must be met to deem an action lawful.[13]

Other potential sources of 'supervaluationism' include when laws prescribe tests using terms with multiple meanings, requiring decision-makers to interpret the meaning of the words used to describe what is required by a law and to evaluate whether the facts meet those requirements.[14] Different interpretations of the law may require lawyers to apply different value systems, thus yielding different conclusions. Multiple value systems may also arise when a situation is regulated by multiple laws, each imposing different, potentially incompatible requirements.

Many laws display a third form of vagueness known as 'fuzzy logic', due to the inability of language to describe precisely characteristics that change by subtle degrees from one state to another.[15] Many lawyers and laypeople intuitively apply Aristotelean truth theory's axiom of 'bivalence', assuming that in law, propositions 'fall into two (mutually exclusive) classes', lawful and unlawful.[16]

10 Hart, *Concept of Law*, 127.
11 Endicott, *Vagueness in Law*, 47.
12 Williamson, 'Vagueness in Reality', 690.
13 Ashley Deeks, 'Multi-part Tests in the *Jus Ad Bellum*', *Houston Law Review*, 53:4 (2016), 1035–64, 1038, 1039.
14 Ibid., 1038, 1039.
15 Williamson, 'Vagueness in Reality', 692.
16 Ronald Dworkin, 'No Right Answer?', *New York University Law Review*, 53 (1978), 1, 4; Pieter Seuren, 'Eubulides as a 20th-Century Semanticist', *Language Sciences*, 27 (2005), 75, 81.

Much law, and the necessary elements of multi-part tests, are 'crafted to have binary (yes/no) answers', assuming all cases fall into these two clear categories.[17] Some national legal systems 'expressly prohibit *non liquet*', forbidding courts from ruling that the law is unclear about whether behaviour examined in a case is lawful or unlawful, 'imposing a duty on judges to decide cases, if necessary, by filling gaps in the law' using analogies, general principles, 'even the elaboration of a new rule'.[18]

However, many laws prescribe tests that cannot be applied bivalently, but are instead vulnerable to the 'sorites paradox', or 'paradox of the heap'.[19] Remove a grain of sand from a heap of sand and it remains a heap. Remove a second or third grain and the heap remains. Continue removing grains and eventually the remaining sand can no longer be described as a heap. However, it is not possible to identify a specific point – a precise number of grains of sand – at which that boundary between 'heap' and 'not heap' has been crossed. Similarly, laws vulnerable to the sorites paradox describe a *continuum* of cases, each slightly different to the next.[20] Most actual and potential cases may encompass behaviours so close to the extremes of such a continuum as to be assessed as clearly meeting or not meeting each test prescribed by the law. However, such plain cases are separated by numerous cases along the continuum, each only slightly different to the next, forming what Hart described as a 'penumbra of uncertainty' rather than sharp boundary between lawfulness and unlawfulness.[21]

'Fuzzy logic' provides a potential solution for assessing cases in the penumbra, rejecting binary categorisations and evaluating cases according to *degrees* of lawfulness.[22] However, even fuzzy logic often cannot quantify the 'degree' to which a case is lawful, because the tests that evaluate lawfulness are often *immensurable* – stipulating 'properties that cannot be quantified', or for which there is no generally accepted method of measurement (see Figure 2.1).[23] Paradigm-based laws are often further complicated because their multi-part tests are *incommensurable* – they require evaluation of characteristics that cannot clearly be measured and compared to each other using the same evaluation standards.[24]

17 Deeks, 'Multi-part Tests', 1039.

18 Daniel Bodansky, 'Non Liquet', *Max Planck Encyclopedia of Public International Law* (Oxford: Oxford University Press, 2006).

19 Seuren, 'Eubulides', 88–9; Endicott, *Vagueness in Law*, 35.

20 Seuren, 'Eubulides', 88–9; Endicott, *Vagueness in Law*, 35.

21 Hart, *Concept of Law*, 131, 134; Endicott, *Vagueness in Law*, 35.

22 Williamson, 'Vagueness in Reality', 693.

23 Endicott, *Vagueness in Law*, 41.

24 Ibid.

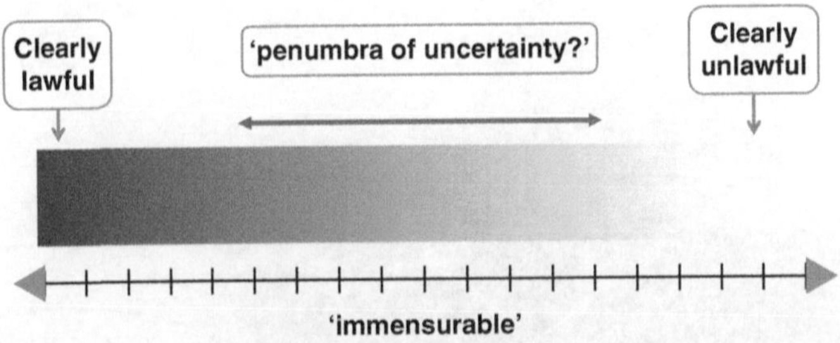

FIGURE 2.1 Fuzzy logic

For example, laws prohibiting 'neglect' of children could be defined by paradigms of lawful 'appropriate childcare', and unlawful 'neglect'.[25] Such laws could be described as multi-part tests with necessary elements concerning food, shelter, safety, healthcare and education.[26] Each of these tests operate according to fuzzy, not bivalent, logic. For example, the test governing 'appropriate food' is not bivalent: giving a child no food would be clearly unlawful, providing sufficient food would be clearly lawful. But that clearly unlawful and clearly lawful behaviour is separated not by a sharp boundary, but by potentially infinite possible cases in which the child receives incrementally different quantities of food.

Figure 2.2 illustrates how paradigms of 'appropriate childcare' and 'neglect' display both fuzzy logic and supervaluationism. The paradigms are identified by multiple tests or necessary elements, overlapping but not entirely co-extensive, immensurable and incommensurable, each operating according to fuzzy logic. The tests are represented as axes radiating from the 'core of application' of appropriate childcare, the narrow arrows indicating the tests interacting. Different 'intensities' of each property and their interaction influence whether an observer evaluates that an action complies with the paradigm either of 'appropriate childcare' or of 'neglect'. Thus giving a child no food, shelter, education, safety or healthcare clearly aligns with the 'neglect' paradigm; providing enough of each clearly aligns with the 'appropriate childcare' paradigm.[27] Yet, because the tests are incommensurable continuums, the paradigms of lawful and unlawful behaviour are not separated by a sharp boundary, but by a fuzzy penumbra of uncertainty.

25 Scott Soames, 'What Vagueness and Inconsistency Tell Us about Interpretation', in Andrei Marmor and Scott Soames, eds., *Philosophical Foundations of Language in the Law* (Oxford: Oxford University Press, 2011), 39–41.

26 Ibid.

27 Ibid.

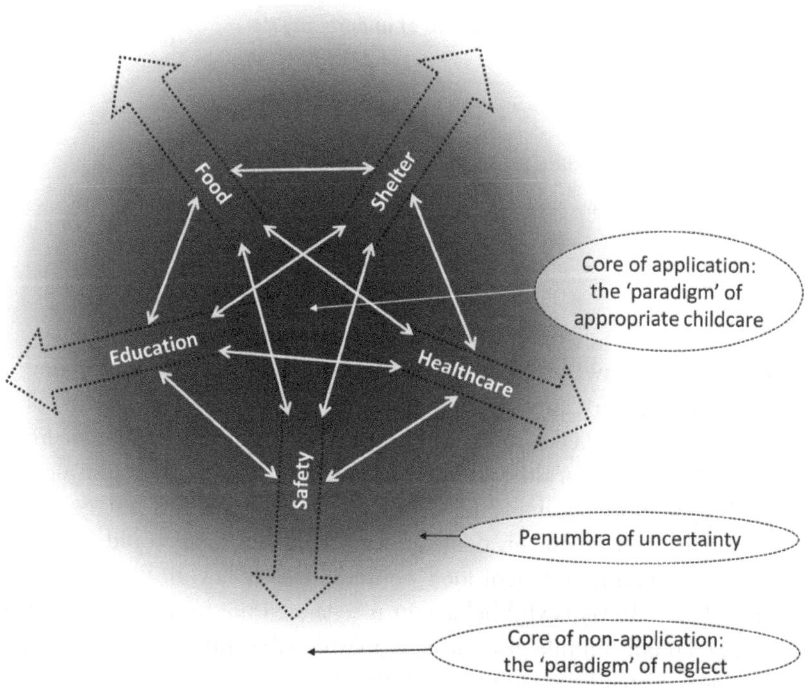

FIGURE 2.2 Incommensurable, fuzzy multi-part test

Such vagueness and uncertainty in law is of course commonplace. All legal systems have evolved canons of interpretation – what Hart described as 'secondary rules' of law – to deal with such cases, prescribing how to interpret law when the words defining it or what it prescribes in a particular case is unclear, or when different rules conflict.[28] Hart argued such secondary rules include legally ultimate 'rules of recognition' specifying how to recognise a valid new or existing rule, often not inferred from other rules, but 'simply accepted as appropriate', as the standard metre bar in Paris is simply accepted as determining metric measurements.[29] However, even well accepted canons of interpretation are often affected by the forms of vagueness described in this section. They often propose paradigms of correct and incorrect ways of interpreting the law, defined by multiple features and thus subject to supervaluationism, and where correct and incorrect interpretive methods are

[28] Hart, *Concept of Law*, 98, 148, 101, 109.
[29] Ibid., 109.

separated not by a sharp boundary but by a continuum of potential methods operating according to fuzzy logic.

All these effects are vividly demonstrated in the 2005 Israel Supreme Court targeted killings judgment, examining when civilians lose immunity from military targeting.[30] The Second Additional Protocol to the Geneva Conventions states that civilians have immunity 'unless and for such time as they take a direct part in hostilities'.[31] The Israel Supreme Court's judgment identified paradigms of civilians who retained and who had lost immunity from targeting, and criteria for what actions constitute 'a direct part in hostilities', what time is 'for such time' and proportionality. At one extreme, civilians clearly immune from targeting spent no time doing anything connected to military attacks; at the other extreme, civilians clearly not immune from targeting spent all their working time planning or conducting attacks and had evaded non-lethal means of capture; many other civilians are distributed between these extremes.[32] The judgment argued there could be no simple test for determining whether a civilian was immune from targeting, and 'each and every case' must be examined using the various criteria that the judgment identified.[33]

Laws may display a fourth form of vagueness, which might be termed 'social supervaluationism'.[34] Different groups can co-exist in the same legal system, holding different shared understandings about law, each with their own, separate 'core' of clearly lawful and clearly unlawful behaviour, and with different penumbra of uncertainty (Figure 2.3). Such groups can operationalise different goals, purposes, value systems and methods of reasoning, and thus apply different boundaries between lawful and unlawful behaviour. Socio-legal scholars assert the prevalence of such varying groups in societies means any legal system's 'secondary rules of law' are 'at least partially constituted by official convergence' by influential groups on 'standards of conduct', 'authoritative texts' and 'basic structural rules'.[35] And so 'Law's basic "truth"' is 'the

30 The Supreme Court Sitting as the High Court of Justice (Israel), HCJ769/02, *The Public Committee against Torture in Israel et al.* v. *Government of Israel et al.*, 11 December 2005.

31 International Committee of the Red Cross, 'Protocol Additional to the Geneva Conventions of 12 August 1949, and Relating to the Protection of Victims of Non-International Armed Conflicts (Protocol II)', 8 June 1977, 1125 UNTS 17513, art 13(3), 615.

32 Israel Supreme Court, *Public Committee against Torture*, paras. 34–46.

33 Ibid., para. 40.

34 John Griffiths, 'What Is Legal Pluralism?', *Journal of Legal Pluralism and Unofficial Law*, 24 (1986), 1, 38, 36.

35 Scott Shapiro, 'What Is the Rule of Recognition (And Does It Exist)?', in Matthew Adler and Kenneth E. Himma, eds., *The Rule of Recognition and the U.S. Constitution* (Oxford: Oxford University Press, 2009), 235, 267.

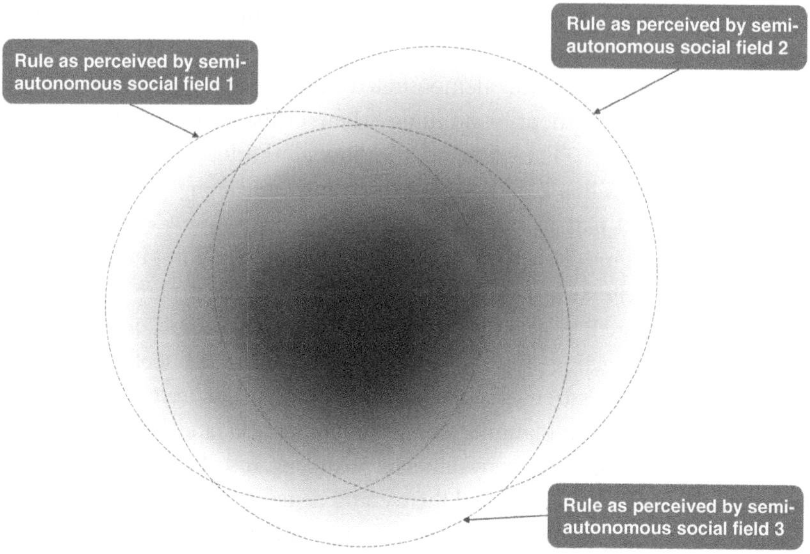

FIGURE 2.3 Fuzzy, overlapping, semi-autonomous social fields

provisional, pragmatic consensus' of legal actors who are 'perceived at any given time to be supported by the highest forms of authority'.[36]

However, even within one jurisdiction, 'ideas, attitudes, opinions, and expectations' about law can diverge.[37] Rawls has suggested that notions of justice within a society arise from a 'reasonable overlapping consensus' of 'a plurality of conflicting reasonable comprehensive doctrines'.[38] Such concepts lead some scholars to observe that legal systems may develop different 'semi-autonomous social fields' or 'legal cultures', functioning as distinct 'interpretive cultures', applying mostly overlapping, sometimes competing shared understandings about legal interpretation and lawfulness.[39] Competing interpretive cultures may heighten legal disagreement, as parties practise 'strategic behaviour in interpretation' – deliberately using different interpretive techniques to advance competing purposes, reaching opposing conclusions in specific cases.[40] This

36 Roger Cotterrell, 'Why Must Legal Ideas Be Interpreted Sociologically?', *Journal of Law and Society*, 25:2 (1998), 171–92, 181.

37 Lawrence M. Friedman, 'The Place of Legal Culture in the Sociology of Law', in Michael Freeman, ed., *Law and Sociology* (Oxford: Oxford University Press, 2006), 185–99, 189.

38 John Rawls, *The Law of Peoples* (Cambridge, MA: Harvard University Press, 2001), 172, 131.

39 Griffiths, 'What Is Legal Pluralism?', 38, 36; Waibel, 'Interpretive Communities', 148; Haas, 'Introduction', 3.

40 Kennedy, *Legal Reasoning*, 159.

affects how law functions as a set of argumentative practices: legal uncertainty provides individuals pursuing competing goals with a wider range of options for both justifying and criticising behaviour as either lawful or unlawful.[41]

Competing legal cultures may create legislative disagreement and thus produce unclear laws, since statutes emerge from interactions between political actors pursuing different goals.[42] Changes in society and technology often require existing laws to be applied to disputes that law-makers never originally envisaged, resulting in competing cultures' value systems and legal understandings evolving in different ways, exacerbating social supervaluationism.[43] Uncertainty about facts can encourage competing interpretive cultures to generate more supervaluationism, as will be discussed in the next chapter.

Some argue law is 'not just a passive receptor' of social and technological changes, but 'plays an active role in the development and design of such changes' by prescribing constraints and rights.[44] Law is applied to, and thus interacts with and evolves in response to social and technological changes, to help determine '(w)hat counts as uncertainty, how uncertainty is framed, and which policy options are available' to deal with that uncertainty, so lawyers actually 'co-produce' the uncertainties they seek to regulate.[45]

Many scholars claim none of these challenges refute 'systemic determinacy', and lawyers and legal systems can always find a single, right answer to legal questions. Fuller advocated interpreting laws in light of their purpose, 'structural integrity' and 'relation with other rules'.[46] Lord Devlin argued every society's moral consensus always suggests a single right answer.[47] Dworkin claimed in complex legal systems, no two theories could 'demand different answers in some case and yet provide equally good fit with the relevant legal materials', and courts must choose the interpretation which best advances 'principles and policies' providing 'the best political justification for the statute

41 Koskenniemi, *From Apology to Utopia*, 67–9.

42 Barry R. Weingast, 'Political Institutions: Rational Choice Perspectives', in Robert E. Goodin and Hans-Dieter Klingemann, *A New Handbook of Political Science* (Oxford: Oxford University Press, 1998), 172–4; Bo Rothstein, 'Political Institutions: An Overview', in Robert E. Goodin and Hans-Dieter Klingemann, *A New Handbook of Political Science* (Oxford: Oxford University Press, 1998), 133–61, 143–8.

43 Hart, *Concept of Law*, 129.

44 Mónika Ambrus, Rosemary Rayfuse and Wouter Werner, 'Risk and International Law', in Mónika Ambrus, Rosemary Rayfuse and Wouter Werner, eds., *Risk and Uncertainty in International Law* (Oxford: Oxford University Press, 2017), 5.

45 Ibid.

46 Lon L. Fuller, 'Positivism and Fidelity to Law – A Reply to Professor Hart', *Harvard Law Review*, 71:4 (1958), 630–72, 670.

47 Lord Devlin, 'Law, Morality and Democracy', *University of Pennsylvania Law Review*, 110:5 (March 1962), 635–49, 638.

at the time it was passed'.[48] Some argue lawyers considering hard cases should rely on their intuitions, since these 'have a cognitive dimension', reflecting genuine reasoning, so that even when lawfulness is hard to define, an experienced judge may assert 'I know it when I see it.'[49] In the longer term, legislation may adapt to a changed reality and thus (re-)establish determinacy as 'an afterthought, after the thing has become obvious enough to set the legislative machinery into motion'.[50] Or judicial decisions can deliver determinacy, as a 'juridical *avant garde*' adapts the law to 'new states of social relations'.[51]

Yet, while all these responses undoubtedly *reduce* indeterminacy, they do not *eliminate* it. Some 'legal realists' and critical legal studies scholars respond by embracing systemic indeterminacy, arguing that experienced advocates know 'the doctrinal regime is sufficiently complex' to provide 'authoritative materials which, through skillful manipulation' can support *any* position.[52] 'Easy cases' undermine such claims: legal assessments such as 'walking one's dog does not violate the antitrust laws' are both determinate and near-impossible to refute.[53] The vast majority of legally regulated interactions are similarly so determinate that even genuine disputes rarely go to court.[54]

The intermediate position of 'specific indeterminacy' aligns with Hart's observation that all laws are *sometimes* indeterminate; 'uncertainty at the borderline' is the price society pays for using language and precedent in law.[55] In fact, it can be argued vagueness and indeterminacies are 'essential features of law'.[56] Hart argued that many legally regulated activities vary so much in important but acceptable ways that 'uniform rules' applied 'without further official direction cannot usefully be framed', and so lawmakers adopt general standards, delegating authority to a body to apply the standard.[57] Even Kelsen argued law often only identifies 'a number of decisions, all of them of equal standing', since '(e)ven a meticulously detailed command must leave

48 Ronald Dworkin, *A Matter of Principle* (Oxford: Oxford University Press, 1985), 145, 129.
49 Paul Gewirtz, 'On "I Know It When I See It"', *Yale Law Journal*, 105 (1996), 1031.
50 Eugen Ehrlich and Nathan Isaacs, 'The Sociology of Law', *Harvard Law Review*, 36:2 (1922), 130–45, 140.
51 Pierre Bourdieu, 'The Force of Law: Toward a Sociology of the Juridical Field', *Hastings Law Journal*, 38 (1987), 805–53, 852.
52 Solum, 'Indeterminacy Crisis', 496; Charles M. Yablon, 'The Indeterminacy of the Law: Critical Legal Studies and the Problem of Legal Explanation', *Cardozo Law Review*, 6 (1985), 917–46, 917, 918.
53 Solum, 'Indeterminacy Crisis', 471–2.
54 Ehrlich and Isaacs, 'Sociology of Law', 141.
55 Hart, *Concept of Law*, 126.
56 Endicott, *Vagueness in Law*, 1.
57 Hart, *Concept of Law*, 131.

a number of determinations to those carrying it out'.[58] And Raz notes that if 'law is exclusively determined by social facts, then the law is gappy', 'there are legal statements which are neither true nor false'.[59] If enough participants in a legal system agree about *most* even if not *all* propositions underpinning law – canons of interpretation, rules of recognition, underlying social purposes, beliefs about causes and consequences of behaviours – then neither systemic determinacy nor systemic indeterminacy seem plausible.

Legal uncertainty in reality can be seen even in highly developed domestic legal systems, and is not confined to marginal or trivial issues. UK laws governing pornography displayed significant uncertainty, from vague formulations in nineteenth-century legislation, inconsistent attempts to enforce the law such as the failed 1960 *Lady Chatterley's Lover* case, up to legislation criminalising 'extreme pornographic images'.[60] The lawfulness of assisted dying has faced similar uncertainty, from the 1961 Suicide Act to controversial court cases forcing the Director of Public Prosecutions to issue guidance incorporating complex, multi-part tests, over which prosecutors and Courts repeatedly disagreed.[61] There are other potential examples – defamation on the Internet, laws governing homosexuality, abortion and heterosexual age of consent are all areas where superficially determinate law has proven difficult to apply in specific cases, displaying a non-trivial penumbra of uncertainty, which expands or contracts in response to social and legal change and the reactions of different sections of society.

Law is always framed or applied in human language, and language has inherently limited precision. Law often deals with complex, multidimensional and fuzzy rather than bivalent activities. Law is always socially constructed, emerging not only from pure doctrinal study but also from the complex, conflicting interactions of human beings with different understandings, beliefs, preferences and value systems. So the vagueness and uncertainty

58 Kelsen, *Introduction*, 80, 81, 78.

59 Joseph Raz, 'Legal Principles and the Limits of Law', in Marshall Cohen, ed., *Ronald Dworkin and Contemporary Jurisprudence* (London: Duckworth, 1983), 73.

60 Ursula Smartt, *Media and Entertainment Law* (Abingdon: Routledge, 2011), 264; Alistair McCleery, 'The Return of the Publisher to Book History: The Case of Allen Lane', *Book History*, 5 (2002), 161–85, 176; HM Government, Criminal Justice and Immigration Act 2008.

61 Jan Neeleman, 'Suicide as a Crime: Legal History, International Comparisons and Present Implications', *Acta Psychiatrica Scandinavica*, 94 (1996), 252–7, 253; *R (on the application of Purdy)* v. *Director of Public Prosecutions* [2009] UKHL 45 (Lords of Appeal, 30 July 2009); Director of Public Prosecutions, *Policy for Prosecutors in Respect of Cases of Encouraging or Assisting Suicide* (London: Crown Prosecution Service, 2010); Sandra Laville, 'Mercy Killing Mother Cleared of Murder after Helping Seriously Ill Daughter Die', *The Guardian* (25 January 2010).

caused by paradigms, fuzzy logic and supervaluationism will apply in at least some cases. In fact, such vagueness and uncertainty are often necessary features of law, enabling it to flex and adapt to the complexities of the activities it seeks to regulate and the communities that seek to apply it. What law requires may sometimes display only *degrees* of truth/falsity – it is *specifically indeterminate*. From this perspective, even domestic law, which many critics of international law hold up as 'true law', might also be described as reliant on informal, decentralised social facts and processes, as vulnerable as international law to Bolton's dismissive description as 'a series of political and moral arrangements' and 'theology and superstition masquerading as law'.[62]

UNCERTAINTY IN IDENTIFYING AND INTERPRETING THE *JUS AD BELLUM*

The rest of this chapter argues that the concepts described so far – paradigms, fuzzy logic, supervaluationism, legal cultures – are all relevant to understanding uncertainty and controversy in international law governing resort to force. That is not obvious from an initial examination of the sources of that law. The UN Charter, signed on 26 June 1945 by the founding members of the United Nations, succinctly and apparently unambiguously articulates the generally accepted rules of international law governing resort to force. Article 2(4) prohibits states 'from the threat or use of force against the territorial integrity or political independence of any state', or 'in any other manner inconsistent with' the UN's purposes.[63] Article 42 permits the UNSC to authorise force 'to maintain or restore international peace and security' should it consider non-forceful measures inadequate. Article 51 preserves states' 'inherent right of individual or collective self-defense if an armed attack occurs'. The prohibition is widely seen as *jus cogens*, 'a norm from which no derogation is permitted', and a norm of customary international law, not only a treaty obligation on states parties to the UN Charter.[64] The 'outlawing of acts of aggression' is widely regarded as an '*erga omnes*' obligation of every state 'towards the international community as a whole', for which all states 'have a legal interest in their protection'.[65] Some lawyers argue that the centrality of the prohibition on force in the charter means it is 'founded on a genuine *jus*

62 Bolton, '"Law" in International Affairs', 48.

63 United Nations Charter.

64 *Nicaragua*, Merits, para. 190; Vienna Convention on the Law of Treaties (VCLT), Vienna, 23 May 1969, in force 27 January 1980, 1155 UNTS 331.

65 *Case Concerning the Barcelona Traction, Light and Power Company, Limited*, Judgment, ICJ Reports 1970, paras. 33, 34.

contra bellum and not on the *jus ad bellum* that characterised earlier periods'.[66]

This post-1945 charter system was a significant development of the existing *jus ad bellum*.[67] The states system that emerged from the treaties making up the 1648 Peace of Westphalia, and from other treaties such as the 1555 Treaty of Augsburg and 1713 Treaty of Utrecht, is widely viewed as having relied on the balance of power enforced by war to maintain international order.[68] That states system incorporated a dichotomy – 'respect for the sovereignty of states, while each State had a sovereign right to destroy the sovereignty of others' through their unconstrained right to make war.[69] The concept of the 'Just War' in the writings of earlier international legal scholars such as Vitoria, Suarez and Grotius had been abandoned.[70] By the nineteenth century, the legality of 'recourse to war was seen to depend upon the formal processes of law' such as a declaration of war, and war entailed legal consequences such as laws of neutrality governing belligerent parties and third states.[71]

But, while countries did enter into bilateral non-aggression treaties, before the twentieth century international law imposed no significant substantive constraints on the rights of states to resort to force.[72] States launched wars against other states to assert hereditary claims to monarchical rule, to prevent the replacement of monarchies by republican rule, to enforce debt payments and to keep markets open.[73] Those weak norms which did regulate war between European states did not prevent those states from using military force to acquire control of extensive territories outside Europe. The 1907 Hague Regulations saw states for the first time accept some general constraints on their right to use force to recover contract debts, but it was not until the carnage of World War I that states accepted more general constraints on their right to use force in their international relations.[74] The 1919 League of Nations

66 Corten, *Law against War*, 2.

67 Peter Malanczuk, *Akehurst's Modern Introduction to International Law*, Kindle ed. (New York: Routledge, 1997), loc. 1631.

68 David Armstrong, Theo Farrell and Helene Lambert, *International Law and International Relations*, 2nd ed. (Cambridge University Press, 2012), 60; Yoram Dinstein, *War, Aggression and Self-Defence* (Cambridge: Cambridge University Press, 2005), 76.

69 Dinstein, *War, Aggression and Self-Defence*, 76.

70 Fisher, *Morality and War*, 80.

71 Shaw, *International Law*, 1120.

72 Dinstein, *War, Aggression and Self-Defence*, 76.

73 Armstrong, Farrell and Lambert, *International Law*, 63; Julia Lovell, *The Opium War: Drugs, Dreams and the Making of China* (London: Picador, 2012); Steven C Topik, 'When Mexico Had the Blues: A Transatlantic Tale of Bonds, Bankers and Nationalists, 1862–1910', *American Historical Review*, 105:3 (June 2000), 714–40, 717.

74 Dinstein, *War, Aggression and Self-Defence*, 79.

required dispute arbitration before resort to force, and the sixty-three adherents to the 1928 Kellogg-Briand or Paris Pact renounced aggressive unilateral force between each other.[75] Yet these treaties failed to prevent World War II.

Nevertheless, it has been argued these various treaties showed that, by 1939, there had emerged a 'custom among civilized peoples to regard a war of aggression as not simply "unjust" or "illegal" but downright criminal'.[76] This was one justification for including 'launching a war of aggression' among the 'criminal violations of International Law' in Article 6(b) of the August 1945 Constitution of the International Military Tribunal of Nuremberg.[77] However, this argument was disputed at the time even by US, UK and French scholars, and the criticisms of 'retroactivity and selectivity' are 'now widely accepted as legitimate complaints against Nuremberg'.[78]

In any case, most commentators in 1945 believed the existing system had failed to prevent war, in part because powerful states had insufficient incentives to support the system or to use force to suppress aggression.[79] The UN Charter's drafters sought to remedy these faults of the previous attempts to regulate force. Their foundational treaty required states to renounce the threat or use of force against the territorial integrity or political independence of other states, introduced a multilateral mechanism to authorise force to confront threats to international peace and security, while preserving states' inherent right of individual and collective self-defence. The charter incentivised the five great powers to maintain the system by safeguarding them from enforcement action through the UNSC veto.

All lawyers also accept that relevant customary international law may have emerged *after* the charter was adopted, as for example the ICJ ruled that by the 1960s the practice had emerged of UNSC resolutions being accepted as valid even with the abstention of any of the Permanent Five UNSC members.[80] Most also accept some pre-charter custom concerning the *jus ad bellum* where it does not contradict the charter, the most famous example being the '*Caroline* criteria', articulated by US Secretary of State Webster in 1842 after British forces destroyed a ship in the United States suspected of supplying

75 Malanczuk, *Akehurst's*, locs. 1582–96.

76 Sheldon Glueck, 'The Nuremberg Trial and Aggressive War', *Harvard Law Review*, 59:3 (1946), 396–456, 412.

77 Ibid., 396.

78 Kirsten Sellars, 'Imperfect Justice at Nuremberg and Tokyo', *The European Journal of International Law*, 21:4 (2011), 1085–102, 1089.

79 Malanczuk, *Akehurst's*, locs. 1582–96.

80 *Legal Consequences for States of the Continued Presence of South Africa in Namibia (South West Africa) notwithstanding Security Council Resolution 276 (1970)*, Advisory Opinion, ICJ Reports 1971, 12, 22.

Canadian rebels.[81] Webster wrote that a state acting in self-defence must demonstrate 'a necessity of self-defence, instant, overwhelming, leaving no choice of means, and no moment for deliberation', doing 'nothing unreasonable or excessive', ensuring its actions were 'limited by that necessity, and kept clearly within it'.[82] The *Caroline* tests of necessity, imminence and proportionality are now often applied by analogy to other legal justifications for use of force beyond self-defence.[83]

Other materials relevant to the law governing resort to force have emerged since 1945, including the UNGA's Declaration on Friendly Relations', 'Definition of Aggression' and 'Uniting for Peace Resolution', as well as ICJ jurisprudence and scholarly writings.[84] The International Criminal Court's (ICC) Crime of Aggression came into force in December 2017, providing additional relevant law for ICC states parties which have ratified the amendment and for any states the UNSC refers to the Court, except for any alleged violations 'committed by a national or on the territory of a State Party that has not ratified or accepted these amendments'.[85] Together, these sources of law and their underpinning institutions constitute a more comprehensive body of international law governing resort to force than at any time in history.

Yet this area of law continues to provoke significant controversy. This controversy is at least partly attributable to the forms of vagueness already identified in this chapter. First, the UN Charter relies on paradigm 'plain cases' of legal and illegal force.[86] The charter's clearest paradigm of *illegal* force is 'an armed attack' (art. 51) or 'use of force', 'against the territorial integrity or political independence of any state' (art. 2(4)), which is not 'in

81 'The *Caroline* Case', in Martin Dixon and Robert McCorquodale, eds., *Cases and Materials on International Law* (Oxford: Oxford University Press, 2003), 530.

82 Ibid., 530.

83 HM Government, 'Chemical Weapon Use by Syrian Regime: UK Government Legal Position' (London: HM Government, 2013).

84 UN General Assembly, Resolution 2625 (XXV), 'Declaration on Principles of International Law concerning Friendly Relations and Co-operation among States in Accordance with the Charter of the United Nations', 24 October 1970, A/RES/2625 (XXV); UN General Assembly, Resolution 3314, 'Definition of Aggression', 14 December 1974, A/RES/3314 (XXIX); UN General Assembly, Resolution 377, 'Uniting for Peace', 3 November 1950, A/RES/377; International Court of Justice, Statute of the International Court of Justice (ICJ Statute), art. 38(1)(d).

85 International Criminal Court, 'The Crime of Aggression', 11 June 2010, ICC-RC/Res. 6; International Criminal Court, 'Activation of the Jurisdiction of the Court over the Crime of Aggression', 14 December 2017, ICC-ASP/16/Res. 5; Dapo Akande, 'The International Criminal Court Gets Jurisdiction over the Crime of Aggression', *EJIL: Talk!*, 15 December 2017, www.ejiltalk.org/the-international-criminal-court-gets-jurisdiction-over-the-crime-of-aggression.

86 Hart, *Concept of Law*, 127.

the common interest' (preamble), not 'individual or collective self-defense' (art. 51), nor authorised by the UNSC, which constitutes a 'threat to the peace, breach of the peace, or act of aggression' (art. 39), and which adversely affects 'international peace and security' (art. 42). Yet there is uncertainty about identifying this paradigm. For example, some ICJ jurisprudence seems to suggest the concepts of 'armed attack' and 'act of aggression' correspond, while 'war and/or crime of aggression' do not necessarily correspond.[87] Kress argues only 'war of conquest' and 'hegemonial war' are clear historical precedents for acts of aggression, the forms of force that arguably have caused most harm to the international system and human security.[88] Another paradigm of illegal force is forceful assistance to any state against which the UN 'is taking preventive or enforcement action' (art. 2(5)).

The UN Charter suggests two clear paradigms of *legal* force. States may use force in 'individual or collective self-defence if an armed attack occurs' (art. 51) on themselves or another UN member by a state not itself acting in self-defence or with UNSC authorisation. States may also use force when the UNSC identifies a 'threat to the peace, breach of the peace, or act of aggression' (art. 39), and authorises military action 'to maintain or restore international peace and security' (art. 42). Article 2(7), protecting matters 'essentially within the domestic jurisdiction of any state', confirms a third generally accepted paradigm of lawful force. States may use force within another state with that government's consent, unless forbidden by a Chapter VII UNSC resolution.

Since the *jus ad bellum* articulates such paradigms, identifying and applying the law is subject to 'supervaluationism'. The law does not prescribe a single test, rather several overlapping but not co-extensive principles, in effect a 'multi-part test' articulating 'specific elements' covering different 'evidentiary questions' against which any use of force must be evaluated to assess its legality.[89] There are various potential ways of framing the *jus ad bellum* tests. For the purposes of this book, they are framed as six tests as follows.

87 Dapo Akande and Antonios Tzanakopoulos, 'The International Court of Justice and the Concept of Aggression', in Claus Kreß and Stefan Barriga, eds., *The Crime of Aggression: A Commentary* (Cambridge: Cambridge University Press, 2015), 214–32, 228.

88 Andreas Paulus, 'Second Thoughts on the Crime of Aggression', *European Journal of International Law* 20 (2009), 1122; Human Security Report Project, *Human Security Report 2009/2010* (Oxford: Oxford University Press, 2011), 7.

89 Jorg Kammerhofer, 'Uncertainties of the Law on Self-Defence in the United Nations Charter', *Netherlands Yearbook of International Law*, 35 (2004), 143; Wilmshurst, 'Chatham House Principles', 963; Dinstein, *War, Aggression and Self-Defence*, 175–273; Deeks 'Multi-part Tests', 1037.

Necessity Actual or impending harm that makes force a necessary response. (Contemporary international lawyers rarely use the term *casus belli*, although policy-makers and commentators still sometimes do.)[90] The *Caroline* criteria describe 'a necessity of self-defence' that is 'overwhelming, leaving no choice of means' to respond.[91] The test is widely interpreted as permitting states to use force if 'no other means would deflect' an attack.[92] It is widely agreed that military invasion constitutes *prima facie* evidence of necessity to use force in self-defence, without requiring peaceful settlement be sought first, if the only alternative is acquiescence to occupation, 'even when a state's use of force in self-defense would be futile, or when it has a more realistic chance of achieving a cessation of the attack by other means'.[93]

The UN Charter does not explicitly define necessity.[94] However, it describes circumstances which may directly or via the UNSC justify force: 'armed attack' (art. 51), 'use of force' (art. 2(4)), 'threat to the peace, breach of the peace' (art. 39), when non-forceful measures 'would be' 'or have proved to be inadequate' (art. 42), and 'such action ... as may be necessary to maintain or restore international peace and security' (art. 42). The charter's preamble, declaring 'force shall not be used, save in the common interest', hints at a possible further circumstance in which force may be necessary: applying the controversial principle '*a contrario sensu*', it might be argued the charter permits force which *is* 'in the common interest'.[95]

90 E.g. Iraq Inquiry, 'Section 3.5: Development of UK Strategy and Options, September to November 2002 – The Negotiation of Resolution 1441', *The Report of the Iraq Inquiry*, vol. 2 (London: HM Stationery Office, 2016), paras. 27, 33, 44, 102, 328.

91 'The *Caroline* Case', 530.

92 UN General Assembly, '*A More Secure World: Our Shared Responsibility*', *Report of the Secretary General's High-level Panel on Threats, Challenges and Change*, 2 December 2004, A/59/565, para. 188; Gray, *International Law*, 150; *Nicaragua*, Merits, para. 237.

93 Oscar Schachter, 'The Right of States to Use Armed Force', *Michigan Law Review*, 82 (1984), 1635; Dapo Akande and Thomas Liefländer, 'Clarifying Necessity, Imminence, and Proportionality in the Law of Self-Defense', *The American Journal of International Law*, 107:3 (2013), 564.

94 *Nicaragua*, Merits, para. 176.

95 *The Corfu Channel Case*, Merits, Judgment, 9 April 1949, ICJ Reports (1949), 4; *Corfu*, Dissenting Opinion of Judge Azevedo, para. 30; Louis Henkin, 'Kosovo and the Law of "Humanitarian Intervention"', *American Journal of International Law*, 3 (1999), 824, 826.

Article 3(g) of the UNGA's 'Definition of Aggression' provides a non-exhaustive list of actions that may constitute armed attack, including invasion, bombardment, blockade of ports, sending 'armed bands, groups, irregulars or mercenaries, which carry out acts of armed force'.[96] The UNSC in 1992 committed to address wider security challenges, including 'international terrorism' and WMD proliferation, and has authorised force to address many such threats, including in Somalia, Afghanistan, the Democratic Republic of the Congo, and Libya.[97]

Victim	Those experiencing actual or impending harm, in whose defence it is lawful for a state to use force. The most uncontroversial victim the UN Charter defines is a state against whom 'an armed attack occurs' (art. 51). The UNGA 'Definition of Aggression' includes attacks against a state's 'land, sea or air forces, or marine and air fleets'.[98]
Attacker	Those against whom it is lawful to use force. The UN Charter implies any actor responsible for 'an armed attack' (art. 51) is a lawful target of military force. The UN Charter clearly also intends 'any state against which the United Nations is taking preventive or enforcement action' (art. 2(5)) with UNSC authorisation to be the lawful target of 'operations by air, sea, or land forces' (art. 42).
Authority	The authorisation that lawful force requires. The UN Charter states that the UNSC may authorise 'such action by air, sea, or land forces as may be necessary to maintain or restore international peace and security' (art. 42). It also states that 'nothing in the present Charter shall impair the inherent right of individual or collective self-defense if an armed attack occurs' against a UN Member (art. 51), clearly preserving states' authority to use force for self-defence

96 UN General Assembly, 'Definition of Aggression'.

97 Greenwood, 'War against Terrorism', 141–2; UN Security Council, 'Note by the President of the Security Council', 31 January 1992, S/23500; James Gow, *Defending the West* (Cambridge: Polity Press, 2005), 37, 56; UN Security Council, Resolution 1973, 17 March 2011, S/RES/1973; UN Security Council, Resolution 1846, 2 December 2008, S/RES/1846; UN Security Council, Resolution 1291, S/RES/1291, 24 February 2000; UN Security Council, Resolution 1386, 20 December 2001, S/RES/1386.

98 UN General Assembly, 'Definition of Aggression'.

without UNSC authorisation. The 1950 UNGA 'Uniting for Peace' resolution stated that the General Assembly could make 'recommendations to Members for collective measures, including in the case of a breach of the peace or act of aggression the use of armed force when necessary', where the UNSC 'fails to exercise its primary responsibility for the maintenance of international peace and security' due to lack of unanimity among its permanent members – although the resolution has not been used for this purpose since the 1950s.[99]

Imminence In large part a test about time scales – how imminent an attack must be for resort to force to be lawful. The *Caroline* criteria specify force is justified when expectation of harm is 'instant', leaving 'no moment for deliberation'.[100] The charter also mentions timing, stating force in self-defence is justified 'if an armed attack occurs', and 'until the Security Council has taken the measures necessary to maintain international peace and security' (art. 51).

Proportionality This requires resort to force to be no more than sufficient to stop the harm being faced, 'limited by that necessity, and kept clearly within it', involving 'nothing unreasonable or excessive'.[101] The UN Charter does not define proportionality for self-defence, although it hints at some sense of proportionality for UNSC-authorised action, stating that the UNSC may take such action 'as may be necessary to maintain or restore international peace and security' (art. 42). The UNGA 'Definition of Aggression' indicates only acts and consequences 'of sufficient gravity' count as aggression.[102] In the *Nicaragua* case, the ICJ decided only actions of 'scale and effects' exceeding 'a mere frontier incident' may be 'classified as an armed attack' justifying force in response.[103] Some lawyers criticise this limitation,

99 UN General Assembly, 'Uniting for Peace'; Dinstein, *War, Aggression and Self-Defence*, 316–18; Gray, *International Law*, 268.

100 'The *Caroline* Case', 530.

101 Ibid., 530.

102 *Nicaragua*, Merits, para. 176, UN General Assembly, 'Definition of Aggression'.

103 *Nicaragua*, Merits, para. 195.

> arguing proportionality dictates *how much* force may be used in self-defence, not *whether* force is a lawful response.[104] Nevertheless, most agree an attack must exceed some '*de minimis* threshold' before the 'victim State' may 'launch war in self-defence'.[105]

Framing the *jus ad bellum* as such a 'multi-part test' shows its similarity to the 'Just War' doctrine prescribed by classical and medieval ethicists such as Aquinas and Augustine, and by sixteenth- and seventeenth-century legal scholars such as Vitoria, Suarez and Grotius, to evaluate justifications for resort to war using criteria such as just cause, right intent, right authority, last resort, reasonable prospects and proportionality.[106] The similarity is unsurprising, since the post-1945 *jus ad bellum* is in some ways a return to the substantive constraints that the Just War doctrine implied for resort to force.[107]

There have been significant attempts to clarify the *jus ad bellum*'s tests through UNGA declarations, ICJ jurisprudence and scholarly writings. The criteria in practice only create controversy when states consider using force in situations that are not self-defence against an ongoing attack or where the UNSC has *not* agreed a UNSCR unambiguously authorising 'all necessary means', the commonly accepted form of words authorising use of military force.[108] For cases that do cause controversy, interpreting these criteria provokes serious disagreements. As the descriptions suggest, the criteria are complex and multifaceted – each imply further tests, which can be defined and interpreted in different ways and are thus subject to further supervaluationism. It is also not possible to draw a sharp boundary between them all – for example, it is difficult distinguishing necessity from proportionality.[109] And they are interdependent, prescribing different boundaries of lawfulness under different paradigms.

The law prescribes no particular ordering for applying these tests, nor any hierarchy indicating which are more or less important; logic suggests they are

104 William H. Taft, IV, 'Self-Defense and the Oil Platforms Decision', *The Yale Journal of International Law*, 29 (2004), 300.

105 Dinstein, *War, Aggression and Self-Defence*, 195, 238.

106 Fisher, *Morality and War*, 80.

107 Dinstein, *War, Aggression and Self-Defence*, 59–77; James Connelly and Don Carrick, 'Ethical and Legal Reasoning About War in a Time of Terror', in Aidan Hehir, Natasha Kuhrt and Andrew Mumford, eds., *International Law, Security and Ethics* (Abingdon: Routledge, 2011), 44–57, 45.

108 Rob McLaughlin, 'The Legal Regime Applicable to Use of Lethal Force When Operating under a United Nations Security Council Chapter VII Mandate Authorising "All Necessary Means"', *Journal of Conflict & Security Law*, 12:3 (2008), 389–417, 389–90.

109 Gray, *International Law*, 150.

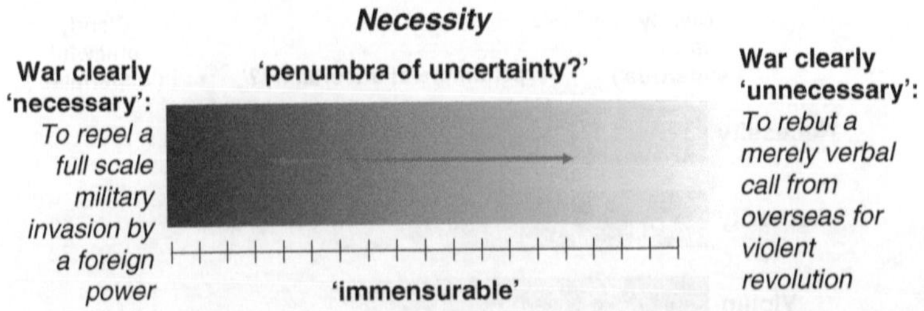

FIGURE 2.4 Fuzzy logic and necessity

'necessary elements' of a multi-part test, and so would all need to be met for force to be lawful.[110] Finally, although these tests appear to be binary 'yes'/'no' questions, in fact they operate according to 'fuzzy logic' – each describes a *continuum* of cases, changing incrementally from clearly lawful to clearly unlawful acts, divided by a fuzzy penumbra rather than sharp boundary (see Figure 2.4).[111] As Franck noted, 'a line of continuity runs from invasions by tanks and divisions through training, arming, sheltering and infiltrating neighboring insurgents, all the way down to hostile radio propaganda calling for revolution'.[112] This form of vagueness is exacerbated by the fact that states no longer declare war when they launch international military action, likely in part because states wish to avoid the constraints of international humanitarian law governing conduct within inter-state conflicts, which has progressively strengthened since 1945.[113]

For the 'attacker' criterion, Cassese observed that the extent of state involvement in an attack required to trigger forceful self-defence is a continuum, encompassing states taking a direct, overt part in attack, to states taking covert measures, to those actively trying to prevent insurgent attacks.[114] This creates uncertainty about whether a state must be shown to exercise 'effective control' or 'overall control' over an attacking force before it can be held responsible for that attack.[115] Although the ICJ and International Criminal Tribunal for the former Yugoslavia originally used 'effective control' and 'overall control' to describe alleged *jus in bello* violations, some scholars now argue these tests be applied in

110 Deeks, 'Multi-part Tests', 1038.
111 Madison, 'Difficulties of the Convention', 183.
112 Thomas Franck, 'Who Killed Article 2(4)?', 813–14.
113 Tanisha M Fazal, *Wars of Law: unintended consequences in the regulation of armed conflict* (Ithaca, NY: Cornell University Press, 2018), 1–5, 23.
114 Antonio Cassese, *International Law* (Oxford: Oxford University Press, 2005), 471–2.
115 Dinstein, *War, Aggression and Self-Defence*, 203; *Prosecutor* v. *Tadic*, Judgment, ICTY Case No. IT-94-1-A, Appeals Chamber, *International Legal Materials*, 38 (1999), 1540–5.

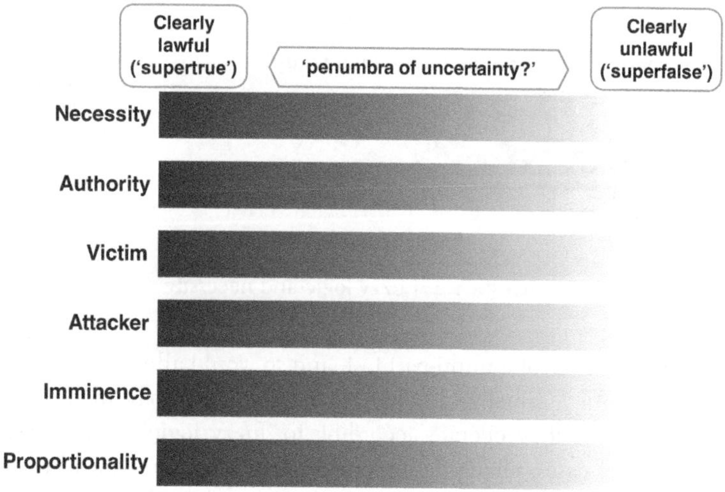

FIGURE 2.5 Fuzzy logic and supervaluationism in the *jus ad bellum*

jus ad bellum decisions too.[116] Similarly, the 'proportionality' threshold of 'scale and effects' separating a 'border incident' from an armed attack is fuzzy, with controversy over whether an accumulation of small attacks may over time create scale and effects amounting to an armed attack justifying self-defence.[117]

The role of fuzzy logic in the *jus ad bellum*'s tests exacerbates the complication caused by supervaluationism (see Figure 2.5). Evaluation is further complicated because the tests are 'immensurable' – no accepted units measure precisely how far a case meets each test; and they are 'incommensurable' – they cannot clearly be measured and compared with each other using the same standards of evaluation.[118]

'HARD CASES' IN THE *JUS AD BELLUM*

The complexity, interdependence and fuzziness of the *jus ad bellum*'s tests enable states and lawyers to assert controversial paradigms of legal force differing from those clearly described in the UN Charter. Uncertainty about the *jus ad bellum* as a system of prescriptive rules and principles also creates opportunities and incentives for states and lawyers to practise 'strategic

[116] *Nicaragua*, Merits, para. 116; *Prosecutor* v. *Tadic*, Judgment, 1540–5; Dinstein, *War, Aggression and Self-Defence*, 203.

[117] Ibid., 195, 238.

[118] Endicott, *Vagueness in Law*, 41.

behaviour in interpretation', and to use the *jus ad bellum* as a system of argumentative practices to deploy 'creative' arguments justifying or criticising the lawfulness of specific behaviour.[119] This section outlines five examples of 'hard cases' engaging the *jus ad bellum*, summarising views about them from interviews and a survey with international lawyers. These justifications were chosen because they provoke significant, persistent disagreement between international lawyers and states about whether the law permits unilateral use of force (i.e. without clear UNSC authorisation) in those circumstances.[120]

The first hard case concerns whether states may use force in self-defence against a non-state armed group in another state without the consent of that host state, as the US-led coalition did in Afghanistan in 2001.[121] The United States and United Kingdom have stated such force is lawful if the host state is 'unable or unwilling' to prevent armed groups on its territory from carrying out attacks.[122] Germany and Belgium justified force in collective self-defence against ISIL because it had 'occupied a certain part of Syrian territory over which the Government of the Syrian Arab Republic does not, at this time, exercise effective control'.[123] However, several states, including France, and many international lawyers disagree with such justifications.[124]

The second hard case concerns whether 'imminence' permits *anticipatory* force against an imminent future attack, or if the UN Charter's words 'if an armed attack occurs' means states must wait for an attack to be underway before responding militarily.[125] The third hard case asks whether, as the US government asserted in 2002, states have a right of *pre-emptive* self-defence against grave threats, such as terrorists or 'rogue states' acquiring WMDs, 'even

119 Koskenniemi, *From Apology to Utopia*, 67–9; Kennedy, *Legal Reasoning*, 159.

120 Dworkin, 'Hard Cases', 1057–109, 1060; Dworkin, *Law's Empire*, 255–6.

121 Gray, *International Law*, 156–160; Wilmshurst, 'Chatham House Principles'; Moir, *Reappraising the Resort to Force*, 41–71.

122 Brian Egan, US State Department Legal Adviser, 'International Law, Legal Diplomacy, and the Counter-ISIL Campaign', *American Society of International Law*, 4 April 2016; UK Attorney General Wright, 'The Modern Law of Self-Defence' (Speech, International Institute for Strategic Studies, 11 January 2017), https://assets.publishing.service.gov.uk/government/uploads/system/uploads/attachment_data/file/583171/170111_Imminence_Speech.pdf; Ashley S. Deeks, 'Unwilling or Unable: Toward a Normative Framework for Extraterritorial Self-Defense', *Virginia Journal of International Law*, 52 (2012), 483.

123 UN Security Council, 'Letter Dated 7 June 2016 from the Permanent Representative of Belgium to the United Nations Addressed to the President of the Security Council', 9 June 2017, S/2016/523; UN Security Council, 'Letter Dated 10 December 2015 from the Chargé d'affaires a.i. of the Permanent Mission of Germany to the United Nations Addressed to the President of the Security Council', 10 December 2015, S/2015/946.

124 Ministère des Armées, *International Law Applied to Operations in Cyberspace* (Paris: Ministère des Armées, 2019) 8–9; Milanovic, 'Accounting', 47–8.

125 Dinstein, *War, Aggression and Self-Defence*, 193–6.

if uncertainty remains as to the time and place' of attack.[126] The United Kingdom and United States have since endorsed Daniel Bethlehem's less expansive definition of imminence, permitting force against threats whose precise timing and target are unknown, if 'there is a reasonable and objective basis for concluding that an armed attack is imminent'.[127]

The fourth hard case is forceful humanitarian intervention, as asserted by the United Kingdom during NATO's 1999 Kosovo intervention and after Syrian chemical weapons attacks in 2013 and 2018.[128] The United Kingdom argues that when a government attacks its own citizens causing 'overwhelming humanitarian catastrophe', and other measures fail to stop those attacks, states are permitted to use proportionate force to end those attacks.[129] The final hard case concerns use of force to enforce counter-proliferation obligations, such as the 2003 US–UK justification that UNSC Resolution 678 (1990) authorising force against Iraq was 'revived' by UNSC Resolution 1441 (2002) declaring Iraq in breach of ceasefire obligations concerning WMDs.[130]

Eighteen interviewees said 'it depends' would be their initial response when asked whether any potential justification for force was lawful.[131] The facts of any case were key to their assessments.[132] One practitioner said a 'range of legal arguments' were available 'in a given scenario', so they were unlikely to see any intervention whose justification was 'not even properly arguable'.[133] One legal scholar argued hard cases often reflected 'a specific moment in time', and may become less difficult as time passes and it becomes clear the justification has been accepted or rejected as settled law.[134]

Several participants[135] stressed 'the underlying primacy' of 'the non-resort to force',[136] 'a presumption of construing exceptions narrowly', an 'extreme

126 The White House, *National Security Strategy September 2002* (Washington, DC: The White House, 2002), 15.

127 Wright, 'Modern Law of Self-Defence'; Egan, 'International Law'; Daniel Bethlehem, 'Self-Defense Against an Imminent or Actual Armed Attack by Nonstate Actors', *The American Journal of International Law*, 106:4 (2012), 769–77.

128 Baroness Symons, 'Kosovo: Use of Military Force' (16 November 1998), *Hansard*, House of Lords, 5th ser., vol. 594, cols. WA 140; Adam Roberts, 'The So-Called "Right" of Humanitarian Intervention', *Yearbook of International Humanitarian Law*, 3 (2000), 3–51, 24; HM Government, 'Chemical Weapon Use'; HM Government, 'Policy Paper: Syria Action – UK Government Legal Position' (London: HM Government, 14 April 2018).

129 Greenwood, 'NATO Intervention in Kosovo', 926.

130 Greenwood, 'War against Terrorism'.

131 Participants 1, 5, 7, 8, 12, 13, 14, 15, 18, 19, 20, 21, 22, 24, 25, 26, 29, 30.

132 Participants 12, 13, 14, 18, 20, 24, 25, 29.

133 Participant 26.

134 Participant 2.

135 Participants 5, 31, 19, 30.

136 Participant 5.

premium' on the prohibition as 'a fundamental norm of international law'.[137] International lawyers needed to start with this presumption and ask 'whether you can bring yourself within an exception', which even the Bethlehem principles described narrowly.[138] One practising international lawyer said the international community may sometimes 'tolerate' force, not condemning the state using force, without necessarily accepting it was legal.[139] In spite of these areas of agreement, the lawyers interviewed and surveyed for this book expressed varying opinions on the lawfulness of the five justifications. Figure 2.6 summarises the survey responses from twenty-three participants.

'Anticipatory or interceptive individual or collective self-defence against imminent armed attack' attracted most approval, 87 per cent of participants rating this justification clearly lawful (39 per cent) or probably lawful (48 per cent). Only 4 per cent described its lawfulness as unclear, and only 8 per cent rated it probably unlawful (4 per cent) or clearly unlawful (4 per cent). One practising lawyer argued the UN Charter 'never intended to make a state sit there and sustain an attack', although it was legitimate to challenge lawyers to explain their justifications in specific cases.[140] A scholar argued almost all self-defence was in some way anticipatory, since invading and occupying territory is probably the only unambiguous example of actual ongoing attack, whereas self-defence usually follows an individual past attack such as Pearl Harbour, which was expected to be the start of an ongoing military campaign.[141] Another scholar argued on the contrary 'interceptive' self-defence is actually defence against ongoing armed attack, since attacks can only be 'intercepted' after being launched.[142]

Several interviewees argued anticipatory self-defence required assessment of multiple 'fact-specific' factors, such as anticipated casualties, readiness of enemy forces, expected timing of attack.[143] For example, a state that learns of a conventional attack planned in six months has less justification for force than a state threatened with nuclear attack in forty-eight hours.[144] One former government lawyer noted even the 'Bethlehem' principles specified a 'high threshold' for anticipatory self-defence, which is always a last resort after 'other options have been exhausted, and you can establish a necessity to act'.[145]

137 Participant 30.
138 Participant 19.
139 Participant 13.
140 Participant 13.
141 Participant 9.
142 Participant 6.
143 Participant 12.
144 Participant 12.
145 Participant 19.

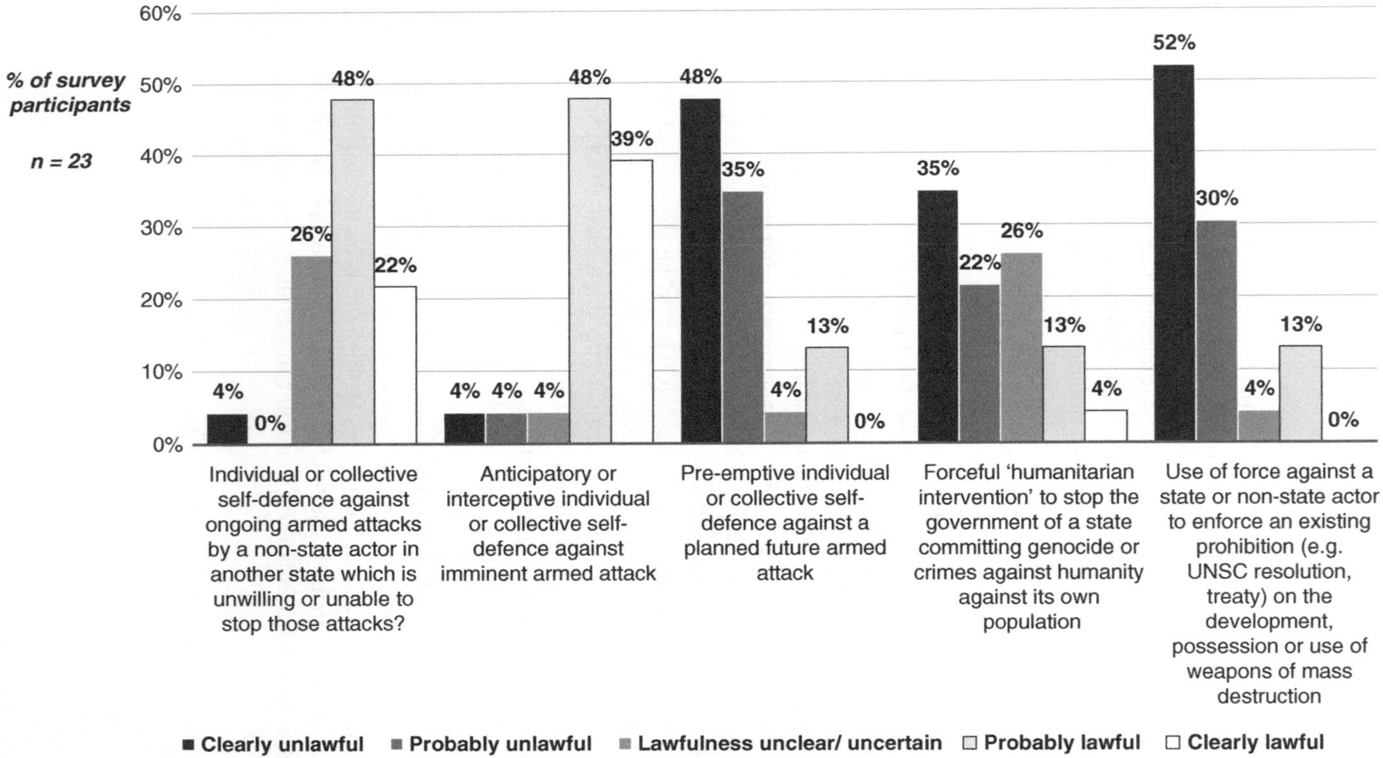

FIGURE 2.6 Distribution of opinion on five hard cases

The majority – 70 per cent – also agreed that 'individual or collective self-defence against ongoing armed attacks by a non-state actor in another state which is unable or unwilling to stop those attacks' was probably lawful (48 per cent) or clearly lawful (22 per cent), only one participant (4 per cent) rated it clearly unlawful. This is less than the 87 per cent who thought anticipatory self-defence was probably or clearly lawful, perhaps because that question did not mention non-state actors. But this justification also attracted the equal highest 'uncertain' rating, of 26 per cent. One former government lawyer mentioned the problem of consent given secretly by host states for such actions, as with Pakistan allegedly taking different private and public positions on US drone strikes against non-state armed groups on its territory.[146]

Interviewees highlighted multiple potential interpretations of the 'unable or unwilling' test in this justification. Three participants argued 'unable or unwilling' was simply part of the necessity test.[147] A practitioner argued 'unwilling' was more important than 'unable' since, for example, during the 1970s IRA campaign the United Kingdom would not have been entitled to launch attacks in Ireland, which was genuinely trying to stop terrorism but was unable to do so completely.[148] One legal scholar argued there simply is a right of self-defence against non-state actors 'because an armed attack is a factual circumstance' regardless of perpetrator.[149]

'Pre-emptive individual or collective self-defence against a planned future armed attack' and use of force 'to enforce an existing prohibition on WMDs, where the prohibition does not explicitly include military enforcement' both elicited similar levels of disapproval. 82 per cent of participants rated use of force to enforce a prohibition on WMD as clearly unlawful (52 per cent) or probably unlawful (30 per cent). Only 4 per cent rated its lawfulness as uncertain, 13 per cent rated it as probably lawful and none rated it as clearly lawful. Many participants identified the 2003 US–UK intervention in Iraq and the April 2017 US use of force against Syria following chemical weapons attacks as examples of this kind of unlawful intervention.[150] One former government lawyer said such cases created a clash of norms, since developing or using WMDs violates international law, but so does unilateral use of force.[151]

Participants expressed slightly more disapproval for 'pre-emptive individual or collective self-defence against a planned future armed attack', with

146 Participant 19.
147 Participants 1, 6, 9.
148 Participant 18.
149 Participant 9.
150 Participant 27.
151 Participant 29.

83 per cent rating this justification as clearly unlawful (48 per cent) or probably unlawful (35 per cent). Only 13 per cent rated it probably lawful, none rated it clearly lawful, and one (4 per cent) rated it as uncertain. One scholar argued 'preventive' self-defence, 'against the threat of a threat of attack' was probably lawful.[152] Israel's 1983 attack on Iraq's Osirak nuclear reactor was an example, justified because Iraq's constitution sought Israel's destruction, Iraq's conflict with Israel had never formally ended, and intelligence suggested delaying any attack would have made it impossible to safely end Iraq's nuclear weapons programme.[153]

A former government lawyer said perceptions of such actions had changed, since even the United States criticised Israel in 1983, yet in 2008 Israel received little condemnation for bombing Syria's alleged nuclear reactor.[154] That interviewee described 'the problem with pre-emption' as the 'invention of language by the Bush administration in 2002' for the purpose of justifying 'unilateral exceptionalism'.[155] A scholar noted that, although the Obama administration had stopped mentioning pre-emption, it had still said 'it would use force when it deems it necessary', which left 'the door wide open' to pre-emptive self-defence, and was 'even more dangerous' than the Bush Doctrine, which 'at least tried to set some boundaries and limitations'.[156]

Interviewees highlighted the multi-faceted nature of the 'imminence' test, which was thus vulnerable to multiple interpretations. Most participants said lawful anticipatory self-defence became unlawful pre-emptive self-defence when exercised against attacks that were temporally or materially so distant that non-forceful measures might still stop them.[157] Several argued imminence that justified lawful anticipatory self-defence was not a fixed time before attack,[158] but had 'an element of elasticity',[159] being 'the last practical opportunity to prevent what is demonstrably an intended attack'.[160] One practising international lawyer argued 'pre-emptive to anticipatory is a spectrum'.[161] A scholar and another practitioner argued the inclusion of the words 'planned future armed attack' in the 'pre-emptive self-defence' question made this justification uncertain, since it may be lawful to use force against actors

152 Participant 9.
153 Participant 9.
154 Participant 19.
155 Participant 19.
156 Participant 1.
157 Participants 6, 10, 17, 13, 5, 19, 8, 11, 25, 20, 3, 29.
158 Participants 13, 10, 19, 8, 11, 25, 3, 20, 17, 29.
159 Participant 25.
160 Participant 13.
161 Participant 10.

whose plans were so advanced they could not be stopped by other means, but where an attack was still temporally distant.[162]

A further practitioner identified as key the 'degree of actual clear threat pertaining to specific identified circumstances against the territory or the nationals' of the state claiming self-defence.[163] A former government lawyer said if the expected attack is a single soldier firing across a border, then a state would need very high certainty before anticipatory action, but 'you'd take fewer risks' if the threat was a WMD attack.[164]

Several interviewees mentioned the 'Bethlehem principles' for anticipatory self-defence. One former government lawyer described them as 'a good effort at setting out what the law should be', and 'general directions in which the law is changing', but it was 'taking it a bit far' to claim 'in all respects they describe current law'.[165] Another said the principles assumed the law had changed significantly, yet lawyers like 'Michael Wood and Elizabeth Wilmshurst are much more cautious'.[166] One practitioner described the principles as 'helpful in aiding thinking', but did not eliminate uncertainty, since while 'one has to apply different thresholds' now that attacks can be conducted from thousands of miles away, there was also a danger of 'loosening it up too much'.[167]

Finally, 'Forceful "humanitarian intervention" to stop the government of a state committing genocide or crimes against humanity against its own population' was rated unlawful by most, but also saw the widest distribution of views. A majority (57 per cent) rated this justification as either clearly unlawful (35 per cent) or probably unlawful (22 per cent), but 26 per cent rated it as uncertain, while 17 per cent rated it probably lawful (13 per cent) or clearly lawful (4 per cent). All who rated the justification probably or clearly lawful accepted it was controversial.[168] One former armed forces lawyer argued it was 'an arguable case' for asserting '*lex ferenda*', but the *lex lata* at present 'doesn't allow for it'.[169] A scholar argued the UK government did not think humanitarian intervention was actually lawful when publishing its justifications, but was making 'state practice that would contribute to legality'.[170]

162 Participants 10, 17.
163 Participant 8.
164 Participant 25.
165 Participant 21.
166 Participant 29.
167 Participant 10.
168 Participants 13, 20, 7, 19, 21.
169 Participant 20.
170 Participant 7.

Participants' reactions to this justification revealed the shifting nature of the tests over time, and the need for at least a degree of social consensus between states about any justification. Most who thought the justification was unlawful argued there was insufficient evidence it had crystallised as customary law.[171] One scholar approvingly quoted 'the 1980s Foreign Office dictum' that 'it perhaps is not unambiguously unlawful'.[172] Another argued the UK parliament's September 2013 decision not to authorise humanitarian intervention against Syria after chemical weapons attacks was a setback for the doctrine; had it been agreed, it would have been a significant example of state practice and *opinio juris*.[173] One former government lawyer observed the UK government had described even Kosovo as 'an "exceptional" measure', yet in 2013 'the Government said there was a general doctrine of humanitarian intervention', which was 'going down a very slippery slope'.[174] One scholar worried 'hard cases make bad law', since justifying 'exceptional situations' makes 'many ordinary violations lawful', and it would be better to develop law to discourage UNSC veto in such situations than to 'legalise humanitarian intervention'.[175]

Fourteen participants viewed humanitarian intervention as unlawful but were regretful about it.[176] One former government lawyer recalled the FCO launched 'a massive diplomatic effort to get other states to accept it' but had failed, 'which is a real shame', and it 'would be a good thing' if the justification became settled customary law.[177] One practitioner argued the justification had 'a strong moral argument, one good precedent' with Kosovo, but as yet was 'legally not particularly strong', and emerging doubts about the facts around Kosovo raised further questions.[178]

Several participants noted that while few states agreed humanitarian intervention was lawful, few called recent uses of force for humanitarian purposes unlawful,[179] which had 'a certain legitimacy' and could help construct 'a tapestry of justification'.[180] A scholar said the April 2017 US air strikes showed many states 'can let things slide' where they see a possible 'greater good', and while 'nobody wants to see an extra justification' and few states have justified actions as humanitarian interventions, many 'prefer to keep quiet', thus

171 Participant 17.
172 Participant 30.
173 Participant 24.
174 Participant 21.
175 Participant 2.
176 Participants 1, 2, 4, 6, 7, 14, 15, 17, 20, 22, 23, 27, 29, 30.
177 Participant 29.
178 Participant 15.
179 Participants 1, 13, 18.
180 Participant 1.

providing 'implicit approval'.[181] A practitioner said such action was 'definitely illegitimate' if a state acted alone, but 'proper analysis' and 'a democratic mandate' domestically and internationally could lend it legitimacy and in time affect 'where the law is going'.[182]

Interviewees mentioned a number of other *jus ad bellum* controversies, which, for reasons of focus, this book does not consider in detail. Debate persists around whether economic coercion and cyber-attack are uses of force prohibited under the UN Charter potentially justifying self-defence.[183] Several participants said it was no longer disputed that cyber-attacks may trigger self-defence, but *when* a cyber-attack could do so remained uncertain.[184] One scholar thought states may be reluctant to express *opinio juris* on this issue, to retain 'freedom of movement within a grey area'.[185] A former armed forces lawyer said cyber-attacks may need 'more severe consequences to be regarded as a use of force' than more traditional attacks.[186] A former government lawyer said cyber-attacks causing deaths, such as opening a dam, remained so theoretical that it was difficult to assess whether they could ever justify 'kinetic response' against a foreign state's cyber command, and 'other reasonable possibilities', including cyber counter-measures, would need to be exhausted first.[187]

Another hard case that interviewees mentioned was foreign interventions in civil wars, sending military forces for combat, or indirect military intervention through training, supporting rebellions and arms sales.[188] One scholar observed that states sending arms to Syrian rebels offered no legal justification, while states supporting the Syrian regime offered little legal criticism of such supplies, which may be because, like cyber-attacks, states want the option of taking such action themselves.[189] Another said 'historically, wars of national liberation are the hardest cases of all', raising difficult questions about the kinds of support that may be lawfully given to either side in such a conflict.[190]

Several participants argued such 'minimal uses of force' were more difficult than the cases examined in this book, since they created uncertainty around

181 Participant 1.
182 Participant 14.
183 Lianne Boer '"Echoes of Times Past": On the Paradoxical Nature of Article 2(4)', *Journal of Conflict and Security Law*, 20 (2015), 5.
184 Participant 2.
185 Participant 2.
186 Participant 11.
187 Participant 19.
188 Participant 30.
189 Participant 2.
190 Participant 30.

whether an action achieved the scale and effects constituting a use of force requiring justification at all.[191] For example, it was difficult identifying when small groups or individuals pose the kind of threat triggering 'an article 51 right of self-defence',[192] whether a plan to kill five or six people was enough, or if many such events was required.[193] One scholar mentioned the worrying effects of drones, which were tempting to use because they were small scale, but which they believed still amounted to clear *jus ad bellum* violations.[194] The March 2018 statement by the UK prime minister declaring the poisoning of the Skripals 'an unlawful use of force by the Russian State against the United Kingdom' is another example of such a minimal use of force, which provoked discussion among international lawyers about the legal implications, including around the right of self-defence.[195]

Disagreement also persists around whether self-defence without UNSC authority is lawful when the victim is a national overseas.[196] A scholar and a former government lawyer wondered whether this was a subset of self-defence or 'some other lawful excuse such as necessity or distress'.[197] Russia's justifications for intervening in Crimea were related, apparently claimed as a pre-emptive unilateral intervention to protect Russian nationals overseas.[198]

Others argued that interpreting a UNSC resolution as authorising force even if it does not explicitly do so was a specific category of hard case.[199] For example, in Kosovo many countries did not rely on humanitarian intervention, but argued they were enforcing a UNSC resolution obligation on the Federal Republic of Yugoslavia authorities to cease attacks on Kosovar civilians.[200] One scholar argued the lawfulness of the Iraq 2003 justification of reviving a previous UNSC authorisation to use force was not clear in 2003 but was now clearly unlawful.[201] A former government lawyer noted that had

191 Participants 17, 19, 27, 30.
192 Participant 19.
193 Participant 17.
194 Participant 27.
195 Theresa May, 'A Statement to the House of Commons by Prime Minister Theresa May Following the Salisbury Incident' (14 March 2018), *Hansard*, House of Commons, 6th ser., vol. 637, cols. 855–7. Dapo Akande, 'The Use of Nerve Agents in Salisbury: Why Does It Matter Whether It Amounts to a Use of Force in International Law?', *Ejil:Talk!* (17 March 2018).
196 Gray, *International Law*, 132–40.
197 Participants 27, 19.
198 Participant 24; Daniel Wisehart, 'The Crisis in Ukraine and the Prohibition of the Use of Force: A Legal Basis for Russia's Intervention?', *EJIL: Talk!* (4 March 2014).
199 Participants 23, 17.
200 Participant 17.
201 Participant 27.

the Iraq war ended quickly and significant WMDs been discovered, many would have agreed it was justified.[202] A practising lawyer argued the UNSC resolutions used to justify the 2003 Iraq invasion were not ambiguous, that the UK/US justification was a 'reasonable answer to the question "what legal arguments could we put up to justify this"', but the chances of the argument succeeding in an international tribunal 'were extremely remote'.[203] Another worried the legal justification for Iraq had been an example of lawyers asserting states had freedom to act because the UNSC was dysfunctional, 'dressing that up as a legal argument'.[204] One scholar said although the US/UK implied authorisation theory 'has a logical sense', it 'relegates the council to spectators in something that individual states decide', which did not 'comport with the purpose of the Charter'.[205]

One practising lawyer wondered if use of force to end a migrant crisis might be a future justification, particularly since many poor countries were most affected by such flows from war-torn neighbouring states.[206] A former government lawyer argued the ICC definition of the crime of aggression was only 'manifest violation of the Charter', and thus political leaders might 'get off the hook' if they had supportive legal advice, allowing them to argue any use of force for which a legal adviser could develop a justification could not be a 'manifest violation'.[207] Another practitioner argued almost all conceivable modern conflicts would be hard cases, since states no longer declared war, and thus it was difficult to identify recent examples of 'traditional' conflict in which all the rules of war applied.[208]

These results do not indicate whether the justifications described are lawful or not, nor do they necessarily reflect the views of UK-based international lawyers as a whole. The participant sample was not large enough, nor selected and assessed using the kinds of methods that could claim to model the distribution of opinion across UK-based international lawyers more widely. This section merely describes the distribution of opinion in this particular group of UK-based international lawyers, providing a baseline to explore how these lawyers' views on legal interpretation and extra-legal factors compare to their opinions on these justifications for force, and to investigate the reasoning these lawyers use to reach their conclusions.

202 Participant 31.
203 Participant 13.
204 Participant 14.
205 Participant 23.
206 Participant 12.
207 Participant 21.
208 Participant 18.

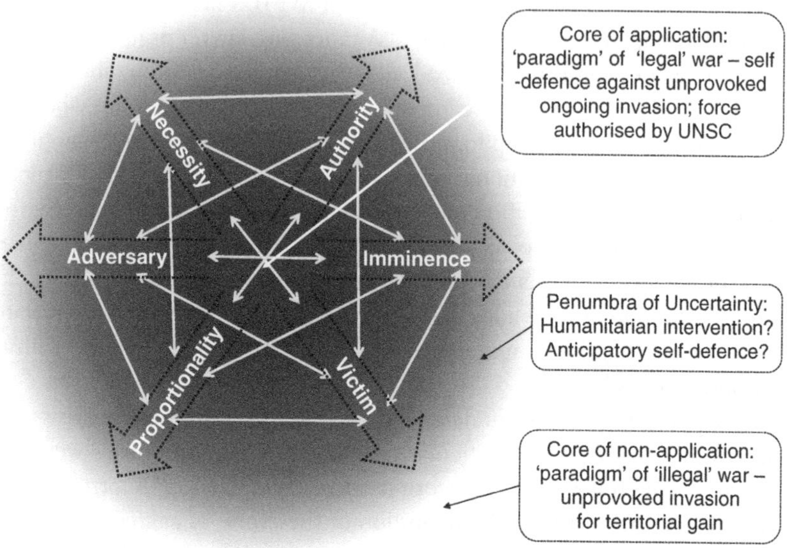

FIGURE 2.7 Paradigms of war

These interview and survey findings do support the contention that the *jus ad bellum* appears to be based around fuzzy, multi-dimensional paradigms (see Figure 2.7). A 'core of application' describes paradigms of legal force. A 'core of non-application' describes paradigms of illegal force. Between these paradigms a 'penumbra of uncertainty' describes force whose legality is unclear. In these terms, the responses from this group of international lawyers suggest they regard anticipatory self-defence and self-defence against an armed attack by a non-state actor as nearest to being clearly lawful justifications for unilateral force. The responses suggest this group views pre-emptive self-defence and use of force to enforce a prohibition on WMDs as nearest to being clearly unlawful justifications for unilateral force. And the group's responses suggest they are most uncertain about the lawfulness of unilateral forceful humanitarian intervention.

The paradigms of clearly lawful and unlawful resort to force in the UN Charter and their underlying assumptions are understandable. In 1945 the Allies believed they had used force lawfully against unjustified attacks. The Nuremberg Tribunal condemned the Axis powers' unprovoked 'wars of aggression', and 'seizure of foreign territories' to secure 'living space' and 'food supplies'.[209] The charter was a significant development of the existing *jus ad*

209 'Judgment and Sentences, International Military Tribunal (Nuremberg)', *American Journal of International Law*, 41 (1946), 172, 186, 199.

bellum, and its institutions of the League of Nations and the Kellogg-Briand or Paris Pact, which most commentators in 1945 believed had failed to prevent war, because they had failed to incentivise powerful states to use military force to suppress aggression.[210] The UN Charter's drafters almost certainly knew some conflicts might differ from the charter's implicit paradigms. But the law they drafted was inevitably less clear about how the rules should apply to forms of war very different from those they most clearly addressed.

INTERPRETIVE PRINCIPLES AND THE *JUS AD BELLUM*

The forms of vagueness identified in the previous section enable the fourth form of vagueness described earlier in this chapter: social supervaluationism. Different groups of lawyers and states may hold different sets of shared intuitions, assumptions, understandings and beliefs about how to identify and interpret the *jus ad bellum* and reach clear legal conclusions about hard cases. Uncertainty about the *jus ad bellum* as a system of prescriptive rules and principles even enables different groups of states and lawyers to practise 'strategic behaviour in interpretation', and so to use the *jus ad bellum* as a system of argumentative practices justifying or criticising the lawfulness of specific behaviour.[211] These different groups of lawyers and states in effect operationalise competing legal theories with different fundamental presuppositions about how international law is formed and how it should be interpreted, enabling some to argue that new justifications for resort to force have emerged while others argue the law remains unchanged. As one scholar puts it, in this area of law 'perhaps more than in others, legal controversies are often inseparable from deeper issues about the methods, or even the theory, of international law'.[212]

A historic, foundational theoretical tension is between positivism and naturalism. Naturalism's focus on law as reflecting morality dominated international law until the eighteenth century, when scientific empiricism inspired the rise of positivism as 'the empirical study of existing law', rather than 'moral theorising' about possible law, distinguishing 'with maximum clarity, law as it is from law as it ought to be'.[213] Yet advocates of modern natural law approaches still challenge positivism's separation of law and morals.[214]

210 Malanczuk, *Akehurst's*, loc. 1631.

211 Koskenniemi, *From Apology to Utopia*, 67–9; Kennedy, *Legal Reasoning*, 159.

212 Corten, *Law against War*, 4.

213 Armstrong, Farrell and Lambert, *International Law*, 79, 80; Hart, 'Positivism', 594.

214 Allen Buchanan, *Justice, Legitimacy, and Self-Determination: Moral Foundations for International Law* (Oxford: Oxford University Press, 2003), 13; Fuller, 'Positivism', 670; Devlin, 'Law, Morality and Democracy', 638; Dworkin, *Matter of Principle*, 129.

These disagreements are reflected in contemporary competition between 'textually-oriented' and 'purposive' approaches to interpretation.[215] During negotiations for the Vienna Convention on the Law of Treaties (VCLT), the United States proposed 'a purposive approach to treaty interpretation', emphasising 'comprehensive examination of the context of any particular treaty' to determine the will of the parties as it evolved over time.[216] Other countries disagreed, preferring to rely on the ordinary meaning of the text of treaties. Article 31(1) of the VCLT reflects that tension, requiring treaties to 'be interpreted in good faith in accordance with the ordinary meaning to be given to the terms of the treaty in their context and in the light of its object and purpose'.[217] It is generally understood that these 'three main elements, wording, context and object and purpose, as well as the guiding principle of good faith, constitute integral parts of that rule and have to be applied in a single combined operation'.[218] UNSC resolutions are not treaties and so not governed by the VCLT, yet the competing interpretations of UNSC resolutions on Iraq displayed the purposive/textual tension, on one side using purposive approaches 'reviving' authorisation for force, on the other using textually oriented approaches to argue the opposite.[219] Linked to these disputes are competing visions of the law's *'telos'* – one extreme seeing multiple, sometimes implicit, legal purposes for force, the other extreme accepting only those purposes explicitly in the UN Charter's text and UNSC resolutions.[220]

Disagreements persist about whether state acceptance or active consent is always required for new rules of customary international law, and how to identify that acceptance/consent. *Opinio juris* is routinely described using human attributes – the 'psychological element', 'a conviction felt by states'.[221] Many lawyers agree 'customary international law is above all a set of shared beliefs, expectations or understandings held by individual human beings who govern and represent states', and so they identify consent or at least acquiescence in formal statements by state officials, aligning with political

215 Michael Byers, *War Law: Understanding International Law and Armed Conflict*, Kindle ed. (New York: Grove Press, 2005), locs. 480–3.

216 Byers, *War Law*, locs. 480–3.

217 VCLT, art. 31(1).

218 Oliver Dorr, Kirsten Schmalenbach, eds., *Vienna Convention on the Law of Treaties: A Commentary* (Heidelberg: Springer, 2012), 523.

219 Byers, *War Law*, locs. 497–949.

220 Michael Byers, 'Agreeing to Disagree: Security Council Resolution 1441 and Intentional Ambiguity', *Global Governance*, 10 (2004), 165–86; Kammerhofer, 'Self-Defence', 197.

221 Anthony D'Amato, *The Concept of Custom in International Law* (Ithaca: Cornell University Press, 1971), 48; Malanczuk, *Akehurst's*, locs. 2122–3.

theories identifying states as 'the empirical behaviours of government officials'.[222] But scholars advocating policy-oriented and transnational legal process approaches argue international law emerges from more wide-ranging interactions between political leaders, officials, judges and non-governmental actors, since any communication between 'politically relevant groups which shapes wide expectations about appropriate future behavior' can be considered 'functional lawmaking'.[223]

As the UK government discovered in 2013 when parliament refused to approve military action against Syria, it is a fact that non-government influences shape *jus ad bellum* decisions in many states.[224] Lawyers outside government can also influence governments directly when advising on specific issues, in ICJ cases, or acting as foreign ministry legal adviser as happens in many countries including the United States.[225] Non-government lawyers shape government legal practice through the International Law Commission's work developing treaties and guidance.[226] And the ICJ Statute itself recognises 'judicial decisions and the teachings of the most highly qualified publicists of the various nations, as subsidiary means for the determination of rules of law'.[227]

Flowing from these tensions are disagreements around how international law changes through customary law. No firm rules prescribe how many instances of state practice and *opinio juris* are required, how widespread, over what period, how clear, in what form, and by whom before a customary international law norm crystallises.[228] Some scholars even view the two 'elements of custom not as fixed and mutually exclusive, but as interchangeable along a sliding scale', and that '(t)he more destabilizing or morally distasteful the activity' being regulated, 'for example, the offensive use of force', then 'the

222 Michael Byers, 'Custom, Power, and the Power of Rules', *Michigan Journal of International Law*, 17 (1995), 137; David Easton, *The Political System* (New York: Knopf, 1953), 316; Bob Jessop, *State Theory: Putting the Capitalist State in its Place* (Cambridge: Polity Press, 1990), 367.

223 Harold H. Koh, 'Is there a "New" New Haven School of International Law?', *Yale Journal of International Law*, 32 (2007), 559–74; Corten, *Law against War*, 14–15.

224 Mark Urban, 'A Fork in the Road for UK Foreign Policy', BBC News (29 August 2013); France 24, 'France Stands Firm on Syria Despite Shock UK Vote', France 24 (30 August 2013).

225 Berman, 'Role of the International Lawyer', 15; Jennings, 'Introduction', xxiii.

226 Berman, 'Role of the International Lawyer', 16.

227 ICJ Statute.

228 Jorg Kammerhofer, 'Uncertainty in the Formal Sources of International Law: Customary International Law and Some of its Problems', *European Journal of International Law*, 15 (2004), 551–2; Stefan Talmon, 'Determining Customary International Law: The ICJ's Methodology between Induction, Deduction and Assertion', *European Journal of International Law*, 26 (2015), 417, 419.

more readily international decision makers will substitute one element for the other' to identify a rule of customary international law.[229] However, scholars holding this view disagree as to how to determine the appropriate 'distribution of weight between the two elements'.[230] So the distinction between *lex ferenda* emerging norms, and *lex lata* settled law is fuzzy rather than sharply binary, and is subject to supervaluationism, since state practice and *opinio juris* are distinct, multi-facetted, incommensurable criteria.[231] Even the distinction between state practice and *opinio juris* is fuzzy; while states' official legal statements can be viewed as clearly *opinio juris*, and participating in action clearly state practice, policy statements and multilateral voting are less clearly categorisable.

Murphy has described disagreements between those who see the *jus ad bellum* as protean and those who apply a form of 'originalism', viewing the law as relatively static.[232] Corten observes more specifically that '(t)he most profound divergences arise over the status and interpretation of the customary prohibition on the use of force'.[233] This originalism/protean tension can be seen in the VCLT.[234] The convention describes the 'preparatory work of the treaty and the circumstances of its conclusion' as supplementary means of interpreting a treaty if the ordinary meaning of its text, its context, object and purpose still leaves 'the meaning ambiguous or obscure' or produces 'a result which is manifestly absurd or unreasonable'.[235] Yet it also specifies that 'subsequent agreement between the parties', 'subsequent practice' in applying the treaty, and 'any relevant rules of international law' shall be taken into account.[236]

Since the *jus ad bellum* is generally seen as *jus cogens*, many international lawyers are reluctant to accept change without formal charter amendment or overwhelming evidence of customary law.[237] However, the *jus ad bellum* has not seen 'extensive and repeated state practice', 'incidents are sparse', their

229 Frederic Kirgis, 'Custom on a Sliding Scale', *American Journal of International Law*, 81 (1987), 146–51, 149.
230 Emmanuel Voyiakis, 'Customary International Law and the Place of Normative Considerations', *The American Journal of Jurisprudence*, 55 (2010), 163–200, 171.
231 Hugh Thirlway, 'Reflections on Lex Ferenda', *Netherlands Yearbook of International Law*, 32 (2001), 4.
232 Murphy, 'Protean Jus Ad Bellum', 24; Guglielmo Verdirame, 'The "Sinews of Peace": International Law, Strategy, and the Prevention of War', *British Yearbook of International Law*, 77:1 (2006), 83–162, 142.
233 Corten, *Law and War*, 6.
234 Dorr and Schmalenbach, *Vienna Convention*, 533–36.
235 VCLT, art. 32.
236 VCLT, art. 31(3).
237 Murphy, 'Protean Jus Ad Bellum', 25.

factual circumstances often unique, with much disagreement about their broader legal significance.[238] Others argue developments such as terrorism, WMD proliferation, new human rights and humanitarian law, evolve 'informal expectations by states and other actors' about the law to allow use of force in wider situations.[239] Most clearly, states' use of force against armed non-state groups internationally still causes lawyers concerns, but draws limited official condemnation, suggesting states use a 'more nuanced legal standard than is captured by the static *jus ad bellum*'.[240]

Hakimi has proposed a more limited concept of 'informal' regulation of the *jus ad bellum*, through UNSC deliberations about contested military operations.[241] Hakimi argues 'the Council's non-authorizing support', for example 'in a press release or presidential statement . . . confers authority', making 'an operation that would otherwise be legally suspect easier to justify and harder to challenge in law'.[242] UNSC statements on the 1990–92 ECOWAS intervention in Liberia, the 2012 French intervention in Mali, and the 2011 intervention by Gulf Cooperation Council states in Yemen are possible examples of this informal regulation.[243] Hakimi speculates that even the contested US 2017 air strikes on Syria after reports of chemical weapons attacks may have received some legitimation after eleven states endorsed the operation and only four condemned it in the UNSC.[244] Such informal regulation 'is more procedural and particularistic' than 'substantive or generalizable', and so allows more military operations to be deemed lawful without creating wide-ranging new *jus ad bellum* justifications.[245]

The evolution of the UNSC P5 abstention – enabling the UNSC to adopt resolutions even if some of its permanent five members abstains – illustrates these uncertainties. For non-procedural UNSC resolutions, including those authorising force, the UN Charter requires 'concurring votes' from all five permanent member states, unless one is 'party to a dispute' under Article 52(3), when it 'shall abstain'.[246] Yet from 1946 many non-procedural UNSC resolutions were passed with at least one permanent member abstaining despite not

238 Ibid., 25.
239 Ibid., 36, 26.
240 Ibid., 42.
241 Monica Hakimi, 'The *Jus Ad Bellum's* Regulatory Form', *American Journal of International Law*, 112:2 (2018), 151–90, 155.
242 Ibid., 155.
243 Ibid., 176, 170, 172.
244 Ibid., 180–1.
245 Ibid., 155.
246 UN Charter.

being party to the dispute.[247] Only in 1971 did the ICJ declare abstention a lawful 'generally accepted' practice.[248] P5 abstention somehow transformed from *lex lata* unlawful to *lex lata* lawful, but *when* or *how* this transformation happened is unclear.

Vagueness may even affect the *jus cogens* status of the prohibition on the use of force. Such peremptory norms may have a *jus cogens* core and non-*jus cogens* penumbra, arising when other *jus cogens* norms are violated, potentially permitting normally prohibited actions under the doctrine of necessity.[249] Alternatively, *jus cogens* norms may be penumbral in cases which are very different from paradigm 'plain cases'.

All these tensions enable disagreements between lawyers and governments about when states can resort to force without explicit UNSC authorisation. In domestic law, court judgments, legislation, and a sovereign state generally accepted as supreme and exercising an effective monopoly on lawful coercion usually narrow interpretive disagreements. And the behaviour of states, international organisations, courts and lawyers do suggest wide-ranging, authoritative rules of legal interpretation have emerged in international law.[250] Most international lawyers regard the ICJ Statute and VCLT as authoritative sources of 'secondary rules' of legal interpretation.[251] The ICJ has adjudicated several disputes engaging the *jus ad bellum*, producing widely accepted jurisprudence. The UN Charter grants the UNGA authority to 'initiate studies and make recommendations' for 'the progressive development of international law and its codification' (art. 13). And the UN Charter confers upon the UNSC 'primary responsibility for the maintenance of international peace and security' (art. 24), authority to 'determine the existence of any threat to the peace, breach of the peace, or act of aggression' (art. 39) and to authorise military force 'to maintain or restore international peace and security' (art. 42).

247 Sydney D. Bailey, 'New Light on Abstentions in the UN Security Council', *International Affairs*, 50:4 (1974), 554–73, 571.

248 *South West Africa*, Advisory Opinion, 22.

249 Oscar Schachter, *International Law in Theory and Practice* (Dordrecht: Martinus Nijhoff, 1991), 20; Rein Mullerson, *Ordering Anarchy: International Law in International Society* (Dordrecht: Martinus Nijhoff, 2000), 156; International Law Commission, 'Second Report on State Responsibility: Addendum', 30 April 1999, A/CN.4/498/Add.2, 25–6.

250 Samantha Besson, 'Theorizing the Sources of International Law', in Samantha Besson and John Tasioulas, eds., *The Philosophy of International Law* (Oxford: Oxford University Press, 2010), 163.

251 International Law Commission, 'State Responsibility', *Report of the International Law Commission on the Work of Its Fifty-Third Session, 23 April–1 June and 2 July–10* August 2001, A/56/10, 59; International Law Commission, *Yearbook of the International Law Commission*, vol. 2, pt 2, A/CN.4/SER.A/2001/Add.1, 31.

But while these rules and institutions help reduce vagueness, uncertainty and disagreement about the *jus ad bellum*, they do not eliminate them. The UNSC has said little to clarify the *jus ad bellum*. The UN Charter describes UNGA resolutions such as the 'Declaration on Friendly Relations' and 'Definition of Aggression' as 'recommendations' rather than legally binding.[252] The ICJ Statute describes the Court's decisions as not setting precedents, and writings of jurists as merely 'supplementary means of determining law'.[253] Since the ICJ requires the consent of states to adjudicate disputes, and the United Kingdom is the only Permanent UNSC Member to accept the Court's compulsory jurisdiction, the ICJ has limited ability to make authoritative rulings on the *jus ad bellum*. Even the VCLT's 'rules of interpretation are not exclusive in a way that they prevent the interpreter from applying other principles compatible with the general rule laid down in Art 31'.[254] None of these formal interpretive resources prescribe a hierarchy of the *jus ad bellum's* criteria, nor do they specify which are necessary and sufficient for legal determination.[255] And all have dealt with too few *jus ad bellum* cases for comprehensive interpretive practices to crystallise.[256]

CONCLUSION: COMPETING INTERPRETIVE CULTURES

The discussion so far does not support a conclusion reached by some, that international law has *no* determinate interpretive rules, except 'in the minds of the scholars'.[257] But the analysis in this chapter suggests a more limited claim: the *jus ad bellum* displays many features – based on paradigms, vulnerable to supervaluationism and fuzzy logic – which suggest it is likely to be 'specifically indeterminate'. While this area of international law will usually provide determinate solutions to disputes about the lawfulness of resort to military force, in specific circumstances it can be weakly or even radically indeterminate.

And this conclusion leads to a further potential claim: when considering 'hard cases' of resort to force, which are very different to the paradigms of clearly lawful and clearly unlawful force in the UN Charter, states and lawyers may consciously or intuitively inhabit competing 'interpretive cultures', separate 'epistemic communities' applying mostly overlapping but sometimes

252 UN Charter, art. 11.
253 ICJ Statute, arts. 59, 36(1)(d).
254 Dorr and Schmalenbach, *Vienna Convention*, 538.
255 See Kammerhofer, 'Self-Defence'.
256 Murphy, 'Protean Jus Ad Bellum', 50.
257 Kammerhofer, 'Sources', 550.

competing shared understandings about legal interpretation and lawfulness.[258] Such opposing interpretive cultures are not transient or novel phenomena. They have deep historical roots, reflecting foundational disagreements about how international law works and how it ought to work – disagreements stretching back at least to the division between positivism and naturalism described in the previous section, emerging in the eighteenth century and crystallising in the nineteenth-century writings of scholars such as Bentham and Austin.[259]

Advocates of interpretive culture as an analytical category do not claim individuals necessarily conform to these cultures consciously, nor that they deliberately coordinate or act collectively. It is likely that interpretive cultures reflect the interaction of structural factors and individuals' own agency in response, reflecting intuitions, presuppositions and preferences which are deeply internalised, unconsciously held, and produced by some combination of individual cognitive characteristics and collective socialisation.[260] As Raz notes, the concept of law that any set of actors operationalises will be shaped by 'the interests and the capacities' of those actors and 'the questions which trouble' them.[261] Similarly, Benda-Beckmann argues different academic and professional groups need 'a different concept of law for different purposes'.[262] Hart's distinction between his 'general and descriptive' concept of law and Dworkin's 'evaluative and justificatory' concept points to the different approaches to law which international lawyers apply in different professional and academic roles.[263]

Key structural factors include the national legal system in which lawyers are educated and gain their professional experience, national approaches to textual and customary sources of law, and dominant attitudes to substantive issues such as the resort to force. Other structural factors could include the institutional environment lawyers work in – academic legal scholars, private practitioners, lawyers working for non-governmental campaign groups and government legal advisers will face different professional priorities and incentives. Interpretive cultures are likely to evolve in response to their interactions

258 Griffiths, 'Legal Pluralism?', 38, 36; Friedman, 'Legal Culture', 189; Waibel, 'Interpretive Communities', 148; Haas, 'Introduction', 3.

259 Hart, 'Positivism', 594.

260 Haas, 'Introduction', 3.

261 Raz, 'Two Views of the Nature of the Theory of Law A Partial Comparison', in Jules L. Coleman, ed., *Hart's Postscript: Essays on the Postscript to 'The Concept of Law'* (Oxford: Oxford University Press, 2001), 10.

262 Benda-Beckmann, 'Who's Afraid of Legal Pluralism?', *Journal of Legal Pluralism and Unofficial Law*, 47 (2002), 40.

263 Hart, *Concept of Law*, 239, 40.

with other cultures and agents outside law – private and public clients and competitors, government, media and other aspects of wider culture and public attitudes. And individual lawyers' preferences and characteristics are likely to shape how they internalise and operationalise these structural factors in their own legal decision-making. The end result is competition and disagreement between more or less coherent schools of thought.

Chapter 7 will discuss national differences in approaches to international law in some more detail. At this point, it is worth noting Anthea Roberts' suggestion in her wide-ranging study that international lawyers appear to constitute 'a "divisible college" whose members hail from different states and regions and often form separate, though sometimes overlapping, communities with their own understandings and approaches, as well as their own distinct influences and spheres of influence'.[264] For example, former FCO legal adviser Franklin Berman has written of a 'dangerous' gap between US lawyers, tending to believe the law 'should allow the United States to use force whenever it feels it must', and European lawyers, believing law should 'outlaw force altogether except in the most extreme circumstances', resolving all disputes in the UNSC.[265] Verdirame has noted differences between US and UK international lawyers' 'fundamental assumptions and methodological choices', how they 'understand, describe and characterize' international law.[266] He argues US lawyers are more ambivalent than Europeans about supra-national rules, more prone to using 'scientific and empirical methods', more influenced by international relations scholarship, and so give higher priority to the 'is' in international law while Europeans are more committed to the 'ought'.[267]

Kammerhofer notes the effects of what he describes as lawyers' national 'cultural prejudice' and 'preconceptions of how a legal system works' – 'every international lawyer a national lawyer first'.[268] Prosper Weil described international law's 'inherent polynormativity', that principles 'of self-interpretation and self-appreciation' enable different states to interpret the law differently, so 'international law as understood by one country is not necessarily the same as that understood by another'.[269] Jouannet argued 'cultural' differences may

264 Anthea Roberts, *Is International Law International?* (Oxford: Oxford University Press, 2017), 2.

265 Sir Franklin Berman QC, 'What Do We Expect of Lawyers in Armed Conflict?', *George Washington International Law Review*, 38 (2006), 628–29.

266 Guglielmo Verdirame, '"The Divided West": International Lawyers in Europe and America', *European Journal of International Law*, 18:3 (2007), 554, 555.

267 Verdirame, 'Divided West', 555–6, 558, 562.

268 Kammerhofer, 'Self-Defence', 552.

269 Prosper Weil, '"The Court Cannot Conclude Definitively . . . " Non Liquet Revisited', *Columbia Journal of Transnational Law*, 36 (1998), 118, 119.

mirror differences between common-law and civil law systems, with US, UK and other common-law jurists more comfortable with the evolutionary features of international law than continental European lawyers, acculturated to interpretation-constraining legal codes.[270] And Koskenniemi has contrasted opposing cultures of rule-focused 'formalism' or 'constitutionalism' compared to largely US rule-sceptical 'dynamism' or 'managerialism'.[271]

Adopting Koskenniemi's terminology, it might be argued that one source and consequence of uncertainty in the *jus ad bellum* is the existence of opposing interpretive cultures of 'formalism' and 'dynamism', which differ over their approach to key principles of legal interpretation.[272] 'Restrictivist' lawyers, who in effect operationalise a *jus contra bellum*, see few valid justifications for resort to force and thus adopt a set of interpretive approaches that might be grouped into a culture of 'formalism'.[273] When assessing the lawfulness of force, formalists emphasise the ordinary meaning of the text of the UN Charter and other formal sources of law. They hold that the law has evolved little since 1945, accept only explicitly legal statements as evidence of *opinio juris*, and require clarity and an overwhelming quantity of state practice as evidence that new customary international law has crystallised.[274] And they regard only the UNSC as permitted to authorise force when the law is unclear.[275]

Opposing them, it may be that 'expansionist' lawyers, who see more justifications for resort to force, adopt approaches to legal interpretation that could be grouped into a culture of 'dynamism'. In assessing the lawfulness of force, dynamists are willing to take account of the UN Charter's wider purposes and other law. They argue law has evolved significantly since 1945, and are willing to accept more forms and smaller numbers of expressions of *opinio juris* and state practice as evidence that new customary international law has

270 Emmanuelle Jouannet, 'French and American Perspectives on International Law: Legal Cultures and International Law', *Maine Law Review*, 58:2 (2006), 292–337; James R. Maxeiner, 'Legal Certainty: A European Alternative to American Legal Indeterminacy?', *Tulane Journal of International and Comparative Law*, 15 (2007), 541–607, 575.

271 Martti Koskenniemi, *The Gentle Civiliser of Nations: The Rise and Fall of International Law, 1870–1960* (Cambridge: Cambridge University Press, 2001), 500–7; Martti Koskenniemi, 'Constitutionalism as Mindset: Reflections on Kantian Themes About International Law and Globalization', *Theoretical Inquiries in Law*, 8:1 (2007), 18–23.

272 Koskenniemi, *Gentle Civiliser*, 500–7; Koskenniemi, 'Constitutionalism as Mindset', 18–23.

273 Corten, *Law and War*, 2, 6.

274 Corten, *Law and War*, 16–27.

275 Murphy, 'Protean Jus Ad Bellum', 22.

crystallised. And they see more discretion for states and bodies outside the UNSC to interpret the *jus ad bellum* as authorising force when the law is unclear.

Part II of this book will consider what evidence there is for such interpretive cultures in key ICJ judgments, in the writings of scholars and UK government legal statements about three US-led military interventions, and in the interviews and survey with UK-based international lawyers conducted for this book. Before that, the next chapter considers how complexity and uncertainty about the *facts* of specific military crises form an important further aspect of uncertainty in the *jus ad bellum*.

3

Uncertainty about Facts in the *Jus Ad Bellum*

INTRODUCTION

Much vagueness in the *jus ad bellum* flows from 'epistemic vagueness' – the inability of decision-makers to be 'perfectly sensitive' to all 'reference-determining factors'.[1] There will be times when lawyers cannot be certain they have correctly perceived and understood basically determinate facts that are necessary for evaluating the legality of an instance of resort to force. And legal evaluation of force is particularly 'fact intensive'.[2] It requires not only evaluation of legal principles, but also factual assessment to 'prove the existence of facts which allow the use of force or which prove the breach of the general prohibition of the threat or use of force'.[3]

Former FCO legal adviser Sir Franklin Berman has noted that 'not just the law, but the facts' are 'of fundamental importance' in such legal decisions, speculating that such decisions may be 80 or 90 per cent fact and only 10 or 20 per cent law.[4] The 'shockingly inadequate' evidence underpinning the 2003 Iraq intervention showed lawyers must 'insist that the facts are properly marshaled and assessed', since later accusations of state responsibility for unlawful behaviour 'may turn on what facts can subsequently be proved in its defense'.[5] The ICJ has stated that in cases engaging the *jus ad bellum*, the Court must make a 'determination of the facts' before applying 'the relevant rules of international law'.[6] In such cases, courts 'must untangle the exact

1 Williamson, 'Vagueness in Reality', 693.
2 Simone Halink, 'All Things Considered: How the International Court of Justice Delegated Its Fact-Assessment to the United Nations in the Armed Activities Case', *International Law and Politics*, 40 (2008), 15.
3 Kammerhofer, 'Self-Defence', 145.
4 Berman, 'Lawyers in Armed Conflict', 631.
5 Berman, 'Lawyers in Armed Conflict', 632.
6 *Congo*, Judgment, 200.

sequence of events, identify the actors involved, and make factual and, ultimately, legal determinations'.[7]

This chapter explores how various forms of epistemic vagueness affect the *jus ad bellum*: how difficulties in identifying and evaluating the facts and consequences of fast moving, confusing military crises shapes uncertainty about what the law prescribes in specific cases. I introduce a fictional military conflict between political leaders Hercules and Thrasymachus, which is used here and elsewhere in the book to examine how international lawyers assess the role of facts in *jus ad bellum* decision-making. In the absence of clear legal rules for resolving factual uncertainties about the use of force, it is possible that lawyers instead rely on their own, contestable assumptions and intuitions about the political and strategic consequences and ethical characteristics of using or not using force, in turn contributing to uncertainty and disagreement both in specific cases and more generally in the law governing resort to force. To lay the ground for this discussion, it is first necessary to take a closer look at the *jus ad bellum*'s tests, to identify what factual assessment they require, and particularly to describe how the tests rely on *forecasting* – a form of assessment subject to irreducible uncertainty.

FACTS AND FORECASTS IN THE *JUS AD BELLUM*

The paradigms prescribed by the *jus ad bellum* describe factual situations. Military invasion of one state by another is a set of facts describing a paradigm of illegal force. An invaded state and its allies using force to expel an invader is a set of facts describing a paradigm of legal force. The tests described by the *jus ad bellum* are factual tests, requiring lawyers to make often complex factual assessments to determine whether a particular situation conforms with the paradigms of legal or illegal force.

Several of the *jus ad bellum*'s tests require even more complex assessments, requiring lawyers to assess and compare the *future* factual consequences of different policy options either using force or not. More generally, since laws intend to create factual future consequences – setting or consolidating precedents, encouraging future compliance, deterring future rule-breaking – lawyers' calculations must grapple with a further layer of future-oriented uncertainty.[8] Such forward-looking assessments are vulnerable to what has been described as 'Parmenides' Fallacy'; the temptation to evaluate policy options by comparing

7 Halink, 'All Things Considered', 15.
8 Mark Tebbit, *Philosophy of Law: An Introduction*, 2nd ed. (London: Routledge, 2005), 192–213.

potential *future* consequences of different policies with *present* conditions, or evaluating a past policy choice by comparing the *present* with the *past*.[9]

In fact, to assess different policy options, decision-makers must compare the alternative possible outcomes of different policies *after* each have been implemented. In other words, a decision-maker considering whether to use force must assess the probability and impact of multiple forecasts of *alternative* future scenarios describing the consequences of policies either involving force or not. Those assessing the legality of such decisions after they have been taken should construct and compare alternative *counter-factual* 'what if' scenarios, recreating the choices and consequences which could feasibly be anticipated by decision-makers at the time force was used.

Considering the *jus ad bellum*'s tests as they were framed in Chapter 2, summarised here are the factual questions each test either explicitly or implicitly requires. These draw on widely used sources of the *jus ad bellum*, and make explicit the forecasting and alternative scenarios some tests require.[10]

Necessity Whether the available facts show an armed attack *has* taken place, *is* taking place, or *will* take place in the future. The decision-maker must compare alternative future scenarios, to assess whether there is 'no practical alternative to the proposed use of force that is likely to be effective in ending or averting the attack', or if the attack can be stopped using non-forceful means, such as diplomacy, support to the victim short of force if the victim of attack is not in the state deciding whether to use force, or if the victim can stop the attack themselves.[11] The decision-maker must assess the likelihood and consequences both of 'false positives' – the risks of wrongly assessing an attack is happening or will happen, and 'false negatives' – wrongly assessing there is or will be no attack.[12] A state facing an attack need not 'exhaust all peaceful measures' before using force, but 'must show *either* that it resorted to

9 Phillip Bobbitt, *The Shield of Achilles: War, Peace and the Course of History* (London: Penguin, 2003), 10.

10 Gray, *International Law*; Dinstein, *War, Aggression and Self-Defence*; Wilmshurst, 'Chatham House Principles', 963–72.

11 Wilmshurst, 'Chatham House Principles', 966.

12 Noam Lubell, 'The Problem of Imminence in an Uncertain World', in Marc Weller, ed., *The Oxford Handbook of the Use of Force in International Law* (Oxford: Oxford University Press, 2014), 19.

	peaceful measures before using force or *that it was not reasonable for it to do so*'.[13]
Victim	Is the victim of the current or imminent attack an individual, group or state that the deciding state has legal standing to protect using military force? The decision-maker must also assess if the victim is itself responsible for an armed attack which justifies its attacker's use of force against it. If the victim is outside the deciding state, the decision-maker must assess whether the victim wants or has asked for military help.[14]
Attacker	The decision-maker must identify who is attacking or about to attack the 'victim'. The decision-maker must assess if another state controls that attacking force, and if that 'attacker' is in another state that must be asked for permission before the deciding state uses force. The decision-maker must also assess non-material, psychological facts: what the 'attacker' knows or believes about their targets, what past facts they believe justifies their attack, what harm they intend to inflict, their ultimate goals. If another state controls the attacker, the decision-maker must establish whether that state is responsible for the attack – if it ordered or is complicit in the attack, or if the 'attacker' acted without the 'sponsor' state's knowledge or against its wishes.[15]
Imminence	The decision-maker must compare multiple future scenarios flowing from alternative policy options, to assess whether there is time to stop the attack using non-forceful means before it causes unacceptable harm, for example, leaving the deciding state unable to defend itself.[16] This includes assessing how much time it is likely to take for options not involving force to stop an attack, how much harm the attack is likely to cause in that time, and whether that is unacceptably greater than the harm caused if force was used. This requires assessments of 'the gravity of the attack, the capability of the attacker, and the

13 Green, *Self-Defence*, 84, 85.

14 *Nicaragua*, Merits, paras. 195, 199.

15 Deeks, 'Unwilling or Unable', 148.

16 Wilmshurst, 'Chatham House Principles', 967.

nature of the threat, for example if the attack is likely to come without warning'.[17]

Proportionality — The decision-maker must assess whether the attack involves means and has caused or *will* cause harm of sufficient scale and effects to be more than a 'mere skirmish' or 'border incident', thus justifying force in response.[18] This test requires the decision-maker to forecast and assess whether the intended use of force in response 'taken as a whole' will cause harm whose scale and effects are sufficient, but no more than sufficient, to stop the attack.[19] Proportionality in self-defence is a balancing test: a defending state may cause as much harm as needed to repel an attack, even if that exceeds the harm the attack causes, but must limit the force used so that its 'physical and economic consequences' 'will not be excessive in relation to the harm expected from the attack'.[20]

Authority — The decision-maker must assess how the deciding state, other states, and legally authoritative institutions have previously assessed the legality of similar uses of force. The decision-maker needs to establish if these past facts suggest this resort to force needs UNSC authorisation, or if the deciding state may act on its own authority, or with authorisation from a regional body, or simply with other states' approval.

Contested and/or emergent paradigms of force set additional, sometimes more demanding, factual tests. Pre-emptive self-defence requires the decision-maker to make more long-ranging, complex forecasts of alternative futures, assessing whether an adversary presents a sufficient medium- or long-term future threat to justify force. Many scholars argue that, while assessing necessity, proportionality and imminence 'can be and is treated more leniently in reactive self-defense', anticipatory self-defense requires a more 'strict application of the rules'.[21] Self-defence against attacks from non-state actors overseas

17 Wilmshurst, 'Chatham House Principles', 968.

18 UN General Assembly, 'Definition of Aggression'.

19 Wilmshurst, 'Chatham House Principles', 968.

20 Dinstein, *War, Aggression and Self-Defence*, 238; Wilmshurst, 'Chatham House Principles', 969.

21 Akande and Liefländer, 'Clarifying Necessity, Imminence, and Proportionality', 563.

without the permission of the 'host' government requires the deciding state to establish whether the host state is so 'unable or unwilling to deal' with the threat that it loses the right to refuse other states permission to use force in its territory against the non-state actor.[22] Again, many argue that, where the host state has not been *complicit* in attacks, and so has 'not made itself liable to defensive force and may not have even been asked for consent, the burden that must be overcome should be greater'.[23]

The highly contested justification for use of force as humanitarian intervention poses particular difficulties. The UK government's most recent statements asserting the doctrine have argued states were permitted to use force to 'alleviate overwhelming humanitarian catastrophe', subject to various factual tests.[24] These included 'convincing evidence, generally accepted by the international community as a whole, of extreme humanitarian distress on a large scale, requiring immediate and urgent relief'; 'it must be objectively clear that there is no practicable alternative to the use of force if lives are to be saved'; and 'the proposed use of force must be necessary and proportionate to the aim of relief of humanitarian need and must be strictly limited in time and scope to this aim (i.e. the minimum necessary to achieve that end and for no other purpose)'.[25]

These are difficult factual evaluations, for which there are no widely accepted thresholds for key variables, such as how many states must agree before evidence can be judged as 'generally accepted by the international community as a whole', or how many people experiencing what kind of harm constitutes 'extreme humanitarian distress on a large scale'.[26] The United Kingdom's published legal position before the April 2018 air strikes on Syria following a use of chemical weapons stated that the relevant chemical attacks had 'killed up to 75 people, and injured over 500 people'.[27] However, the complexity of the tests in the statement suggest these figures were not intended to be interpreted as numerical thresholds generally applicable to future decisions to use force.[28] The tests also require forecasts of alternative scenarios assessing how much humanitarian distress would be caused if force is used or not: whether humanitarian distress requires 'immediate and urgent relief', whether the proposed force is 'necessary and proportionate', and whether

22 Wilmshurst, 'Chatham House Principles', 967.
23 Akande and Liefländer, 'Clarifying Necessity, Imminence, and Proportionality', 564.
24 HM Government, 'Chemical Weapon Use'.
25 Ibid.
26 Ibid.
27 HM Government, 'Policy Paper: Syria Action'.
28 Ibid.

'there is no practicable *alternative* to the use of force if lives are to be saved' (emphasis added).[29]

Clearly, such factual tests are open to multiple interpretations and complex interactions. For example, one state may observe atrocities in another state causing civilian deaths of a scale it assesses to be 'extreme humanitarian distress on a large scale' justifying the use of force. But the relative capabilities of both states' militaries may leave the deciding state uncertain as to whether using force would end the atrocities, or instead cause even more suffering. Most commentators who support humanitarian intervention argue it should involve military action 'more narrowly focused and targeted than all out warfighting', and 'even higher standards should apply' than for self-defence, so that states using such force should cause *less* harm than the humanitarian crisis is expected to cause.[30] Others go further, making the justification explicitly dependent on a strategic assessment: 'A right to use force on humanitarian grounds can only exist if, in that particular context, there is a military option that can improve the humanitarian situation. Where there is no such option, there is no right.'[31]

Decision-makers considering whether to rely on contested paradigms to justify force must make other, longer-term factual forecasts. They must assess whether other states are likely to accept or reject that justification, whether their decision may face and lose legal challenge, whether states' and other actors' responses will embed or weaken the norm on which they are relying, and the benefits or harms that norm may cause more generally if it were to crystallise. Any state using force in situations where facts are contested must forecast and assess the probability and potential consequences of 'false positives' and 'false negatives' – possible futures where the factual basis of action or inaction is shown to be false.[32]

Figure 3.1 illustrates the complex multi-scenario analysis the various tests in the *jus ad bellum* require, using a 'MECE' tree, an analytical tool developed

[29] Ibid.

[30] International Commission on Intervention and State Sovereignty, *The Responsibility to Protect: Report of the International Commission on Intervention and State Sovereignty* (Ottawa: International Development Research Centre, 2001), 37; Brownlie and Apperley, 'Kosovo Crisis Inquiry', 910; Greenwood, 'NATO Intervention in Kosovo', 933; Chinkin, 'Legality of NATO's Action', 921–2; Lowe, 'Kosovo Crisis', 941.

[31] Guglielmo Verdirame, 'The Law and Strategy of Humanitarian Intervention', *EJIL: Talk!* (blog), 30 August 2013.

[32] Noam Lubell, 'Problem of Imminence', 18–19; Lord Butler of Brockwell, *Review of Intelligence on Weapons of Mass Destruction (HC898)* (London: The Stationery Office, 2004), paras. 208, 209, 453, 454, 603, 604; Iraq Inquiry, *The Report of the Iraq Inquiry: Executive Summary* (London: Her Majesty's Stationery Office, 2016), paras. 566–70.

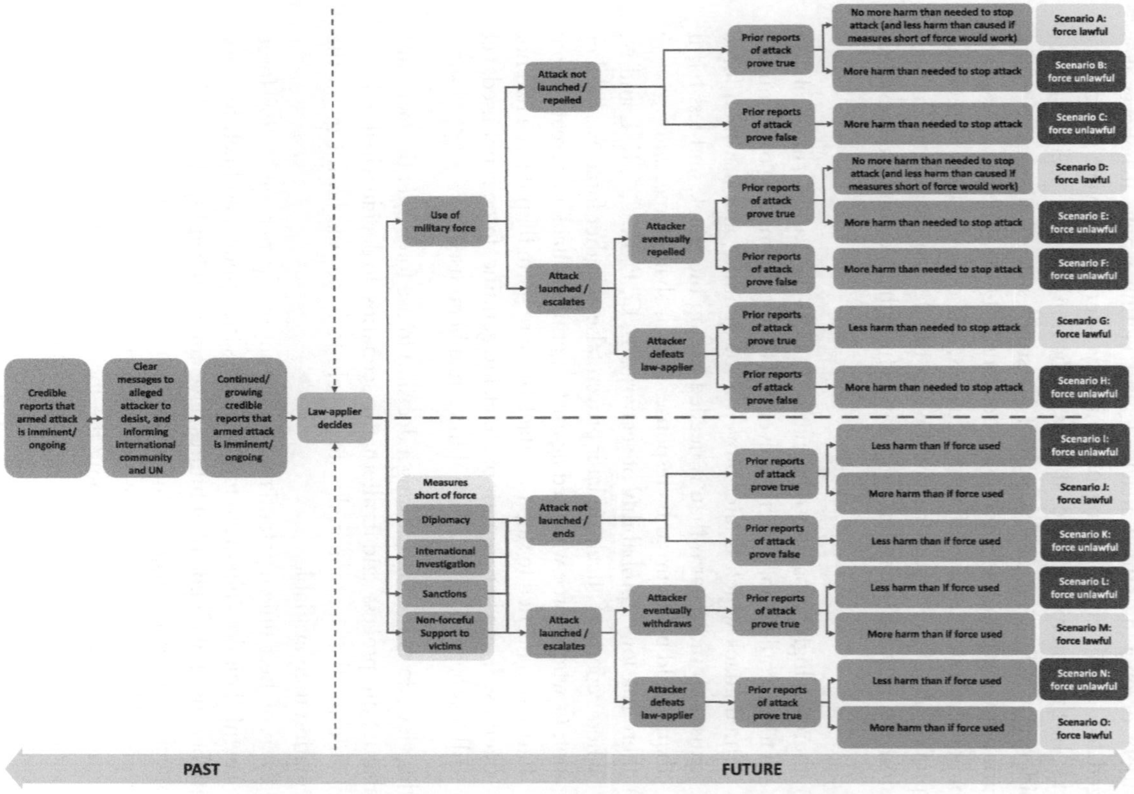

FIGURE 3.1 *Jus ad bellum* MECE decision-tree

by McKinsey and Company seeking to anticipate the 'mutually exclusive, collectively exhaustive' ways in which a situation may unfold.[33] The figure illustrates a situation where a state receives persistent, credible reports of imminent or ongoing armed attacks against victims whom it believes it is obliged to defend, after making non-military efforts to prevent or end the attacks. In this interpretation of the *jus ad bellum's* tests, a decision-maker considering whether to use force must construct sixteen alternative future scenarios flowing from different policy responses. Different harm flows from the policies adopted in the different scenarios, and different facts are eventually proven about the reports received when the decision-maker made their decision. Using this analysis, force may be lawful *if* the decision-maker assesses that:

(a) there is a high probability of scenarios A, D, G, J, M and O, in which use of force would stop, prevent or even fail to stop an ongoing or imminent armed attack which is later proven to be genuine, and in which force causes no more harm than is needed to stop the attack, and less harm than would be incurred by responses not involving force; *and*
(b) there is a lower probability of scenarios B, C, E, F, H, I, K, L and N, where reports of attack are later proven false, whether force was used or not; or where force was used against a genuine attack but creates *more* harm than needed to stop the attack or more harm than if force had not been used; or where reports of attack are genuine, force is not used, yet still less harm is caused than if force had been used.

On this view, an evaluator assessing a decision to use force *after* the fact must reconstruct this process, and its alternative scenarios, to decide whether it was reasonable for the decision-maker to conclude force was lawful given the information then available.

Only six of these fifteen potential future scenarios – 40 per cent – show force to be lawful. This does *not* mean force is always the option least likely to prove lawful, because not all potential futures have equal probability. The evidence in a specific case may suggest futures in which force is lawful are collectively more probable than futures in which force is unlawful. Nevertheless, the diagram shows that simply mapping the logical potential futures following a decision to use or not to use force generates more scenarios in which force is unlawful than lawful. The 'idea of going to war on the basis of probabilities' may be 'repugnant to many', as one scholar notes, but probabilities are 'the

33 Hugh Courtney, *20/20 Foresight: Crafting Strategy in an Uncertain World* (Boston: Harvard Business School Press, 2001), 25, 120–1.

only reality we can realistically work with' when faced with uncertainty about the future consequences of different policy choices.[34]

It should also be clear that these complex factual assessments are vulnerable to the various other forms of vagueness and uncertainty described so far. All the tests are vulnerable to *epistemic vagueness* – uncertainty about facts causing 'irremediable ignorance in borderline cases', our limited powers of discrimination meaning 'we cannot make our judgements perfectly sensitive to all the reference-determining factors'.[35] Belligerent parties in the military crisis will have exclusive access to different information critical to such evaluation, 'exercising indirect control over the fact-finding process'.[36] Belligerents are typically secretive about their actions and strategic in their communications, hiding facts revealing their own strengths and weaknesses, seeking advantage by misleading and shaping others' perceptions.[37] They often seek to conceal facts revealing culpability for violations, or incompetence or ignorance that could provoke legal, media or political attacks. As Judge Schwebel argued in the *Nicaragua* case, the Nuremberg Tribunal examined captured files to reach its judgments, but it was much harder to assess the policies and motives of the states involved in almost all contemporary conflicts, since any such state will be 'unwilling, for security reasons, to reveal information it treats as secret'.[38]

In addition, as Kammerhofer notes, 'the "fog of war" often makes a determination of who did what, when and to whom in a military conflict very difficult, if not impossible'.[39] Such military crises are often chaotic and confusing. Contemporaneous records may be wrong or contradictory. Witnesses may misinterpret, forget, confuse events or be 'influenced by what other people say' through 'memory conformity or social contagion', so even those directly involved may disagree about relevant facts.[40] Forensic and other material evidence is often incomplete, destroyed or lost. Key witnesses may die during the conflict or afterwards.

Jus ad bellum assessments also rely on non-material, psychological facts, which are often even more difficult to establish. The Rome Statute specifies that to hold someone criminally responsible, including for the crime of

34 Lubell, 'Problem of Imminence', 18.
35 Williamson, 'Vagueness in Reality', 693.
36 Halink, 'All Things Considered', 20.
37 Kammerhofer, 'Self-Defence', 146.
38 *Nicaragua*, Schwebel, 295.
39 Kammerhofer, 'Self-Defence', 146.
40 Daniel B. Wright, Amina Memon, Elin M. Skagerberg and Fiona Gabbert, 'When Eyewitnesses Talk', *Current Directions In Psychological Science*, 18:3 (2009), 173–8, 173.

aggression, they must be shown to have acted 'with intent and knowledge' that they will cause unlawful consequences.[41] 'Hostile intent' or *mens rea* may also be relevant for determining whether an armed attack has occurred. As the International Law Association has argued, 'while hostile intent is not an essential element of an armed attack, the existence of mistake or accident is highly relevant in deciding whether the use of force in self-defence is necessary'.[42] For example, a state which immediately admits its forces fired on a neighbour, claims it was a mistake, pays compensation, prosecutes personnel involved and does not repeat such action is less likely to be considered responsible for an armed attack than a state that denies responsibility for such an incident, rewards the personnel involved, and repeats such actions. The French government has explicitly stated that a cyber-attack must be a '*deliberate*, offensive and malicious action' (emphasis added) before it 'may reach the threshold of an armed attack to which France may respond in self defence under Article 51' of the UN Charter.[43]

And the kinds of forecasts the *jus ad bellum* requires are inherently uncertain. As one seminal study observed, 'point prediction in international relations is virtually impossible'.[44] Another wide-ranging study of forecasting noted that, while scientists have more knowledge and 'data-crunching power' than ever before, they continue to lack confidence about the prospects for predicting socio-political events.[45] Such events, including those involving force, emerge from complex, 'non-linear' causal chains involving social, economic and political factors of varying volatility.[46] Such situations are not 'clock-like', operating under predictable laws and causal mechanisms, but 'cloud-like' in their complexity and contingency.[47] They involve networks of independent actors with imperfect information about the situation and each other, pursuing incompatible goals through competitive, interdependent decision-making, adapting their goals and behaviour over time.[48] As

41 Dinstein, *War, Aggression and Self-Defence*, 136; ICC Statute, Article 30.

42 ILA Committee on Use of Force, *Draft Report on Aggression and the Use of Force (May 2016)*, 4; Tom Ruys, *Armed Attack and Article 51 of the UN Charter* (Cambridge: Cambridge University Press, 2010), 29; Dinstein, *War, Aggression and Self-Defence*, 203.

43 Ministère des Armées, *International Law*, 6.

44 Steven Weber, Steven Bernstein, Richard Ned Lebow and Janice Gross Stein, 'God Gave Physics the Easy Problems: Adapting Social Science to an Unpredictable World', *European Journal of International Relations*, 6:1 (2000), 43–76, 53.

45 Philip Tetlock and Dan Gardner, *Superforecasting: The Art and Science of Prediction* (London: Random House, 2015), locs. 177–9 (Kindle).

46 Weber et al., 'God Gave Physics the Easy Problems', 53–9.

47 Tetlock and Gardner, *Superforecasting*, locs. 221–2.

48 M. L. R. Smith and John Stone, 'Explaining Strategic Theory', *Infinity Journal*, 4 (2011), 27–30.

Clausewitz observed, in military conflicts, '[e]ach of the adversaries forces the hand of the other, and a reciprocal action results which in theory can have no limit', pushing any conflict towards 'the utmost exertion of forces'.[49] Changes in any causal factor affects others, shaping events in unpredictable ways, playing out over time-scales beyond the military crisis itself, ultimately creating outcomes no party to a conflict may have envisaged.

The *jus ad bellum's* factual assessments are also vulnerable to *fuzzy logic*. The law does not prescribe clear factual boundaries dividing lawful from unlawful force, nor does it specify how thorough assessments must be, what range of options and consequences they must consider, how far into the future to forecast. Although there 'is a far-reaching consensus that a threat with a very low likelihood of materialization' or below 'some threshold of gravity' does not justify anticipatory self-defense, it is not clear what those thresholds or cut-off points are, how they interact – whether less severe threats require a higher probability while lower probabilities justify force responding to severe threats, and how these affect calculations of imminence.[50] One scholar has proposed a 'reasonableness' test – a state must show *'it was not reasonable'* for it to resort to peaceful measures before using force because of the scale and effects of the attack.[51] But the law specifies no thresholds for reasonableness, how much factual uncertainty is permitted to remain reasonable, what probability of accuracy an assessment of attack must reach for resort to force to be reasonable and therefore lawful.[52]

Supervaluationism is a further source of uncertainty in factual assessments – the facts may meet some tests but not others. Each test requires the decision-maker to use *multiple variables* to assess past, present or future facts, including the scale, timing and location of attack, the future behaviour of the attacking forces, the past behaviour and present and future resilience of the victim, the likely legal and other responses of other states. These different variables are incommensurable, sometimes immensurable, and often suggest different conclusions about whether force is lawful.

Multiple, fragmentary and conflicting evidence can also create supervaluationism, as it can be interpreted in different ways, generating competing explanations about what has happened and what *might* happen if force is used or not. The tests require decision-makers to deal with multiple potentially contradictory information sources to establish the facts, each of which

49 Carl von Clausewitz, *On War* (trans and ed. Michael Howard, Peter Paret and Beatrice Heuser) (Oxford: Oxford University Press, 2007), 5.

50 Akande and Liefländer, 'Clarifying Necessity, Imminence, and Proportionality', 565.

51 Green, *Self-Defence*, 85.

52 Lubell, 'Problem of Imminence', 18–19.

may suggest the use of force being evaluated is lawful or unlawful, creating another form of supervaluationism. The UN Charter and other formal sources do not specify valid sources of evidence for such factual evaluations, but states, scholars and the ICJ have used many obvious sources for establishing facts in specific cases.[53] These include: government reporting and secret intelligence; non-governmental reports, including from aid organisations, campaigning groups, academics, the media; legal, military, forensic or other expert testimony or reports; reports from international and regional organisations such as the UN, the Organisation for Security and Co-operation in Europe (OSCE) or the African Union, their special rapporteurs or regional missions; and international and domestic courts and tribunals.

Since many modern military operations are part of an international alliance or coalition, the interaction of the differing views of allies when new operations are being considered can add to these complications. The difficult evolution of NATO decision-making to intervene in Kosovo in 1999, and the failure to persuade a similarly extensive coalition of nations to intervene in Iraq in 2003, demonstrate how different allies made different calculations of current and future facts in these situations, the likely consequences of different courses of action, and thus whether force was an advisable policy course.[54] These situations also revealed different attitudes between allies as to what constituted lawful use of force – and indeed differences about the need for states to articulate a legal justification at all.[55] The United Kingdom appeared more concerned than most

53 Halink, 'All Things Considered', 18.

54 Bruno Simma, 'NATO, the UN and the Use of Force: Legal Aspects', *European Journal of International Law*, 10 (1999), 1; Antonio Cassese, '*Ex Inuria Ius Oritur*: Are We Moving Towards International Legitimation of Forcible Humanitarian Countermeasures in the World Community?' *European Journal of International Law*, 10 (1999), 23, 29; Michael Wood, 'The Law on the Use of Force: Current Challenges', *Singapore Year Book of International Law*, 11 (2007), 11.

55 UN Security Council, Document S/2003/351 (United States), 'Letter Dated 20 March 2003 from the Permanent Representative of the United States of America to the United Nations Addressed to the President of the Security Council', 20 March 2003, S/2003/351; Document S/2003/350 (United Kingdom) 'Letter Dated 20 March 2003 from the Permanent Representative of the United Kingdom of Great Britain and Northern Ireland to the United Nations Addressed to the President of the Security Council', 20 March 2003, S/2003/350; Document S/2003/352 (Australia), 'Letter Dated 20 March 2003 from the Permanent Representative of Australia to the United Nations Addressed to the President of the Security Council', 20 March 2003, S/2003/350; UK Attorney General Goldsmith, 'The Use of Force Against Iraq', *International and Comparative Law Quarterly*, 52:3 (2003) 811–12; Australian Attorney-General, 'Memorandum of Advice on the Use of Force against Iraq', *Australian Yearbook of International Law*, 24 (2003), 415; William H. Taft and Todd F. Buchwald, 'Preemption, Iraq, and International Law', *The American Journal of International Law*, 97 (2003), 557–63, 553; Gray, *International Law*, 355; Matthew Craven, Susan Marks, Gerry Simpson and Ralph Wilde, 'We are Teachers of International Law', *Leiden Journal of International Law*, 17 (2004), 363–74.

of its allies about explaining the lawfulness of its action in Kosovo, while it adopted a narrower and perhaps less ambitiously expansionist legal justification than the United States for its intervention in Iraq.

Uncertainty of fact in specific cases can affect uncertainty about the wider law too. Facts do not necessarily make law: as Kammerhofer put it, there exists a 'duality of norm and fact', law 'is not (necessarily) a description of reality' but 'a prescription for future behaviour'.[56] However, as Stern notes, controversies about customary law focus on 'the fundamental question of the relationship between fact and law'.[57] If the facts underpinning a novel justification for force are uncontested, compelling and demonstrate sufficiently serious threat, more states and commentators are likely to express their support for it, strengthening arguments for it to be accepted as customary law.[58] States and commentators are less likely to accept a justification where the facts underpinning it are contested and unpersuasive.

For example, before the 11 September 2001 terrorist attacks, it was widely accepted that use of force against terrorists overseas required the consent of the state on whose territory the terrorists were located.[59] Yet overwhelming state approval for and wide participation in the US-led intervention in Afghanistan in 2001, sustained acceptance that Al-Qaeda in Afghanistan was responsible for the 11 September 2001 attacks, and later action by the United States and other states against terrorists without host nation consent elsewhere suggest the 'right of self-defence in case of a non-state armed attack now occupies a place within the "light grey" area' of the *jus ad* bellum, even though many lawyers and some states still disagree.[60] The discredited factual assessment about Iraqi WMDs underpinning the 2003 US-led intervention in Iraq, and persistent conflict and deaths after the intervention,[61] undermined support both for the legal theory

56 Kammerhofer, 'Formal Sources of International Law', 537.

57 Brigitte Stern, 'Custom at the Heart of International Law', *Duke Journal of Comparative and International Law*, 11 (2001), 89.

58 Ibid., 95.

59 Claus Kress, 'Major Post-Westphalian Shifts and Some important Neo-Westphalian Hesitations in the State Practice on the International Law on the Use of Force', *Journal on the Use of Force and International Law*, 1 (2014), 42; *Wall*, Higgins, 215; Rosalyn Higgins, *Problems and Process: International Law and How We Use It* (Oxford: Clarendon Press, 1994), 250.

60 Kress, 'Major Post-Westphalian Shifts', 53; Wilmshurst, 'Chatham House Principles'; Antonio Cassese, 'Terrorism Is Also Disrupting Some Crucial Legal Categories in International Law', *European Journal of International Law*, 12 (2001), 993; J. Charney, 'The Use of Force against Terrorism and International Law', *American Journal of International Law*, 95 (2001), 835; Myjer and White, 'Twin Towers Attack', 5.

61 Iraq Inquiry, *Executive Summary*, 77.

that 'material breach' of ceasefire conditions could revive UNSC resolution authorisation to use force long after the initial operation without explicit UNSC authorisation, and for the 'purposive' method of interpreting UNSC resolutions underpinning that justification.[62]

Many argue NATO's 2011 intervention in Libya, hailed as the first UNSC-authorised operation under the 'Responsibility to Protect' doctrine, caused more instability than would have otherwise occurred, went beyond what was necessary to protect civilians, and thus undermined prospects for future similar UNSC resolutions, for example in Syria.[63] But it is possible the facts about the Kosovo intervention help sustain some support for the doctrine of humanitarian intervention, despite what Kress argues as 'neo-Westphalian resistance' leaving the doctrine in a 'dark grey' zone.[64] Although some facts underpinning the intervention in Kosovo remain contested, International Criminal Tribunal for the former Yugoslavia (ICTY) convictions support the claim that serious war crimes were committed there.[65] Despite political instability, Kosovo has not seen serious violent conflict, and the ICJ has refused to find its independence claim unlawful.[66] The UK government continues to assert a doctrine of humanitarian intervention, other governments may be growing more supportive of it, and the doctrine continues to find support among commentators.[67]

HERCULES, THRASYMACHUS AND THE CONFOUNDING EFFECTS OF FACTUAL DETAIL

The claim that such uncertainties and dilemmas about facts and forecasting create disagreement between lawyers about the legality of specific cases of

62 Byers, *War Law*, loc. 514.

63 Alex J. Bellamy and Paul D. Williams, 'The New Politics of Protection? Côte d'Ivoire, Libya and the Responsibility to Protect', *International Affairs*, 87:4 (2011), 845; Alan Kuperman, 'A Model Humanitarian Intervention? Reassessing NATO's Libya Campaign', *International Security*, 38:1 (2013), 105–36; Anders Henriksen and Marc Schack, 'The Crisis in Syria and Humanitarian Intervention', *Journal on the Use of Force and International Law* 1 (2014), 127.

64 Kress, 'Major Post-Westphalian Shifts', 52, 53.

65 Gray, *International Law*, 34; ICTY Appeals Chamber, 'Press Release: Convictions for Kosovo Crimes Upheld for Four Senior Serbian Officials', MS/CS/1594e (The Hague: ICTY, 2014).

66 *Accordance with International Law of the Unilateral Declaration of Independence in Respect of Kosovo*, Advisory Opinion, ICJ Reports 2010, 403, para. 122.

67 Organisation of African Unity, 'Constitutive Act of the African Union', 1 July 2000, 2158 UNTS 37733, art. 4(h); HM Government, 'Chemical Weapon Use'; Charlie Savage, 'Obama Tests Limits of Power in Syria Conflict', *The New York Times* (8 September 2013); Harold Koh, 'Syria and the Law of Humanitarian Intervention (Part II: International Law and the Way Forward)', JustSecurity (2 October 2013).

resort to force can be observed in the results of one part of the survey of international lawyers conducted for this book. That part asked lawyers for their opinions about the lawfulness of force in fictional scenarios involving Hercules and Thrasymachus, leaders of states 'H' and 'T'.[68] The states had a long history of conflict, and both have close allies who are permanent UNSC members. Hercules and Thrasymachus have a poor relationship, while diplomatic relations between their states ended years ago, and politico-military tensions have steadily grown. Military clashes on the border have increased in recent months, causing occasional military deaths, each state blaming the other. Against this background, the survey asked the lawyers for their opinions on the legality of examples of resort to force relying on four contested justifications, or 'hard cases', described in Chapter 2: anticipatory self-defence, pre-emptive self-defence, self-defence against a non-state actor, and humanitarian intervention. Figure 3.2 summarises the responses from the twelve participants who completed this part of the survey.

Anticipatory self-defence. Participants were first invited to consider at what if any point in the following four-hour chain of events Hercules should consider it legally permissible to authorise force in self-defence against State T.

X_8 An unmanned aerial vehicle (UAV) of a type known to be in State T's armed drone programme is ready for take-off, weapons status unclear.

X_9 The UAV is flying in T airspace, but its destination and weapons status are unclear.

X_{10} The UAV is still in T airspace, but its trajectory shows it will definitely enter State H airspace, although its weapons status remains unclear.

X_{11} The UAV enters H airspace, H air-defence sensors detect a missile on the UAV.

X_{12} The UAV launches its missile, but it is unclear if the missile will strike H territory or the surrounding sea.

X_{13} H air defence sensors show the missile is on course to impact H territory. The missile has evaded anti-missile defences, although may still self-destruct before impact.

X_{14} The missile detonates on H territory, causing significant casualties and damaging military facilities.

68 Inspired by 'Hercules and the Quietest Rave' in Endicott, *Vagueness in Law*, 160; Dworkin, *Law's Empire*, 239; Plato, *The Republic*, 2nd ed. (trans. Alan Bloom) (New York: Basic Books, 1991), 16.

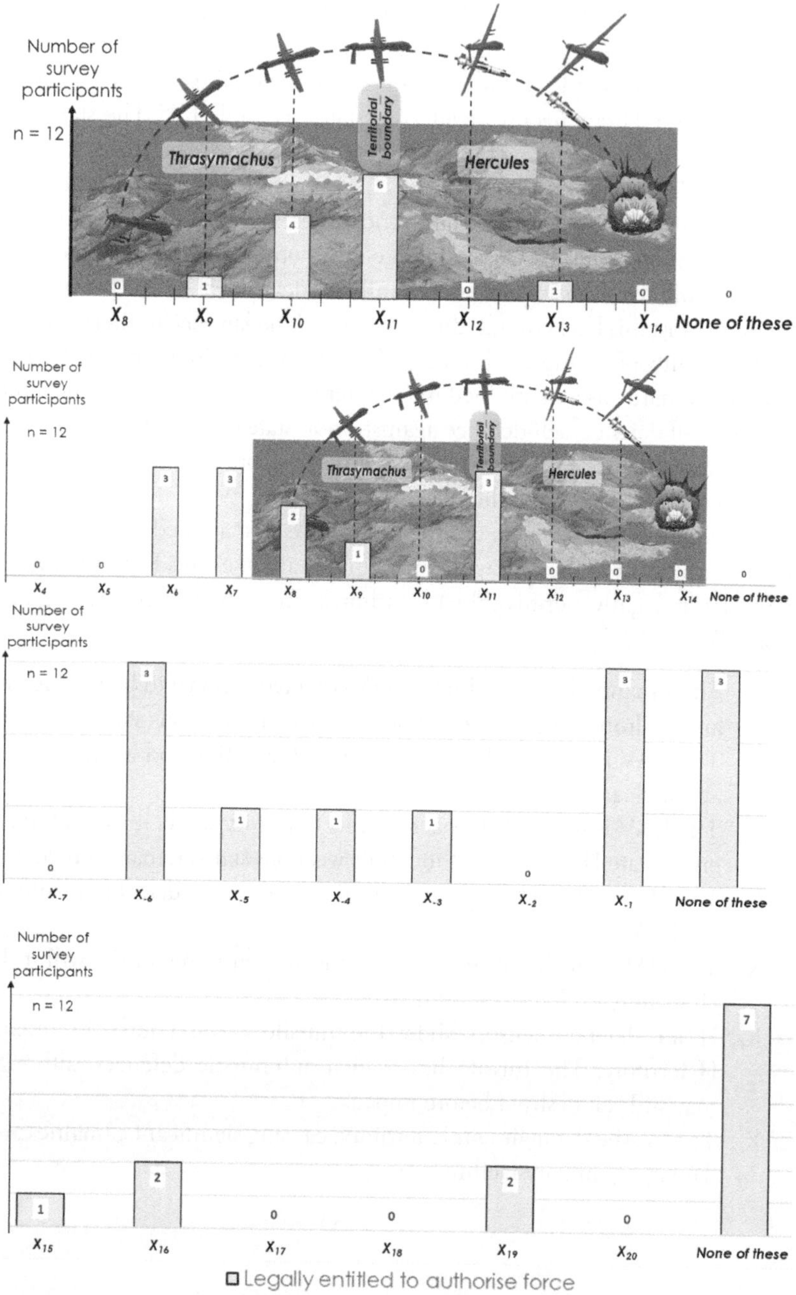

FIGURE 3.2 Scenarios (from top): anticipatory self-defence; anticipatory or pre-emptive self-defence; self-defence against non-state actor; humanitarian intervention

As Figure 3.2 shows,[69] when presented with a concrete drone attack with little specific prior information, a large minority – five of twelve participants – approved some form of anticipatory self-defence. One legal scholar who described anticipatory self-defence as probably unlawful when asked about it in principle approved resort to force in this scenario without waiting for the missile to hit State H territory.[70] The second most popular point for approving force (four participants) was clearly anticipatory, the UAV still in State T airspace but definitely entering State H airspace, even though its weapons status remained unclear. One scholar approved force even earlier, when the UAV had taken off, but its destination and weapons status were unclear.[71] The most popular response (six of twelve participants) approved force when the drone had just entered H airspace and its missile was detected. This was arguably the earliest point that could be described as self-defence against ongoing attack, as the UAV had violated H airspace, although since it had not discharged weapons the response might still be seen as anticipatory. Only one participant, a scholar, approved force when the UAV was well within H airspace and had fired a missile that was definitely going to hit H territory.[72]

Pre-emptive self-defence. Participants were then invited to consider the following chain of events over the twelve months before the 'drone strike'.

- X_1 Thrasymachus's media, politicians and public demand the development of armed drones capable of defeating H air defences.
- X_2 Thrasymachus's political party passes a resolution calling for attacks on H.
- X_3 Thrasymachus secretly authorises planning for drone strikes on H.
- X_4 Thrasymachus makes public statements raising the prospect of an attack on H.
- X_5 Thrasymachus launches a secret programme to build weaponised drones.
- X_6 Thrasymachus secretly makes a strategic decision to attack H.
- X_7 Thrasymachus secretly orders a specific drone strike on H.

Participants were asked at what if any point in the *whole* new timeline Hercules should consider it legally permissible to authorise force against

69 'Predator Type Drone' image by boscorelli3D, from 3DExport.com; 'Sea Dart Missile' image by Hristov, from 3DExport.com; 'Explosion' image by Oceloti, from Vectorstock; Island generated using *Polygon Map Generator* by Amit Patel, Red Blob Games (www.redblobgames.com/maps/mapgen2/).

70 Participant 27.

71 Participant 9.

72 Participant 24.

State T in self-defence, assuming he learns of these developments as they happen.

As Figure 3.2 shows, a large majority – nine of twelve participants – accepted clearly anticipatory and arguably pre-emptive self-defence when presented with this information. One practising international lawyer who supported anticipatory self-defence stated in interview that the right 'comes into play when there is the last practical opportunity to prevent what is demonstrably an intended attack'.[73] Even with the information in this scenario, the 'last practical opportunity' to prevent the attack may be as late as when the UAV is at the airfield (chosen by two of twelve participants). Yet half the participants said force was lawful before then, either when Thrasymachus secretly gave the order for the strike (three participants), or when he made a less specific strategic decision to attack (three participants). Three participants authorised force as soon as the UAV entered H airspace, and none waited for the drone to fire. This scenario suggested that revealing more information about the situation *increased* rather than *reduced* contestation; unlike the earlier scenario, no point was most popular – three points each attracted three participants and another point attracted one participant.

Self-defence against non-state actors. Participants were then invited to consider the following events in the twelve months before Thrasymachus faced calls for an offensive drone programme.

- X_{-7} Thrasymachus faces a violent insurgency, headquartered in a region of State H where Hercules has lost control. Thousands of State T civilians and combatants have been killed by insurgents. Hercules decides to interdict the insurgents.
- X_{-6} Hercules cannot secure parliamentary approval to use force against T's insurgents within H, his parliament fearing civilian suffering and sympathising with the rebels.
- X_{-5} The local population in that region of H facilitates the insurgency's logistics.
- X_{-4} Local officials from Hercules' party and members of his cabinet help the insurgents, including training them in official facilities, without Hercules' knowledge.
- X_{-3} Hercules suspects this support is being provided, orders that it stop, but his instructions are ignored.
- X_{-2} Hercules knows the support is continuing, and acquiesces covertly.
- X_{-1} Hercules announces publicly that his government is supporting the insurgents.

[73] Participant 13.

Assuming Thrasymachus learns of these developments as they happen, participants were now asked at what point from X_{-1} to X_{-7}, Thrasymachus might consider it legally permissible to authorise force in self-defence against attacks from a non-state actor located in State H, which Hercules is 'unable or unwilling' to deal with.

Responses to this scenario showed the widest spread of responses (see Figure 3.2), even more contestation than when asking participants about self-defence against non-state actors in principle. No point in the scenario was most popular. Three participants only approved force when Hercules publicly confirmed support for the insurgents. Three chose different points in the timeline at which Hercules appeared willing but unable to stop the insurgents. And three chose the point when Hercules' parliament refused to approve military action against the insurgents, but before the government or population started supporting them. Three said use of force was not lawful at all in this scenario, one of three equally most popular answers, and more than the one participant – a legal scholar – who declared self-defence against non-state actors clearly unlawful when asked about this justification in principle, suggesting opposition to this justification *hardened* when faced with at least this set of concrete facts.

Humanitarian intervention. Finally, participants were invited to consider the following events, describing an apparent humanitarian catastrophe in State T weeks after the 'drone strike'.

X_{15} Media reports suggest State T's armed forces plan mass killings of the insurgents' ethnic group.
X_{16} Television footage shows mass killings of civilians from the insurgents' ethnic group.
X_{17} Defectors from State T corroborate these reports.
X_{18} A regional organisation to which T and H both belong calls for use of force in a humanitarian intervention against T to stop the mass killings.
X_{19} An UNGA resolution endorses this call for humanitarian intervention.
X_{20} A draft UNSC resolution authorising intervention in State T gains votes from all UNSC members apart from one P5 state, which vetoes.

Participants were asked at which if any point in this chain Hercules should consider it legally permissible to authorise force against State T to prevent a humanitarian catastrophe. Responses to this scenario (see Figure 3.2) showed a clear majority – seven of twelve participants – regarding humanitarian intervention unlawful, but a significant minority declaring it lawful (five participants) if supported by an UNGA resolution (two participants), or when television footage showed mass killings (two participants), or even when media reports suggested State T's forces were planning mass killings (one participant). This variation in views clearly reflects the wide variety of views expressed in the interview comments reported in Chapter 2.

Comparing how the twelve participants who completed this part of the survey replied to the questions about force in principle asked in Chapter 2 and these questions about force in this concrete albeit fictional case reveals that these international lawyers did find themselves giving legal opinions that were broadly as 'interventionist' in this 'concrete' case as their opinions of the *jus ad bellum* in the abstract. At the same time, half the participants who replied to both sets of questions gave significantly different answers to questions of resort to force in principle and in a concrete scenario; and those differences did not all point in the same direction. Two participants seemed more cautious about force in the scenarios than in principle, only willing to declare force lawful fairly late in the scenarios, scoring significantly less than the replies they gave about the lawfulness of force in principle; a 'real' case seemed to make them more cautious.[74] But four participants seemed significantly less cautious about using force in the scenarios than in principle.[75] Only three participants gave answers yielding almost exactly the same 'restrictive/permissive' score for both the in-principle and scenario questions.[76]

These scenarios suggest four overall conclusions about how facts may affect disagreements about contested legal justifications for force. First and most obviously, these scenarios confirmed that these international lawyers continued to disagree about contested justifications even when presented with facts. Participants remained opposed to humanitarian intervention and became even more opposed to self-defence against non-state actors when presented with these 'facts'. Second, more facts revealing more detail and complexity about the military confrontation *increased* rather than reduced disagreement around contested justifications for self-defence. Participants gave four different answers to the 'simplest' scenario of self-defence against Thrasymachus' drone strike, five different answers to the scenario revealing more about Thrasymachus' preparation for the strike, and six different answers to the scenario revealing both more information and more complexity by suggesting Hercules' actions may have justified Thrasymachus's attack.

Third, these lawyers were fairly consistent in their answers about the justification of force in the abstract and in these hypothetical factual scenarios.

74 Participants 1, 17.
75 Participants 4, 23, 24, 27.
76 Participants 2, 9, 18.

But, fourth, that consistency was not perfect, and the inconsistency does not point in one direction – significant numbers of participants were either more interventionist or less interventionist when asked about resort to force in the abstract and in factual scenarios. These conclusions and the analysis preceding it raise questions about how lawyers actually deal with factual uncertainty. What guidance does the law provide for assessing facts?

RESPONSES IN LAW TO UNCERTAINTY OF FACT

Chapter 2 described how lawyers draw on canons of legal interpretation, including those in the VCLT and ICJ Statute, to address uncertainty in interpreting the law in specific cases. No equivalent authoritative legal guidance exists for dealing with factual uncertainties; as one commentator notes 'in reality there is very little hard law on evidence'.[77] Even the ICJ's basic documents fail to explain how the Court 'will weigh evidence or what standard of proof the parties need to satisfy'.[78] In its early years, the Court avoided extensive discussion of facts, instead deciding cases on points of law. However, since the 1980s the ICJ has through its examination of specific cases developed rules of evidence in case law.[79] The legal principles of due diligence and reasonableness may also shed light on a state's obligations to establish the facts when deciding whether to use force.

The ICJ's rules of evidence are not legal obligations on itself, on other tribunals, or on states considering force or assessing another state's actions. It is generally accepted that the ICJ does not apply the principle *stare decisis* in its decision-making, so its case law does not create binding precedents. Nevertheless, the ICJ does practice '*jurisprudence constante*', citing and seeking consistency with its own decisions, procedural choices, evidence doctrines and statements on evidence from previous judgments.[80] So the Court's past rules of evidence provide some insight into how it may assess facts in future cases, and thus states and commentators have at least pragmatic reasons to refer to them in use of force decisions which may be challenged in the Court. The ICJ set out its approach to assessing evidence in particular detail in the *Nicaragua*, *Tehran Hostages*, *Oil Platforms*, *Congo*, and *Genocide Convention* cases.[81] Riddell and Plant, and separately Halink, have identified from these

77 Simon De Smet, 'Book Review', *The Cambridge Law Journal*, 68:3 (2009), 664–7.

78 Halink, 'All Things Considered', 25.

79 Anna Riddell and Brendan Plant, *Evidence before the International Court of Justice* (London: British Institute of International and Comparative Law, 2009), 186.

80 Riddell and Plant, *Evidence*, 30, 31, 31.

81 Riddell and Plant, *Evidence*, 187, 190–1.

cases the following broad factors for assessing the probative value and reliability of evidence.

Sources	The number of sources indicating a particular alleged fact, whether those sources are partisan or independent, and whether they are corroborated by other sources.[82] Identifying the sources of reports is particularly important, since '[w]idespread reports of a fact may prove on closer examination to derive from a single source', meaning those multiple reports have no greater evidentiary value than the original source.[83] The Court found in the *Congo* case that media reports were often partial and unreliable.[84]
Interest	Whether sources of evidence have an interest in the case, and whether they provide 'admissions against the interest of the party submitting it'.[85] The Court has given particular weight to 'Reliable evidence acknowledging facts or conduct unfavourable to the state represented by the person offering the evidence'.[86]
Relation to Events	Whether evidence 'records direct observations or hearsay', giving particular weight to 'evidence from persons with direct knowledge' of relevant events.[87]
Method	How evidence has been collected and analysed before being submitted, for example giving more weight to reports deriving from 'a careful, judicial-like process' such as ICTY judgments, and less weight to anonymous reports whose methods of analysis are unclear.[88]
Verification	Giving more weight to evidence subjected to cross-examination by experienced judges with specialist knowledge, and verified by other expert, independent sources.[89] The Court also gives more weight to

82 Riddell and Plant, *Evidence*, 192.
83 Halink, 'All Things Considered', 22.
84 Halink, 'All Things Considered', 23.
85 Riddell and Plant, *Evidence*, 192.
86 Halink, 'All Things Considered', 22.
87 Riddell & Plant, *Evidence*, 192; Halink, 'All Things Considered', 22.
88 Riddell & Plant, *Evidence*, 192; Halink, 'All Things Considered', 23.
89 Riddell & Plant, *Evidence*, 192; Halink, 'All Things Considered', 22–3.

	uncontested facts, and evidence whose accuracy is unchallenged 'by impartial persons'.[90]
Contemporaneity	Giving more weight to documents or statements prepared 'at a time close to the facts' they attest to, and less weight to evidence prepared later or specifically for litigation.[91]
Form	The Court has generally preferred written to oral evidence, since it is not procedurally well equipped to deal with testimony.[92] Riddell and Plant also argue witnesses have often not contributed much to cases, and so are 'somewhat of a waste' of time and money.[93] Pietrowski notes that the 'frailty of human contingencies' make witness testimony 'liable to arouse distrust', while documents are 'of higher probative value'.[94] In domestic court cases, judges can assess witness reliability by considering their demeanour and relationship to the parties to a case, but in international cases witnesses are often experienced professionals, whose demeanour is less likely to signal reliability in this way.[95] And since witness testimony is only ever provided within a court case, it is more likely to be tailored to the needs of one party than documents prepared for other purposes.[96]
Procedure	Whether evidence was submitted according to the ICJ rules of procedure.[97]

A particular challenge for the Court or any party outside government attempting to assess that government's decision to use military force is the importance of classified information in such decisions. Article 49 of the ICJ Statute allows the Court to take 'formal note' if parties refuse to produce material when requested, which is generally accepted as permitting the court to draw 'adverse inferences from a refusal to provide requested

90 Halink, 'All Things Considered', 22, 22–3.
91 Riddell and Plant, *Evidence*, 192; Halink, 'All Things Considered', 22.
92 Riddell and Plant, *Evidence*, 192–3.
93 Riddell and Plant, *Evidence*, 192–3.
94 Robert Pietrowski, 'Evidence in International Arbitration', *Arbitration International*, 22:3 (2006), 391.
95 Riddell and Plant, *Evidence*, 193.
96 Riddell and Plant, *Evidence*, 193.
97 Riddell and Plant, *Evidence*, 192.

documents'.[98] However, the Court has not so far stated that it has drawn such adverse inferences in decisions on cases where a party refused a request to provide documents, for example in the *Corfu Channel* case when the United Kingdom refused to disclose classified documents, and in the *Genocide Convention* case, when Serbia and Montenegro refused to disclose unredacted classified documents.[99] In any case, the Court cannot *compel* parties to produce classified evidence, and has not developed procedures for protecting such information.[100]

The ICJ's Statute and rules say nothing about standards of proof. It is unclear *how much evidence and how much certainty* is sufficient for legal evaluation of a case against the *jus ad bellum* tests. As one scholar puts it, requiring 'a high threshold' for evidence 'would lead to fewer unwarranted uses of force (false positives), but raise the risk of inaction due to insufficient proof of an imminent attack that does materialise (false negatives)'.[101] A lower threshold would more easily allow force, and 'reduce chances of negligent inaction (false negatives), but increase the chance of unnecessary force (false positives)'.[102] The commentary to the ICJ statute argues the Court's practice shows it is impossible to set a standard, since 'all depends on the norms at stake'.[103] Judge Krylov in his dissenting opinion in the ICJ *Corfu Channel* case argued: '[O]ne cannot condemn a State on the basis of probabilities. To establish international responsibility, one must have clear and indisputable facts.'[104] And yet, as has already been noted, in decision-making about military crises, probabilities are often 'the only reality we can realistically work with'.[105]

ICJ case law has used various standards of proof even in the same judgment, with individual judges advocating different approaches, the overall standard of proof usually only revealed 'when the Court delivers its judgment'.[106] This challenge has been exacerbated by different attitudes to standards of proof in different legal systems. Judges from the civil law tradition have been less concerned with establishing a standard of proof, since in that tradition proof is 'not a question of probability', rather 'the personal appreciation of the judge' – *'l'intime conviction du juge'*.[107] Common law judges have been

98 ICJ Statute; Halink, 'All Things Considered', 19.
99 Riddell and Plant, *Evidence*, 217.
100 Riddell and Plant, *Evidence*, 217.
101 Lubell, 'Problem of Imminence', 21.
102 Ibid.
103 Halink, 'All Things Considered', 24.
104 *Corfu*, Dissenting Opinion of Judge Krylov, ICJ Reports (1949), 72.
105 Lubell, 'Problem of Imminence', 18.
106 Halink, 'All Things Considered', 25.
107 Riddell and Plant, *Evidence*, 125.

more concerned with establishing a standard, given common law's two well-established standards, 'preponderence of evidence' or 'balance of probabilities' in civil cases, and 'beyond reasonable doubt' in criminal cases.[108]

Case law suggests the Court applies 'a sliding scale for the standard of proof', depending on the gravity of the claims and seriousness of the allegations.[109] The Court has used the balance of probabilities for boundary disputes, cases which do not seek attribution of international responsibility, or in straightforward disagreements over treaty interpretation.[110] However, the Court has said claims 'involving charges of exceptional gravity must be proved by evidence that is fully conclusive', requiring a high level of certainty.[111] In the *Genocide Convention* case, the Court rejected the claim that Serbia and Montenegro was responsible for the Srebrenica Massacre because it was 'not established *beyond any doubt*' that Serbia and Montenegro knew that Republika Srbska forces intended to carry out the massacre.[112]

In most *jus ad bellum* cases, the Court has used standards between these extremes, suggesting it sees violations of the *jus ad bellum* as serious violations of international law, but less serious than genocide. In the *Oil Platforms* case, the Court applied a 'convincing proof standard' to conclude the United States had provided insufficient evidence that Iran was responsible for a missile attack on a US tanker.[113] In the *Congo* case, the Court required 'sufficient and convincing' evidence that Uganda's armed forces were stationed in particular locations in the DRC, and had substituted their authority for that of the DRC, a higher standard of proof than 'balance of probabilities' or 'sufficiency'.[114]

As one scholar has noted, statements and practice by states and scholars also propose different views about the standard of proof necessary for resort to force.[115] The factors Daniel Bethlehem proposed for assessing imminence say a state may conclude 'an armed attack is imminent for purposes of the exercise of a right of self defense, provided that there is a *reasonable and objective basis* for concluding that an armed attack is imminent' (emphasis added), a test

108 Riddell and Plant, *Evidence*, 124.
109 Halink, 'All Things Considered', 24.
110 Riddell and Plant, *Evidence*, 133.
111 *Application of the Convention on the Prevention and Punishment of the Crime of Genocide (Bosnia and Herzegovina* v. *Serbia and Montenegro)*, Judgment, ICJ Reports 2007, 43, para. 209.
112 *Genocide*, Judgment, para. 422 (emphasis added).
113 Halink, 'All Things Considered', 25.
114 *Congo*, Judgment, para. 173; Riddell and Plant, *Evidence*, 133.
115 Jasmin Johurun Nessa, 'Self-Defense in International Law: What Level of Evidence?', JustSecurity (8 July 2019).

which the United Kingdom and the United States have endorsed.[116] A footnote in Bethlehem's article clarifies that '[t]he "reasonable and objective basis" formula . . . requires that the conclusion is capable of being reliably supported with a high degree of confidence on the basis of credible and all reasonably available information'.[117] But even this clarification does not specify if this test requires evidence to meet the standard of 'clear and convincing', that the allegation is 'substantially more probable to be true than not', nor the lower standard of 'preponderance of the evidence' or 'balance of probabilities', that the allegation is 'more likely to be true than not'.[118]

And the UK government itself has used different words to describe the evidence underpinning its use of force decisions, suggesting it does not have a settled standard of proof for such decisions.[119] For example, in September 2015 the UK prime minister declared there was 'clear evidence' against two British nationals killed by UK air strikes in Syria, invoking the right of 'self-defence'. But in November 2015 the prime minister referred to a 'solid basis of evidence' for use of force in self-defence against ISIL in Syria.[120]

Humanitarian intervention poses its own difficult questions about 'the legal standard that should apply to the question of whether the intended humanitarian objective . . . can be achieved through the proposed use of force'.[121] As one scholar has put it: 'If, for example, the Chiefs and the Intelligence Services advise that it is more likely than not that the particular objective can be achieved, would that be enough? Or should a higher likelihood of success be required? And how should the consequences of failure be factored into the legal analysis?'[122]

The international law principle of 'due diligence' may provide additional guidance about the degree of factual certainty decision-makers must reach before using force. The 'due diligence' principle applies a standard of 'reasonable care' to assess whether a state has met its obligation 'to take all measures it could reasonably be expected to take' to avoid wrongful consequences of actions it commissions or fails to prevent.[123] Another scholar has proposed

116 Bethlehem, 'Self-Defense'; Wright, 'Modern Law of Self-Defence'; Egan, 'International Law'.

117 Bethlehem, 'Self-Defense', 6.

118 Nessa, 'Self-Defense in International Law'.

119 Ibid.

120 David Cameron, 'Syria: Refugees and Counter-terrorism' (7 September 2015), *Hansard*, House of Commons, 6th ser., vol. 599, cols. 23–7; David Cameron, 'Syria' (26 November 2015), *Hansard*, 6th ser., vol. 602, cols. 1489–94.

121 Verdirame, 'Law and Strategy'.

122 Ibid.

123 International Law Association Study Group on Due Diligence in International Law, *Second Report* (International Law Association, July 2016), 2, 9.

a 'reasonableness' test for a state to 'show *either* that it resorted to peaceful measures before using force or *that it was not reasonable for it to do so*', and if the nature of the attack meant 'it would not be reasonable to expect a state to seek alternative non-forcible means' of response.[124]

The principle of 'due diligence' requires diligence 'appropriate and proportional to the degree of risk' of harm, and to the significance of the rule concerned, thus expecting more diligence to prevent genocide, a *jus cogens* violation, than to prevent harm to property.[125] Elizabeth Wilmshurst has argued '(t)he more far-reaching, and the more irreversible' the actions, 'the more a State should accept (internally as well as externally) the burden of showing that its actions were justifiable on the facts'.[126] A state can only be expected to prevent harm if it 'has knowledge of the situation', although it may be obliged 'to use best efforts' to gain relevant knowledge.[127] The principle of reasonableness takes account of 'what could be expected from a State', taking into account its level of development.[128] And the principle of due diligence may allow states that are victims of an international wrong to rely more on 'inferences' and 'circumstantial evidence'.[129]

The notion of diligence has also been referred to in judicial opinions in ICJ cases considering the resort to force. For example, in the *Nicaragua* case, the Court argued it was unreasonable to expect Nicaragua to exercise 'a higher degree of diligence' than its neighbours in preventing arms from flowing to rebels.[130] Judges Kooijmans and Tomka, in their dissenting opinions in the *Congo* case, argued the DRC had breached its 'duty of vigilance' to prevent armed groups from attacking Uganda from its territory.[131]

This discussion suggests any state considering resort to force overseas, an act engaging a *jus cogens* norm and potentially causing significant international harm, is obliged to make best efforts to establish the relevant facts to a high degree of confidence. The discussion also suggests *less* effort and confidence will be required from less capable states, and from states expecting or already experiencing extensive harm from attack. As one scholar puts it, since there can never be 100 per cent certainty about future events, we might expect states to wait until 'they are 95% certain that a specific enemy attack is imminent' for a moderate

124 Green, *Self-Defence*, 85.
125 ILA Study Group, *Second Report*, 12, 20.
126 Wilmshurst, 'Chatham House Principles', 968.
127 ILA Study Group, *Second Report*, 12.
128 ILA Study Group, *Second Report*, 9.
129 *Corfu*, Merits, 18.
130 *Nicaragua*, Merits, para. 157.
131 *Congo*, Kooijmans, 306; *Congo*, Tomka, 351.

conventional attack, but 'faced with WMD they might decide to move ahead when they are 80% certain' given the much greater harm of a 'false negative'.[132]

At the same time, the ICJ's rules of evidence and the principle of due diligence have important weaknesses. First, past cases suggest the ICJ does not apply these rules of evidence consistently. Halink argues that in the *Congo* case, the Court failed 'to engage in independent fact-assessment', accepted UN reports 'as proven facts', and did not 'articulate a clear standard of proof'.[133] Riddell and Plant observe the Court 'enjoys virtually unfettered discretion in determining and applying the standard of proof', in seeking, admitting and using different forms of evidence, and in developing procedures 'to address novel or unexpected questions relating to evidence'.[134]

Second, these rules and principles are vulnerable to the forms of vagueness described in Chapter 2. As Figure 3.3 illustrates, the ICJ's rules of evidence are not bivalent tests; each describes a continuum operating according to fuzzy logic. Judges Bedjaoui, Ranjeva, and Koroma of the ICJ referred to the paradox of the heap when they argued that, when considering evidence, 'degrees of quantity must not conceal variations in quality', and 'a pile of wheat remains a pile of wheat if you take away one grain, then another grain, and so on. And yet there becomes a time when, by removing one grain, there is no longer any pile.'[135] As Jeremy Bentham noted in his treatise on judicial evidence, 'nobody can be ignorant that belief is susceptible to different degrees of strength or intensity'.[136] Similarly, judgements about due diligence, reasonableness, effort and confidence clearly operate according to fuzzy rather than bivalent logic, and are context-specific. An International Law Association study noted due diligence and reasonableness are 'difficult to determine *in abstracto*', leaving states 'much discretion'.[137]

These principles are also susceptible to supervaluationism, because they are multi-part tests taking account of multiple factors which can be evaluated using various different standards. The different principles are overlapping but not co-extensive – evidence may meet all the principles, or only some. The Court's jurisprudence suggests 'no discernible hierarchy among these factors' to guide lawyers.[138] And they are susceptible to social supervaluationism, when

132 Lubell, 'Problem of Imminence', 20.
133 Halink, 'All Things Considered', 16.
134 Riddell and Plant, *Evidence*, 411.
135 *Maritime Delimitation and Territorial Questions between Qatar and Bahrain*, Joint Dissenting Opinion of Judges Bedjaoui, Ranjeva and Koroma, ICJ Reports 2001, para. 83.
136 Jeremy Bentham and Etienne Dumont, *Treatise on Judicial Evidence* (London: JW Paget, 1825), 40.
137 ILA Study Group, *Second Report*, 9.
138 Riddell and Plant, *Evidence*, 192.

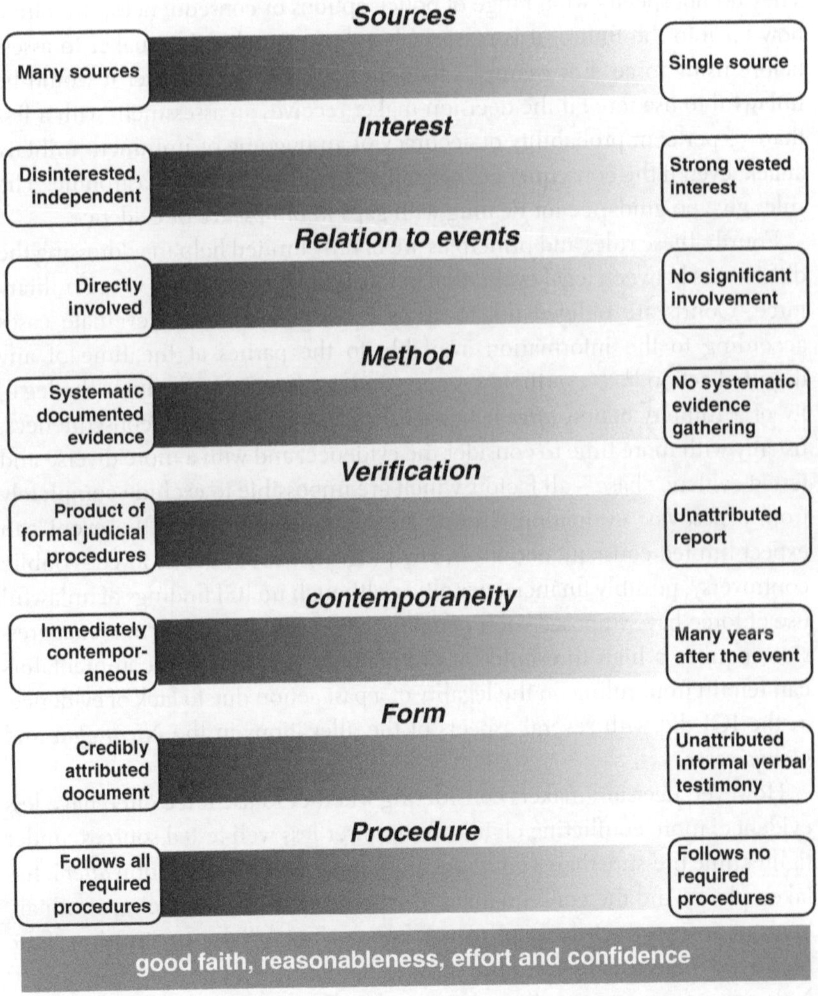

FIGURE 3.3 Vagueness in ICJ rules of evidence

there are competing claims about relevant facts, future consequences and the absence of evidence about facts. As Riddell and Plant note, 'one judge may believe a certain allegation has been proven, whilst another does not', and ICJ jurisprudence does not make it clear how much evidence amounts to proof.[139]

Third, these rules provide no guidance for constructing or comparing the alternative factual scenarios and forecasts that the *jus ad bellum*'s tests require.

[139] Riddell and Plant, *Evidence*, 123.

They do not specify what range of policy options or consequences, stretching how far into the future, it is reasonable to expect a decision-maker to assess before using force. For example, they do not prescribe whether it would be unlawful to use force if the decision-maker receives an assessment with a less than 50 per cent probability of accuracy of an ongoing or imminent military attack, even if the consequences of such an attack would be catastrophic. The rules give no guidance for dealing with gaps in or *absence* of evidence.

Fourth, these rules and principles are of only limited help in addressing the differences between legal evaluation before and after a decision to use military force. Courts are obliged not to apply hindsight, and must evaluate cases according to the information available to the parties at the time of any disputed action.[140] Nevertheless, courts and commentators evaluate the legality of a military action *after* it has taken place, knowing the consequences, usually with more time to consider the evidence, and with a more diverse and tested evidence base – all factors which are impossible to exclude completely from a *post hoc* evaluation. Courts and commentators after the event can expect limited consequences from any judgment about use of force – public controversy, possibly financial penalties, although no ICJ findings of unlawful use of force have imposed such penalties, and even the ICC crime of aggression requires a high threshold for prosecution.[141] Courts and commentators can refrain from ruling on the legality of a past action due to lack of evidence, as the ICJ did with several aspects of the allegations in the *Nicaragua* and *Congo* cases.

However, decision-makers considering whether to use force often have less evidence, more conflicting claims, from fewer less well-tested sources, under tighter time pressure than a court or commentator evaluating action *after* it has taken place. And the consequences to state decision-makers facing a military crisis of an incorrect decision to use force or not – 'false positives' or 'false negatives' – are usually far more serious than for judges or commentators.[142] Not using force in a military crisis risks allowing serious harm to those a decision-maker is obliged to protect if an attack is genuine. Yet using force risks causing serious wrongful harm if reports of attack are false, exposing the decision-maker to accusations of violating a *jus cogens* norm, and potentially exposing the decision-maker's state to use of force in self-defence.

140 J. G. Merrills, Judge Sir Gerald Fitzmaurice and the Discipline of International Law: Opinions on the International Court of Justice, 1961–1973 (The Hague: Kluwer Law International, 1998), 65–6.

141 Dinstein, *War, Aggression and Self-Defence*, 136.

142 Lubell, 'Problem of Imminence', 19.

All this analysis suggests the ICJ's rules of evidence, its approach to the standard of proof, and the principles of due diligence and reasonableness offer lawyers and states guidance about how to assess evidence, and about the effort and confidence required in establishing the facts when considering resort to force. They can help to reduce uncertainty about the facts relevant to *jus ad bellum* decisions. But they do not provide lawyers with authoritative guidance for resolving all such factual uncertainties, for choosing between multiple interpretations of fact, and for the forecasting that the *jus ad bellum*'s tests require. Nevertheless, international lawyers and states still routinely make determinations about the lawfulness of even controversial cases of the resort to force. How do lawyers resolve the factual uncertainties such cases present, in the absence of authoritative legal rules and principles for doing so?

EXTRA-LEGAL REASONING IN THE *JUS AD BELLUM*

The discussion so far has described legal and factual uncertainties that the *jus ad bellum* presents, and the absence of authoritative legal rules for dealing with those uncertainties. This analysis suggests the *jus ad bellum* sometimes fits Kelsen's description of law as 'a frame', which identifies 'a number of decisions', meaning '[e]very method of interpretation' leads 'merely to a possible result' not 'a single correct result'.[143] As Hart described, sometimes within law's framework 'there jostle too many alternatives' to identify one clear decision, in some cases 'law imposes only limits on our choice', and *in extremis* the law 'forces us to choose between the lesser of two evils'.[144] In such cases, there is 'room for cognitive activity beyond discovering the frame', not 'positive law' but 'cognition of other norms', and decision-makers inevitably apply 'some concept of what the law ought to be'.[145] In other words, legal decision-making in such complex cases may be only *partially autonomous* of extra-legal factors.

Many scholars have observed that in the *jus ad bellum*, as in other areas of law, legal decision-making is frequently politicised. Gray describes how states reporting use of force to the UNSC spend more effort asserting political and factual justifications rather than legal reasoning, and states often accept UNSC resolutions authorising force for political rather than legal reasons.[146] Byers describes how, particularly in justifying its 2003 Iraq intervention, the

143 Kelsen, *Introduction*, 80, 78, 81.

144 Hart, 'Positivism', 629, 620.

145 Kelsen, *Introduction*, 83; Hart, 'Positivism', 608.

146 Gray, *International Law*, 119, 198.

United States used its power to try to drive customary legal change, embed purposive approaches to legal interpretation and create a norm of pre-emption serving its geopolitical interests.[147] Koskenniemi has described 'international law's obsession about military crises, war and humanitarianism' as 'politics by those who have the means to strengthen control on everyone else', and observed that moral concerns about Kosovo meant 'most lawyers – including myself' took the 'ambivalent position' that NATO's intervention 'was both formally illegal and morally necessary', even though Koskenniemi believed it served US geopolitical interests.[148]

These analyses also suggest that, when states, their leaders and legal advisers advance controversial legal justifications for resort to force, they may not always *believe* their justifications actually represent the law as it is. Instead, such justifications may be forms of 'strategic behaviour in interpretation', whether 'cynical manipulation of legal rules' to advance politico-strategic goals, or more idealistic attempts to change the law by breaking – or at least bending – it.[149] However, as Gray has commented, it remains important to examine the words states use to justify their military actions, and 'in the absence of empirical evidence', assertions that states are being cynical, 'are no more plausible than the opposite version that states are in fact influenced by law'.[150]

Many lawyers argue for 'the need to maintain a clear distinction between law and politics or morals'.[151] However, others argue that 'in hard cases of indeterminacy' in the *jus ad bellum*, scholarly opinions are 'motivated by political choices', and 'the weight of doctrinal arguments' 'vanishes almost completely', so 'extra-legal (in the sense of not-doctrine based) background assumptions determine our decisions'.[152] Kammerhofer has observed that 'differences over "technicalities"' in the *jus ad bellum* indicate '"higher-order" problems', disagreements about law's '*telos*' or fundamental political or moral goals.[153] Another scholar argues that 'there is no neat distinction between the political factors inherent in law and the political views (conscious or unconscious)' of ICJ judges, and that '[t]he less well defined an area of law, the more that political and ideological viewpoints' about '*the principle(s) of*

147 Byers, *War Law*, locs. 469–521.

148 Martti Koskenniemi, '"The Lady Doth Protest Too Much": Kosovo, and the Turn to Ethics in International Law', *The Modern Law Review*, 65:2 (2002), 159–75, 160, 162.

149 Kennedy, *Legal Reasoning*, 159; Gray, *International Law*, 7.

150 Gray, *International Law*, 30.

151 Corten, *Law against War*, 18.

152 Marxsen, 'Indeterminacy', 80.

153 Kammerhofer, 'Self-Defence', 197.

law underlying the system are likely to influence' legal opinion.[154] Another argues it is 'rare indeed to find a lawyer' who thinks 'uses of force against non-State actors are unwise but still legally permissible or a lawyer who thinks that they are very helpful but are unfortunately unlawful'.[155] Choices about such political principles as 'sovereignty and human rights', 'the territorial integrity of one state and the security concerns of another' are 'value loaded and connect to underlying political and theoretical preferences'.[156] As a further scholar argues, any attempt to determine customary international law must rely 'on some criteria that identify which facts about the behavior and attitudes of international agents count in favor of or against' any given customary rule, and '(t)he only plausible criteria for that job are normative considerations'.[157]

It would lack credibility to claim that self-consciously strategic behaviour never explains lawyers' and states' decisions to advance controversial legal justifications for resort to force. But it can also be argued that such opinions are determined in more subtle ways, by lawyers' and policy-makers' underlying extra-legal political and ethical objectives, preferences, ideologies, intuitions and presuppositions determining the factual assessments and legal opinions they reach in specific hard cases of resort to force, and thus shaping their opinions about the *jus ad bellum* more generally. As a scholar of political analysis has noted, interpretations of incomplete information, counterfactual judgements and multi-scenario forecasts rely on specific 'assumptions about how the world works', and 'about how events would have unfolded' with different 'key factors'.[158]

In other words, decision-makers use at least intuitive, implicit 'extra-legal' theories of politico-strategic causation to explain current evidence, make inferences filling gaps in evidence, and to construct the forecasts needed for complex decision-making. Such implicit politico-strategic theories concern the ways and means states and other actors use to pursue their interests, the effects of 'bargaining and persuasion', 'threats and pressure, psychological as well as physical', 'words as well as deeds' and 'the art of creating power'.[159] And in choosing between competing theories of causation and policy options in hard cases, decision-makers apply at least intuitive, implicit normative or ethical theories about how the world *ought* to work.[160] Such ethical theories

154 Green, *Self-Defence*, 176, 184.
155 Milanovic, 'Accounting for Complexity', 41.
156 Peters and Marxsen, 'Editors' Introduction', 11.
157 Voyiakis, 'Customary International Law', 181.
158 Tetlock, *Expert Political Judgement*, 145, 146.
159 Freedman, *Strategy*, xii.
160 Fisher, *Morality and War*, 60.

seek to identify when force might be considered right behaviour, helping 'enable us to live together well in communities and so flourish as human beings'.[161] The notion of legitimacy, which has become prominent in *jus ad bellum* debates, encompasses both procedural and substantive acceptability – whether a law is created and applied according to processes acceptable to a political community, and whether it conforms with substantive moral and political rationales.[162]

Some scholars argue 'there is no neat distinction between the political factors inherent in law and the political views (conscious or unconscious)' of legal decision-makers.[163] Dworkinian jurists may view such factors as legitimate components of legal decision-making, seeking the legal interpretation that best advances 'principles and policies' providing 'the best political justification for the statute at the time it was passed'.[164] Nevertheless, this book argues there are factors that can be described as 'extra-legal reasoning' '(in the sense of not-doctrine based) background assumptions', since even Dworkinian jurists usually seek some legal anchoring (a UNSC resolution, a UNGA declaration, another existing body of international law) for the political and other principles that can be legitimately invoked when interpreting the law.[165]

The competing theories advanced by different scholars of international politics, strategy and ethics capture many of the opposing intuitions and presuppositions about how the world works and how it ought to work that lawyers grapple with. Lawyers may well apply these theories as 'non-inferential' beliefs, held intuitively, rather than consciously inferred from formal knowledge of political, strategic or ethical theories.[166] Different politico-strategic and normative theories are likely to produce different alternative factual analyses and forecasts, yielding different answers as to whether victims, attackers and other states are likely to respond in ways showing force is or is not necessary, proportionate, timely and therefore lawful compared to non-forceful options.

One important area of disagreement between politico-strategic theories is around the role of power, security and competition compared with institutions, norms and cooperation in relations between states.[167] Political

[161] Fisher, *Morality and War*, 60.
[162] Franck, *Fairness in International Law*, 27; Chinkin, 'Rethinking Legality/Legitimacy', 221–2; Falk, 'Introduction', 9.
[163] Green, *Self-Defence*, 176.
[164] Dworkin, *A Matter of Principle*, 145, 129.
[165] Marxsen, 'Indeterminacy', 80; Murphy, 'Protean Jus Ad Bellum', 36, 26.
[166] Elizabeth Tropman, 'Non-Inferential Moral Knowledge', *Acta Analytica*, 26 (2011), 355–66, 357.
[167] Gow, *Defending the West*, 20–3.

realists and critical theorists are often regarded as representing opposing political ideologies, yet both sets of theorists generally hold that power drives international behaviour in an anarchical international system lacking overarching governing authority. International relations is 'a struggle for power', driven by political leaders' fear and competitiveness, in which 'armed strength as a threat or potentiality is the most important material factor' for states.[168] Power is distributed unevenly, forcing states to compete, and so states use force only to benefit their own power and security rather than to serve common interests.[169] From this analysis many realists perhaps surprisingly prescribe caution about using force.[170] States *should* only use force to serve their power and security, by maintaining an acceptable balance of power or by making a currently unacceptable balance of power more favourable.[171] States should not use force if their power is not at stake or if it risks shifting the current balance of power in unfavourable directions.[172] Critical theorists are committed to resisting the uneven distribution of power between states and groups that enables rich capitalist powers to exploit poorer countries, so they too usually oppose powerful states using force in less powerful countries.[173]

Opposing the material determinism of realists and critical theorists, theorists of liberal institutionalism, interdependence, international society and some constructivists argue economic and social interdependence, formal and informal institutions, non-state actors, ideas and norms can and do constrain and shape state behaviour, encouraging cooperation between states even where that contradicts pure calculations of power.[174] States' identities and interests, international institutions and norms are 'inter-subjective beliefs', constructed over time by social interactions between states, non-state actors and individuals.[175] International politics is not driven solely by states' material capabilities, rational calculations and self-seeking zero-sum competition;

168 Hans J. Morgenthau, *Politics among Nations: The Struggle for Power and Peace* (New York: McGraw-Hill, 2006), 17, 31.

169 Kenneth N. Waltz, *Theory of International Politics* (New York: Random House, 1979), 88–99.

170 David M. Edelstein, 'Why Realists Don't Go for Bombs and Bullets', Foreign Policy (21 July 2010).

171 Morgenthau, *Politics among Nations*, 9.

172 Kenneth N. Waltz, 'The Politics of Peace', *International Studies Quarterly*, 11:3 (1967), 199–211, 204–5.

173 Naomi Head, 'Critical Theory and Its Practices: Habermas, Kosovo and International Relations', *Politics*, 28:3 (2008), 150–9; Andreas Bieler and Adam David Morton, 'A Critical Theory Route to Hegemony, World Order and Historical Change: Neo-Gramscian Perspectives in International Relations', *Capital and Class*, 82 (2004), 85–113.

174 Robert O. Keohane and Joseph S. Nye, 'Power and Interdependence Revisited', *International Organization*, 41:4 (1987), 725–53, 729–33; Gow, *Defending the West*, 22–6.

175 Armstrong et al., *International Law and International Relations*, 101.

rather '[a]narchy is what states make of it'.[176] Under some circumstances, 'states, conscious of certain common interests and common values, form a society' in which 'they conceive themselves to be bound by a common set of rules'.[177] Many writers of these schools are sceptical of use of force in international relations, arguing 'international society presupposes the intrinsic value of all states and accommodates their inward diversity'.[178] But others have advocated force to support international institutions, to advance common interests and to enforce international norms such as those prohibiting genocide.[179]

There are parallel tensions in ethical and normative theories. One set of ethical conceptions focuses on war's inherent wrongness, from 'pacificists' wishing to limit war incrementally, to 'pacifists' advocating immediate rejection of all intentional killing.[180] They argue war's fundamental acts – intentional killing and causing harm – contravene basic deontological rules governing the sanctity of human life, the avoidance of suffering and respect for others' autonomy.[181] Few ethical values are universal enough to justify force – for example, different cultures, groups, even individuals disagree about how to define unjustified killing.[182] The teleological consequences of war are unethical, since all wars 'simply add to the numbers of innocent dead, cause untold suffering, political and economic instability on a global scale, increase racism and result in attacks on civil liberties'.[183] And war enables and exploits human vices and 'spiritual evil', as Bertrand Russell put it, 'the hatred, the injustice, the repudiation of truth, the artificial conflict', 'the blindness of atavistic instincts and the sinister influence of anti-social interests'.[184] As Norman writes, 'even if

176 Alexander Wendt, 'Anarchy Is What States Make of It: The Social Construction of Power Politics', *International Organization*, 46:2 (1992), 391–425, 395.

177 Hedley Bull, *The Anarchical Society* (London: MacMillan, 1977), 13.

178 Robert H. Jackson, 'Martin Wight, International Theory and the Good Life', *Millennium – Journal of International Studies*, 19:2 (1990), 261–72, 267.

179 Robert O. Keohane, 'Political Authority after Intervention: Gradations in Sovereignty', in J. L. Holzgrefe and Robert O. Keohane, *Humanitarian Intervention: Ethical, Legal and Political Dilemmas* (Cambridge: Cambridge University Press, 2003), 298; Nicholas Wheeler, *Saving Strangers* (Oxford: Oxford University Press, 2002), 12–13; Gow, *Defending the West*, 35–6.

180 Martin Ceadel, *The Origins of War Prevention: The British Peace Movement and International Relations 1730–1854* (Oxford: Oxford University Press, 1996), 45–6.

181 Richard Norman, *Ethics, Killing and War* (Cambridge: Cambridge University Press, 1995), 40–60.

182 Gilbert Harman and Judith J. Thomson, *Moral Relativism and Moral Objectivity* (Oxford: Blackwell, 1996), 8.

183 Stop the War Coalition, 'Constitution', www.stopwar.org.uk/constitution; Michael Howard, *War and the Liberal Conscience* (London: Hurst, 2008), 25–35.

184 Bertrand Russell, 'The Ethics of War', *International Journal of Ethics*, 25:2 (1915), 127–42, 133.

wars can sometimes be just, it's only in very limited circumstances, and subject to conditions much more stringent than are typically applied to decisions to go to war. Most wars are unjust.'[185]

The dominant alternative ethical approach is the contemporary Just War tradition, which 'holds that war is inherently an evil and can only be justified when it is the lesser evil'.[186] This tradition tends to view various ethical values as sufficiently universal to sometimes justify force, since 'even fundamental social and political transformations ... leave the moral world intact or at least sufficiently whole so that we can still be said to share it'.[187] The Just War tradition proposes deontological, eudaemonic and consequentialist tests for assessing whether resort to force is ethical.[188] War must have a just cause, such as to protect innocents, and must also have right intent – it must be motivated primarily by the just cause and not other, selfish motives. It requires right authority and a proper declaration, it should be the last resort at least logically if not temporally, its harmful consequences must be proportionate to the harm averted by using force, and it must have reasonable prospects of successfully achieving its just cause.[189] Most Just War writers would require all these considerations to be met for force to be ethically justified; others prioritise some considerations over others – for example, the balance of good and bad consequences of using force.[190] The key point is that 'Just War theory, even when it demands a strong critique of particular acts of war, is the doctrine of people who do expect to exercise power and use force'.[191]

The concept of legitimacy in international law includes many of these politico-strategic and ethical concepts. It encompasses the perceptions of a community that a law that governs them has been originally created and is applied in specific cases according to 'right process' as defined by that community.[192] The Kosovo Commission declared that NATO's 'military intervention in Kosovo was illegal but legitimate', arguing there was a 'gap between legality and legitimacy', and prescribing tests for assessing legitimacy

185 Norman, *Ethics, Killing and War*, 208.

186 James A. Stroble, 'Justification of War in Ancient China', *Asian Philosophy*, 8:3 (1998), 165–90, 166.

187 Michael Walzer, *Just and Unjust Wars: A Moral Argument with Historical Illustrations*, 3rd ed. (New York: Basic Books, 2000), 16; Connelly and Carrick, 'Ethical and Legal Reasoning', 45.

188 Fisher, *Morality and War*, 80.

189 Ibid.

190 Wheeler, *Saving Strangers*, 37.

191 Michael Walzer, *Arguing about War* (New Haven, CT: Yale University Press, 2004), 14.

192 Thomas M. Franck, 'Legitimacy in the International System', *American Journal of International Law*, 82:4 (1988), 706; Franck, *Fairness in International Law*, 27.

going beyond 'right process' to include substantive humanitarian and ethical considerations, such as preventing suffering, protecting victimized populations and avoiding self-interested goals such as territorial acquisition.[193] Some argue assessments of legitimacy should include moral and politico-strategic assessment, evaluating 'conformity with the justifying moral imperative that prompted action in the first place, and validation of the political rationale based on feasible costs relative to the goals achieved'.[194]

CONCLUSION: COMPETING STRATEGIC CULTURES

What this discussion suggests is that political, strategic and ethical theories and reasoning potentially offer lawyers more guidance than legal rules and principles for resolving the uncertainties of factual analysis and forecasting in difficult cases engaging the *jus ad bellum*. This provides one obvious way in which legal decision-making in complex *jus ad bellum* cases may be only partially autonomous of extra-legal political, strategic and ethical reasoning. However, it is clear that such extra-legal analytical methods are just as amenable to contestation and disagreement as legal reasoning. This creates obvious opportunities for *social supervaluationism* in factual assessments of cases involving force, as different decision-makers interpret and reach different conclusions from the available evidence. These differences of analysis are partly due to self-serving strategic behaviour, as opposing parties to a conflict present different versions of the facts to serve their own ends. ICJ voting records and the ICJ provision for parties to a dispute to nominate judges *ad hoc* show that even the Court's judges are not immune to at least the suspicion of national partiality.[195]

Any decision-maker's partisan political affiliations and preferences must surely play some role in the conclusions they reach about facts and law in a conflict. But it seems implausible to claim that partisan affiliations and preferences entirely determine decision-makers' legal and factual conclusions. Opposing parties to a conflict, and their supporters, often genuinely believe their own versions of the facts, reflecting the evidence and analysis available to

193 IICK, *Independent International Commission on Kosovo: The Kosovo Report* (Oxford: Oxford University Press, 2000), 4, 10, 293.

194 Falk, 'Introduction', 9.

195 Green, *Self-Defence*, 179; Thomas R. Hensley, 'National Bias and the International Court of Justice', *Midwest Journal of Political Science*, 12 (1968), 568; Il Roh Suh, 'Voting Behaviour of National Judges in International Courts', *American Journal of International Law*, 63 (1969), 224, 228; Adam M. Smith, 'Judicial Nationalism in International Law: National Identity and Judicial Autonomy at the ICJ', *Texas International Law Journal*, 40 (2004), 197.

them, and their underlying intuitions about how the world actually works and how it *ought* to work. As this chapter has already noted, even allies sharing the same strategic goals and outlook can reach different conclusions about both facts and law underpinning potential military operations, and can even disagree about the very need to advance legal justifications for such operations.

This book is most interested in how these underlying extra-legal intuitions shape legal choices, rather than political affiliations. The key dividing lines between the opposing sets of politico-strategic and ethical-normative theories described in the previous section point to the kinds of competing extra-legal intuitions that lawyers might at least implicitly apply to resolve the factual and forecasting uncertainties they face when considering hard cases of resort to force. This suggests a second potential explanation for how lawyers' methods of reasoning when faced with uncertainty in the *jus ad bellum* may sustain and exacerbate uncertainty and disagreement. Lawyers with restrictivist and expansionist approaches to the *jus ad bellum* may in effect form competing 'strategic cultures', each with consistent, mutually reinforcing 'extra-legal' intuitions, assumptions and beliefs about the political, ethical and strategic implications of force – shared understandings, expectations, and beliefs about conflict, 'pervasive and long lasting strategic preferences' about 'what is right and what works in war'.[196]

As with interpretive cultures, advocates of strategic culture do not claim individuals necessarily conform to these cultures consciously, nor that they deliberately coordinate or act collectively. Adherence to a strategic culture may reflect deeply internalised and unconsciously held intuitions, presuppositions and preferences, likely the product of some combination of individual cognitive characteristics and collective socialisation.[197] As with interpretive cultures, strategic cultures are likely to reflect the interaction of structural factors and individuals' own agency in response. National experiences are likely to be key. As one writer puts it, 'different security communities think and behave somewhat differently about strategic matters', due to their 'distinctive histories and geographies'.[198] Strategic cultures represent distinct 'modes of thought and action with respect to force', reflecting a range of distinctive national conditions, including 'perception of the national historical experience, aspiration for self-characterization (e.g., as an American, what am I?, how should I feel, think, and behave?)', and 'geography, political philosophy',

196 Farrell, 'World Culture', 450; Gray, 'National Style in Strategy', 22; Johnston, 'Thinking about Strategic Culture', 46.

197 Haas, 'Introduction', 3.

198 Colin Gray, 'Out of the Wilderness: Prime Time for Strategic Culture', *Comparative Strategy*, 26:1 (2007), 1–20, 6.

'civic culture, and "way of life"'.[199] As with interpretive cultures, institutional settings also likely shape strategic culture – academia, the private sector, non-governmental campaign groups and government – all provide different frameworks of priorities, norms and incentives for decision-makers, and are likely to evolve in interactions with other cultures and agents.

And individual preferences and characteristics are likely to shape how individual lawyers internalise these structural factors into their own legal decision-making. Both interpretive cultures and strategic cultures may well represent groups of individuals who share broadly similar, coherent patterns of what psychologists term 'cognitive biases', 'motivated biases' and 'heuristics'.[200] Such biases and heuristics are inherent or learned intuitions, presuppositions and rules of thumb 'which reduce the complex tasks of assessing probabilities and predicting values to simpler judgmental operations'.[201] Heuristics and intuitions are often economical and effective ways of making rapid decisions, particularly in situations that recur frequently and conclude rapidly, allowing decision-makers to practice thoroughly and learn effective intuitive judgment and thus accurately predict consequences from observable cues.[202] But in complex, idiosyncratic and infrequently recurring situations, biases and heuristics can 'lead to severe and systematic errors'.[203]

The end result is likely to be competition and disagreement between more or less coherent strategic cultures representing distinct 'modes of thought and action with respect to force'.[204] When it comes to decision-making about military crises, lawyers within competing strategic cultures are likely to choose different explanations of past events, different conclusions about the likelihood and desirability of future consequences of different policy options, and reach different legal opinions on factually complex cases. Lawyers' implicit theories about how conflicts arise and their consequences are also likely to underpin their choices and beliefs about how far the *jus ad bellum* prohibits and permits force more generally too.

Thus, it might be the case that lawyers with a 'restrictivist' approach to the *jus ad bellum* when considering a 'hard case' of resort to force, will tend to apply a set of politico-strategic and ethical assumptions, intuitions and beliefs that

199 Gray, 'National Style in Strategy', 22.
200 Tversky and Kahneman, 'Judgment under Uncertainty', 1124.
201 Ibid.
202 Daniel Kahneman and Gary Klein, 'Conditions for Intuitive Expertise: A Failure to Disagree', *American Psychologist*, 64:6 (2009), 515–26, 254.
203 Tversky and Kahneman, 'Judgment under Uncertainty', 1124.
204 Gray, 'National Style in Strategy', 22.

could be grouped under the broad heading of a 'pacificist' strategic culture. When faced with a case in which the requirements of the law are contested, pacificists will tend to choose the legal interpretation that minimises the potential for future legal uncertainty and abuse, which best protects less powerful states rather than trusting militarily and economically dominant states, and which holds that the prohibition on force is always the most important principle. When assessing different interpretations of complex, incomplete or contradictory factual evidence, and when constructing forecasts about the consequences of using or not using force unilaterally, pacificists tend to proceed on the basis that such force almost always causes more harm than it prevents for the state using force and for the international community, that only self-interested states use force unilaterally, and thus only a few interests and ethical values are sufficiently widely shared to guide decisions about unilateral force. And thus, this explanation proposes that 'pacificist' lawyers who tend to see little political, strategic and ethical justification for unilateral use of force in specific cases will also tend to see strong political, strategic and ethical reasons to support a restrictivist *jus contra bellum* in general.

And opposing them, it may be that when lawyers with an 'expansionist' approach to the *jus ad bellum* consider a 'hard case' of resort to force, they tend to apply a set of politico-strategic and ethical assumptions, intuitions and beliefs that could be grouped under the broad heading of an 'interventionist' strategic culture. When faced with a case in which the requirements of the law are contested, 'interventionists' tend to choose the interpretation of the law that best fits with changes in the character of conflict since the UN Charter was adopted, and which holds that principles such as human rights, preventing genocide, fighting terrorism or countering WMD proliferation can be more important than the prohibition on force. When assessing different interpretations of complex, incomplete or contradictory evidence, and when constructing forecasts about the consequences of using or not using force unilaterally, interventionists tend to proceed on the basis that such force may often prevent more harm than it causes for the state using force and for the international community, that states that use force unilaterally can often advance common interests as well as self-interest, and that more interests and ethical values are sufficiently widely shared to guide decisions about unilateral force. And thus 'interventionist' lawyers who tend to see more such extra-legal political, strategic and ethical justifications for force in a range of individual cases, will also see more political, strategic and ethical reasons to support an expansionist approach to the *jus ad bellum* in general as well.

It might even be argued that competing interpretive and strategic cultures, and uncertainties about the future outcome of specific cases of force and about the future evolution of conflict more generally, are reasons why vagueness in the *jus ad bellum*, like in all law, is both essential and inevitable. When activities regulated by law vary significantly in socially important ways, 'uniform rules' applied 'without further official direction cannot usefully be framed', so lawmakers – such as the drafters of the UN Charter – must adopt general standards, delegating authority to a body such as the UNSC to apply those standards.[205] As Kelsen said, '(e)ven a meticulously detailed command must leave a number of determinations to those carrying it out'.[206] Vagueness and uncertainty may be necessary features of the *jus ad bellum*, enabling it to flex and adapt to the complexities of both the conflicts it seeks to regulate and the international community which seeks to apply it.

Part II of this book will consider what evidence there is for such strategic cultures, as well as the interpretive cultures proposed in Chapter 2, in systematic textual analysis of key ICJ judgments, in the writings of scholars and UK government legal statements about three US-led military interventions, and in interviews and a survey with UK-based international lawyers conducted for this book.

[205] Hart, *Concept of Law*, 131.
[206] Kelsen, *Introduction*, 80, 81, 78.

PART II

THE INTERNATIONAL COURT OF JUSTICE, UK-BASED LAWYERS AND THE JUS AD BELLUM

4

Competing Interpretive Cultures of War

All laws are promulgated for this end, that every man may know his duty; and therefore the plainest and most obvious sense of the words is that which ought to be put upon them, since a more refined exposition cannot be easily comprehended, and would only serve to make the laws useless.

Thomas More, *Utopia*[1]

Therefore is the name of it called Babel; because the Lord did there confound the language of all the earth: and from thence did the Lord scatter them abroad upon the face of all the earth.

Genesis, 11:9[2]

INTRODUCTION

The first part of this book examined the nature and sources of legal and factual uncertainty and specific rather than systemic indeterminacy in the *jus ad bellum*. It proposed two potential explanations for how international lawyers reach determinate legal opinions in hard cases engaging the *jus ad bellum*. In such cases, legal opinions on resort to force may be associated with specific views about methods of legal interpretation, or with views about the politics, strategy and ethics of force – in some sense, opinions about the *jus ad bellum* may be only partially autonomous of extra-legal factors. This second part of the book considers whether these explanations are valid, and if so under what conditions and with what limitations. To do this, the next two chapters

[1] Thomas More, *Utopia* (eBook ed.) (H. Morley, ed.) (The Project Gutenberg, 2005), 85.
[2] King James Version.

consider the writings of legal scholars, ICJ judgments and interview and survey research with UK-based international lawyers, to assess how lawyers' assumptions, beliefs and intuitions about methods of legal interpretation and about extra-legal factors align with their conclusions about the lawfulness of force, and about alternative interpretations of facts and forecasting in hard cases of resort to force.

This chapter uses these research methods to examine how far uncertainty and disagreement about the law governing resort to force is produced by disagreements about principles of legal interpretation. It tests whether and under what conditions the explanation proposed in Chapter 2 might be valid: that, when considering hard cases of resort to force, lawyers who support more restrictive approaches to the *jus ad bellum* tend to apply a broadly 'formalist' approach to legal interpretation, while those with a more expansionist approach to force apply a 'dynamist' approach to legal interpretation. Chapter 2 proposed that lawyers of the 'formalist' interpretive culture assessing the lawfulness of resort to force tend to emphasise the ordinary meaning of the text of the UN Charter and other formal sources of law. They hold that the law has evolved little since 1945, accept only explicitly legal statements as evidence of *opinio juris*, and require clarity and an overwhelming quantity of state practice as evidence that new customary international law has crystallised. And they regard only the UNSC as permitted to authorise force when the law is unclear. Opposing them, lawyers of the 'dynamist' interpretive culture assessing the lawfulness of resort to force tend to be more willing to take account of the charter's wider purposes and other law. They argue that law has evolved significantly since 1945, and are willing to accept a wider variety and smaller numbers of expressions of *opinio juris* and state practice as evidence that new customary international law has crystallised. And they see more discretion for states and bodies outside the UNSC to interpret the *jus ad bellum* as authorising force when the law is unclear.

This chapter first summarises textual analysis of the writings of eight respected UK-based international lawyers and UK government statements concerning the legality of military interventions in Kosovo in 1999, Afghanistan in 2001 and Iraq in 2003, considering whether those legal opinions align with specific interpretive methods. The scholarly writings analysed were fifteen legal assessments written by Christopher Greenwood, Vaughan Lowe, Christine Chinkin, Christine Gray, Ian Brownlie and Brian Apperley, Lindsay Moir and Nigel White (writing with Eric Myjer).[3] These

[3] Greenwood, 'NATO Intervention in Kosovo', 926; Lowe, 'Kosovo Crisis', 934; Chinkin, 'Rethinking Legality/Legitimacy', 910; Gray, *International Law*, 132–40, 156–60, 216–22, 354–69;

scholars were selected using 'reputational' and 'decisional' criteria, as having influence among UK lawyers, representing different approaches to the *jus ad bellum*, and reaching differing opinions on the interventions examined.[4]

The chapter next summarises textual analysis of the three majority judgments and twenty-eight separate or dissenting opinions written by a total of twenty-two judges in the ICJ cases *Nicaragua* (1986), *Wall* (2004) and *Congo* (2005), considering how far they display specific interpretive methods. These cases were chosen because they dealt with significant questions concerning the *jus ad bellum* – alleged *jus ad bellum* violations were central to the *Nicaragua* and *Congo* cases. Analysing these cases provides evidence of several national legal cultures, since the judges who wrote opinions on these cases came from nineteen countries.[5] These cases are key sources of jurisprudence for the *jus ad bellum*, since the ICJ is currently the only Court that comes close to being authoritative final adjudicator of international disputes concerning resort to force.[6] And the cases map the evolving jurisprudence of a contentious legal justification for force: self-defence against armed attacks by non-state actors. The chapter finally reports perhaps the most novel form of research conducted for this book: surveys and interviews with thirty-one UK-based international lawyers, considering how their opinions about interpretive principles correlate with their views on the lawfulness of force as reported in Chapter 2.

These different sources of research represent lawyers engaging with the *jus ad bellum* from different perspectives. The UK government legal statements are written by international lawyers working on behalf of that state: it could be argued those lawyers are fulfilling the role of '*counselor*', constructing legal arguments to help the UK government justify military action it wishes to take to achieve its political objectives.[7] Judges, on the other hand, are generally expected to make impartial, objective, 'authoritative determinations' of what the relevant legal rules are and whether those rules have been broken in cases they adjudicate – identifying and applying

Brownlie and Apperley, 'Kosovo Crisis Inquiry', 878; Greenwood, 'War against Terrorism', 301; Chinkin, 'Rethinking Legality/Legitimacy', 220; Moir, *Reappraising the Resort to Force*, 40; Myjer and White, 'Twin Towers Attack', 5; Greenwood, 'War against Terrorism', 301–17; Lowe, 'Iraq Crisis', 859–71; Brownlie, 'Memorandum'; Greenwood, 'Pre-emptive Use of Force', 7–38.

4 Hoffmann-Lange, 'Methods of Elite Research'.

5 Argentina, Belgium, Brazil, Egypt, Germany, India, Italy, Japan, Jordan, Netherlands, Nigeria, Poland, People's Republic of China, Sierra Leone, Slovakia, Tanzania, United Kingdom, United States and Venezuela.

6 Green, *Self-Defence*, 173.

7 Harold Hongju Koh, 'The State Department Legal Adviser's Office: Eight Decades in Peace and War', *Georgetown Law Journal*, 110 (2012), 1758.

international law as it is.[8] Finally, legal scholars and commentators can be expected to play some combination of these roles. The writings of such lawyers may indicate what society agrees the law actually is, since, as D'Amato has noted, lawyers with high professional standing have 'some right to claim, on the basis of professional training and experience, an ability' to predict 'what a judge would decide' on controversial issues.[9] Scholars can also play a more justificatory role in advocating for 'some concept of what the law ought to be', whether as applied in a particular case, or as it ought to evolve in future.[10]

This chapter and the next are structured to enable the reader to engage with the evidence in two ways. Separate sections report analysis of legal writings, ICJ judgments, and the interviews and survey research conducted for this book. Each section has an introduction, a narrative reporting how the materials assessed displays either different legal interpretation techniques in this chapter or different forms of extra-legal reasoning in the next, and a conclusion providing an overall assessment of the evidence. Each narrative section includes examples of wording used by the legal scholars, judges and interviewed lawyers, alongside diagrams illustrating the analysis. Readers who wish to examine the textual detail of the evidence can read through these chapters in their entirety. Others could read the introductions and conclusions of each section, using the diagrams to gain a more synoptic understanding of the evidence.

The analyses of ICJ judgments, scholarly writings and government statements identified phrases in the texts that appeared to evaluate the tests of necessity, authority, victim, attacker, imminence and proportionality identified in Chapter 2. The analyses also identified phrases applying those principles of legal interpretation proposed in Chapter 2 as associated with the 'formalist' and 'dynamist' interpretive cultures. The judges and scholars were ranked along a continuum between the extreme positions for each *jus ad bellum* test or interpretive principle based on their writings, and these positions represented visually on linear spectra. For example, the second spectrum in Figure 4.2 illustrates views on customary legal change: lawyers at one pole of the spectrum believe law is highly protean, those at the other pole believe law is static. Between those poles lawyers hold views of varying intensity.

In this chapter I demonstrate that there does seem to be a correlation between these lawyers' views about legal interpretation and about the extent to which the *jus ad bellum* permits resort to force. Broadly speaking, those

8 Hart, *Concept of Law*, 96–7.

9 D'Amato, 'Legal Uncertainty', 1.

10 Hart, 'Positivism', 608.

lawyers who adopted a restrictive *jus contra bellum* tended to apply a 'formalist' approach to legal interpretation, while those with a more expansionist approach tended to apply a 'dynamist' interpretation. But this chapter reveals important caveats to this relationship, and no evidence suggesting that legal principles guide how lawyers interpret factual evidence or make the forecasts required by the *jus ad bellum*. This suggests these lawyers' intuitions and preferences about interpretive techniques might explain some but not all the variation in views they express about the *jus ad bellum*.

LEGAL SCHOLARS AND LEGAL INTERPRETATION: KOSOVO, AFGHANISTAN AND IRAQ

Introduction

The legality of NATO's intervention in Kosovo provoked significant international disagreement. The non-governmental Kosovo Commission declared the intervention 'illegal but legitimate'.[11] The UK government declared the intervention legal.[12] Russia, China and Namibia declared it illegal in a draft UNSC resolution, as did the Non-Aligned Movement.[13] The United States and Germany privately believed the operation was unlawful and should not set a precedent.[14] International lawyers were divided in their assessment of the intervention's legality, although most at the time probably assessed it to be unlawful.[15] Serbia challenged the action in the ICJ, but only Belgium advanced a legal justification for the intervention during proceedings, and although the Court expressed 'profound concern' it did not rule on the intervention's legality.[16] In contrast, the US-led intervention in Afghanistan after the 11 September 2001 terrorist attacks received immediate and almost

11 IICK, *Kosovo Report*, 4.

12 Symons, 'Kosovo'; Roberts, 'So-Called "Right"', 24.

13 UN Security Council, Press Release SC/6659, 'Security Council Rejects Demand for Cessation of Use of Force against Federal Republic of Yugoslavia', 26 March 1999; UN Press Release GA/SPD/164, 18 October 1999; Non-Aligned Movement, 'Final Communique of the Meeting of Ministers for Foreign Affairs and Heads of Delegation of the Non-Aligned Movement, Held in New York on 23 September 1999', www.nam.gov.za/minmeet/newyork com.htm, para. 171.

14 Simma, 'NATO', 1; Wood, 'Law on the Use of Force', 11.

15 Cassese, '*Ex Inuria Ius Oritur*', 29.

16 *Legality of use of Force (Yugoslavia* v. *Belgium)*, Verbatim Record, 10 May 1999, ICJ CR99/15; *Legality of Use of Force (Yugoslavia* v. *United States of America)*, Order, 2 June 1999, ICJ Reports (1999) 916, at 922.

universal state approval, while provoking significant disagreement among international lawyers.[17]

Finally, the legality of the US-led intervention in Iraq provoked significant international disagreement, dwarfing that for either Kosovo or Afghanistan. The United States, United Kingdom and Australia asserted that the intervention was lawful, arguing UNSC Resolution 1441 (2002) 'revived' the authorisation to use force in UNSC Resolution 678 (1990) by declaring Iraq in material breach of the ceasefire conditions in UNSC Resolution 687 (1991).[18] The US letter to the UNSC reporting the action also referred to self-defence.[19] Some states, such as Saudi Arabia, Italy, Japan and Turkey broadly supported the coalition, but France, Germany, Russia, China and many other NATO, EU and non-aligned states, as well as many international lawyers strongly disagreed.[20]

Textual analysis of scholarly writings and UK legal statements about these three military interventions revealed a similar range of opinions, as Figure 4.1 illustrates. These analyses suggest that these lawyers operate different paradigms of legal and illegal force. The lawyers' opinions ranged across a continuum for each *jus ad bellum* test, consistent with this book's claim that the tests operate according to fuzzy logic.

The lawyers agreed that the Kosovo intervention was not justified by the UN Charter's explicit exceptions – self-defence and UNSC authorisation, but they disagreed about whether the intervention had another legal basis. The UK government said the action was lawful under 'the accepted principle that force may be used in extreme circumstances to avert a humanitarian catastrophe'.[21] Greenwood pronounced the intervention 'consistent with international law' under a customary right of humanitarian intervention.[22] Lowe found 'no clear legal justification' for the action, but argued it was 'desirable that such a justification be allowed to emerge' in customary law.[23] Chinkin appeared

17 Kammerhofer, 'Self-Defence', 203.

18 UN Security Council, Document S/2003/351 (United States); S/2003/350 (United Kingdom); S/2003/352 (Australia); UK Attorney General Goldsmith, 'The Use of Force Against Iraq', *International and Comparative Law Quarterly*, 52:3 (2003), 811–12; Australian Attorney-General, 'Memorandum of Advice on the Use of Force against Iraq', *Australian Yearbook of International Law*, 24 (2003), 415.

19 UN Security Council, Document S/2003/351 (United States); W. H. Taft and T. F. Buchwald, 'Preemption, Iraq, and International Law', *The American Journal of International Law*, 97 (2003), 557–63, 553.

20 Gray, *International Law*, 355; Craven et al., 'Teachers of International Law', 363–74.

21 George Robertson, 'Kosovo' (25 March 1999), *Hansard*, House of Commons, 6th ser., vol. 328, col. 617.

22 Greenwood, 'NATO Intervention in Kosovo', 926.

23 Lowe, 'Kosovo Crisis', 941.

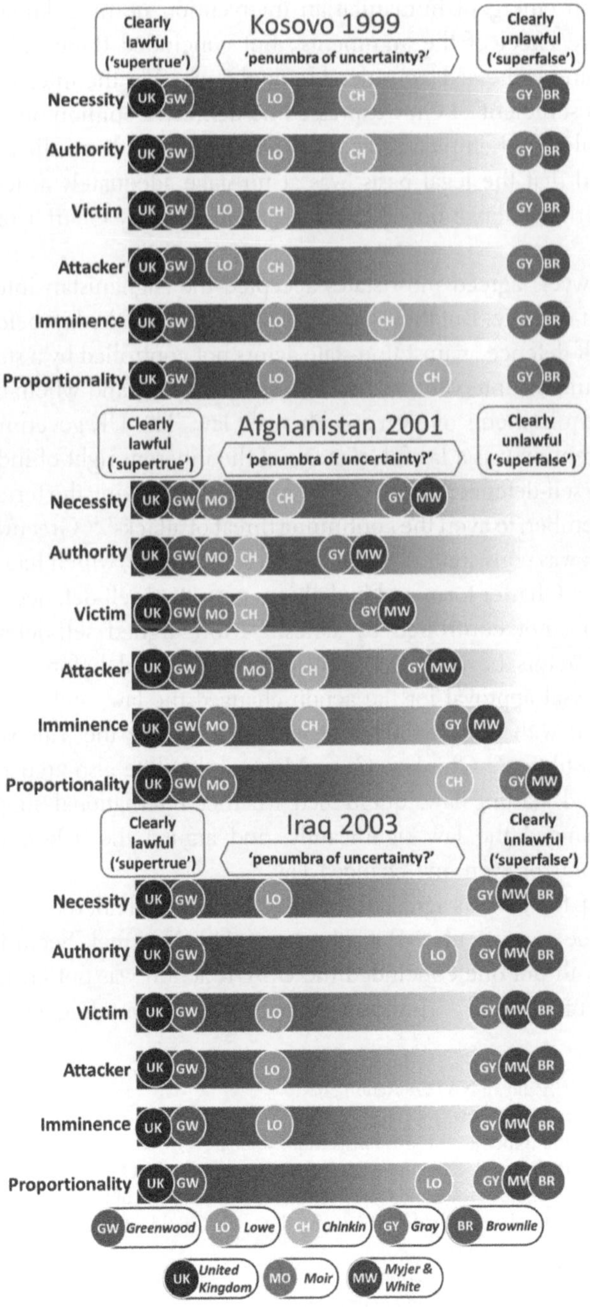

FIGURE 4.1 Evaluating Kosovo, Afghanistan and Iraq

open to an emergent humanitarian intervention norm, acknowledged 'the cumulative effect of the arguments', but concluded these did not 'bestow legality', and expressed 'considerable doubt' whether the intervention's legal basis 'was sufficient'.[24] Gray expressed no definitive opinion on the intervention's legality, but emphasised arguments against it.[25] Brownlie and Apperley concluded that the legal basis 'was at no stage adequately articulated', and humanitarian intervention 'has no place' in the UN Charter or customary law.[26]

The lawyers agreed most states accepted the Afghanistan intervention as lawful self-defence. But they disagreed about whether the law before 2001 permitted self-defence against non-state actors not controlled by a state, whether the Afghanistan intervention had changed that law, and whether the action met all requirements of even any changed law. The UK government argued the intervention was a lawful 'exercise of the inherent right of individual and collective self-defence, recognized in Article 51, following the terrorist outrage of 11 September, to avert the continuing threat of attacks'.[27] Greenwood argued the action was consistent with the law on self-defence, which had persisted in its pre–UN Charter form and had always permitted self-defence against non-state actors not controlled by states.[28] Moir argued self-defence against non-state actors beyond state control was unlawful before 2001, but the near-universal approval for the action changed the law, and the action itself was lawful, with the possible exception of targeting the Taleban from the start of hostilities.[29] Chinkin, Gray, Myjer and White also argued the action contravened existing law, questioned whether international support for the action changed the law significantly, and argued the action contravened requirements of even any changed law.[30]

On Iraq, the lawyers agreed the United States could not rely on pre-emptive self-defence as articulated in the 2002 US National Security Strategy. However, all but one concluded the US/UK action was not lawful. The UK government claimed '[a]uthority to use force against Iraq exists from the

24 Chinkin, 'Legality of NATO's Action', 925.

25 Gray, *International Law*, 47–51.

26 Brownlie and Apperley, 'Kosovo Crisis Inquiry', 904.

27 UN Security Council, Document S/2001/947, 'Letter Dated 7 October 2001 from the Chargé d'affaires a.i. of the Permanent Mission of the United Kingdom of Great Britain and Northern Ireland to the United Nations Addressed to the President of the Security Council', 7 October 2001, S/2001/947.

28 Greenwood, 'War against Terrorism', 307–8.

29 Moir, *Reappraising the Resort to Force*, 71.

30 Chinkin, 'Rethinking Legality/Legitimacy', 225; Gray, *International Law*, 203; Myjer and White, 'Twin Towers Attack', 6.

combined effect of Resolutions 678, 687 and 1441'.[31] Greenwood endorsed the UK argument, while recognising 'others have taken a different view'.[32] Lowe accepted that Iraq had breached its obligations and represented a threat, but argued 'the invasion lacked any legal justification' as there was no new UNSC resolution 'explicitly authorising' force.[33] Gray emphasised the justification's weaknesses, that 'the doctrine of implied authorisation' is 'controversial', many states continued to argue the intervention 'was not legal', and even the UN secretary general publicly described the invasion as illegal.[34] Myjer and White described the US/UK justifications as 'spurious claims by some states to be acting under UN authority', with 'no basis in law' or previous UNSC resolutions.[35] Brownlie was clear that '[c]ompulsory disarmament of the type envisaged could only be lawful if based upon a SC Resolution'.[36]

Narrative

Further textual analyses suggested the lawyers had applied different, competing principles of legal interpretation, appearing to vary broadly although not entirely with the lawyers' opinions about the interventions' lawfulness.[37] The lawyers agreed on some interpretive principles: the UN Charter is the central source of the *jus ad bellum*, and customary law can also play a role. Beyond these fundamentals, as Figure 4.2 illustrates, the lawyers displayed significant differences in legal interpretation, their opinions ranging across continuums, suggesting fuzzy boundaries between clearly valid and clearly unacceptable approaches.

Purposive or textual interpretation? The texts show tensions between *purposive* and *textually oriented* interpretation, competing visions of the law's *'telos'* – one extreme seeing multiple, sometimes implicit legal purposes for force, the other extreme finding few purposes explicitly in the UN Charter's text and UNSC resolutions.[38] On Kosovo, in various ways the UK government, Greenwood, Lowe and Chinkin argued the charter has purposes beyond sovereignty, potentially justifying force to stop extreme

31 Goldsmith, 'Use of Force against Iraq'.
32 Greenwood, 'Pre-emptive Use of Force', 36.
33 Lowe, 'Iraq Crisis', 866.
34 Gray, *International Law*, 366, 364, 364.
35 White and Myjer, 'Editorial', 1.
36 Brownlie, 'Memorandum', Ev22.
37 Kammerhofer, 'Self-Defence', 197.
38 Byers, 'Agreeing to Disagree', 165–86; Kammerhofer, 'Self-Defence', 197.

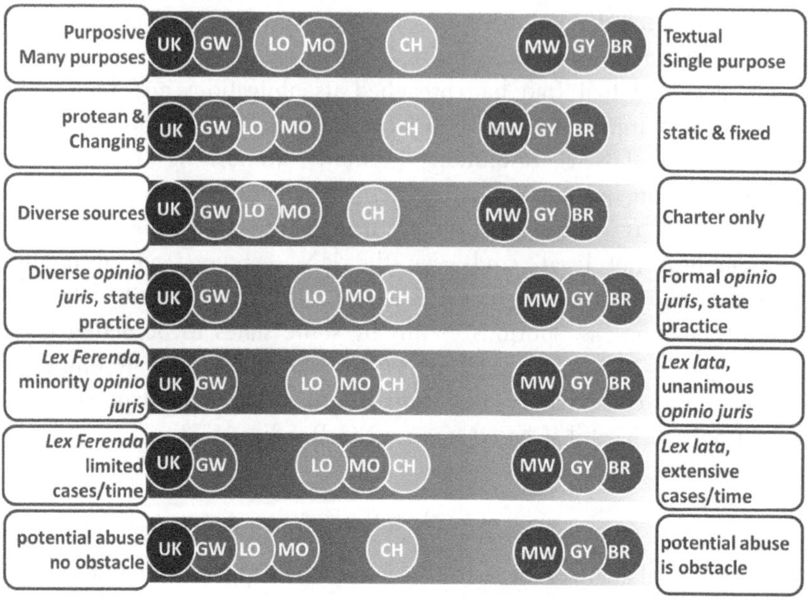

FIGURE 4.2 Competing interpretive techniques

violations of fundamental rights.[39] The UK government argued such force was permitted 'as an exceptional measure in support of purposes laid down by the UNSC, but without the Security Council's express authorisation, when that is the only means to avert an immediate and overwhelming humanitarian catastrophe'.[40] Chinkin however acknowledged the charter 'gives priority to State sovereignty'.[41] Gray doubted 'states as a whole' agreed force can be used to protect human rights.[42] Brownlie and Apperley argued the justifications 'do not reflect the clear text of the UN Charter', and 'sources of international law' provide no 'support for the legality of humanitarian intervention'.[43]

On Afghanistan, Chinkin, Gray, Myjer and White relied on textual arguments to in effect specify narrow purposes for self-defence, doubting whether this intervention complied with them, since it relied on a claim of self-defence against a non-state actor while the UN Charter explicitly 'regulates relations

39 Greenwood, 'NATO Intervention in Kosovo', 929; Chinkin, 'Legality of NATO's Action', 920.
40 Robertson, 'Kosovo'.
41 Ibid.
42 Gray, *International Law*, 48.
43 Brownlie and Apperley, 'Kosovo Crisis Inquiry', 884, 893, 886.

between sovereign states', without mentioning conflict 'outside the inter-state paradigm'.[44] There was no UNSC resolution explicitly recognising 11 September 2001 as an 'armed attack' nor authorising 'all necessary means' to respond.[45] Myjer and White further claimed UNSC resolutions showed 'clear' UNSC 'preference' for a 'criminal justice' rather than 'military' response.[46] Gray argued the operation's failure to end terrorism meant its necessity was questionable, and reliance on air strikes and targeting of Taleban was not proportionate.[47] Greenwood and Moir however observed that the text of the UN Charter does not limit self-defence only to state attacks, and UNSC resolutions after the 11 September attacks acknowledged 'the inherent right to self-defense', indicating the UNSC supported the US-led action.[48] The United Kingdom observed that military action 'against Usama Bin Laden's Al-Qaeda terrorist organization and the Taliban regime that is supporting it' was an 'exercise of the inherent right of individual and collective self-defence, recognized in Article 51'.[49] Moir did however view targeting the Taleban from the start of the operation as stretching beyond the action's purpose, as there was no evidence of Taleban involvement in Al-Qaeda's attacks.[50]

On Iraq, the United Kingdom and Greenwood displayed a purposive approach, emphasising that UNSC Resolutions 678 (1990), 687 (1991) and 1441 (2002) in combination 'authorised force against Iraq, to eject it from Kuwait and to restore peace and security in the area', which 'went beyond the goal of liberating Kuwait' to include 'the express purpose of restoring international peace and security in the area'.[51] They also deployed what the UK attorney general's detailed 2003 legal advice described as a 'narrow textual reading' of UNSC Resolution 1441 (2002), claiming it would have explicitly required a further UNSC resolution authorising force 'if that had been intended', and so only required 'reporting to and discussion by the Security Council of Iraq's failures, but not an express further decision to authorise force'.[52] Lowe endorsed a generally purposive approach ('Substantive rules are

44 Chinkin, 'Rethinking Legality/Legitimacy', 225.

45 Ibid.

46 Myjer and White, 'Twin Towers Attack', 6.

47 Gray, *International Law*, 203.

48 Greenwood, 'War against Terrorism', 307–8; Moir, *Reappraising the Resort to Force*, 47.

49 UN Security Council, Document S/2001/947.

50 Moir, *Reappraising the Resort to Force*, 59.

51 Goldsmith, 'Use of Force against Iraq'; Greenwood, 'Pre-emptive Use of Force', 34.

52 UK Attorney General Goldsmith, 'Iraq: Resolution 1441', *International and Comparative Law Quarterly*, 54:3 (2005), 767–78, para. 26; Goldsmith, 'Use of Force against Iraq'.

means to an end'), and agreed Iraq's behaviour was 'in breach of its international obligations' and 'prejudicial to international peace and security'.[53] But he noted 'the express views' of UNSC members when discussing UNSC Resolution 1441 (2002) clearly did not endorse force, while the wording of UNSC Resolution 686 (1991) and UNSC Resolution 687 (1991) suggested the earlier authorisation was 'only for the duration of the military operation to expel Iraq from Kuwait'.[54]

Myjer and White, Brownlie and Gray rejected any suggestion that enforcing UNSC resolutions or counter-proliferation were valid purposes for force without 'clear and unambiguous' UNSC resolution authorisation, that the UNSC debates made clear that 'it was not the intention of the council' that UNSC Resolution 1441 (2002) 'revived' UNSC Resolution 678 (1990)'s authorisation of force, some Council members explicitly saying 'the purpose of the resolution' was disarmament through inspections, not force.[55] Gray pointedly asked 'how could Resolution 678 (1990) provide authority to use force twelve years after it was originally passed and in very different circumstances?'[56] Brownlie argued that '[t]he phrase, "if an armed attack occurs" was really carefully chosen by the draftsman' of the UN Charter, who had not intended 'a loose regime', while alternative interpretations of UNSC Resolution 678 (1990) are 'problematical', because the purpose of that resolution relates to 'threats to Kuwait', and the situation in 2003 was 'very difficult to tuck under the umbrella of the former conflict between Iraq and Kuwait'.[57]

Linked to purposive arguments, the potential for force to *draw on legal instruments not themselves authorising force* – human rights law, genocide law – was accepted by the United Kingdom, Greenwood, Lowe and to some extent Chinkin in relation to the Kosovo intervention, 'as an exceptional measure in support of purposes laid down by the UN Security Council, but without the Council's express authorisation'.[58] Greenwood and Moir inferred states' approval for the Afghanistan action from references to the inherent right of self-defence in UNSC resolutions after 11 September.[59] On Iraq, Greenwood and the United Kingdom relied on UNSC Resolution 1441 (2002)'s determination that Iraq was in material breach of ceasefire conditions

53 Lowe, 'Iraq Crisis', 863, 864.
54 Lowe, 'Iraq Crisis', 866, 865.
55 White and Myjer, 'Editorial', 4; Gray, *International Law*, 356, 361.
56 Gray, *International Law*, 356, 361.
57 Brownlie, 'Memorandum', Ev22, Ev25.
58 Greenwood, 'NATO Intervention in Kosovo', 931; Robertson, 'Kosovo'.
59 Greenwood, 'War against Terrorism', 308; Moir, *Reappraising the Resort to Force*, 52–54; UN Security Council, Document S/2001/947.

to revive UNSC Resolution 678 (1990)'s authorisation to use force, also using the VCLT's definition of material breach of international obligations.[60] But on Iraq, Lowe argued it was 'unacceptable' that action 'as serious and important as a massive military attack upon a state should be launched on the basis of a legal argument dependent upon dubious inferences drawn from the silences in Resolution 1441 and the muffled echoes of earlier resolutions'.[61] Gray, Brownlie and Apperley, and Myjer and White consistently discounted arguments relying on legal instruments not explicitly authorising force, seeing explicit UNSC authorisation as the only valid authority for force in situations that are not clear cases of self-defence against ongoing armed attack by another state.[62]

Protean or static law? Disagreements around whether the law is relatively *protean* and changing, or is relatively *static* and in its *'original'* form, are linked to these tensions about purposes. On Kosovo, Greenwood, Lowe and Chinkin argued the *jus ad bellum* 'includes customary international law', which is 'not static' and had been shaped by human rights and Genocide law since 1945.[63] The United Kingdom also implicitly applied a protean view, declaring that although there was 'no general doctrine of humanitarian necessity in international law', cases had 'nevertheless arisen (as in northern Iraq in 1991) when, in the light of all the circumstances, a limited use of force was justifiable'.[64] Greenwood argued humanitarian intervention was already a lawful justification for force.[65] Lowe argued such a right should be 'encouraged to develop', but agreed with Chinkin it had not yet clearly emerged, but rather was 'an emerging concept'.[66] Gray, Brownlie and Apperley argued proponents of customary change bore the 'burden of proof', 'there is a presumption against a radical change' in international law, and there was 'very little evidence' that a new norm of humanitarian intervention had emerged and crystallised.[67]

On Afghanistan, Greenwood was clear that pre–UN Charter custom had always permitted self-defence against non-state actors, and the charter had preserved this 'inherent right of self-defense'; denying such a view

60 Goldsmith, 'Use of Force against Iraq'; Greenwood, 'Pre-emptive Use of Force', 29.

61 Lowe, 'Iraq Crisis', 866.

62 Brownlie and Apperley, 'Kosovo Crisis Inquiry', 891–4; White and Myjer, 'Editorial', 3, 4; Gray, *International Law*, 356, 364, 369; Brownlie, 'Memorandum', Ev23.

63 Greenwood, 'NATO Intervention in Kosovo', 929, 926–7.

64 Symons, 'Kosovo'.

65 Greenwood, 'NATO Intervention in Kosovo', 926.

66 Lowe, 'Kosovo Crisis', 941; Chinkin, 'Legality of NATO's Action', 920.

67 Brownlie and Apperley, 'Kosovo Crisis Inquiry', 894, 909, 894.

would be 'a strange formalism'.[68] The United Kingdom's justification asserted that international law permitted force in self-defence against Al Qaeda and the Taleban.[69] Moir accepted that custom had crystallised before 2001 requiring state involvement in non-state attacks to trigger the legal right of self-defence, but argued this was reversed by the near-universal approval for the Afghanistan operation.[70] Gray, Myjer and White and to some extent Chinkin argued pre–UN Charter custom was superseded by the charter's inter-state paradigm, and had been confirmed by UNGA declarations and ICJ judgments.[71] They were reluctant to accept that the US-led intervention had caused the law to evolve, which Myjer and White feared would permit force 'in so many instances that the regulation of it no longer makes any sense'.[72]

On Iraq, the United Kingdom and Greenwood displayed a protean approach in their support for the 'revival' argument, which had been used only in 1993 and 1998. They argued that '[a] material breach of Resolution 687 revives the authority to use force under Resolution 678', and since UNSC Resolution 1441 (2002) had determined Iraq was 'in material breach of Resolution 687', it revived 'authority to use force'.[73] Lowe accepted 'international law develops unevenly', 'developments in one area may lag behind' others, and even 'constitutional development' of UNSC processes can occur, but he saw no evidence for the development of the revival doctrine.[74] Myjer and White accepted that law can change, including how the UNSC authorises force if the whole council agrees, but 'clearly there was no such consensus' to suggest UNSC Resolution 1441 (2002) revived UNSC Resolution 678 (1990)'s authorisation for force, which had 'no basis in law'.[75] Brownlie and Gray displayed a relatively static approach, arguing UNSC resolutions can authorise force only for specific purposes, and further resort to force required a 'more tailor-made' resolution supported by 'the international community'.[76]

Identifying* opinio juris *and state practice. Arguments about whether customary change requires evidence of the *active, formal opinio juris* and

68 Greenwood, 'War against Terrorism', 307.
69 UN Security Council, Document S/2001/947.
70 Moir, *Reappraising the Resort to Force*, 49–54.
71 Gray, *International Law*, 195–9, Myjer and White, 'Twin Towers Attack', 7–8; Chinkin, 'Rethinking Legality/Legitimacy', 225.
72 Myjer and White, 'Twin Towers Attack', 18.
73 Goldsmith, 'Use of Force against Iraq'; Greenwood, 'War against Terrorism', 35.
74 Lowe, 'Iraq Crisis', 862, 868.
75 White and Myjer, 'Editorial', 2, 2, 7.
76 Brownlie, 'Memorandum', Ev26; Gray, *International Law*, 361.

state practice of a *majority of states* in numerous *cases over time* often underpin these tensions between protean and static approaches. Greenwood argued change 'does not require unanimity', and a humanitarian intervention norm had emerged from relatively few cases in the 1990s.[77] The United Kingdom also implied a less demanding approach to *opinio juris* and state practice, citing 'no-fly-zones' in Northern Iraq in 1991 as evidence of a humanitarian intervention norm justifying resort to force as 'an exceptional measure'.[78] Moir accepted customary law had changed rapidly after the Afghanistan action, legalising self-defence against non-state actors.[79]

Chinkin and Lowe also saw potential for relatively rapid customary change,[80] but concluded state practice was insufficient 'to conclude definitively' that a humanitarian intervention norm had emerged.[81] Brownlie and Apperley required 'general practice', and 'conviction' among 'the preponderance' of states before such a norm could be viewed as having crystallised, reporting that NATO legal advisers had privately opposed the action in Kosovo.[82] Gray required new custom to be 'widely recognized' by 'states as a whole', rejected earlier alleged precedents of humanitarian intervention, noted the Non-Aligned Movement's continued opposition to the norm, describing 'instant custom' as 'fiction', and that those who argued the law on self-defence had changed cite only Afghanistan as state practice.[83] Myjer and White saw any evolution of the law following the Afghanistan intervention as dangerous, taking self-defence 'outside the limits of the Charter' and beyond UNSC supervision, and, like Gray, emphasised formal, textual sources of law including UNGA declarations and ICJ cases.[84]

On Iraq, the United Kingdom and Greenwood were willing to accept the revival doctrine after only cases in 1993 and 1998, even though the UK attorney general had himself described it as, 'controversial' and 'not widely accepted' by commentators, with 'several States expressing the view that it was not' lawful.[85] Lowe emphasised only 'the market-place of State Practice', can confer 'the status of formally binding law', and since 'the express views of Security Council Members' during the debate on UNSC Resolution 1441 (2002) had showed the council did not endorse the US/UK legal theory, 'there is no

77 Greenwood, 'NATO Intervention in Kosovo', 930, 929–30.
78 Robertson, 'Kosovo'.
79 Moir, *Reappraising the Resort to Force*, 49–54.
80 Chinkin, 'Legality of NATO's Action', 925.
81 Ibid., 920; Lowe, 'Kosovo Crisis', 938.
82 Brownlie and Apperley, 'Kosovo Crisis Inquiry', 909.
83 Gray, *International Law*, 48, 49, 52, 198, 201.
84 Myjer and White, 'Twin Towers Attack', 16, 7; Gray, *International Law*, 199–200.
85 Goldsmith, 'Iraq: Resolution 1441', paras. 4, 10; Greenwood, 'War against Terrorism', 32, 33.

known doctrine of the revival of authorisations' in UNSCRs.[86] Myjer and White argued 'there was no such consensus' within the UNSC for the revival doctrine, and the 'critical reaction of many states and other actors' to the US/UK intervention showed lack of support for 'a new interpretive rule' allowing 'individual states to unilaterally interpret and enforce Security Council resolutions'.[87] Brownlie argued Kuwait and Iraq's other neighbours did not support military action or by implication the US/UK interpretation of UNSC resolutions.[88] And Gray argued the coalition case was 'essentially unilateral', the US/UK justification 'ultimately failed to convince the vast majority of states', and UNSC Resolution 1441 (2002)'s drafting history showed most states did not accept the US/UK legal theory.[89]

Conclusions

These analyses broadly supported Chapter 2's proposition that lawyers tend to align with competing interpretive cultures. Lawyers who tended to support a restrictive *jus contra bellum* tended to apply 'formalist' legal interpretation techniques, more likely to stick to the letter of the law, applying more stringent tests for *opinio juris* and state practice before accepting legal change, and wanting explicit UNSC authorisation for all use of force apart from straightforward self-defence. Lawyers applying a more expansionist *jus ad bellum* tended to apply 'dynamist' interpretation techniques, more willing to invoke wider purposes and other international law to justify force, requiring less stringent *opinio juris* and state practice before accepting legal change, and seeing more discretion for states to authorise force outside the UNSC.

There were anomalies however, where expansionists deployed formalist arguments, while restrictivists deployed dynamist arguments. The UK attorney general described the justification for resort to force in Iraq as relying on a 'narrow textual reading' of UNSC Resolution 1441 (2002).[90] Meanwhile criticisms of this justification emphasised the more limited purposes evident in UNSC members' statements and the contextual evidence of UNSC Resolution 1441 (2002)'s negotiating history. The expansionist justification for force in Afghanistan at least partially relied on a textual reading of the UN Charter – that Article 51's words did not confine self-defence to attacks by states. Restrictivist critics of that intervention deployed purposive, protean

86 Lowe, 'Iraq Crisis', 860, 866, 865.
87 White and Myjer, 'Editorial', 2, 7, 8.
88 Brownlie, 'Memorandum', Ev22.
89 Gray, *International Law*, 362, 364, 355, 359, 369.
90 Goldsmith, 'Iraq: Resolution 1441', para. 26.

arguments – that the law was originally intended to apply only to conflict between states, which subsequent UNGA declarations and ICJ judgments confirmed.

The analysis also supports this book's more general argument that the *jus ad bellum* displays 'specific indeterminacy'. Lawyers reached multiple, overlapping but not entirely coincident conclusions about the different interpretive principles, displaying supervaluationism. Lawyers' approaches to each principle were distributed along a continuum, displaying fuzzy rather than bivalent logic. Lawyers displayed 'social supervaluationism', distributed on a continuum between the two interpretive cultures rather than forming coherent, clearly separated groups. And of course, the lawyers' disagreed about the overall lawfulness of the interventions themselves. To the extent that convergent opinions of qualified, knowledgeable international lawyers signifies determinacy in international law, these three interventions displayed varying degrees of specific indeterminacy in the *jus ad bellum*.

THE ICJ AND LEGAL INTERPRETATION: *NICARAGUA, WALL, CONGO*

Introduction

In the seminal 1986 *Military and Paramilitary Activities in and against Nicaragua* case, the ICJ decided by twelve votes to three that US involvement in military and paramilitary activities in Nicaragua was a 'breach of its obligation under customary international law not to intervene in the affairs of another State', 'not to use force against another State' and 'not to violate the sovereignty of another state'.[91] The same margin rejected US justifications of its actions as 'collective self-defence' responding to Nicaragua's support for rebels in El Salvador and Honduras, as those states had not declared themselves victims of attack at that time, the United States could have used other non-forceful measures, and its actions were disproportionate.[92] But, by fourteen votes to one, the Court decided not to hold the United States responsible for acts by armed groups it supported, since the United States could not be shown to have exercised 'effective control' over those groups.[93]

91 *Nicaragua*, Merits, para. 292.
92 Ibid.
93 Ibid.

Judge Schwebel argued US actions were lawful collective self-defence, and Nicaragua was responsible for aggression.[94] Judges Jennings and Oda questioned whether Nicaragua was more culpable for aggressive action than the majority had found.[95] Judges Ago and Lachs shared the majority's overall conclusions, but felt the Court should have considered more evidence of Nicaragua's potential culpability.[96] Schwebel, Jennings and Oda also argued the case should not have proceeded due to the US 'Multilateral Reservation', which excluded from ICJ jurisdiction any disputes involving the United States that were governed by multilateral treaties, since the United States claimed its dispute with Nicaragua was governed by the UN Charter and other multilateral treaties regulating use of force.[97]

Although the *jus ad bellum* was not central to the 2004 ICJ advisory opinion on the *Legal Consequences of the Construction of a Wall in the Occupied Palestinian Territory* case, the judgment and several separate opinions addressed the question of self-defence against armed non-state actors. The Court decided by large majorities that the wall and 'its associated regime' were 'contrary to international law', Israel was obliged to dismantle them and make reparation for damage caused, the UNGA and UNSC should consider action to end this illegal situation which all states were obliged 'not to recognize' or assist.[98] In addition, all states parties to the Fourth Geneva Convention should 'ensure compliance by Israel' with that convention, while respecting wider international law.[99] International law governing self-defence became relevant because Israel claimed the wall was 'consistent with Article 51' of the UN Charter, a claim the majority rejected, concluding Article 51 enshrined a right of self-defence only from 'armed attack by one State against another State'.[100] Judges Buergenthal and Kooijmans argued the charter did not make self-defence 'dependent upon an armed attack by another State', while Judge Higgins expressed concerns about the conclusion.[101]

Finally, the 2005 ICJ *Armed Activities on the Territory of the Congo* case addressed the Democratic Republic of Congo (DRC)'s claims that Uganda's activities in the DRC between April 1998 and June 2003 were an 'act of aggression' which violated principles 'of non-use of force in international

94 *Nicaragua*, Schwebel, 269–70, 344, 392.
95 *Nicaragua*, Jennings, 544; *Nicaragua*, Oda, 240, 243.
96 *Nicaragua*, Ago, 187; *Nicaragua*, Lachs, 161.
97 *Nicaragua*, Jennings, 534; *Nicaragua*, Schwebel, 286–7; *Nicaragua*, Oda, 217–19.
98 *Wall*, Opinion, 201–2.
99 *Wall*, Opinion, 201–2.
100 *Wall*, Opinion, 194.
101 *Wall*, Buergenthal, para. 6; *Wall*, Kooijmans, para. 35; *Wall*, Higgins, 215.

relations'.[102] The Court found by sixteen votes to one that Uganda's military activities, occupation of territory, and support for irregular forces 'violated the principle of non-use of force in international relations and the principle of non-intervention'.[103] By fourteen votes to three, the Court rejected Uganda's counter-claim that the DRC's support to non-state actors who carried out attacks on Uganda were 'acts of aggression' violating UN Charter principles of 'non-use of force' and non-intervention.[104] Judges Kooijmans, Tomka and Judge Ad Hoc Kateka dissented; as Judge Tomka put it, the DRC had 'breached its duty of vigilance during the period 1994-1997 by tolerating Ugandan rebel movements' use of the DRC's territory to launch attacks on Uganda'.[105] Judges Kooijmans, Kateka and Simma, argued attacks on Uganda by non-state actors in the DRC from June to August 1998 'amounted to an armed attack in the sense of Article 51', entitling Uganda to exercise self-defence, and that its actions during this period were not 'unnecessary or disproportionate'.[106]

Figure 4.3 illustrates the judges' disagreements about the lawfulness of the actions considered in these cases. The diagrams for *Nicaragua* and *Congo* illustrate the Judges' opinions using the tests identified in Chapter 2. The diagram for *Wall* focuses on the narrower question of whether self-defence against non-state actors is lawful. It is worth noting that, as has often been observed, ICJ majority judgments normally reflect a compromise between judges' different positions, so they are often less explicit about their underlying reasoning and may be less fruitful than dissenting or separate opinions for the textual analysis this research uses.[107] Detailed analysis of the texts suggested systematic disagreements between the judges about principles of legal interpretation (see Figure 4.4), which apparently varied broadly but not entirely with the restrictiveness of the judges' opinions about the *jus ad bellum*.

Narrative

Broad or narrow purposes? The texts show disagreements about the fundamental purposes of the law, whether accepting multiple, broad purposes or fewer, narrower purposes for self-defence in the UN Charter and other sources. In *Nicaragua*, the majority saw narrow purposes for self-defence.

102 *Congo*, Judgment, 180, 181.
103 *Congo*, Judgment, 280.
104 *Congo*, Judgment, 259.
105 *Congo*, Tomka, 351.
106 *Congo*, Kateka, 372; *Congo*, Kooijmans, 315; *Congo*, Simma, 337–8.
107 Green, *Self-Defence*, 177–8; Talmon, 'Determining Customary International Law', 434.

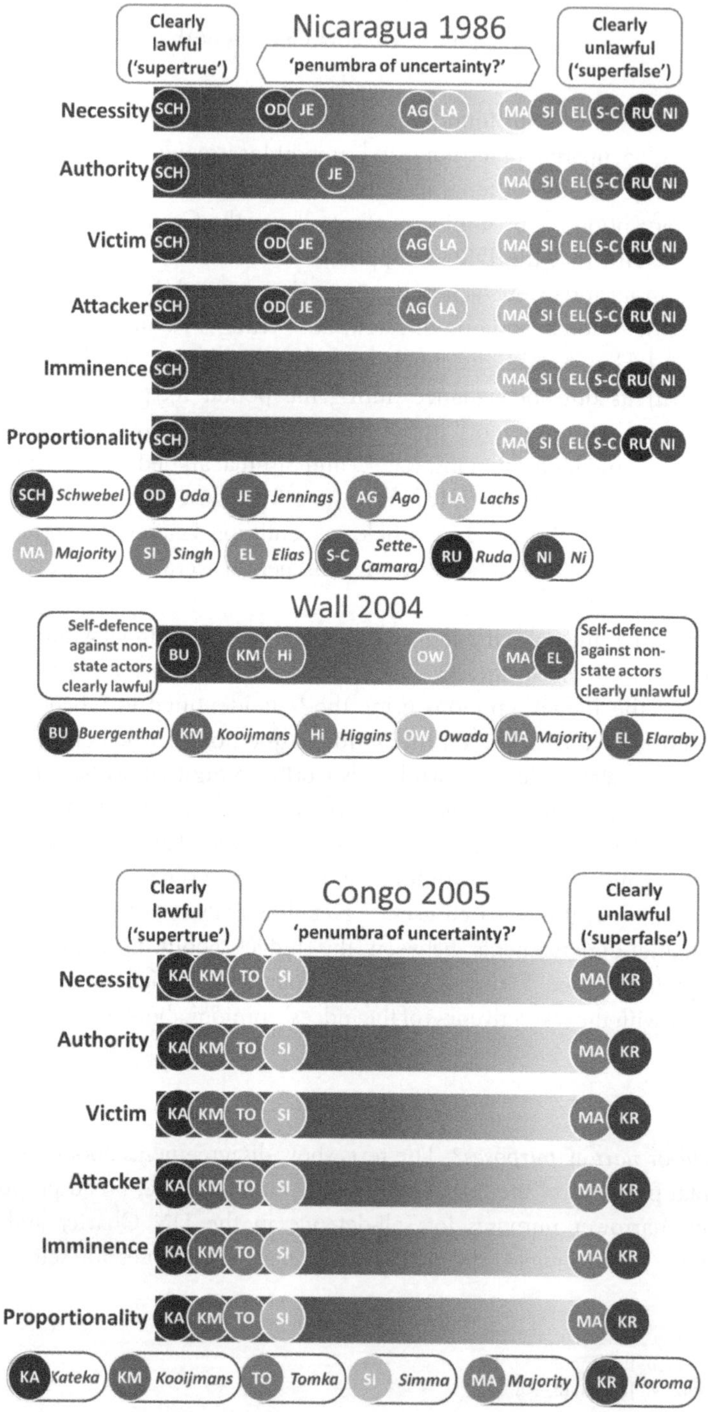

FIGURE 4.3 Analysis of ICJ opinions on *Nicaragua*, *Wall*, *Congo*

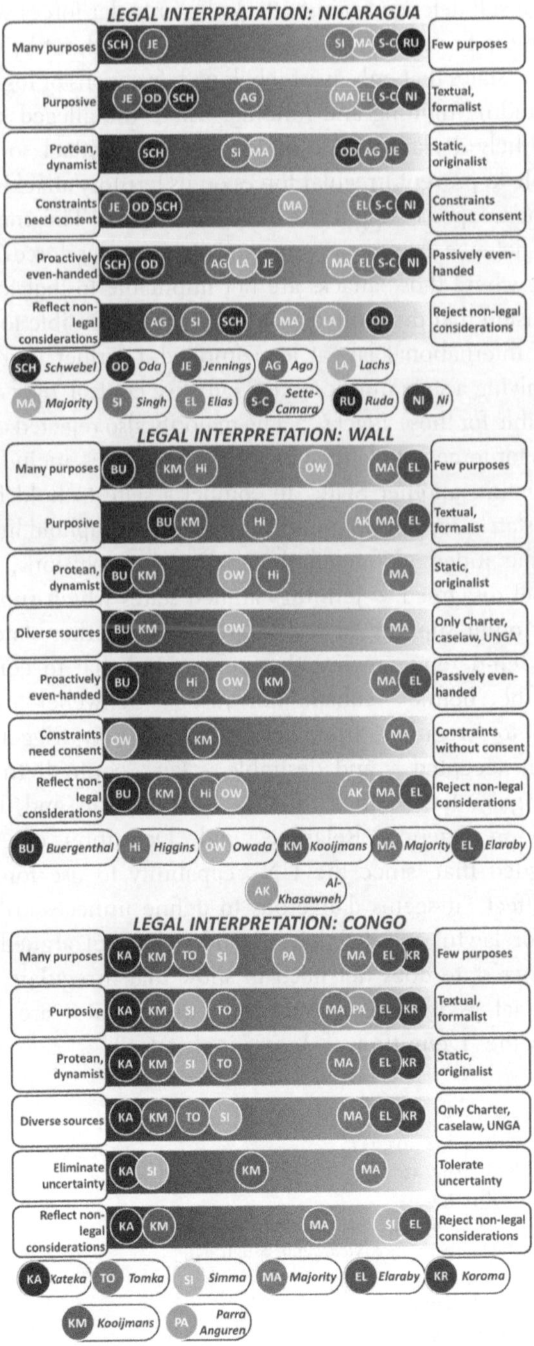

FIGURE 4.4 *Nicaragua, Wall, Congo* – principles of legal interpretation

They rejected self-defence against attacks by irregular forces with 'scale and effect' of 'a mere frontier incident had it been carried out by regular armed forces'; against states that only assist rebels with 'weapons or logistical or other support' including training and funding; where the alleged 'attacked' state does not publicly declare itself experiencing armed attack; or against states merely unable to prevent irregular forces on its territory attacking other states or to prevent weapons supplies to rebels abroad.[108] The majority at least implied self-defence cannot be triggered by irregular forces' attacks from another state where those attacks are not imputable to that foreign state.[109] Their conclusion that the United States was not responsible for the Contras' violations of international law at least implied a further narrowing of self-defence, implying a state must exercise 'effective control' over attackers to be held responsible for those attacks.[110] The majority also rejected other potential justifications for force not claimed by the United States, including to support 'opposition within another State', to compel a state to hold free elections, because of a state's 'ideology or political system', or to uphold human rights.[111]

Most of the judges defended the majority conclusions, but Jennings and Schwebel disagreed.[112] Jennings argued states which supply arms and 'logistical or other support' to armed groups in another state may trigger the right of self-defence against themselves, and that to conclude otherwise would be 'neither realistic nor just'.[113] Schwebel argued that to exclude 'aid to irregulars' from actions which may trigger self-defence 'departs from accepted – and desirable – law', contradicting arguments from Nicaragua, the United States, El Salvador and the UNGA's 'Declaration on Friendly Relations' and 'Definition of Aggression'.[114] Jennings argued that, since the UN's capability to use force had never come into effect, 'it seems dangerous to define unnecessarily strictly the conditions for lawful self-defence'.[115] And Schwebel argued self-defence against another state does not need to show that 'irregulars operating on its territory' act as its agents, only 'that those States are "substantially involved"' as the 'Definition of Aggression' states.[116]

108 *Nicaragua*, Merits, paras. 195, 157.
109 *Nicaragua*, Merits, para. 230.
110 *Nicaragua*, Merits, para. 115.
111 *Nicaragua*, Merits, paras. 209, 262, 263, 268.
112 *Nicaragua*, Sette-Camara, 199; *Nicaragua*, Singh, 151.
113 *Nicaragua*, Jennings, 543.
114 *Nicaragua*, Schwebel, 332, 342.
115 *Nicaragua*, Jennings, 544.
116 *Nicaragua*, Schwebel, 344.

In *Wall*, the majority asserted a narrow purpose for self-defence, saying Article 51 enshrined self-defence only for 'armed attack by one State against another State'.[117] Higgins accepted the majority opinion 'as a statement of the law as it now stands', but maintained concerns she had raised separately that the interpretation was 'operationally unworkable', incorrectly applying the description of armed attack by irregulars in the UNGA's 'Definition of Aggression'.[118] Buergenthal and Kooijmans disagreed with the majority, arguing the UN Charter's articulation of self-defence 'does not make its exercise dependent upon an armed attack by another State'.[119]

In *Congo*, the majority seemed to view safeguarding a state's sovereignty as a higher purpose than a state's 'duty of vigilance' to stop irregulars on its territory from attacking neighbouring states, accepting the DRC's difficult and expansive terrain meant its failure to prevent non-state attacks did not amount to '"tolerating" or "acquiescing"' to such attacks.[120] By declaring all Uganda's actions unlawful after the DRC withdrew its consent for Ugandan military presence on its territory, the majority rejected the possibility that some Ugandan actions may have served the lawful purpose of self-defence against non-state armed groups.[121] Kooijmans and Tomka disagreed, arguing the 'duty of vigilance' to prevent such attacks was an important purpose of the law, and the DRC had failed to show it had complied with that duty.[122] Kooijmans and Simma argued self-defence had wider purposes, by accepting that attacks on Uganda by non-state actors from the DRC between June and August 1998 were 'an armed attack in the sense of Article 51, thus entitling Uganda to the exercise of self-defence', and Uganda's actions in the DRC in this period were not 'unnecessary or disproportionate to the purpose of repelling the persistent attacks'.[123] They argued Uganda only 'overstepped the limits' after 1 September.[124] Judge Kateka argued the DRC's inability to control its territory gave Uganda a more general justification to use force in self-defence in the DRC.[125]

Purposive or textual interpretation? The texts also showed tensions between textual and purposive, creative legal interpretation techniques.

[117] *Wall*, Opinion, para. 139.
[118] *Wall*, Higgins, 215; Higgins, *Problems*, 250–1.
[119] *Wall*, Buergenthal, para. 6; *Wall*, Kooijmans, para. 35.
[120] *Congo*, Judgment, 268.
[121] *Congo*, Judgment, 269.
[122] *Congo*, Kooijmans, 306, 325; *Congo*, Tomka, 351.
[123] *Congo*, Kooijmans, 315; *Congo*, Simma, 337–8.
[124] *Congo*, Kooijmans, 315.
[125] *Congo*, Kateka, 372.

In *Nicaragua*, the majority derived the customary law of self-defence by relying on formal textual sources, including the UNGA's 'Declaration on Friendly Relations' and 'Definition of Aggression', texts from the Conference of American States, Conference on Security and Co-operation in Europe, the Montevideo Convention on Rights and Duties of States, International Law Commission writings and the UN Charter.[126] The majority interpreted the 'Declaration on Friendly Relations' as signifying States' acceptance 'of the rule or set of rules declared by the resolution'.[127] Judge Sette-Camara specifically argued for a textual approach, saying the court should have even applied the UN Charter.[128]

Schwebel disagreed, saying the majority view makes 'a fetish of literalism', warning that the 'Definition of Aggression' 'is not a treaty text' and its significance 'should not be magnified'.[129] Jennings described the majority approach as 'somewhat formalistic', warning their approach of using the 'treaty interpretation process' to determine custom 'must raise a suspicion that it is in reality the treaty itself that is being applied'.[130] Ago accepted the majority judgment, but doubted states' acceptance of UNGA or other 'resolutions or declarations' are 'proof conclusive' of States' *opinio juris* for a customary rule.[131] Oda, Jennings and Schwebel used purposive arguments to say the Court should not have accepted jurisdiction in the case, since the purpose of the US multilateral reservation was to exclude from ICJ jurisdiction 'disputes arising under multilateral treaties', and the Nicaragua case clearly engaged the UN Charter, a multilateral treaty.[132]

In *Wall*, the majority did not describe the rationale underpinning their conclusion that self-defence applied only 'in the case of armed attack by one State against another State', but made clear their reliance on the text of the UN Charter and the 'Declaration on Friendly Relations'.[133] In his separate opinion, Judge Elaraby described the 'Declaration on Friendly Relations' as 'an agreed interpretation of Article 2(4)', citing ICJ judgments and UNGA declarations as clear and authoritative sources of law.[134] Judge Al-Khasawneh argued UNGA declarations, 'while not binding, nevertheless produce legal effects and

[126] *Nicaragua*, Merits, paras. 188–91.
[127] *Nicaragua*, Merits, para. 188.
[128] *Nicaragua*, Sette-Camara, 199.
[129] *Nicaragua*, Schwebel, 335, 345.
[130] *Nicaragua*, Jennings, 544, 532.
[131] *Nicaragua*, Ago, 184.
[132] *Nicaragua*, Jennings, 533; *Nicaragua*, Oda, 217.
[133] *Wall*, Opinion, paras. 139, 87.
[134] *Wall*, Elaraby, 254, 236.

indicate a constant record of the international community's *opinio juris*'.[135] Buergenthal, Kooijmans and Higgins also used textual argument to counter the majority opinion, saying 'nothing in the text of Article 51 . . . stipulates that self-defence is available only when an armed attack is made by a State'.[136] Buergenthal regretted '[t]he Court's formalistic approach'.[137] Higgins regretfully accepted the Majority's restrictive interpretation, but described it as 'formalism of an un-evenhanded sort'.[138]

In *Congo*, the majority displayed a textual approach in applying UN Charter Article 2(4) and the 'Definition of Aggression' to designate Uganda's military activities in the DRC 'an act of aggression'.[139] The majority also appeared to give higher priority to these texts establishing the prohibition on force and protecting a state's sovereignty than to other texts asserting states' 'obligation not to allow knowingly its territory to be used for acts contrary to the rights of other States', reflected in the UNGA's 'Declaration on Friendly Relations' and the 1949 ICJ *Corfu Channel* case.[140] Simma, Kooijmans and Kateka displayed a more purposive approach in describing some of Uganda's actions as justifiable self-defence against non-state armed groups, even if that right was not explicitly set out in the UN Charter, UNGA resolutions or ICJ judgments.[141]

Protean or static law? The texts also show tensions between a static, 'originalist' approach to legal interpretation, and more protean, dynamist interpretation, sometimes in unexpected ways. In *Nicaragua*, the majority deployed protean arguments for a restrictive *jus ad bellum*, claiming the text governing force in the UN Charter, the 'Declaration on Friendly Relations' and the 'Definition of Aggression' had already become customary international law.[142] Schwebel accepted UN Charter provisions governing resort to force reflected customary law, and argued from a protean perspective that support to irregular forces can trigger the right of self-defence, since '[w]hatever legal doubts may have existed prior to World War II were dispelled by the events of the post-war period'.[143] While Jennings, Ago and Oda sympathised with a less restrictive *jus ad bellum*,

135 *Wall*, Al-Khasawneh, 236.
136 *Wall*, Buergenthal, para. 6; *Wall*, Kooijmans, para. 35; *Wall*, Higgins, para. 33.
137 *Wall*, Buergenthal, para. 6.
138 *Wall*, Higgins, para. 34.
139 *Congo*, Judgment, 180.
140 *Congo*, Tomka, 352.
141 *Congo*, Kateka, 372; *Congo*, Kooijmans, 315; *Congo*, Simma, 336–8.
142 *Nicaragua*, Merits, paras. 188–91.
143 *Nicaragua*, Schwebel, 303, 334.

they also argued for a more static approach, doubting 'there is a virtual identity of content' between customary international law on self-defence and the UN Charter.[144]

In *Wall*, the Majority again adopted a protean approach in accepting the 'Declaration on Friendly Relations' and *Nicaragua* judgment as sources of law from which they derive their restrictive interpretation of self-defence.[145] They also implied a boundary to their protean approach, arguing that Israel could not invoke as justification for the wall UNSC Resolutions 1368 (2001) and 1373 (2001), which reaffirmed the right of self-defence in the context of terrorism.[146] Buergenthal and Kooijmans however adopted a protean critique of the majority, observing those UNSC resolutions 'made clear that "international terrorism constitutes a threat to international peace and security" while "*reaffirming* the inherent right of individual or collective self-defence as recognized by the Charter of the United Nations"', without limiting that right to attacks by state actors only, '(i)n fact, the contrary appears to have been the case'.[147] Kooijmans regretted that the Court 'by-passed this new element', whose legal implications 'cannot as yet be assessed but which marks undeniably a new approach' to self-defence.[148]

In *Congo*, the majority applied a relatively static approach in accepting the principle implicit in the *Nicaragua* judgment that attacks by irregulars only trigger self-defence if they had substantial state involvement. Judge Elaraby explicitly argued the Court should have applied the customary law evident in the 'Definition of Aggression' to declare Uganda's activities as aggression, while Judge Koroma defended the majority as 'consistent with' the Court's previous jurisprudence, particularly *Nicaragua*.[149] Kooijmans, Simma and Kateka adopted a relatively protean approach in saying more recent developments, including UNSC Resolutions 1368 (2001) and 1373 (2001), showed states believed 'large-scale attacks by non-state actors can qualify as "armed attacks" within the meaning of Article 51'.[150]

Authority and consent. The *Nicaragua* texts showed disagreements about the kind of authority required to approve lawful resort to force, and how far law can constrain states without their consent. The majority concluded a state had

144 *Nicaragua*, Jennings, 530; *Nicaragua*, Ago, 183; *Nicaragua*, Oda 253, 256.
145 *Wall*, Opinion, para. 87.
146 *Wall*, Opinion, para. 139.
147 *Wall*, Buergenthal, para. 6; *Wall*, Kooijmans, para. 35.
148 *Wall*, Kooijmans, para. 35.
149 *Congo*, Elaraby, 331; *Congo*, Koroma, 288.
150 *Congo*, Kooijmans, 314; *Congo*, Simma, 337; *Congo*, Kateka, 365–8.

authority to use force in collective self-defence only if the alleged 'attacked' state formally declares itself a victim of attack and requests assistance.[151] The majority also concluded that, while customary law does not require states invoking self-defence to report to the UNSC as required by UN Charter Article 51, 'absence of a report' may indicate whether that State 'was itself convinced that it was acting in self-defence'.[152] Jennings disagreed, arguing such a formal declaration and request for assistance 'might sometimes be unrealistic'.[153] Schwebel argued such a reading of Article 51 implied aggressors are 'free to act covertly, but those who defend themselves against aggression are not'; and that the better view is that states under covert attack may 'informally and quietly seek foreign assistance', while states committing covert aggression should not 'complain' if 'States acting in self-defence to that aggression respond covertly' since 'no legal right can spring from a wrong'.[154]

The majority showed some support for law to constrain states without consent, concluding that the US multilateral treaty reservation did not prevent the Court from considering the case under customary international law without US consent, even if the relevant treaty norm and customary norm had 'exactly the same content'.[155] Judges Elias, Sette-Camara and Ni went further, arguing the Court should have applied the UN Charter as well as customary law.[156] Oda, Jennings and Schwebel disagreed, arguing the US multilateral treaty reservation should have prevented the Court from considering the case at all without US consent.[157]

Even-handedness. The texts also revealed disagreements about what a Court must do to be even-handed in a case. In *Nicaragua*, the majority argued the United States must accept the consequences of declining to take part in the case, including forfeiting opportunities to rebut factual allegations, saying a party which refuses to appear must not 'profit from its absence', which 'would amount to placing the party appearing at a disadvantage'.[158] But the majority also emphasised the Court's duty to be even-handed, not 'automatically' ruling 'in favour of the party appearing', and declined to declare compensation for Nicaragua, wanting to

151 *Nicaragua*, Merits, paras. 195, 199.
152 *Nicaragua*, Merits, para. 200.
153 *Nicaragua*, Jennings, 545.
154 *Nicaragua*, Schwebel, 373, 356, 373.
155 *Nicaragua*, Merits, para. 175.
156 *Nicaragua*, Elias, 178; *Nicaragua*, Ni, 209–10; *Nicaragua*, Sette-Camara, 197.
157 *Nicaragua*, Jennings, 534; *Nicaragua*, Oda, 219; *Nicaragua*, Schwebel, 304.
158 *Nicaragua*, Merits, paras. 28, 30, 31.

give the United States opportunity to argue that point.[159] Nevertheless, several judges thought the Court should have done more to be even-handed. Lachs wanted 'the Court to have dealt in greater detail with the question of assistance from or through Nicaragua to opposition forces in El Salvador', and should have 'granted El Salvador a hearing on its declaration of intervention'.[160] Jennings and Oda doubted Nicaragua's support to Salvadorian rebels was as limited as the majority had concluded, although Jennings blamed the United States for refusing to appear and present evidence, while Oda argued the majority did not adequately consider evidence available from the Untied States and El Salvador.[161] Schwebel was most concerned, arguing Nicaragua's status as aggressor and its misrepresentation of facts should have meant its claims should fail, saying the judgment 'might reinforce the suspicion' of 'politicization of judicial proceedings and anti-Western bias'.[162]

In *Wall*, Buergenthal, Kooijmans, Higgins and Owada criticised the majority for not being sufficiently even-handed in considering Israel's claim that the wall was necessary self-defence. Buergenthal rejected the whole judgment for this reason, saying 'the Court did not have before it the requisite factual bases for its sweeping findings'.[163] Higgins criticised the opinion's 'un-evenhanded' 'formalism', arguing 'Palestine cannot be sufficiently an international entity to be invited to these proceedings, and to benefit from humanitarian law, but not sufficiently an international entity' to be bound by the prohibition on armed attack.[164] Owada argued the case needed 'material explaining the Israeli side of the picture', and the majority should have addressed Israel's claims, even though these were articulated elsewhere rather than submitted as evidence.[165] Kooijmans felt the Court had sufficient evidence to reach a judgment, but also argued it 'could have reflected in a more satisfactory way the interests at stake for all' in the region.[166] Higgins and Kooijmans also hinted at concerns that the UNGA's request for this advisory opinion reflected states' wish to use the ICJ to apply political pressure on Israel, rather than seeking authoritative legal advice.[167]

159 *Nicaragua*, Merits, paras. 28, 284.
160 *Nicaragua*, Lachs, 161, 170–1.
161 *Nicaragua*, Jennings, 544; *Nicaragua*, Oda, 243–4.
162 *Nicaragua*, Schwebel, 392, 313.
163 *Wall*, Buergenthal, para. 1.
164 *Wall*, Higgins, para. 34.
165 *Wall*, Owada, paras. 22, 23.
166 *Wall*, Kooijmans, para. 13.
167 *Wall*, Higgins, 210; *Wall*, Kooijmans, 525.

Koroma defended the majority opinion, expressing understanding 'that a prolonged occupation would engender resistance', while calling 'on all parties to the conflict to respect international humanitarian law'.[168] Al-Khasawneh argued 'Israel's prolonged military occupation with its policy of creating *faits accomplis* on the ground' was what prevented the Palestinians' 'right of self-determination from being fulfilled'.[169] Elaraby argued the Court should have been even firmer, since 'the illegality of the Israeli occupation regime itself set off an escalatory spiral of resistance and repression, and under these conditions all considerations of morality and reason establish a right of resistance inherent in the population'.[170]

What role for extra-legal considerations? Finally, the judges' different opinions revealed varying approaches to the role of extra-legal considerations in such cases. In *Nicaragua*, Oda argued that, although legal and political issues may overlap, highly political disputes had never been dealt with by the Court or its predecessors, and the ICJ Statute and state practice showed states believed cases involving use of force were too politically sensitive for legal adjudication, and should be dealt with by political organs such as the UNSC.[171] He argued the United States believed the dispute too politically charged for judicial adjudication, which should only take place in those cases where the states involved voluntarily submit to the Court's jurisdiction.[172] Lachs argued the Court was right to handle the case, but also acknowledged that links between law and politics made it difficult to identify when a political dispute may be justiciable, which was why regional talks and mediation remained 'the best way' to resolve the conflict.[173] Ago supported the majority judgment, but worried it insufficiently considered political factors, particularly Nicaragua's authoritarian political changes, and the conflict between Nicaragua's Sandinista government and opposition forces who were authentically Nicaraguan, not merely agents of foreign powers.[174]

Nevertheless, the majority concluded the case did 'fall into the category of "legal disputes"' under Article 36(2) of the ICJ Statute, and appeared to argue

168 *Wall*, Koroma, 206.
169 *Wall*, Al-Khasawneh, 237.
170 *Wall*, Elaraby, 256.
171 *Nicaragua*, Oda, 238–40.
172 *Nicaragua*, Oda, 236.
173 *Nicaragua*, Lachs, 168, 178.
174 *Nicaragua*, Ago, 186–7.

that political-strategic assessment was unnecessary to decide this case.[175] At the same time the majority evaluated evidence about the parties' claims and counter-claims in detail using apparently politico-strategic assessments, for example about the value of press and media reports, public reports from governments, and evidence from senior officials.[176] President of the Court Singh justified the prohibition on force with explicitly politico-strategic and ethical assessments of the 'disastrous consequences' of a looser *jus ad bellum*.[177] Schwebel agreed with the majority in rejecting assertions that self-defence 'is a "political" and hence non-justiciable question', and claimed his assessment of the facts and law did not imply judgment on politics or the policies pursued by the parties, which were not proper functions of an ICJ judge, yet his assessment also apparently contained considerable politico-strategic analysis.[178] However, Schwebel went on to claim the case was not justiciable, and the Court should not have exercised jurisdiction, because it required evaluation of policies and motives concerning use of force for which the Court had too little evidence without access to the 'secret' internal documents of the governments concerned.[179]

In *Wall*, Buergenthal regretted that the Court had failed 'to address any facts or evidence specifically rebutting Israel's claim' that the wall served security requirements.[180] Kooijmans argued the majority 'should have given more explicit attention to the general context of the request', should have worked 'within the wider political context', and should have left 'issues of self-determination' to the Roadmap 'political process'.[181] Higgins also regretted that the majority neglected the 'immensely complex' 'law, history and politics of the Israel-Palestine dispute'.[182] Owada argued the Court should 'engage in an in-depth scrutiny of all aspects of the particular circumstances' of the case, 'if necessary going beyond what has been argued by the participants'.[183] But Al-Khasawneh argued legality and respect for the prevailing law were vital prerequisites to any negotiated political settlement, which must not be sacrificed to assist negotiations.[184] Elaraby argued politics must be subservient to law, and too many important decisions on the Palestinian question had been

175 *Nicaragua*, Merits, paras. 33, 60–3.
176 *Nicaragua*, Merits, paras. 74, 230.
177 *Nicaragua*, Singh, 156.
178 *Nicaragua*, Schwebel, 284, 268.
179 *Nicaragua*, Schwebel, 266, 295.
180 *Wall*, Buergenthal, 243.
181 *Wall*, Kooijmans, 221, 223, 228.
182 *Wall*, Higgins, 210.
183 *Wall*, Owada, 261.
184 *Wall*, Al-Khasawneh, 238–9.

'taken on the basis of political expediency, without due regard for the legal requirements'.[185] He wanted the majority to include more historical context to show how Palestine's treatment had undermined international law, warning that political processes or negotiations cannot remove Palestine's legal right to the Occupied Territories.[186]

In *Congo*, the majority recognised the wider complexities in the Great Lakes region, but concluded the Court must 'respond, on the basis of international law, to the particular legal dispute brought before it', to interpret and apply the law 'mindful of context' but not going beyond the law.[187] Simma said 'by dodging the issue of "aggression"' the Court appeared uncomfortable with 'questions of utmost importance in contemporary international relations', and, while the Court should keep political context in mind, it must not desist 'from stating what is manifest out of regard for such non-legal considerations'.[188] However, Kooijmans argued the court 'inadequately reflects the structural instability and insecurity in the region', and should have shown it was 'fully aware of the wider context' and 'complexity of the issues involved'.[189] Kateka also argued the Court should have considered 'existing realities', including the Rwandan genocide and 'terrible history of unscrupulous dictators' supported from abroad.[190]

The *Congo* case also suggested different approaches to uncertainty in the *jus ad bellum*. The majority argued it had 'no need to respond' to parties' claims about when 'contemporary international law provides for a right of self-defence against large-scale attacks by irregular forces', thus appearing to accept this continuing area of legal uncertainty.[191] Kooijmans, Simma and Kateka criticised the Court for creating this uncertainty through the *Nicaragua* and *Wall* judgments, and for not clarifying that confusion in the *Congo* case.[192] Elsewhere, Simma argued the Court must affirm that there are 'no gaps' in the law, and not leave people in a 'legal void'.[193]

Conclusions

The analysis of these cases again broadly supports Chapter 2's proposed explanation that judges' approaches to the *jus ad bellum* form distinct

185 *Wall*, Elaraby, 247.
186 *Wall*, Elaraby, 249, 259.
187 *Congo*, Judgment, 190.
188 *Congo*, Simma, 338, 335.
189 *Congo*, Kooijmans, 307, 310.
190 *Congo*, Kateka, 363.
191 *Congo*, Judgment, 223.
192 *Congo*, Kateka, 364, 367; *Congo*, Kooijmans, 316; *Congo*, Simma, 336.
193 *Congo*, Simma, 340.

interpretive cultures. Those judges who supported a more restrictive *jus contra bellum* also tended to see limited, narrow purposes for self-defence, privileging the most obvious reading of the texts of formal legal documents such as the UN Charter, UNGA declarations and ICJ judgments over the wider actions of states and even UNSC resolutions. They tended to see law as relatively static, only acknowledging change supported by such formal, widely-approved texts. They were more willing to adjudicate cases without the consent of one party, more ready to take only limited steps to explore evidence defending states that refused to participate in cases, and were less overtly willing to take account of extra-legal factors in their opinions.

In *Nicaragua*, Judges Oda and Schwebel explicitly opposed considering non-legal issues in legal judgments, unlike judges who supported a more expansionist right of self-defence in other cases, yet Schwebel went on to cite many strategic and ethical justifications for his position and against the majority.[194] In *Congo*, the majority's decision not to describe Uganda's actions as aggression, and acknowledgement of 'the complex and tragic situation' in the Great Lakes region, showed willingness to 'be mindful of context' in the region, but also determination that 'its task cannot go beyond' its obligation 'to respond, on the basis of international law, to the particular legal dispute brought before it'.[195] Simma and Elaraby, in criticising the court for not calling Uganda's action aggression, argued against regional political considerations overly influencing the court's decisions.[196] Simma argued that, 'by dodging the issue of "aggression", the Court creates the impression that it somehow feels uncomfortable being confronted with certain questions of utmost importance in contemporary international relations', and, while the Court should reflect political context, it must not desist 'from stating what is manifest out of regard for such *non-legal* considerations' (emphasis added).[197]

Judges supporting a more expansionist *jus ad bellum* generally took opposing positions on these issues. They tended to see wider permissible purposes for self-defence, and were more willing to look at alternative, less obvious reading of the texts of formal legal documents such as the UN Charter, UNGA declarations and ICJ judgments. They tended to see law as relatively protean and dynamic, more likely to evolve in response to the wider actions of states, and more ready to accept a wider range of texts as evidence of change. They tended to be more willing to oppose adjudicating cases that lacked both

194 *Nicaragua*, Oda 238; *Nicaragua*, Schwebel, 268, 300, 332, 392.
195 *Congo*, Judgment, para. 190.
196 *Congo*, Elaraby, 331–2; *Congo*, Simma, 338.
197 *Congo*, Simma, 338, 335.

parties' consent, more ready to argue for exploring evidence defending states that refused to participate in cases, and more willing to take account of extra-legal factors in their opinions.

However, again there were anomalies. Throughout these cases, expansionist judges sometimes used formalist arguments, while restrictivist judges sometimes used dynamist arguments. Some judges used textual arguments that the words of Article 51 of the UN Charter do not specify that only states can conduct armed attacks. They advanced less protean arguments that the *Nicaragua* case and UNGA declarations had not changed the law to require that states be involved in armed attacks to trigger the right of self-defence. Restrictivist judges argued the opposite, using purposive and protean arguments – that the UN Charter was intended to regulate only inter-state conflict, and that this legal position had been confirmed in UNGA Declarations and ICJ jurisprudence.

The analysis again supports this book's more general argument that the *jus ad bellum* displays 'specific indeterminacy' and various forms of vagueness. Judges' interpretive techniques displayed supervaluationism, involving multiple, overlapping but not necessarily coincident interpretive principles. They displayed fuzzy logic, their approaches to each principle distributed along a continuum rather than separated into binary categories. They displayed 'social supervaluationism' – judges were distributed on a continuum between the two interpretive cultures, not clearly divided into two separate groups. And of course, the judges disagreed about the actual lawfulness of resort to force in the *Nicaragua* and *Congo* cases.

UK INTERNATIONAL LAWYERS AND LEGAL INTERPRETATION

Introduction

Finally, this section reports the results of survey and interview research with UK-based international lawyers. This research investigated the lawyers' views about the contested principles of legal interpretation which this book has already identified, and which were refined using the analysis of scholarly writings and ICJ cases reported in this chapter. The lawyers were asked whether legal interpretation should rely only on the ordinary meaning of the text of the UN Charter and other formal *jus ad bellum* sources, or could also take account of the UN Charter's wider purposes and other law. They were asked whether the law governing resort to force had evolved significantly since 1945, whether new customary international law requires only clear, explicitly legal statements of *opinio juris*, and overwhelming numbers of state practice, or whether custom could crystallise on the basis of a wider range of evidence and smaller numbers of state practice and *opinio juris*. And they were asked whether only the UNSC may authorise force in situations where the requirements of the law are unclear, or whether states and other bodies have discretion to interpret the *jus ad bellum* in such circumstances.

Figure 4.5 summarises the survey responses. As can be seen, participants' views varied to differing degrees across the questions. The interviews revealed more about these variations. In combination, this research suggested four overarching observations. First, this sample of international lawyers had a relatively strong preference for moderation about principles of legal interpretation. Second, this sample was relatively open to change in international law governing resort to force. Third, despite the popularity of moderation, the lawyers clearly differed in their preferences for either formalist or dynamist approaches to legal interpretation. And fourth, the data suggested a relatively strong correlation between lawyers' preferred legal interpretation techniques and their attitudes to the lawfulness of force – formalist lawyers tended to be more restrictivist, while dynamist lawyers tended to be more expansionist.

Narrative

The first overall observation was the popularity of moderation about legal interpretation in this sample of lawyers. The most popular choices were that law had undergone some evolution since 1945 (52 per cent), that sometimes official and sometimes political statements could be interpreted as *opinio juris* (43 per cent), and that new rules of customary international law sometimes do and sometimes do not require overwhelming numbers of *opinio juris* and state practice (43 per cent). The moderate option was second most popular for the remaining three questions. In hard cases engaging the *jus ad bellum*, 25 per cent said the UNSC is supreme but states and other bodies sometimes have discretion; 22 per cent said legal interpretation about such cases must sometimes rely on the plain meaning of legal texts and can sometimes look to wider purposes as well; and 22 per cent thought new custom sometimes does and sometimes does not require clear *opinio juris* and state practice.

The second overall observation is that this sample was relatively open to change in the law governing resort to force. The survey showed 96 per cent of participants thought the law had evolved somewhat (52 per cent), significantly (39 per cent) or a great deal (4 per cent). Only 4 per cent thought the law had evolved little since 1945. The survey also showed 86 per cent thought the crystallisation of new rules of customary international law concerning use of force sometimes do not (43 per cent) or usually do not (43 per cent) require the

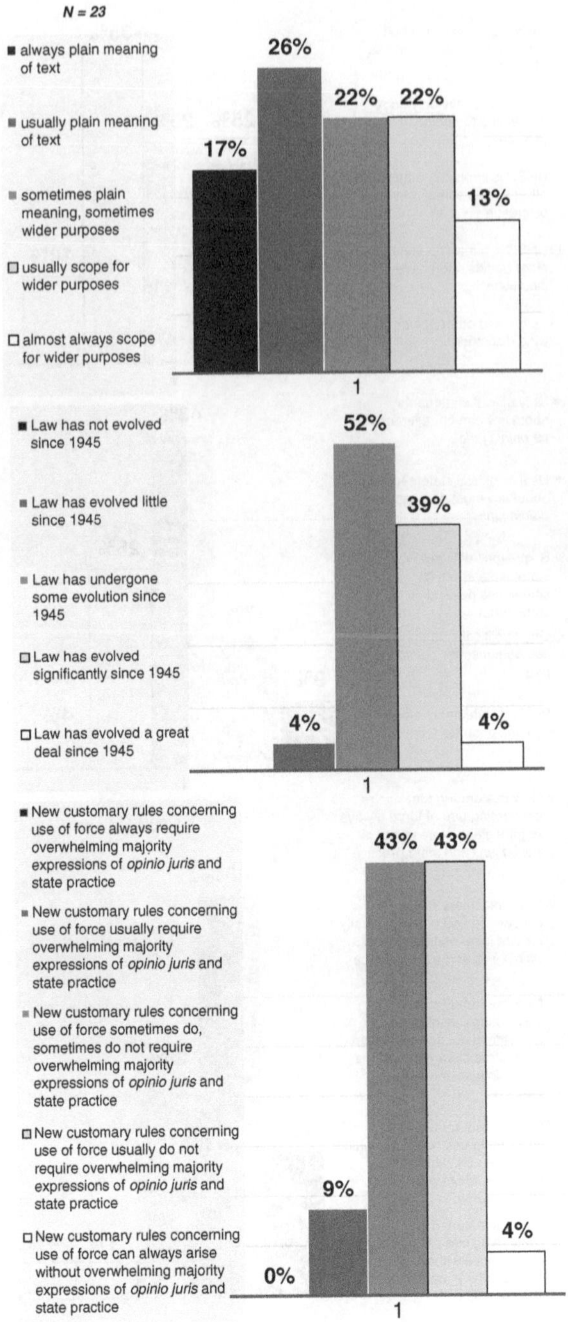

FIGURE 4.5 Opinions on principles of legal interpretation

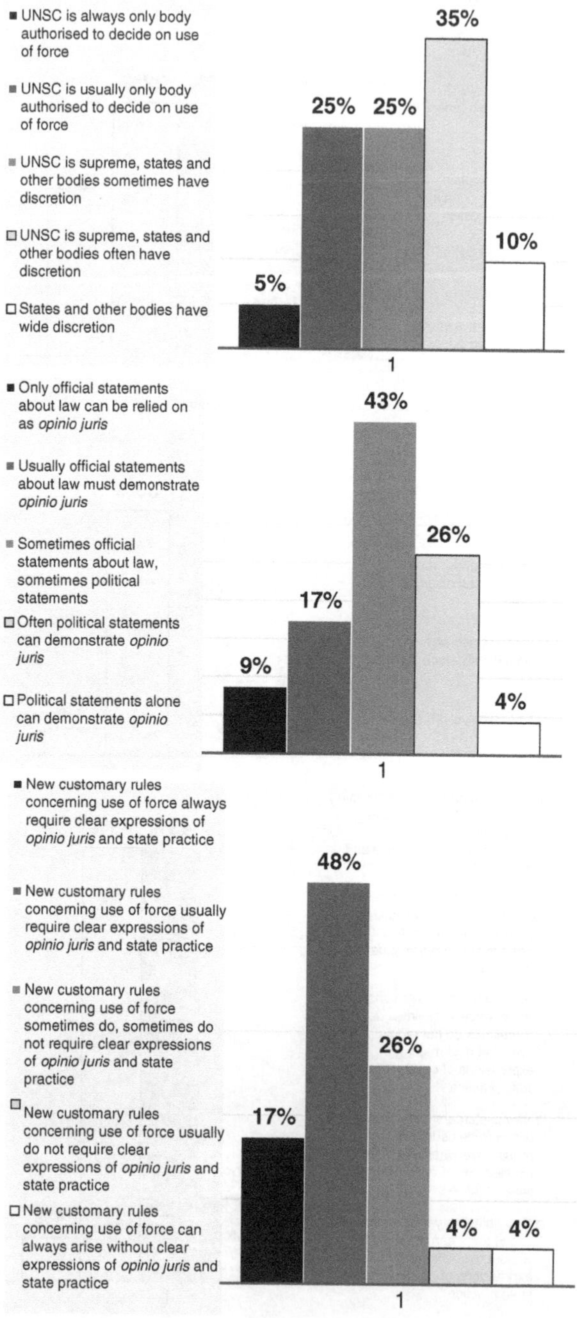

FIGURE 4.5 (Cont.)

overwhelming majority of states to express state practice or *opinio juris*. Only 8 per cent thought an overwhelming majority was usually required, and only 4 per cent thought it was never required.[198]

In interviews, all participants agreed the law governing resort to force had evolved at least somewhat since 1945, and more evolution was possible. One legal scholar said law did not develop only by 'interpretation of the words', you must also 'look at the practice of the majority of states', and law can evolve for many other reasons, from 'complete cock up', to 'policy activism' including on issues such as the 'Responsibility to Protect'.[199] A practitioner described the Bethlehem Principles as an example of how scholarly writing shapes law, describing the article as 'a proxy of what the UK thinks' which may shape practice, but may also lead to 'mistakes' leading to 'push back', and fears that change had 'gone too far'.[200] A former government lawyer warned against 'a very originalist approach to treaty interpretation' as the United States had adopted with human rights law, since if a treaty has been reinterpreted and applied in a certain way by some states and the organisation established by the treaty or by courts, and other states are quiet, 'then things change'.[201] Furthermore, articles 2(4) and 51 of the UN Charter are clearly governed by customary international law, since they do not establish 'all the requirements of self-defence', while humanitarian intervention could be 'an emerging exception'.[202] Another former government lawyer observed that, although the UN Charter had not changed, the law had, since '[t]he Charter is flexible', and treaties may be interpreted 'in light of new facts'.[203] For example self-defence against non-state actors may not have been foreseen in 1945, but Article 51 does not preclude it, most states now regard it as lawful, and even humanitarian intervention could through custom 'be superimposed on the Charter, if there is general acceptance'.[204]

Openness to change was tempered by strong support for clear *opinio juris* and state practice, attracting the second highest level of support in the survey. Out of the participants, 91 per cent believed that for new rules of customary international law to crystallise, clear expressions of *opinio juris* or state practice were needed usually (48 per cent), sometimes (26 per cent) or always

198 The original survey asked about unanimity, but feedback showed no participants thought customary change required unanimity and they interpreted the answer not as unanimity but as overwhelming majority; so this question was changed and answers interpreted in that light.

199 Participant 27.

200 Participant 18.

201 Participant 19.

202 Participant 19.

203 Participant 21.

204 Participant 21.

(17 per cent). Only 8 per cent of participants thought such clarity was not usually required (4 per cent) or was never required (4 per cent). The interviews showed this was a key reason for disagreement about whether humanitarian intervention or self-defence against non-state actors were lawful justifications for resort to force.[205] One scholar, sympathetic to such justifications, argued that the way the *jus ad bellum* 'is structured makes evolution very difficult'.[206] The UN Charter clearly articulates a right of self-defence, and the requirements of that right may thus evolve to encompass self-defence against non-state actors; but the charter allowed no such obvious scope for the emergence of a humanitarian intervention norm, which thus required much clearer evidence.[207] Another scholar argued it was particularly difficult for new *jus ad bellum* exceptions to evolve, because they needed to overcome the system's underlying *jus cogens* prohibition, while stronger human rights or international humanitarian law protections evolve more readily because they align with the legal system's underlying principle protecting individuals.[208]

The survey showed moderate variation of opinion on whether only the UNSC may authorise force when the law is unclear. Forty-five per cent thought that, while the UNSC is supreme, states and other bodies often have discretion (35 per cent) or have wide discretion (10 per cent) to decide whether force is lawful then the law is unclear. Twenty-five per cent thought the UNSC is supreme but states and other bodies sometimes have discretion. Thirty per cent thought the UNSC is usually (25 per cent) or always (5 per cent) the only body permitted to authorise force when the law is unclear. The interviews clearly underlined the primacy of the UNSC, alongside strong arguments for some discretion for states to decide whether to use force when the UNSC does not decide and the law was unclear or contested, such as for humanitarian intervention.[209] One practising international lawyer said 'the UN is supreme' but often 'the UNSC says nothing because they're deadlocked', and where it 'doesn't act or is unclear either deliberately or not, then others have some scope'.[210]

These observations of moderation might indicate that the UK community of international lawyers, from whom this sample was drawn, is relatively pragmatic and averse to theoretical disputes.[211] And in fact most participants

205 Participant 15.
206 Participant 17.
207 Participant 17.
208 Participant 3.
209 E.g. participants 13, 14, 23.
210 Participant 8.
211 Participants 25, 21.

gave no answer when asked what theories of law they thought were accurate or useful in applying the law. Many interviewees said international lawyers were not particularly theoretical.[212] One practising international lawyer said 'insofar as I have any general view of law' it is 'rather pragmatic and instrumentalist'.[213] Some admitted they knew little about legal theories.[214] One former government lawyer did 'not think much of' theories such as realism or naturalism, which were 'very abstract' and 'offer little guidance on how to provide legal advice', arguing that few UK lawyers thought about legal theory, unlike 'lawyers from the continent'.[215] Another former government lawyer thought German lawyers answering this question 'might follow Kelsen and look for a grundnorm', and adopt a 'very positivist' and 'rules based' approach, while lawyers from different traditions would take other things into account.[216] A scholar referred to their 'doctrinal upbringing' in Germany as encouraging them to work within the existing canons of interpretation.[217] Another scholar said they had observed in their work divisions across 'national and regional boundaries', with some German and Swiss scholars taking 'a more value-based approach' and so arguing for the lawfulness of humanitarian intervention.[218]

However, the third overall observation suggested real differences of theoretical approach even within this pragmatic, largely Anglo-Saxon group. Some participants said all lawyers inevitably operationalise a theory of law, which can vary according to national legal cultures.[219] And this sample did show a division between lawyers who took a more formalist approach to legal interpretation, and those favouring a more dynamist approach. There was greatest variation around one of the most crucial principles dividing the groups: the importance of the plain meaning of legal texts against wider purposes. Forty-three per cent thought the plain meaning of the text must prevail usually (26 per cent) or always (17 per cent) when interpreting the law. But 35 per cent favoured scope to rely on wider purposes to interpret the law usually (22 per cent) or almost always (13 per cent). And 22 per cent thought sometimes the plain meaning of the text and sometimes wider purposes could prevail. One practising international lawyer noted that the letter co-signed by sixteen UK international lawyers in 2003 opposing the Iraq intervention

212 Participants 5, 6, 23, 26.
213 Participant 13.
214 Participants 28, 29.
215 Participant 21.
216 Participant 25.
217 Participant 30.
218 Participant 4.
219 Participant 4.

revealed fundamental methodological differences. Some signatories had 'wanted it to be much more robust' and detailed in refuting the government's justification for force, but the signatories were unable to agree such a detailed text, and had to keep the letter simple.[220]

In interviews, all participants emphasised the need to start with the ordinary meaning of the words of the UN Charter when assessing the legality of force. One scholar argued the charter text was 'very clear', and needed no 'textual magic', it 'just says what it says' and 'you have to go through contortions' to 'make it say something else'.[221] But several participants said it was essential to go beyond the text in hard cases.[222] Some said in the charter 'you don't always know what the plain meaning of the text is, or the plain meaning doesn't deal with a particular situation', such as anticipatory self-defence or self-defence against non-state actors.[223] Several pointed out the VCLT itself advises interpreting treaties according to the plain meaning of the text in light of context, object and purposes, and subsequent practice.[224] Other texts such as UNGA resolutions and ICJ judgments, which potentially addressed these issues, were contested and not clearly legally binding.[225] One practising international lawyer argued treaties and custom are 'relatively modest attempts to lay down a few basic rules', not 'a comprehensive moral code', so they obviously 'leave a lot unresolved'.[226]

Another practitioner argued there was 'room for logical extensions' in interpreting law, albeit more limited in international law than common law.[227] Lawyers could draw on materials and principles from different areas of law by analogy where the law itself was unclear, particularly if in other areas of law 'it seems blindingly obvious that this is what we always say is right in this context'.[228] A former government lawyer said 'there's a spectrum': some were 'playing fast and loose with the law', but a better distinction was between those 'who are rigid and only accept black letter law', and 'those who consider that the practice of states has to be taken into account'.[229] They said they 'would not trust the lawyer' who confidently advised 'there is a right to humanitarian

220 Participant 13.
221 Participant 24.
222 Participants 31, 25, 20, 22, 12, 13, 19, 21.
223 Participants 25, 20.
224 Participants 22, 12, 13, 19, 21.
225 Participant 25.
226 Participant 13.
227 Participant 10.
228 Participant 10.
229 Participant 19.

intervention', since this was 'too bald a statement' which was 'not supported by the settled authorities'.[230]

The survey showed moderate variation of opinion about whether political statements could demonstrate *opinio juris* with or without explicitly legal statements. Thirty per cent of participants thought political statements could demonstrate *opinio juris* either alongside legal statements (26 per cent) or on their own (4 per cent). Twenty-six per cent thought official legal statements must be available to demonstrate *opinio juris* usually (17 per cent) or always (9 per cent). Forty-three per cent of participants thought political statements could sometimes demonstrate *opinio juris* with or without legal statements.

In interviews, the differences were evident. Several participants insisted that evidence of *opinio juris* should rely on explicitly legal statements. A former government lawyer preferred documents 'drafted with a legal provision in mind, such as a letter to the Security Council'.[231] The weight of such statements depends 'on the care with which it's been drafted, the details, the reasoning, also the speaker', for example an attorney general's statement would be 'more significant' than statements by other non-legal officials.[232] They warned that 'what lawyers advise and what governments say is not always the same', and there have been 'situations where legal advisers to governments' have advised an act 'is completely unlawful' without affecting their government's actions.[233] A scholar warned not to necessarily 'ascribe the status of *opinio juris*' to 'clearly political or policy statements', since '[m]any politicians talk in terms which are not necessarily technically legal'.[234] Several participants mentioned the potential for confusion if different ministers from the same government offered different media justifications for an action. It might be impossible to identify a state's *opinio juris* on a particularly controversial question, so it was best to 'stick to a document which has been published and clearly refers to the law'.[235] All participants who expressed a view regarded off-the-cuff media comments as poor evidence of *opinio juris*.[236]

However, many participants said it was important to accept at least some politicians' statements as evidence of *opinio juris*.[237] Of particular legal

230 Participant 19.
231 Participant 25.
232 Participant 25.
233 Participant 25.
234 Participant 5.
235 Participant 2.
236 Participant 25.
237 Participants 25, 10, 13, 6.

significance were well prepared, formal statements such as, 'set piece speeches by Prime Minister and Foreign Secretary which laid out very clearly what the government's position was', for example on drone strikes in Syria.[238] One practitioner said statements from prime ministers or attorneys general were of equal weight, since both were senior representatives of the state.[239] Some were willing to accept such well-prepared statements as evidence of *opinio juris* even if they did not explicitly express a legal opinion, if other statements did make a clear link to law.[240] However, one former government lawyer said both Tony Blair's Chicago and Sedgewick constituency speeches were not informed by formal government legal advice, yet were important expressions of *opinio juris*; after those speeches government legal advisers had asked to provide legal advice on future similar speeches.[241] One practitioner downplayed the distinction between political and legal statements, saying *opinio juris* 'doesn't depend on whether one categorises the statement as political or legal', but rather 'whether or not a state behaves or abstains from acting' because it 'regards itself as being under a legal obligation'.[242] That practitioner argued international courts had been too willing to declare custom purely based on statements without action.[243] One legal scholar contrasted *opinio juris*, which was akin to 'discourse analysis', and state practice, which was in contrast 'about brute facts'.[244]

Some participants argued *opinio juris* needed to reflect the views of 'specially affected states'.[245] A former government lawyer argued rules cannot 'arise by majority if it's the minority who are specially affected', as for example non-nuclear weapons states cannot make *erga omnes* law about nuclear weapons without states that possess nuclear weapons agreeing.[246] Another former government lawyer argued many states 'not involved in armed conflict can afford to be black letter positivists', since they fear attack more than they wish to use force, yet restrictive rules were unlikely to be effective if states likely to use force did not also agree.[247]

238 Participant 19.
239 Participant 10.
240 E.g. Participant 8.
241 Participant 21.
242 Participant 22.
243 Participant 22.
244 Participant 24.
245 Participants 20, 25.
246 Participant 25.
247 Participant 20.

Conclusions

To seek to assess if any relationship could be observed between these international lawyers' opinions on the restrictiveness of the *jus ad bellum* and their preferred legal interpretive techniques, responses to the survey were analysed as follows. The lawyers' answers to each survey question were given scores between zero and 100. For the questions about the five 'hard cases' of resort to force, the most 'restrictivist' answers scored zero while the most 'expansionist' answers scored 100. For the questions about principles of legal interpretation, the most 'formalist' answers scored zero, while the most 'dynamist' answers scored 100. Scores for participants' answers to both sets of questions were then averaged to give overall 'hard cases' and 'legal interpretation' scores. So a 'hard cases' score of zero was the most restrictive approach to the *jus ad bellum*, regarding all hard cases as clearly unlawful, while 100 was most expansionist, viewing all hard cases as clearly lawful. 'Legal interpretation' scores of zero were the most 'formalist' and 100 were the most 'dynamist'.

Using these averaged 'hard cases' and 'legal interpretation' scores, the participants were plotted on the scatterplot graph in Figure 4.6 with 'restrictive-expansive' on the X axis, and 'textual-purposive' on the Y axis, and a correlation coefficient for the two sets of values was then calculated using IBM SPSS (Statistical Package for the Social Sciences). A correlation is defined as 'an interdependence of two or more variable quantities such that a change in the value of one is associated with a change in the value or the expectation of the others'.[248] A 'correlation coefficient' is defined as 'a number between −1 and 1 calculated so as to represent the linear interdependence of two variables or two sets of data'.[249] A correlation coefficient of 1 would indicate a perfect linear correlation between the two sets of data – participants' scores for the expansiveness of the *jus ad bellum* would vary (increase or decrease) by the identical proportion to their scores for dynamism in interpretive techniques. A coefficient of 0 would indicate no correlation – there was no such relationship between the participants' scores for each test.[250]

The analysis also identified whether a correlation is statistically significant, which occurs if the correlation's '2-tailed statistical significance' is less than 0.05 – implying a probability of only 5 in 100 'that the results could have arisen by chance (that is, due to sampling error)'.[251] For sample sizes of less than

248 'Correlation, n.' OED Online. Oxford University Press. www.oed.com/view/Entry/41934?redirectedFrom=correlation (accessed 9 November 2021).

249 Ibid.

250 Bryman and Teevan, *Social Research Methods*, 267.

251 Ibid., 274.

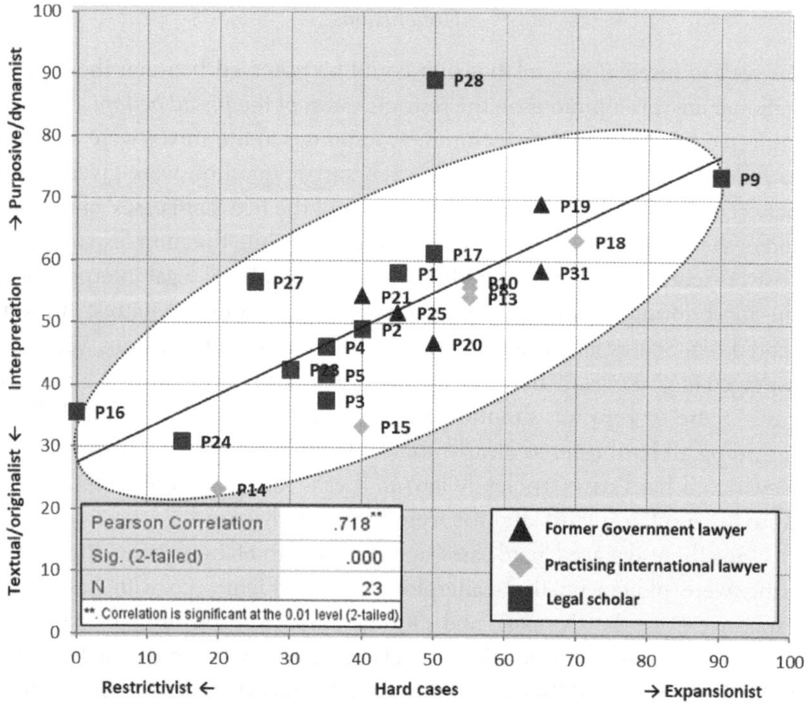

FIGURE 4.6 Correlating views on hard cases and legal interpretation

twenty-five, such as in this research, the statistical significance test assumes independent observations (i.e. that the participants did not influence each other). This is plausible, as I approached participants separately, and found no evidence that they communicated with each other about their participation in this study. For such sample sizes, the test also assumes both variables follow a bivariate normal distribution in the wider population – a greater assumption, since I am not aware of comparable data on the distribution of opinions on these questions across international lawyers in the United Kingdom or elsewhere.

This analysis produces the fourth, and concluding overall observation from this part of the research: a strong correlation of 0.718 between lawyers' legal interpretation techniques and their attitudes to lawfulness of force. In the social sciences, 0.718 is a strong correlation; the correlation is statistically significant at the 0.01 level, meaning there is 'a risk of only 1 in 100 that the results could have arisen by chance (that is, due to sampling error)'.[252] In other

[252] Ibid., 274.

words, for this sample of UK-based international lawyers, answering these questions about these principles of legal interpretation and these hard cases of resort to force, there was a strong but not perfect correlation suggesting formalist lawyers tended to prefer a restrictive *jus contra bellum*, while dynamist lawyers tended to prefer an expansionist *jus ad bellum*.

Many participants who took both relatively restrictivist and relatively expansionist approaches to the *jus ad bellum* also expected a correlation between lawyers' interpretive techniques and their openness to force.[253] A scholar and a practitioner thought it would be 'difficult to establish the cause and effect', whether lawyers reach a conclusion 'because they are black letter literalist interpreters or whether they adopt black letter literal interpretation' because that produces the conclusion they want.[254] The scholar thought 'the cause is extraneous' – whether the lawyer believed that 'unilateral force was a good or bad thing'.[255]

Yet the interviews also suggested why the correlation was not perfect.[256] Formalism would not always be effective in justifying a restrictivist opinion on resort to force in specific cases; similarly, dynamism would not always yield the best arguments for expansionist opinions in every case. As one scholar put it, all lawyers are 'somehow object' or 'result driven'.[257] Those who favour a wide prohibition 'will be more textualist' when that leads 'to a restrictive result', and less textual 'when looking at the exceptions' and trying to construe them narrowly.[258] A practitioner noted this was true beyond the *jus ad bellum*; in most areas of law, lawyers who want 'certain outcomes resort to certain techniques'.[259]

Formalist, textual arguments support the lawfulness of self-defence against non-state actors, since the text of Article 51 of the UN Charter does not specify that only states can conduct armed attacks triggering the right of self-defence, and the *Caroline* criteria describing the customary right of self-defence originated in a case concerning use of force in self-defence against a non-state actor.[260] One scholar noted they were both a dynamist adherent of the New Haven policy process school of legal interpretation *and* a restrictivist concerning the *jus ad bellum*.[261] Another scholar said the link between interpretive

253 Participants 17, 4.
254 Participants 23, 13.
255 Participant 23.
256 Participants 6, 30.
257 Participant 30.
258 Participant 30.
259 Participant 15.
260 Participants 4, 1, 30; Webster, 'Caroline Case', 530.
261 Participant 27.

techniques and expansionism or restrictivism was 'on a spectrum': 'there are those who are quite restrictive' about the *jus ad bellum*, but have 'looser approaches to *opinio juris*, textualism and treaty interpretation'.[262] In other words, many participants in this research expected imperatives other than preferences and beliefs about interpretive principles to drive lawyers' opinions about hard cases in the *jus ad bellum*.

CONCLUSION

This chapter's analysis of scholarly writings, ICJ cases, surveys and interviews broadly supported the explanation proposed in Chapter 2 of competing interpretive cultures. Lawyers who tended to support a more restrictive *jus contra bellum* tended to display 'formalist' principles of legal interpretation. They were more likely to stick to the letter of the law in assessing hard cases of resort to force, apply stringent tests for *opinio juris* and state practice before accepting new custom, and look to the UNSC to explicitly authorise all force apart from straightforward self-defence. Lawyers with a more expansionist approach tended to display more 'dynamist' interpretive principles. They were more open to applying wider purposes of international law in assessing hard cases of resort to force, more open to change in the law by being less stringent about *opinio juris* and state practice, and more willing to see discretion to authorise resort to force outside the UNSC.

The survey and interviews showed this sample of UK-based international lawyers as a pragmatic, atheoretical group, given to moderation about legal interpretation, quite open to legal change. However, the research also showed even this group dividing between formalists and dynamists. And correlation analysis showed a strong correlation with high statistical significance supporting the argument that more dynamist lawyers tended to be more expansionist about the *jus ad bellum*, while more formalist lawyers tended to be more restrictivist about international law governing resort to force.

All the analyses supported the more general argument of this book that the *jus ad bellum* displays specific indeterminacy and various forms of vagueness. Interpretation of the law displays supervaluationism, as it involves multiple, overlapping but not necessarily coincident interpretive principles. It displays fuzzy logic, as lawyers' approaches to each principle were distributed along a continuum rather than separated into binary categories. It displays 'social supervaluationism', as lawyers clearly disagreed about the interpretive principles. In addition, the lawyers did not form polarised, clearly defined

262 Participant 4.

interpretive cultures. Instead, lawyers' views about legal interpretation were distributed on a continuum between the two interpretive cultures, as were their views on the restrictiveness of the *jus ad bellum*.

There were important caveats to these findings. Lawyers did not always display the full set of interpretive preferences grouped under the broad headings of 'formalism' and 'dynamism'. And these preferences did not always align with opinions about the *jus ad bellum* proposed in Chapter 2. Expansionists deployed textual arguments to support a more permissive *jus ad bellum* in Afghanistan, *Congo*, *Wall* and Iraq. The scholarly writings showed the justification for resort to force in Iraq relied on a 'narrow textual reading' of UNSC Resolution 1441 (2002) to argue that it revived UNSC Resolution 687 (1991)'s authorisation to use force in Iraq.[263] Arguments against this justification emphasised the limited purposes implicit in UNSC members' statements, and contextual evidence of the resolution's negotiating history. Scholarly justifications for resort to force in Afghanistan used the textual argument that the words of the UN Charter do not limit the right of self-defence only to attacks by states. Criticisms of this intervention used arguably dynamist arguments to assert developments in international law since 1945 had clarified that the right of self-defence could only be claimed against attacks by states.

In the ICJ cases, less restrictive judges similarly argued that the words of Article 51 of the UN Charter do not limit self-defence only to attacks by states, alongside less protean arguments that the *Nicaragua* case and UNGA declarations did not change the *jus ad bellum* to require states to be involved in attacks triggering self-defence. Restrictivists deployed dynamist arguments to argue for a restrictive *jus contra bellum* in these cases, arguing the law had evolved to include UNGA declarations implying self-defence only justifies force against non-state actors controlled by states. The survey data and interviews also did not show a perfect correlation – some formalists found ways of justifying an expansionist *jus ad bellum*, while some dynamists found ways of justifying a restrictivist *jus contra bellum*. Many expected lawyers to deploy either formalist or dynamist arguments to support the decision that they favoured in any specific hard case engaging the *jus ad bellum*. So if there is any causal link between interpretive principles and willingness to assess force as lawful, it cannot explain all the variation seen – some other imperative must also drive lawyers' decisions about hard cases of resort to force.

Furthermore, this analysis of legal interpretation principles revealed no legal guidance for lawyers to interpret unclear, ambiguous or contradictory

263 Goldsmith, 'Iraq: Resolution 1441', para. 26.

evidence of fact, or to make the forecasts required by the *jus ad bellum*. Nor do these interpretive principles specify the factual thresholds for the *jus ad bellum*'s tests: how much force used in an attack, causing how many casualties and how much damage satisfies the 'scale and effects' test; how brief must be the advance warning of an attack to meet the imminence test; how high must be the probability of force succeeding; how many casualties constitute an overwhelming humanitarian catastrophe. The next chapter will assess how far lawyers use 'extra-legal' reasoning to answer such questions, applying 'some concept of what the law ought to be', relying on 'cognitive activity beyond discovering the frame', not 'positive law' but 'cognition of other norms'.[264] To what extent are legal opinions on the resort to force driven by lawyers' intuitions, assumptions, beliefs and biases about politics, strategy and ethics?

264 Hart, 'Positivism', 608; Kelsen, *Introduction*, 83.

5

Competing Strategic Cultures of Law

They detest war as a very brutal thing, and which, to the reproach of human nature, is more practised by men than by any sort of beasts. They, in opposition to the sentiments of almost all other nations, think that there is nothing more inglorious than that glory that is gained by war.

Thomas More, *Utopia*[1]

What sit we then projecting Peace and War?
War hath determined us, and foiled with loss
Irreparable; terms of peace yet none
Vouchsafed or sought; for what peace will be given
To us enslaved, but custody severe,
And stripes, and arbitrary punishment
Inflicted?

John Milton, *Paradise Lost*[2]

INTRODUCTION

This chapter recounts empirical research exploring to what extent uncertainty and disagreement about the law governing resort to force is associated with disagreements about politico-strategic and ethical opinions about military crises. The chapter considers how, as Kelsen put it, when law functions as 'a frame' identifying 'a number of decisions' and not 'a single correct result', there may be 'room for cognitive activity beyond discovering the frame', not 'positive law' but 'cognition of other norms'.[3] Or, as Hart described, when

[1] More, *Utopia*, 89.
[2] John Milton, *Paradise Lost* (Oxford: Oxford University Press, 2005), II. 329–35.
[3] Kelsen, *Introduction*, 80, 78, 81, 83.

within law's framework 'there jostle too many alternatives', and 'law imposes only limits on our choice', lawyers may inevitably apply 'some concept of what the law ought to be' to reach a conclusion.[4]

The chapter assesses whether and under what conditions the law might be described as only partially autonomous of extra-legal factors, as proposed in Chapter 3: that lawyers hold consistent, mutually reinforcing political, strategic and ethical beliefs and intuitions about conflicts, broadly aligning with competing strategic cultures representing distinct 'modes of thought and action with respect to force'.[5] According to the explanation proposed in Chapter 3, in decision-making about military crises, lawyers within competing strategic cultures are likely to choose different explanations of past events, different conclusions about the likelihood and desirability of future consequences of different policy options, and reach different legal opinions on factually complex cases. Lawyers' implicit theories about how conflicts arise and their consequences are likely to underpin their beliefs about how far the *jus ad bellum* prohibits and permits force more generally too. Thus disagreements between lawyers about these extra-legal intuitions may be consistent with their disagreements about the *jus ad bellum*. And thus Chapter 3 proposed that lawyers with a restrictivist approach to the *jus ad bellum* will conform with a 'pacificist' strategic culture, seeing little political, strategic and ethical justification for force. On the other hand, lawyers with an expansionist approach will align with an 'interventionist' strategic culture, seeing more political, strategic and ethical justifications for force.

Chapter 3 proposed that lawyers within the 'pacificist' strategic culture, when faced with a case where the requirements of the law are contested, tend to choose the interpretation of the law that minimises the potential for future legal uncertainty and abuse, which best protects less powerful states rather than trusting militarily and economically dominant states, and which holds that the prohibition on force is always the most important principle. When assessing different interpretations of complex, incomplete or contradictory factual evidence, and when constructing forecasts about the consequences of using or not using force unilaterally, pacificists tend to proceed on the basis that such force almost always causes more harm than it prevents for the state using force and for the international community. They tend to assume only self-interested states use force unilaterally, and that only a narrow range of interests and ethical values are sufficiently widely shared to guide decisions about unilateral force. And thus, 'pacificist' lawyers who tend to see little

[4] Hart, 'Positivism', 629, 620, 608.
[5] Gray, 'National Style in Strategy', 22.

political, strategic and ethical justification for force in specific cases will also prefer a more restrictivist approach to the *jus ad bellum* in general. In other words, this explanation proposes that lawyers who believe unilateral use of force is almost always politically, strategically and morally unwise in individual cases, will also see strong political, strategic and ethical reasons to support a restrictivist *jus contra bellum* in general.

Chapter 3 also proposed that lawyers aligning with the 'interventionist' strategic culture, when faced with a case where the requirements of the law are contested, will tend to choose the interpretation of the law that best fits with changes in conflict since the adoption of the UN Charter, and which holds that principles such as human rights, preventing genocide, fighting terrorism or countering WMD proliferation can be more important than the prohibition on force. When assessing different interpretations of complex, incomplete or contradictory evidence, and when constructing forecasts about the consequences of using or not using force unilaterally, interventionists tend to proceed on the basis that such force can prevent more harm than it causes for the state using force and the international community. They tend to assume states that use force unilaterally can advance common interests as well as self-interest, and that a wide range of interests and ethical values are often sufficiently widely shared to guide decisions about unilateral force. And thus 'interventionist' lawyers who tend to see more such extra-legal political, strategic and ethical justifications for the unilateral use of force in various specific cases, will also see more extra-legal reasons to support an expansionist approach to the *jus ad bellum* as law in general as well.

This research investigates whether uncertainty about the *jus ad bellum* as a system of prescriptive rules and principles encourages these different groups of lawyers to practise 'strategic behaviour in interpretation', and use the law as a set of argumentative practices to justify or criticise the lawfulness of specific behaviour with arguments which align with their extra-legal beliefs and intuitions.[6] Of course, when states, their legal advisers and other international lawyers advance controversial legal justifications for resort to force, they may not always *believe* those justifications represent the law as it is. Instead, those justifications may be various forms of 'cynical manipulation of legal rules' to advance other politico-strategic goals, or more idealistic attempts to change the law by breaking – or at least bending – it.[7] Even so, this research assesses whether and to what extent such controversial legal arguments – and criticisms of them – whether sincere or not, advance or rely on specific principles of legal interpretation and extra-legal intuitions.

6 Kennedy, *Legal Reasoning*, 159; Koskenniemi, *From Apology to Utopia*, 67–9.
7 Kennedy, *Legal Reasoning*, 159; Gray, *International Law*, 7.

This chapter summarises what evidence may be inferred for these strategic cultures in the three kinds of empirical research recounted in Chapter 4. First this chapter reports the results of systematic textual analysis of scholarly writings and UK government statements concerning interventions in Kosovo, Afghanistan and Iraq, assessing how those texts display different politico-strategic and ethical assumptions and presuppositions. Then the chapter reports the results of similar systematic textual analysis of ICJ opinions on *Nicaragua* (1986), *Wall* (2004) and *Congo* (2005). Finally, the chapter summarises the findings of a survey and interviews with thirty-one UK-based international lawyers, examining how their opinions about the politico-strategic and ethical dimensions of force correlate with their views on the lawfulness of force as reported in Chapter 2.

Using a similar approach to the textual analysis reported in Chapter 4, the analyses of ICJ judgments and scholarly writings reported in this chapter identified phrases in the texts that appeared to express extra-legal assumptions and presuppositions, including those proposed in Chapter 3 as constituting the 'pacificist' and 'interventionist' strategic cultures. Sometimes the texts explicitly made moral, political or strategic statements, at other times politico-strategic or ethical reasoning could be inferred from the texts' description of the likely factual consequences of different courses of action, or the motivations and other qualities of the actors involved in the military crisis being considered. The judges and scholars were ranked along a continuum between the extreme positions for each extra-legal principle observed in their writings, and these positions represented visually on linear spectra. For example, the first spectrum in Figure 5.1 illustrates views on whether unilateral force may be necessary to safeguard human rights. Lawyers at one pole of the spectrum believe unilateral force may sometimes be necessary to safeguard human rights, those at the other pole believe unilateral force is never necessary to safeguard human rights. Between those poles are lawyers expressing views of varying intensity about the need to use force unilaterally to safeguard human rights.

As described in Chapter 3, this book views strategy as concerned with the ways and means a state uses to pursue its national interests. This aligns with Freedman's conception of strategy as 'bargaining and persuasion', 'threats and pressure, psychological as well as physical', 'words as well as deeds' and 'the central political art', 'the art of creating power'.[8] This definition accommodates debate – about what constitutes national interests, what actions are more or less likely to enhance those interests, about how and if interests are affected by ideas and relationships or purely by material capabilities. This book views the ethics of

[8] Freedman, *Strategy*, xii.

force as concerned with identifying when force might be considered right behaviour, when it might help 'enable us to live together well in communities and so flourish as human beings'.[9] The analysis investigates tensions between different conceptions of ethics and forms of ethical reasoning – whether ethical principles are subjective and personal or universal and shared, whether ethical reasoning should privilege deontological rules prescribing right behaviour, eudaemonic 'virtues' concerning an actor's internal motives and other qualities, or teleological calculations about the consequences of actions.[10] These tensions also reflect competing notions of legitimacy, whether the creation and application of the law accords with processes acceptable to a political community and with substantive moral and political rationales.[11]

In this chapter I demonstrate that there does seem to be a correlation between these lawyers' 'extra-legal', politico-strategic and ethical views about force and their views on the *jus ad bellum*, and that their specific areas of extra-legal disagreement broadly align with those proposed in Chapter 3. Lawyers who favour a more restrictivist *jus contra bellum* tend to express views consistent with a 'pacificist' strategic culture, seeing few politico-strategic and ethical justifications for force. Those applying a more expansionist approach tend to express an 'interventionist' strategic culture, seeing more politico-strategic and ethical justifications for force. Such strategic and ethical disagreements are particularly evident in factual assessments and forecasts of consequences in the scholarly writings and judgments analysed. But, as with the findings of Chapter 4, there are caveats, which together suggest that, in hard cases, lawyers' assessments of the legality of force are partially but not wholly shaped by their extra-legal assumptions, intuitions and biases about the resort to force in general and in the specific case they are considering.

LEGAL SCHOLARS AND EXTRA-LEGAL REASONING: KOSOVO, AFGHANISTAN AND IRAQ

Introduction

This section summarises textual analysis of extra-legal intuitions expressed in the scholarly writings and UK legal statements examined in Chapter 4, considering the legality of military interventions in Kosovo, Afghanistan and

9 Fisher, *Morality and War*, 60.

10 Fisher, *Morality and War*, 5–6; Brian Orend, *The Morality of War* (Peterborough, Ontario: Broadview Press, 2006), 49, 61.

11 Falk, 'Introduction', 9.

Iraq. As this section will show, implicit and sometimes explicit in all the texts are distinct, varying politico-strategic and ethical assumptions about the conflicts concerned, illustrated in Figure 5.1. These extra-legal assessment broadly mirror the authors' legal assessments of those conflicts.

Narrative

What interests and values justify force? The first sets of strategic disagreements concerned *what issues count as foreign policy interests that make strategic sense to defend using force*. Closely linked are ethical disagreements around *what values are sufficiently universal to justify force*, and whether *force is always the greatest ethical wrong*. The United Kingdom stated that its objectives in Kosovo were 'to avert an impending humanitarian catastrophe' by disrupting Yugoslav forces' attacks on Kosovar Albanians and 'their ability to conduct such repression in future'.[12] The United Kingdom further observed that NATO's nineteen member states and the European Union supported the action.[13] Greenwood argued mass killings were legitimately a 'matter of international concern', and it would contradict international law's basic principles to stop states from preventing 'something as terrible as the Holocaust'.[14] Lowe asserted there was a 'moral justification for unilateral intervention' to stop humanitarian catastrophe if 'some exceptional factor' justified it.[15] Chinkin agreed such interventions could be 'morally justified', but noted that action in Kosovo did not achieve its goals 'in the short term'.[16] Gray doubted human rights were widely accepted as justifying force, and noted a Non-Aligned Movement statement at that time opposing unilateral humanitarian intervention.[17] Brownlie and Apperley conceded no justification for such intervention even 'as a matter of morality'.[18]

All the assessments of Afghanistan at least implicitly accepted that *states have an interest in countering terrorism*, which *is a value sufficiently widely shared to justify force*, while expressing different factual assumptions about *whether force is effective for these purposes*. Greenwood and Moir agreed with the United Kingdom that the United States and its allies had strategic justification to use force in 'individual and collective self-defence, recognized in Article 51', after

12 Robertson, 'Kosovo'.
13 Robertson, 'Kosovo'.
14 Greenwood, 'NATO Intervention in Kosovo', 926, 929, 930.
15 Lowe, 'Kosovo Crisis', 940.
16 Chinkin, 'Legality of NATO's Action', 918, 920, 922, 923.
17 Gray, *International Law*, 48, 52.
18 Brownlie and Apperley, 'Kosovo Crisis Inquiry', 909, 905.

the 11 September terrorist attacks, 'to avert the continuing threat of attacks', given evidence of further attack planning and the Taleban's refusal to hand over Al-Qaeda.[19] Although Moir argued the coalition should not have targeted the Taleban initially, he accepted the Taleban would probably have resisted and thus become legitimate targets.[20] However, Chinkin and Gray assessed the operation had not ended terrorism and was unlikely to do so.[21]

The assessments of Iraq diverged sharply in their views about *whether states have an interest in using force unilaterally to enforce UNSC resolutions* prohibiting WMDs, *whether these values are sufficiently widely shared to justify force*, and *whether such force is effective*. These disagreements often hinged on factual assessments of whether Iraq had a WMD programme posing a threat justifying force. Greenwood and the United Kingdom clearly saw such force as in states' interests, effective, and reflecting widely shared values, referring to the unanimous adoption of UNSC Resolution 1441 (2002) declaring Iraq in breach of its obligations.[22] They argued Iraq posed a threat since chief UN inspector Blix 'found Iraq's cooperation on matters of substance wanting', Iraq never took 'the steps required of it by the Council', and when UNSC Resolution 1441 (2002) was passed Iraq was 'in material breach' of its ceasefire obligations.[23] Lowe saw circumstances in which unilateral force may be strategically necessary, and agreed that lawyers had a 'duty' to 'ensure' a 'gap does not open up' so that 'law becomes detached from its roots in common morality'.[24] He agreed Iraq's behaviour was 'in breach of its international obligations' and 'prejudicial to international peace and security'.[25] However, unlike with Kosovo, Lowe argued the security and moral imperatives in Iraq in 2003 did not 'warrant overriding the Charter limitations on the use of force'.[26] Myjer and White, Brownlie and Gray showed no sign of accepting strategic or ethical justifications for such unilateral force, Brownlie noting that Kuwait and Iraq's other neighbours did not feel sufficiently threatened to support the intervention by late 2002.[27] These scholars

19 Greenwood, 'War against Terrorism', 308; Moir, *Reappraising the Resort to Force*, 52–4, 58–61; UN Security Council, Document S/2001/947.

20 Moir, *Reappraising the Resort to Force*, 59.

21 Gray, *International Law*, 201, 203; Chinkin, 'Rethinking Legality/Legitimacy', 227–8.

22 Greenwood, 'War against Terrorism', 31, 34; Goldsmith, 'Use of Force against Iraq'; Goldsmith, 'Iraq: Resolution 1441', paras. 10–11.

23 Greenwood, 'War against Terrorism', 31, 34; Goldsmith, 'Use of Force against Iraq'; Goldsmith, 'Iraq: Resolution 1441', para. 10.

24 Lowe, 'Iraq Crisis', 867, 871.

25 Ibid., 864.

26 Ibid., 868.

27 Gray, *International Law*, 364, 221; Brownlie, 'Memorandum', Ev22; White and Myjer, 'Editorial', 5.

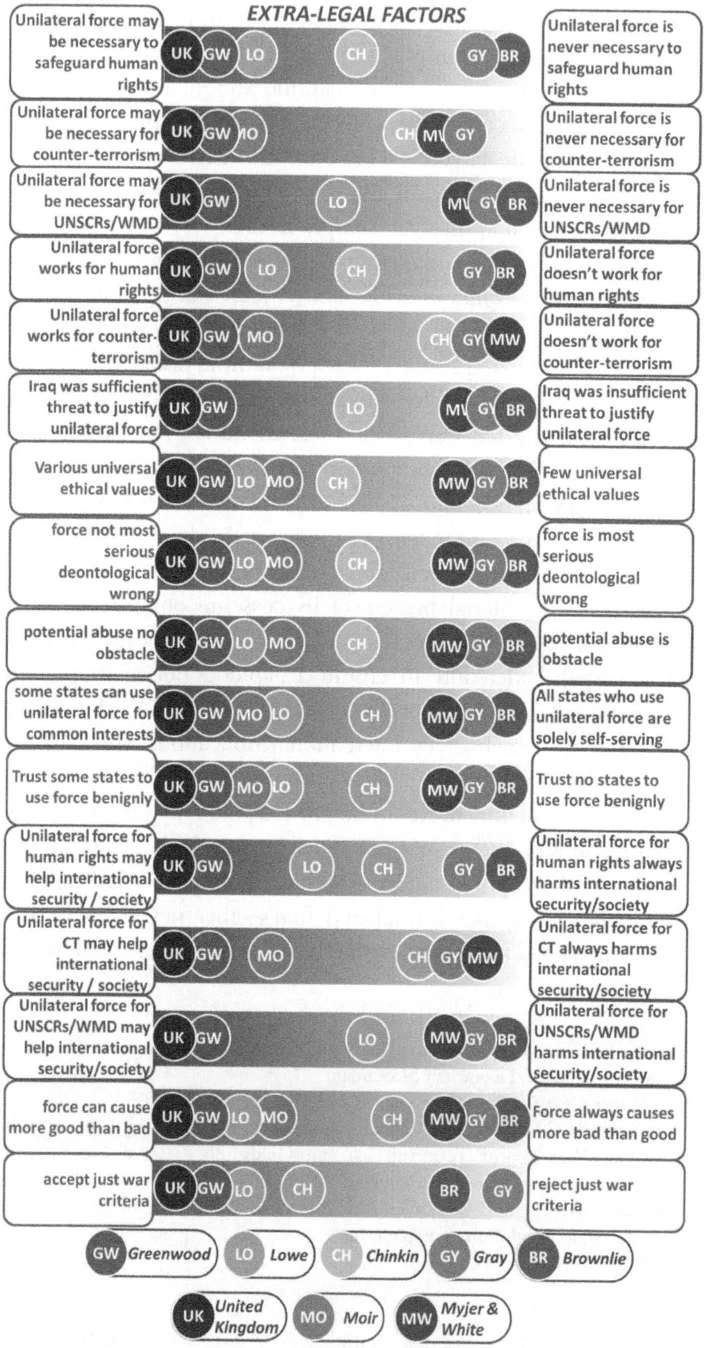

FIGURE 5.1 Competing methods of strategic and ethical evaluation

argued the US/UK allegations about Iraq's WMD 'had not been substantiated', the US/UK evidence was 'unconvincing' when the intervention began and, as Gray observed, disproven shortly after.[28]

Controversy, uncertainty, potential for abuse. The United Kingdom, Greenwood, Lowe and Moir accepted that *controversy* and *uncertainty* and thus implicitly *potential for abuse* (an assessment of future outcomes) should not necessarily prevent the use of legal justifications for force.[29] Greenwood observed that self-defence persists despite frequent abuse.[30] Lowe preferred 'to define a narrow principle' of humanitarian intervention and risk abuse than do nothing when confronted with atrocities, or act without defining a principle and encourage *greater* abuse.[31] Moir endorsed self-defence against imminent attack despite the difficulties in evaluating its proportionality.[32] Chinkin expressed more concern about potential abuse, arguing unilateral action weakened the prohibition against force and the UN Charter's authority.[33]

Gray, Brownlie and Apperley saw potential abuse as an argument against humanitarian intervention.[34] Myjer and White criticised the United States and the UNSC for not excluding 'any possible doubt' that the US-led action in Afghanistan was UNSC-endorsed self-defence, even finding the UNSC authorisation for the NATO-led International Security Assistance Force (ISAF) too 'opaque'.[35] On Iraq, Brownlie warned that the revival argument was 'pseudo-legality which could be used on almost any occasion' by powerful states.[36] Gray argued it was 'dangerous', 'risks undermining the authority of the United Nations' and made the UNSC 'unwilling to pass resolutions under Chapter VII condemning state action' to avoid implying authorisation for future unilateral force.[37] Lowe was concerned that the 'revival' doctrine set no clear 'limits upon the [UNSC's] 1991 authorisation to States'.[38]

Can states be trusted to use unilateral force? Further disagreements concerned strategic and ethical assessments of *whether states can be trusted to use force for legitimate, virtuous and/or community ends and not purely for*

28 Gray, *International Law*, 364, 221; Brownlie, 'Memorandum', Ev22; White and Myjer, 'Editorial', 5.
29 Goldsmith, 'Iraq: Resolution 1441'.
30 Greenwood, 'NATO Intervention in Kosovo', 934.
31 Lowe, 'Kosovo Crisis', 939.
32 Moir, *Reappraising the Resort to Force*, 57.
33 Chinkin, 'Rethinking Legality/Legitimacy', 925.
34 Gray, *International Law*, 34, 38; Brownlie and Apperley, 'Kosovo Crisis Inquiry', 905.
35 Myjer and White, 'Twin Towers Attack', 10–14.
36 Brownlie, 'Memorandum', Ev27.
37 Gray, *International Law*, 366.
38 Lowe, 'Iraq Crisis', 866.

self-interest without UNSC authorisation, or if all states are untrustworthy. The United Kingdom, Greenwood and Lowe clearly accepted that NATO's goals in Kosovo were confined to ending the humanitarian catastrophe and did not include 'defeating the Yugoslav army'.[39] Lowe argued the UNSC must determine the existence of a crisis and establish the purposes of such interventions, to ensure they are 'on behalf of the international community'.[40] Chinkin however questioned whether NATO pursued only 'humanitarian objectives' in Kosovo.[41] Gray argued humanitarian ends are 'almost always mixed with other, less laudable motives'.[42] Brownlie and Apperley more directly claimed NATO in reality pursued a 'geopolitical and collateral agenda' to depose the Yugoslav government, which was 'impossible to reconcile' with 'humanitarian intervention'.[43]

With Afghanistan, Greenwood and Moir accepted the United Kingdom's assertion that it and the United States believed they faced future attacks, and that most other countries agreed with that assessment.[44] The United Kingdom stressed its benign motives, 'proud to be a multicultural, multiracial country', whose 'operations are not directed against the Afghan population, or against Islam'.[45] Chinkin, Gray, Myjer and White expressed clear discomfort that the UNSC had neither declared 11 September 2001 an armed attack nor controlled the intervention.[46] Gray described US efforts to involve other states as a cynical 'quest for legitimacy' which rejected 'the constraints of acting through NATO or the UN'.[47] Chinkin described the action as 'reminiscent of colonial "civilizing" missions', that the coalition had hypocritically tolerated previous abuses in Afghanistan, and ongoing abuses in Pakistan and Saudi Arabia, and described the UNGA's endorsement of the operation as 'an outstanding feat of misrepresentation'.[48] Myjer and White accused the UNSC of neglecting 'its primary duty to restore and maintain peace and security'.[49]

39 Greenwood, 'NATO Intervention in Kosovo', 928–30; Lowe, 'Kosovo Crisis', 941; Robertson, 'Kosovo'.
40 Lowe, 'Kosovo Crisis', 940, 941.
41 Chinkin, 'Rethinking Legality/Legitimacy', 922.
42 Gray, *International Law*, 34.
43 Brownlie and Apperley, 'Kosovo Crisis Inquiry', 887–91, 883, 904, 909, 905.
44 UN Security Council, Document S/2001/947.
45 Ibid.
46 Chinkin, 'Rethinking Legality/Legitimacy', 227; Myjer and White, 'Twin Towers Attack', 13; Gray, *International Law*, 206.
47 Gray, *International Law*, 206.
48 Chinkin, 'Rethinking Legality/Legitimacy', 227.
49 Myjer and White, 'Twin Towers Attack', 16.

On Iraq, Greenwood accepted the United Kingdom's assertion that it used force to advance the common interests of enforcing UNSC Resolution 687 (1991) and disarming Iraq, rather than for economic gain as others claimed.[50] Lowe sympathised with UK/US security concerns, but worried whether another 'elusive motive' including 'oil' might also be in play, condemned the 'conflation of moral and political argument' in the UK/US justifications, and argued that 'rooting international law in the exigiencies of national political objectives' is 'one of the defining characteristics of imperialism'.[51] Myjer and White condemned 'spurious claims' from the United Kingdom and United States of 'acting under UN authority', and their duplicity in telling the UNSC there was 'no automaticity' in UNSC Resolution 1441 (2002), yet afterwards 'repeatedly stating' another resolution was not needed before using force.[52] Gray also noted UK/US acceptance of 'no automaticity', observed that Iraqi cooperation had improved when the United States and United Kingdom claimed it remained in breach of the resolution, and emphasised claims that the United States and United Kingdom's real intention was 'regime change in a sovereign state contrary to the UN Charter'.[53] Brownlie claimed the action's 'long-term objectives' were 'not clearly linked, for my money, to a simple restoration of the cease-fire regime', and warned that even action with UNSC authorisation must not include 'regime change' or 'support of ethnic minorities or indigenous groups'.[54]

Does force cause more harm and international discord than it prevents? The texts displayed further extra-legal disagreements about whether using force unilaterally beyond unambiguous self-defence *harms international peace and security and international relations*, and *generates more good than bad consequences* compared to non-forceful measures – competing counter-factual assessments or forecasts of the consequences of using force compared with not using force. The United Kingdom argued the military action in Kosovo was accepted by many countries, that even discussions with Russia 'were perfectly friendly', and that military action would alleviate humanitarian suffering.[55] Greenwood cited successful unilateral humanitarian interventions in the 1990s.[56] He argued the Kosovo intervention had stopped more harm than it caused, as Yugoslav atrocities during the operation had been pre-planned, and

50 Greenwood, 'Pre-emptive Use of Force', 31–2, 36.
51 Lowe, 'Iraq Crisis', 861, 863.
52 White and Myjer, 'Editorial', 1, 2.
53 Gray, *International Law*, 364.
54 Brownlie, 'Memorandum', Ev23, Ev28.
55 Robertson, 'Kosovo'.
56 Greenwood, 'NATO Intervention in Kosovo', 930.

asserted that the risk of setting harmful precedents was 'not sufficient' to prevent interventions when they were the only option to stop atrocities.[57] Lowe acknowledged some interventions may cause harmful disruptions to international relations, so he proposed requiring UNSC assessment before such interventions and multilateral participation in them.[58] He also recommended states 'stand aside' until violence reaches a scale justifying 'exceptional rights of intervention' overriding sovereignty.[59]

Chinkin supported 'proportionate' force to stop extreme abuses, implying such action can be compatible with international peace and security, but worried about the future consequences of NATO's action 'leading international law into new areas', and 'weakens the prohibition on the use of force and the authority of the Charter'.[60] Gray argued most states accept 'the risk of inaction' in the face of abuses within another country as 'the price to pay' for the UN security system, and the Kosovo Force (KFOR) did not prevent abuses.[61] Brownlie and Apperley argued NATO killed and injured thousands more civilians, women and children than would have otherwise been harmed, claiming such interventions hamper non-proliferation and make human rights abuses worse than they otherwise would have been.[62]

All the assessments of Afghanistan acknowledged its initial international support and the threat that it targeted. The United Kingdom stressed that Al-Qaeda targeted not only the United States and United Kingdom, but 'other countries around the world', and the action was 'part of a wider international effort'.[63] Greenwood and Moir, while acknowledging 'mistakes in identifying targets', clearly assessed the US-led action as justified given the likely consequences of other options.[64] However, Myjer and White argued the absence of explicit UNSC authorisation suggested some UNSC members had doubts about the intervention.[65] Gray, Chinkin, Myjer and White described growing international disapproval for the intervention, regional tensions it had caused, and potential future harm to international peace and security through the loosening of limitations on self-defence after the operation.[66] They

57 Greenwood, 'NATO Intervention in Kosovo', 931.
58 Lowe, 'Kosovo Crisis', 939.
59 Lowe, 'Kosovo Crisis', 940, 941.
60 Chinkin, 'Legality of NATO's Action', 920, 921, 923, 925.
61 Gray, *International Law*, 369, 343, 48.
62 Brownlie and Apperley, 'Kosovo Crisis Inquiry', 898, 905, 909.
63 UN Security Council, Document S/2001/947.
64 Greenwood, 'War against Terrorism', 315.
65 Myjer and White, 'Twin Towers Attack', 6,10.
66 Gray, *International Law*, 204–7; Chinkin, 'Rethinking Legality/Legitimacy', 228; Myjer and White, 'Twin Towers Attack', 16–17.

emphasised the operation's failure to end terrorism or improve human rights, the large numbers of civilians killed, instability in Afghanistan and increased extremism.[67] They questioned the operation's proportionality, Myjer and White arguing that invading all of Afghanistan was a disproportionate response to an attack on 'a small part' of the United States.[68]

On Iraq, the United Kingdom claimed it had international support, saying the UNSC had determined Iraq was 'in material breach of Resolution 687, because it has not fully complied with its obligations to disarm'.[69] Greenwood accepted that disagreement among UNSC members and other states about the strategic need for the US-led action prevented explicit UNSC resolution authorisation, and prompted outright opposition from several states.[70] But he argued previous actions to enforce UNSC Resolution 687 (1991) showed at least international acquiescence to such action, and 'the only possible interpretation' of UNSC Resolution 1441 (2002)'s preamble was that 'the Council (unanimously) considered that the earlier resolution was still in force'.[71] Lowe warned the intervention showed 'exceptional powers now claimed by governments', posing a 'risk of a serious and indefinite erosion of fundamental legal rights, and indeed erosion of the Rule of Law itself'.[72] He feared such action 'in disregard of settled international procedures and institutions' would make it more likely that 'governments become regarded, in the conduct of foreign affairs, as being above the law'.[73]

Myjer and White predicted that the US/UK approach in Iraq was likely to damage the UNSC, since interpreting resolutions in ways 'contrary to the consensus (which may be an agreement to disagree)' would 'undermine the council as a forum'.[74] Brownlie compared the action unfavourably to peaceful resolution of the Cuban missile crisis, forecasted that it would create a doctrine that only 'strong states within a given region will have the privilege of using', and emphasised the harm it was doing to international relations, as shown by opposition in the UNSC, the Non-Aligned Movement and even, in 2002, Iraq's neighbours, including Kuwait.[75] Gray observed there was serious international disapproval of the intervention for years afterwards, and that in

67 Chinkin, 'Rethinking Legality/Legitimacy', 228.
68 Myjer and White, 'Twin Towers Attack', 7.
69 Goldsmith, 'Use of Force against Iraq', para. 4.
70 Greenwood, 'War against Terrorism', 35.
71 Ibid., 35.
72 Lowe, 'Iraq Crisis', 871.
73 Ibid., 864.
74 White and Myjer, 'Editorial', p.2.
75 Brownlie, 'Memorandum', Ev27, Ev28.

Iraq there was 'civil disorder', 'attacks on occupying forces' and the rise of Al-Qaeda–linked terrorists who previously had not operated in Iraq.[76]

Just War criteria? Finally, the Kosovo assessments explicitly addressed the *Just War doctrine*, and *criteria for humanitarian intervention*. Greenwood, Lowe and Chinkin suggested criteria for such actions.[77] These included *just cause* – large scale loss of life, violations of *jus cogens* rights.[78] Greenwood and Lowe described a form of *right authority* in requiring objective, preferably UNSC verification of the crisis, Lowe adding a requirement for the UNSC to set 'specific policies' guiding the intervention.[79] Greenwood's *last resort, balance of consequences* and *reasonable prospects* criteria included requiring force to be 'the only practicable means' to stop loss of life.[80] Lowe required that states stand aside until 'the scale of violence demands' that sovereignty be overridden exceptionally.[81] Chinkin required the UN be 'unable or unwilling to act' before such an intervention.[82] Her *proportionality* and *last resort* tests required 'overwhelming necessity', domestic authorities no longer willing to end gross human rights violations, and 'all other means' of ending violations to be exhausted.[83] Gray proposed no criteria, instead noting the difficulties in balancing scope, legal basis, the role of the UNSC and the modalities of action when considering such interventions.[84] Brownlie and Apperley's criteria 'as a matter of morality' rejected any unilateral action, requiring 'a short term operation', 'in co-ordination with the lawful Government', using limited military means.[85]

Conclusions

As with the assessment of legal interpretation techniques reported in Chapter 4, this analysis seems to show a relationship between the writers' opinions of the interventions' legality and their underlying politico-strategic and ethical assumptions. The writers did seem to express consistent, mutually reinforcing political, strategic and ethical beliefs, intuitions, factual assessments and

76 Gray, *International Law*, 365, 221.
77 Fisher, *Morality and War*, 66–76.
78 Greenwood, 'NATO Intervention in Kosovo', 931; Lowe, 'Kosovo Crisis', 939; Chinkin, 'Legality of NATO's Action', 921.
79 Lowe, 'Kosovo Crisis', 939.
80 Greenwood, 'NATO Intervention in Kosovo', 931.
81 Lowe, 'Kosovo Crisis', 940, 941, 939.
82 Chinkin, 'Legality of NATO's Action', 922.
83 Ibid., 922, 921.
84 Gray, *International Law*, 50.
85 Brownlie and Apperley, 'Kosovo Crisis Inquiry', 909, 910.

forecasts about these conflicts, broadly aligning with the competing strategic cultures of 'pacifism' and 'interventionism' proposed in Chapter 3. Those writers who argued against the legality of the interventions in Kosovo, Afghanistan and Iraq also tended to express 'pacificist' extra-legal opinions about those conflicts in particular and about conflicts in general. Opposing them, writers who supported the legality of these interventions tended to express 'interventionist' extra-legal opinions about those and other conflicts. In some ways, there was a stronger relationship between these writers' extra-legal views about force and the conclusions they drew about the legality of force than the relationship between their choices of interpretive techniques and the legality of force.

Greenwood's texts and the UK government statements conveyed most obvious politico-strategic and ethical justification for all three interventions and the evidence underpinning them. This mirrored their legal justifications of the interventions, which drew on broadly dynamist techniques, but also relied on textual arguments to justify the intervention in Iraq and to interpret Article 51 of the UN Charter. Moir conveyed substantial politico-strategic rationale and ethical justification for the Afghanistan intervention, while doubting the rationale for targeting the Taleban as well as Al-Qaeda from the start of hostilities, mirroring his legal assessment, which combined dynamist interpretation alongside a textual reading of article 51 of the Charter. Lowe's texts argued that law needed to align with morality, and conveyed significant politico-strategic justifications and positive effects of the Kosovo intervention, while acknowledging important questions about it. He saw decisive politico-strategic and ethical arguments against action in Iraq, while acknowledging some arguments in favour. These assessments mirrored his legal assessments, which use broadly dynamist interpretive techniques to conclude on Kosovo that it was 'desirable' that humanitarian intervention 'be allowed to emerge' as customary law, and that the Iraq intervention was unlawful.[86]

Chinkin's assessment of Kosovo displayed tension between politico-strategic and ethical justifications for the action and the evidence underpinning it, alongside significant concerns, reflecting her ambivalent legal assessment using dynamist and textual interpretation techniques. Gray, Chinkin, Myjer and White acknowledged some strategic justification and evidence for the Afghanistan intervention, but substantial strategic and ethical concerns, mirroring their legal condemnation of the intervention. Gray, Brownlie and Apperley, and Myjer and White accepted almost no politico-strategic or

[86] Lowe, 'Kosovo Crisis', 941.

ethical justification or evidence for the Iraq and Kosovo intervention, much harm flowing from them, and more general politico-strategic and ethical concerns about humanitarian intervention and other unilateral resort to force. This mirrored their legal condemnations of these interventions, which had used largely 'formalist' legal interpretation techniques.

These analyses also suggested a further significant conclusion. The writers' extra-legal opinions about force displayed similar forms of vagueness and disagreement as their legal opinions and choices of legal interpretation. They displayed supervaluationism – their politico-strategic and ethical assessments seemed to depend on multiple evaluation principles, which were overlapping but not entirely co-extensive. These principles seemed to operate according to fuzzy rather than bivalent logic – cases that were clearly ethical or politico-strategically advisable were separated from cases that were clearly unethical or politico-strategically unsound by a fuzzy penumbra of uncertainty rather than sharp dividing line. Together, the principles described paradigms of ethical or politico-strategically advisable examples of resort to force. And the writers' extra-legal opinions displayed social supervaluationism – they were arranged on a spectrum between opposing interventionist and pacificist strategic cultures, rather than forming distinct, clearly separated opposing groups.

THE ICJ AND EXTRA-LEGAL REASONING: *NICARAGUA, WALL* AND *CONGO*

Introduction

This section summarises textual analysis of extra-legal intuitions expressed in the judgments and individual judges' separate or dissenting opinions in the three ICJ cases examined in Chapter 4 – *Nicaragua, Wall* and *Congo*. As this section will show, the analysis suggested similar conclusions (see Figure 5.2) to those suggested by the analyses of scholarly assessments reported in the previous section. Distinct, varying politico-strategic and ethical assumptions and intuitions about the resort to force could be observed in the judgments and opinions, and these extra-legal intuitions were broadly consistent with the restrictivist or expansionist legal conclusions the judges had reached on the cases themselves.

Narrative

What threats justify force? The judges appeared to disagree about the range of *threats that offer strategic or ethical justification for states to use force in self-defence,* and *whether supporting rebels in a neighbouring country, or using force in self-defence to prevent that support is the more serious wrong*. In the *Nicaragua* case, the majority regarded Nicaragua's support to Salvadorean rebels as not a sufficiently serious wrong to justify US force in collective self-defence, yet they regarded US use of force and support to rebels in Nicaragua, supposedly to end Nicaragua's support, as clearly unjustified.[87] Judge Singh clearly sees limits on justifications for self-defence, saying force must not be used to respond to 'minor provocations'.[88] He described the 'principle of non-use of force' in ethical and strategic language, 'the very cornerstone of the human effort to promote peace in a world torn by strife', 'a sanctified absolute rule of law', a 'pivotal fact of inter-state law, life and relations', which 'no reservations could ever suppress', and 'vital for the peace and progress of the international community'.[89] Judges Ruda and Sette-Camara refuted the actions the United States claimed as self-defence as neither necessary nor widely accepted for self-defence.[90]

Dissenting judges emphasised the strategic and normative unacceptability of such restrictions. Jennings described such restrictions as not 'realistic', that 'it seems dangerous' defining self-defence 'unnecessarily strictly', leaving 'a large area where both a forcible response to force is forbidden' and yet the UN military capability 'intended to fill that gap, is absent'.[91] This made it 'difficult to understand' what a state is forbidden from doing to other states 'short of direct attack' by its own forces without expecting lawful use of force in response.[92] Schwebel claimed the majority 'departs from accepted – and desirable – law', emphasising strategic dangers in the majority's ruling that a state facing covert attack must have 'declared itself' victim of an attack before claiming collective self-defence, producing a 'bizarre result' leaving aggressors 'free to act covertly' but not those defending themselves.[93] Schwebel argued that a more reasonable interpretation would permit states to respond covertly against covert aggression, since covert measures cannot be reported to the UNSC without undermining their 'security and effectiveness'.[94]

In *Wall*, the majority's conclusion – that states may lawfully only use force in self-defence against attacks by states – at least implicitly assumed violent

87 *Nicaragua*, Merits, para. 292.
88 *Nicaragua*, Singh, 151.
89 *Nicaragua*, Singh, 153, 156, 157.
90 *Nicaragua*, Ruda, 176; *Nicaragua*, Sette-Camara, 197.
91 *Nicaragua*, Jennings, 543, 544.
92 *Nicaragua*, Jennings, 543.
93 *Nicaragua*, Schwebel, 332, 373.
94 *Nicaragua*, Schwebel, 374.

non-state actors do not pose such a threat that states *need* to use force against them.[95] In his separate opinion, Elaraby explicitly described the 'prohibition of the use of force' in Article 2(4) of the UN Charter as 'the most important principle that emerged in the twentieth century'.[96] Those who dissented expressed opposing strategic opinions – Kooijmans and Buergenthal citing UNSC resolutionss after 11 September 2001 as signalling states' acceptance that attacks from non-state terrorists could justify a forceful response,[97] while Higgins assessed the restriction as 'operationally unworkable'.[98]

In *Congo*, the majority accepted that irregular forces in the DRC had attacked Uganda, and the DRC had been unable to prevent those attacks. But they rejected Uganda's claim of self-defence against those attacks, clearly viewing those attacks as insufficiently serious to override the DRC's sovereignty.[99] Judge Koroma cited the *Nicaragua* decision's 'distinction between cases of armed attack and "other less grave forms" of the use of force' against which force in self-defence was not necessary, such as less significant support to irregular forces.[100] The majority said the territorial integrity of States such as the DRC must be respected, even if they were unable to prevent non-state groups attacking other states from their territory.[101] Koroma described as a 'moral' principle 'the fundamental and customary law principle of *pacta sunt servanda*' underpinning the prohibition on use of force.[102] However, Judge Tomka argued sovereignty 'does not involve only rights but also obligations' including a 'duty of vigilance' on the DRC 'to exert all good efforts in order to prevent its territory from being used to the detriment of Uganda'.[103] Judges Simma, Kooijmans and Kateka argued that in such situations it 'would be *unreasonable* to deny the attacked State the right to self-defence merely because there is no attacker State' (emphasis added).[104] They argued the DRC's sovereignty should not require Uganda to endure attacks by non-state actors, citing UNSC resolutions since the 11 September 2001 attacks in New York, wider state practice and *opinio juris* to show this justification's wide acceptance.[105]

95 *Wall*, Opinion, para. 139.
96 *Wall*, Elaraby, 254.
97 *Wall*, Buergenthal, para. 6; *Wall*, Kooijmans, para. 35.
98 Higgins, *Problems*, 250–1.
99 *Congo*, Judgment, 280–1.
100 *Congo*, Koroma, 288.
101 *Congo*, Judgment, 280–1.
102 *Congo*, Koroma, 291.
103 *Congo*, Tomka, 351, 352.
104 *Congo*, Simma, 336–38; *Congo*, Kooijmans, 314, 315; *Congo*, Kateka, 372.
105 *Congo*, Simma, 336–38; *Congo*, Kooijmans, 314, 315; *Congo*, Kateka, 372.

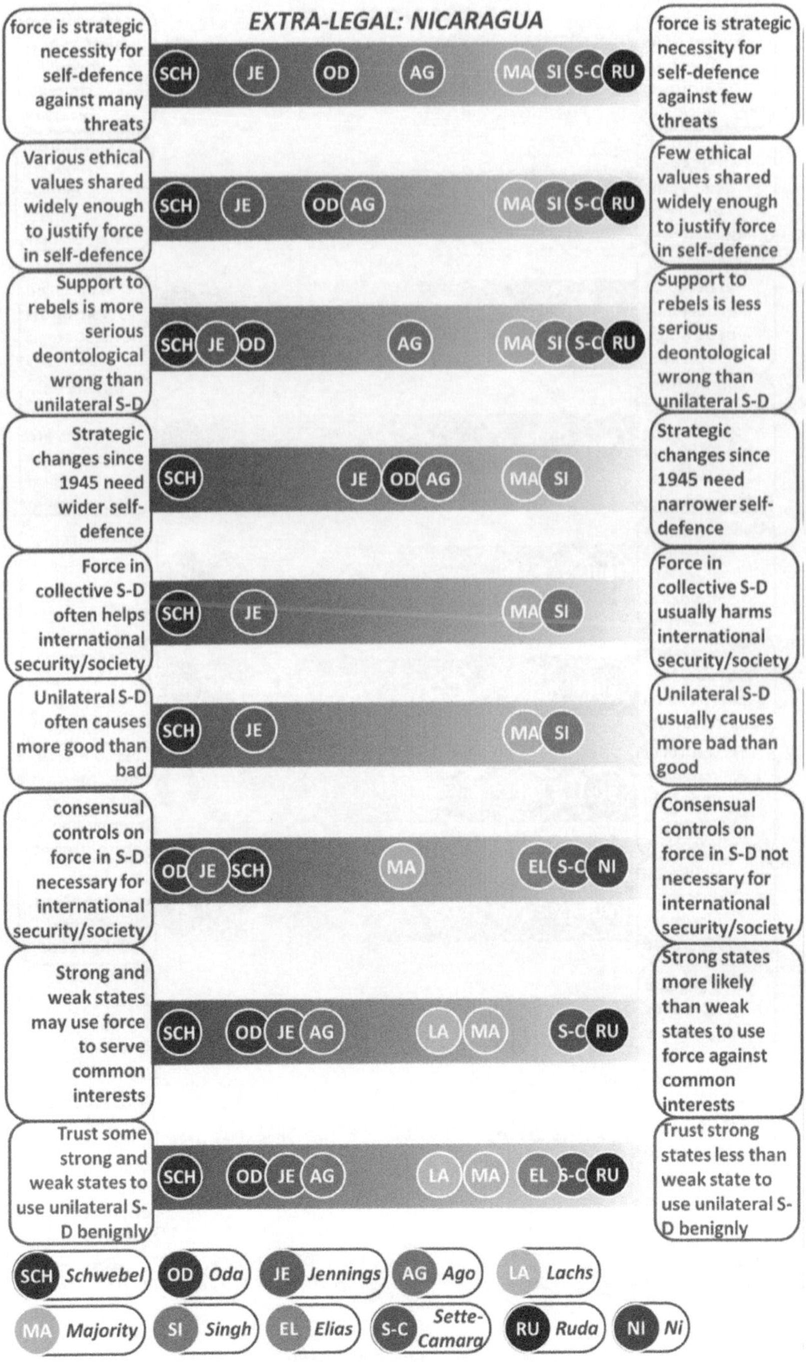

FIGURE 5.2 Nicaragua, Wall, Congo: extra-legal assumptions

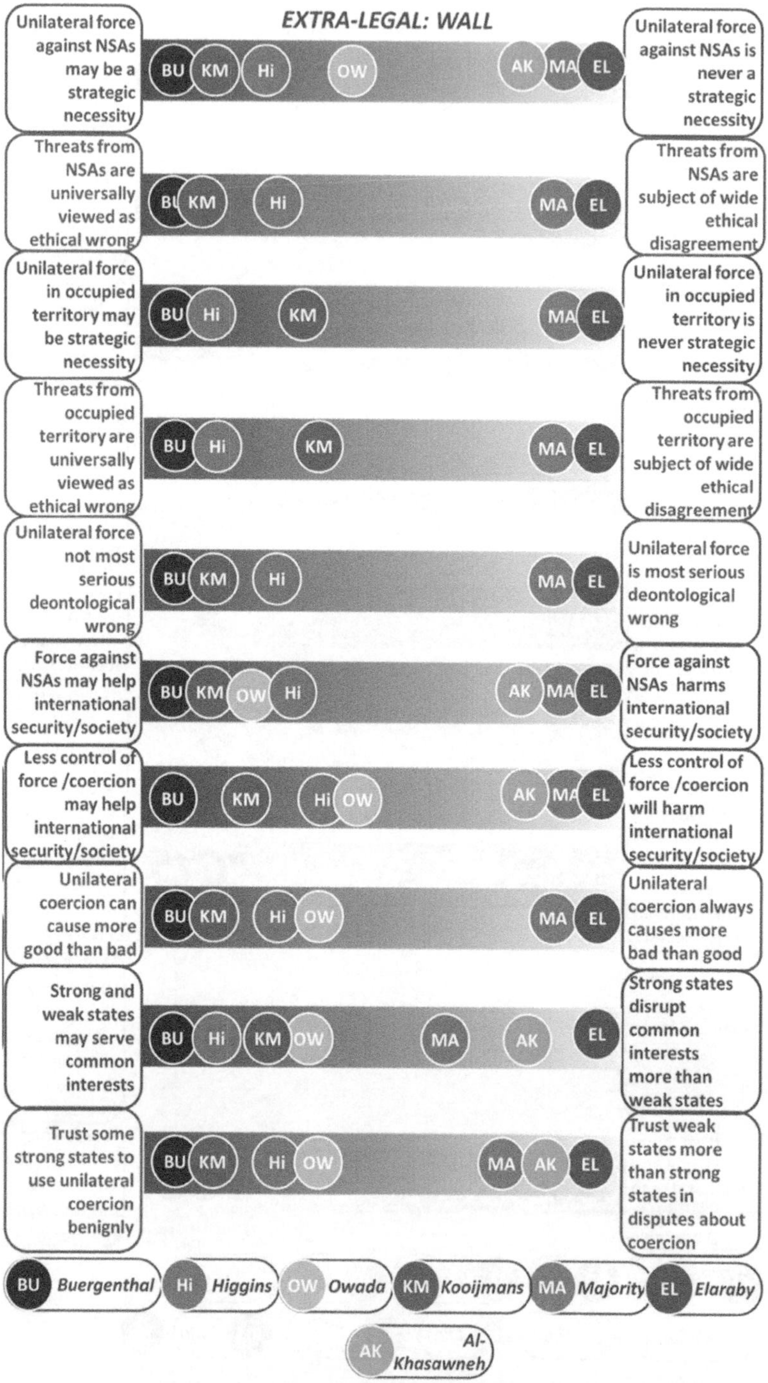

FIGURE 5.2 (Cont.)

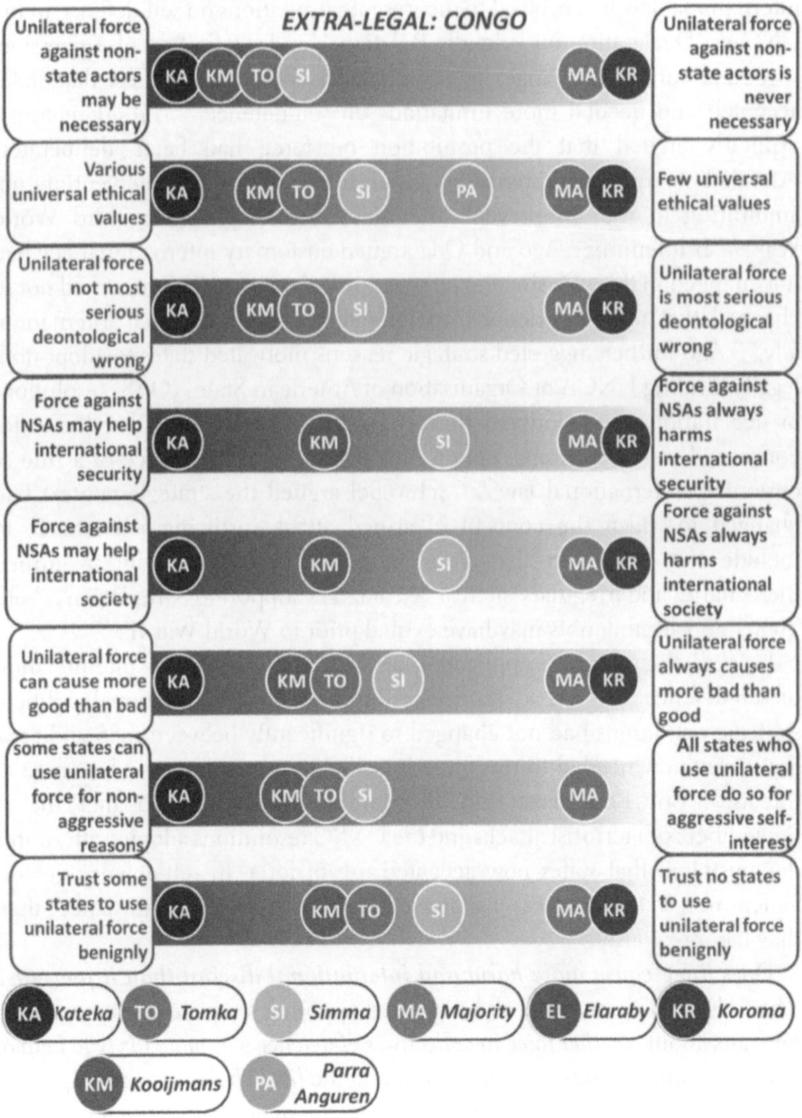

FIGURE 5.2 (Cont.)

Have strategic changes altered the requirements for lawful force? The judges' different views about change in customary international law also suggest *views about whether strategic changes since 1945 had altered the requirements for self-defence*. In *Nicaragua*, the majority's acceptance that customary international law had evolved to incorporate limitations on self-defence in the UNGA's 'Declaration on Friendly Relations', and 'Definition of Aggression' suggested sufficient changes in the strategic context since 1945 that states accepted and needed more limitations on self-defence.[106] President Singh explicitly argued that the prohibition on force had been 'deliberately extended' to outlaw reprisals 'or other forms of armed intervention not amounting to war' to prevent 'the major catastrophe of a third World War'.[107] But Jennings, Ago and Oda argued customary international law had not changed in this way since 1945, suggesting the strategic context had not so changed that more restrictions on self-defence were accepted internationally.[108] Ago further suggested strategic reasons motivated states to adopt non-legally binding UNGA or Organisation of American States (OAS) resolutions or declarations, and doubted these were 'proof conclusive' that the states concerned were expressing '*opinio juris* possessing all the force of a rule of customary international law'.[109] Schwebel argued the strategic context had changed to *widen* the concept of armed attack justifying self-defence to include the 'new and dangerous mode of military activity by armed mercenaries and irregulars' such as Nicaragua's support to Salvadorian rebels, '(w)hatever legal doubts may have existed prior to World War II'.[110]

In *Wall*, the majority's application of *Nicaragua*'s restrictive interpretation of self-defence suggests a strategic assumption that international politico-strategic conditions had not changed so significantly between 1986 and 2004 that states now needed to use force in self-defence against a wider range of threats.[111] But Kooijmans and Buergenthal clearly argued that the 11 September 2001 terrorist attacks and the UNSC resolutions adopted afterwards demonstrated that states now accepted use of force in self-defence against violent non-state actors was a strategic necessity in more circumstances than they had previously.[112]

Does force cause more harm and international discord than it prevents? The judges' disagreements also suggested opposing strategic assessments and forecasts about *whether force in collective self-defence was more likely to help or harm international security and society*, and the *likely balance of consequences of a wider right of self-defence*. In *Nicaragua*, the majority's arguments to limit

106 *Nicaragua*, Merits, paras. 188–95.
107 *Nicaragua*, Singh, 151.
108 *Nicaragua*, Jennings, 530–2; *Nicaragua*, Ago, 184; *Nicaragua*, Oda, 256–7.
109 *Nicaragua*, Ago, 184.
110 *Nicaragua*, Schwebel, 334–5.
111 *Wall*, Opinion, para. 139.
112 *Wall*, Buergenthal, para. 6; *Wall*, Kooijmans, para. 35.

self-defence assumed such force was unlikely to serve international security and international relations.[113] Singh explicitly warned that if force were permitted following 'minor provocations', then 'the day would soon dawn when the world would have to face the major catastrophe of a third World War – an event so dreaded in 1946 as to have justified concrete measures being taken forthwith to eliminate such a contingency'.[114] But Schwebel described the changed international security environment fostering great power consensus for a wider definition of armed attack via proxies.[115] Jennings defined collective self-defence more narrowly, but described the majority's restrictions as unrealistic and dangerous for international security, and doubted international society had accepted such restrictions.[116]

In *Congo*, the majority argued the harmful consequences of Uganda using force against hostile non-state actors in the DRC outweighed the harms of Uganda enduring attacks by those non-state actors.[117] Koroma stated ethical and strategic opinions that the prohibition on force was 'not only moral, but serves an important role in maintaining peace and security between neighbouring states and in preventing military conflicts between them'.[118] Kooijmans and Simma both acknowledged risks to regional security if one state uses force against rebels in another in the complex conflicts across the Great Lakes region, and noted the 'reprehensible behaviour' of all parties involved in these conflicts, but they assessed some Ugandan actions against non-state groups in the DRC as proportionate and necessary even in that context.[119] They, Kateka and Tomka found it unreasonable to expect a state to endure attacks by non-state actors in a neighbouring state that had not taken reasonable measures to end those attacks.[120]

Should legal constraints be consensual or compulsory? The disagreements in these cases also suggested the judges held opposing assessments about *whether international security and society are better served by consensual or compulsory controls on self-defence*. In *Nicaragua*, the majority's decision to proceed with the case despite US opposition, although only using customary law and not multilateral treaties, suggested an assessment that international society is served by the Court giving some but not complete consideration to a

[113] *Nicaragua*, Merits, para. 188–95.
[114] *Nicaragua*, Singh, 151.
[115] *Nicaragua*, Schwebel, 340–2.
[116] *Nicaragua*, Jennings, 543–4.
[117] *Congo*, Judgment, 280.
[118] *Congo*, Koroma, 291.
[119] *Congo*, Kooijmans, 307, 310; *Congo*, Simma, 334–5.
[120] *Congo*, Simma, 336–8; *Congo*, Kooijmans, 314, 315; *Congo*, Kateka, 372; *Congo*, Tomka, 314.

state's wishes.[121] Judges Elias, Sette-Camara and Ni argued even multilateral law should be applied in the case in spite of the US 'Multilateral Reservation', implying state consent for such adjudication was unnecessary.[122] However Judge Oda said the Court considering the case 'against the wish of a respondent State' would obstruct 'genuine solution of the dispute'.[123] Schwebel said judicial scrutiny of force required assessment of 'policies – and motives' of the states involved, which the Court would not do with the United States and other concerned states absent and 'unwilling, for security reasons, to reveal information it treats as secret'.[124] Lachs supported the majority, but acknowledged that close links between law and politics made it difficult to identify when political disputes such as that between Nicaragua and the United States may be justiciable, and commended the consensual 'Contadora' regional talks as the best way of resolving the conflict.[125] In *Wall*, the majority's restrictive interpretation of self-defence, and willingness to draw wide conclusions about Israel's actions, suggested assumptions that international peace and security were best served by constraining states' ability to use force and other forms of coercion, even beyond constraints those states had consented to, and requiring strong states to tolerate some military harm.[126]

Trust states? Finally, the disagreements suggested competing assessments about *whether strong states are more likely than weak states to use force to serve or disrupt common interests, whether states can be trusted to use unilateral force for benign motives*, and *whether strong states are less trustworthy than weak states*. In *Nicaragua*, the majority's findings suggested an assessment that force by strong states was more dangerous than military actions by weaker states. For example, they concluded that arms flows from Nicaragua to rebels in El Salvador 'would not constitute such armed attack', even 'assuming the participation of the Nicaraguan Government', and that, if Honduras, El Salvador and the United States could not stop these arms flows, 'it would clearly be unreasonable' to demand 'a higher degree of diligence' of Nicaragua.[127] Sette-Camara and Ruda distrusted the United States' claim to be defending the interests of countries not involved in the case when invoking its multilateral treaty reservation, rather than protecting its own interests and obstructing international justice.[128] The majority's

121 *Nicaragua*, Merits, paras. 56, 172, 175–82.
122 *Nicaragua*, Elias, 178; *Nicaragua*, Sette-Camara, 197; *Nicaragua*, Ni, 208–10.
123 *Nicaragua*, Oda 246.
124 *Nicaragua*, Schwebel, 295.
125 *Nicaragua*, Lachs, 168, 178.
126 *Wall*, Opinion, para. 139.
127 *Nicaragua*, Merits, paras. 230, 157.
128 *Nicaragua*, Ruda, 194; *Nicaragua*, Sette-Camara, 194.

discussion of ideological intervention to change a country's political system or international alliances, or to stop human rights abuses, even though the US Congress rather than the US government had referred to these justifications, suggested the majority considered these, and not only defence of El Salvador, may have been US motives for military action.[129]

Schwebel's defence of US actions, his accusation that Nicaragua had 'odiously unclean' hands, had committed aggression and 'compounded its sins by misrepresenting them to the Court', were clearly assessments grounded in ethics and his opinion that Nicaragua rather than the United States was in the wrong.[130] Schwebel criticised the majority's apparent willingness to permit some states to take covert military action, while insisting that a state experiencing covert attack must declare itself a victim of attack before claiming collective self-defence.[131] Jennings was also 'doubtful' Nicaragua's involvement did not include 'some forms of "other support"' to Salvadorian rebels besides providing weapons 'officially or unofficially', while also criticising the United States for not taking part in the case's substantive phase.[132] Ago worried the judgment gave too little weight to events in Nicaragua, particularly the Soviet-aligned, politically repressive Sandinista government's displacement of the democratic, internationally non-aligned coalition that had initially overthrown Nicaragua's Somoza dictatorship.[133] Oda worried the majority had failed to consider more evidence of Nicaraguan wrong-doing, emphasising that *both* Nicaragua and the United States must respect principles of non-intervention, prohibition of force and respect for sovereignty.[134] Lachs argued the Court should have examined further 'the question of assistance from or through Nicaragua to opposition forces in El Salvador', and should have heard El Salvador's claim of armed attack by Nicaragua.[135]

In *Wall*, the majority's willingness to draw conclusions about Israel's actions without seeking more evidence for their justifications suggested an assumption that *strong states are more likely than weak states to act in self-serving ways causing military crises and disrupting common interests*, and that a military crisis is more likely to be sustainably resolved by protecting the rights of weaker states rather than stronger states. Elaraby argued 'all considerations of morality and reason establish a right of resistance inherent in the population' of the

129 *Nicaragua*, Merits, paras. 257–68.
130 *Nicaragua*, Schwebel, 392.
131 *Nicaragua*, Schwebel, 373.
132 *Nicaragua*, Jennings, 544.
133 *Nicaragua*, Ago, 186.
134 *Nicaragua*, Oda 240, 243–4.
135 *Nicaragua*, Lachs, 161.

Palestinian territories, that Israel must return all territory acquired since 1967 as required by UNSC Resolution 242 (1967), and that '[i]t is legally wrong and politically unsound to transform this obligation of result into a mere obligation of means, confining it to a negotiating process'.[136]

In *Congo*, the majority seemed to trust the alleged aggressor state Uganda less than the 'victim' state, the DRC, rejecting Uganda's claim to be acting in self-defence and rejecting much Ugandan evidence as lacking 'the quality or character to satisfy the Court', yet they did not require DRC to present evidence of its efforts to prevent attacks by irregular forces from its territory.[137] However, while Kooijmans and Simma agreed many Ugandan actions breached the prohibition on force, they showed at least some trust in Uganda by accepting some of its actions as legitimate self-defence.[138] Kooijmans regretted the Court's 'lack of balance' in favouring the DRC over Uganda.[139] Kateka was more explicitly trusting of Uganda, complaining 'the Court has not been even-handed in its treatment of the materials submitted by the two Parties'.[140]

Conclusions

Of the ICJ cases examined here, *Nicaragua* provided the most comprehensive and detailed material about potential extra-legal reasoning around the lawfulness of self-defence, while *Wall* provided the least. Not all judges made explicit their underlying strategic and ethical assumptions, just as not all were explicit about their views on all the contested principles of legal interpretation. Nevertheless, these analyses of majority judgments and dissenting and separate opinions did suggest clear differences between the judges in these areas of extra-legal reasoning. As with the findings of the textual analyses in the previous section, the judges seemed to express consistent, mutually reinforcing political, strategic and ethical beliefs, intuitions, factual assessments and forecasts about these conflicts, broadly aligning with the competing strategic cultures of 'pacifism' and 'interventionism' proposed in Chapter 3.

Those judges who supported the findings of unlawful use of force in *Nicaragua* and *Congo*, and who supported the opinion in *Wall* that only attacks by states could trigger the right of self-defence, also tended to express 'pacificist' extra-legal opinions about those conflicts in particular and about

136 *Wall*, Elaraby, 256, 259.
137 *Congo*, Judgment, para. 220.
138 *Congo*, Kooijmans, 314–16; *Congo*, Simma, 336–8.
139 *Congo*, Kooijmans, 324.
140 *Congo*, Kateka, 361–2.

conflicts in general. Judges who argued against these findings of unlawful use of force and the restrictive interpretation of self-defence in *Wall* tended to express 'interventionist' extra-legal opinions about those and other conflicts. The analyses also demonstrated competing lines of argument re-emerging in all three cases around the extent to which justification for force in self-defence could be based on a state's support to or tolerance of non-state groups based on their territory while attacking neighbouring states.

In *Nicaragua*, unlike the other cases, there were serious disagreements about material facts, particularly the extent of Nicaragua's support to El Salvador's rebels, and its efforts to stop others on its territory supporting those rebels. There were also disagreements about motives and perceptions, particularly whether El Salvador and Honduras regarded themselves as victims of armed attack by Nicaragua; whether Nicaragua genuinely intended to stop support to El Salvador's rebels; most significantly, whether the United States genuinely acted on concern for El Salvador and Honduras or hostility to the Nicaraguan regime's communist political system, and its pro-Soviet alliances.

In *Congo*, the analysis suggests the judges' disagreements flowed less from different conclusions about matters of fact. But the ways in which the Court assessed evidence also suggested politico-strategic and ethical assumptions about the relative reliability of different actors. The Court regarded as most reliable evidence that had been tested by skilled and experienced judges through cross-examination, and they assumed evidence not quickly challenged by either party was reliable, implying both parties can and will quickly identify and challenge evidence they regard as unreliable.[141] The Court assessed evidence from media articles as not reliable unless it could be shown as deriving from multiple sources.[142] And it viewed evidence from state representatives as inherently less reliable when it defends that state than when it incriminates it.[143]

These are all reasonable rules of evidence, grounded in what most would regard as justifiable scepticism of the claims made by states and their representatives when accused of wrongdoing. Nevertheless, they also reflect politico-strategic and ethical presuppositions about how and why actors actually behave and ought to behave. Politico-strategic considerations seem to have played a more general role in shaping Judge Kateka's argumentation; his opinion diverged furthest from the majority on many aspects of the case.

141 *Congo*, Judgment, para. 201.
142 *Congo*, Judgment, para. 204.
143 *Congo*, Judgment, paras. 201, 203.

Kateka was a judge *ad hoc* appointed at Uganda's request under Article 31 of the ICJ Statute, implying different obligations to other judges, as Kateka himself explained: 'I am bound to exercise my function impartially and conscientiously while also discharging the special obligation to endeavour to ensure, so far as is reasonable, that argument in favour of the Party that appointed me "is reflected – though not necessarily accepted – in [this] dissenting opinion".'[144]

The analysis suggests the judges' intuitions about strategy and ethics may have shaped their overall conclusions about the lawfulness of force in these cases in ways which were more significant than their choices about legal interpretation: that the judges' legal opinions on these cases were not entirely autonomous of extra-legal considerations. For example, purposive and textual approaches to interpretation were used to justify both expansionist or restrictivist conclusions about cases. In *Nicaragua*, the restrictivist majority seemed to apply a purposive, dynamist approach to accept more restrictions on self-defence than the UN Charter stipulated. Yet in *Wall* and *Congo*, the majority adopted formalist interpretive techniques to accept the *Nicaragua* ruling's restrictions. And judges supporting wider rights of self-defence adopted formalist interpretation in the *Nicaragua* case and a mix of textual and purposive interpretation in the *Wall* and *Congo* cases.

So it could be argued that the judges' views on the politico-strategic and ethical implications of self-defence may have influenced them to use both dynamist and formalist arguments to justify the restrictivist or expansionist conclusions that best aligned with their extra-legal intuitions about force. As one scholar has argued 'there is no neat distinction between the political factors inherent in law and the political views (conscious or unconscious)' of ICJ judges, and 'The less well defined an area of law, the more that political and ideological viewpoints of the judges *as to the principle(s) of law underlying the system* are likely to influence' their conclusions.[145]

Finally, as with the analyses of scholarly writings in this chapter, the judges' extra-legal opinions about force displayed similar forms of vagueness and disagreement as their legal opinions and choices of legal interpretation. They displayed supervaluationism – their politico-strategic and ethical assessments seemed to use multiple, overlapping but not entirely co-extensive evaluation principles. These principles seemed to operate according to fuzzy rather than bivalent logic – clearly ethical or politico-strategically advisable cases were separated from clearly unethical or politico-strategically unsound

144 *Congo*, Kateka, 361.

145 Green, *Self-Defence*, 176, 184.

cases by a fuzzy penumbra of uncertainty rather than sharp dividing line. Together, the principles described paradigms of ethical or politico-strategically advisable examples of resort to force. And the judges' extra-legal opinions displayed social supervaluationism – distributed across a spectrum between interventionist and pacificist strategic cultures, rather than forming distinct, clearly separated opposing groups.

UK INTERNATIONAL LAWYERS AND EXTRA-LEGAL REASONING

Introduction

Finally, this section reports survey and interview research with UK-based international lawyers, investigating views they express about politico-strategic and ethical principles relevant to the *jus ad bellum*. The survey and interviews asked lawyers in different ways if, in cases where the requirements of the law are contested, they would choose the interpretation of the law that minimised potential for future legal uncertainty and abuse, which protected the interests of less powerful states or which was willing to trust more powerful states, and whether the prohibition on force is always or only sometimes the most important principle. The questions also asked if, when assessing incomplete, contradictory, or uncertain factual evidence about unilateral force, the lawyers would proceed on the basis that such force causes more harm than it prevents for the state using force and the international community, whether only self-interested states use force unilaterally or whether states pursuing common interests also use such force, and which goals and values are sufficiently universal to underpin decisions about unilateral force.

Figure 5.3 summarises the survey responses. This analysis suggests four key observations. The first is war aversion and ideological moderation. In response to questions asking whether force was associated with *positive* politico-strategic or ethical features, 'usually not' was the most popular answer to five of the fourteen questions asked – three on its own, two equal with another answer. In eleven of those questions, answers that were politico-strategically and ethically 'pessimistic' about force received more support than 'optimistic' answers; in four questions 'optimistic' answers received no support. Ideological moderation was also popular – answers saying force was politico-strategically or ethically justified 'sometimes, sometimes not' were most popular in eleven of fourteen questions, suggesting pragmatism in this sample. Second, nevertheless, there was again observable politico-strategic and ethical variation, and third, a relatively strong correlation between political-ethical beliefs and legal opinions. But, fourth, these results saw law exerting *some* constraining effect

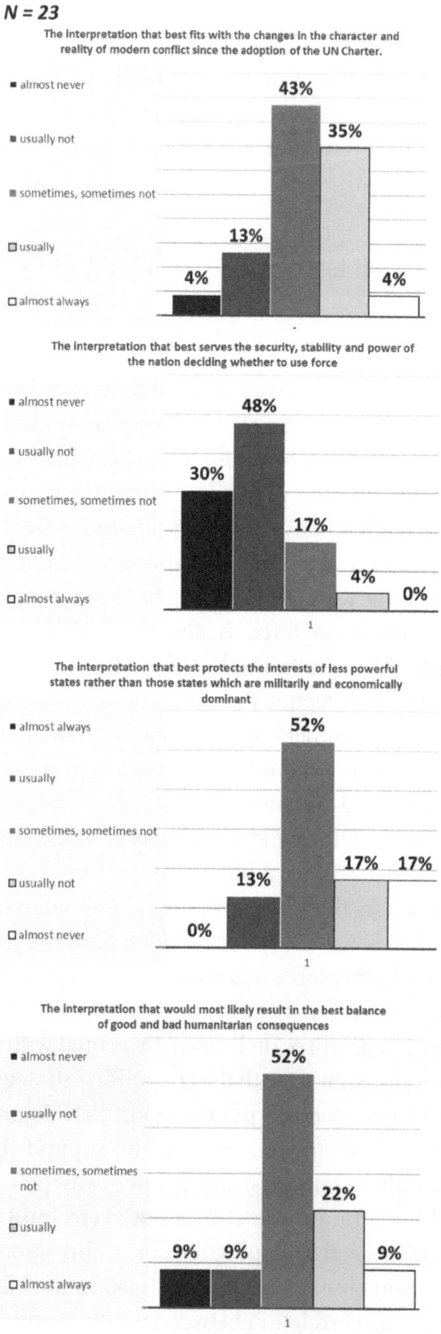

FIGURE 5.3 Opinions on 'extra-legal' factors in legal interpretation

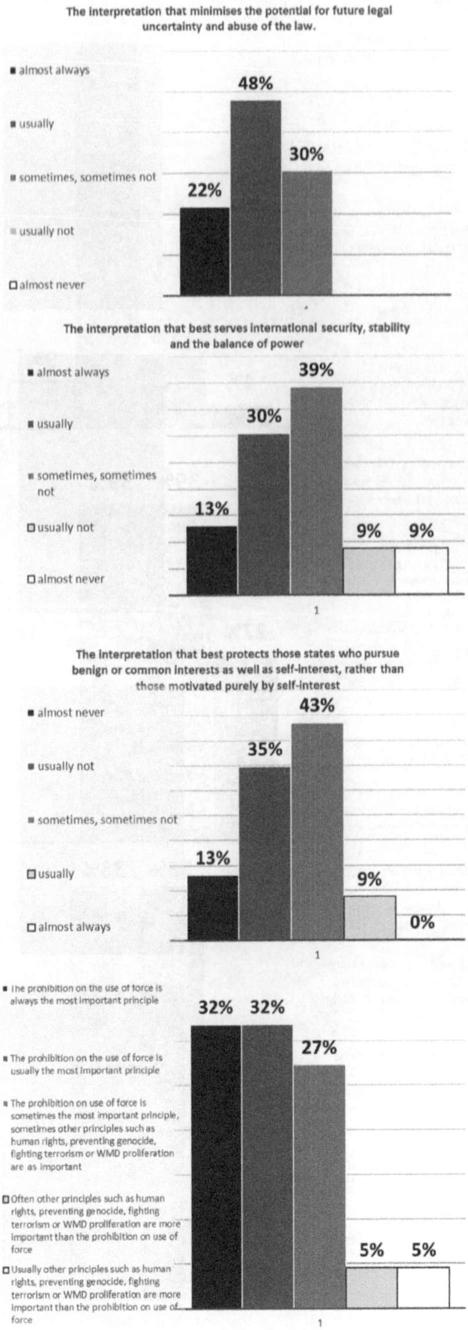

FIGURE 5.3 (Cont.)

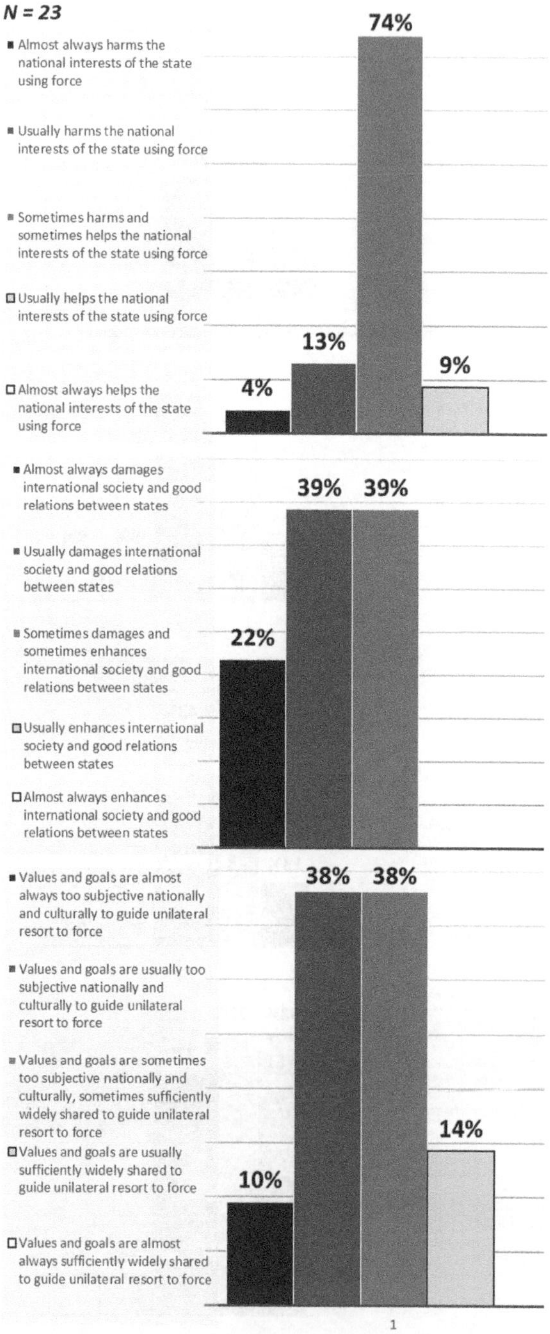

FIGURE 5.3 (Cont.)

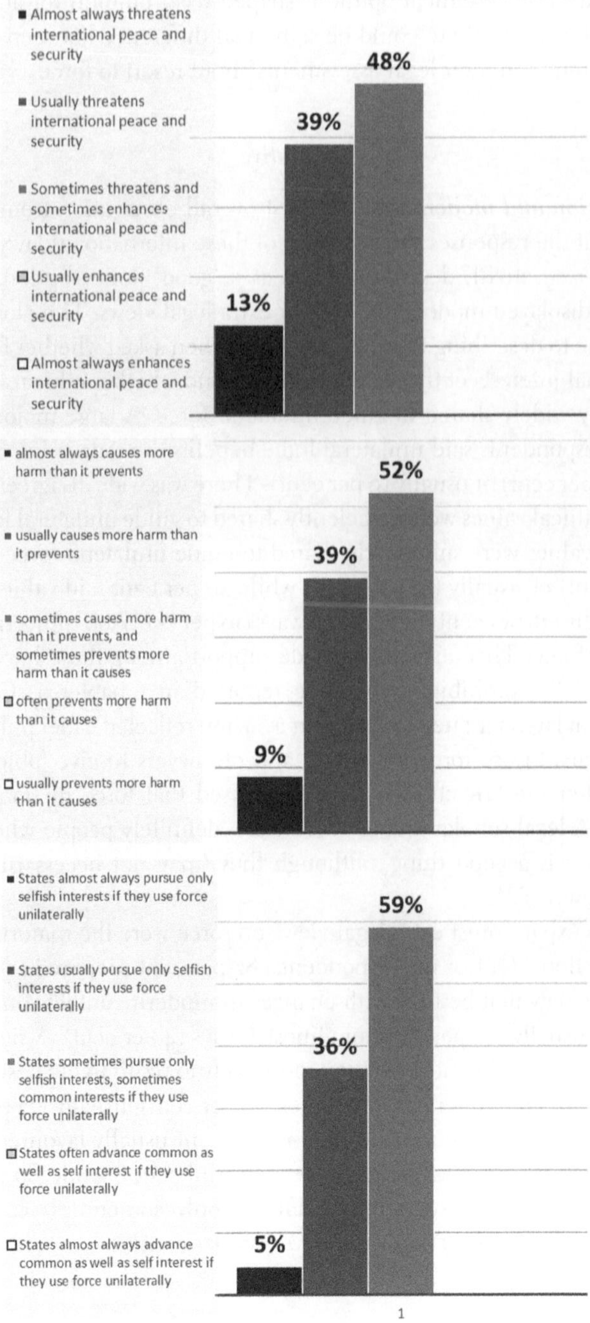

FIGURE 5.3 (Cont.)

on how far political-ethical opinions shaped legal opinion for at least some lawyers – for whom there could be some real difference between their extra-legal opinions and their legal assessments about resort to force.

Narrative

War aversion and moderation. The first overall observation from these analyses is that the responses showed none of these international lawyers, expansionist or restrictivist, describing force as a 'good' policy option, and most generally displayed moderation in their extra-legal views. The closest participants came to describing force as 'good' was when asked whether force served the national interests of the state using force and whether ethical values were sufficiently widely shared to guide unilateral force. A large majority (83 per cent) of respondents said unilateral force benefits the state using force sometimes (74 per cent) or usually (9 per cent). There was wide disagreement about whether ethical values were sufficiently shared to guide unilateral force: 52 per cent said values were sufficiently shared to guide unilateral force sometimes (38 per cent) or usually (14 per cent), while 48 per cent said values and goals were usually (38 per cent) or almost always (10 per cent) too subjective to guide unilateral force. This fits with the wide support among these lawyers for the primacy of the prohibition on force reported in Chapter 4. One former government lawyer argued lawyers' war aversion reflected wider public distrust of politicians to use force effectively and of lawyers to give 'objective legal advice', after the UK attorney general advised that force in Iraq would be lawful.[146] A legal scholar argued there were 'definitely people who think the use of force is a good thing', although they 'may not necessarily be international lawyers'.[147]

Broadly expansionist extra-legal views on force were the majority on three other questions. Out of the respondents, 82 per cent preferred the interpretation of the law that best fits with changes in modern conflict sometimes (43 per cent), usually (35 per cent) or almost always (4 per cent). A significant 83 per cent preferred the interpretation most likely to result in the best balance of humanitarian consequences sometimes (52 per cent), usually (22 per cent) or almost always (9 per cent). And only 14 per cent usually favoured the interpretation of law that best protects less powerful states, while 86 per cent of respondents preferred such interpretations only sometimes (52 per cent), usually not (17 per cent) or almost never (17 per cent).

146 Participant 31.
147 Participant 3.

Opposing extra-legal opinions. The second overall observation is that, despite war aversion and moderation, opinions still varied – and more so than on legal interpretation. Four questions received answers in all five available categories, five questions saw answers in four of the five categories, and only five questions received answers in three categories. This suggested that, unsurprisingly, this group of lawyers held varied views about the politics and ethics of force, both relatively open to it and relatively opposed, as would be expected of any group of professionals dealing with international affairs.

As Figure 5.4 shows, survey responses to the Hercules and Thrasymachus conflict scenarios showed the spread of politico-strategic and ethical-normative views even more starkly. In all four scenarios, participants chose more options about ethics than options about lawfulness, and in three of the four scenarios they chose more options about politics and strategy than lawfulness. There are several possible explanations for this. International lawyers can be expected to receive training and experience covering the same legal principles and materials. However, they are likely to have less convergent education, experience and wider media and social influences on their opinions about the politico-strategic and ethical aspects of force. In addition, law's mechanisms for resolving disagreements – treaties, UNGA resolutions, Courts, *opinio juris* and state practice – may make it more likely that lawyers want to and do converge on legal positions than they are likely to seek or reach consensus on the ethics, politics or strategy of force.

The scenario on self-defence against a non-state group provoked least disagreement about the politico-strategically optimal point to use force,

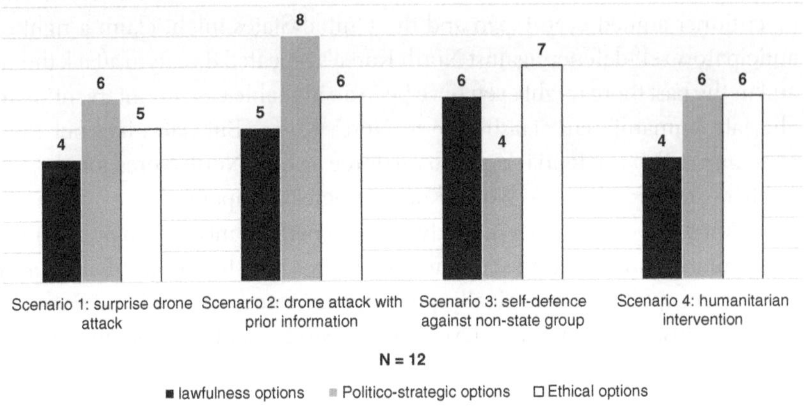

FIGURE 5.4 Scenarios – numbers of legal and extra-legal options chosen

although this scenario attracted most disagreement about the legally and ethically optimal points to use force. There was almost equal disagreement about the politico-strategically and legally optimal point to use force in the scenarios on self-defence against surprise attack and humanitarian intervention. The widest disagreement about the politico-strategically optimal point to use force was in the scenario about self-defence against an attack for which there were many warning signs.

In the two scenarios about self-defence against a drone attack, several participants thought it was politico-strategically optimal to resort to force *earlier* than it was legally or ethically justifiable, suggesting they believed politico-strategic considerations may argue for more aggressive, earlier military action than law or ethics allow. But in interviews, some said it may be politically advisable to use force *later* than when it would be legal. One practising international lawyer said if the state was confident that anti-missile defences can be effective, then it would be better to authorise force when 'the UAV has invaded H airspace' and 'it is known the UAV is carrying a weapon', which may be *later* than when force was judged lawful, since waiting would mean the aggressor 'can undoubtedly be seen to be T'.[148] Another practitioner mentioned drone strikes against terrorists in Syria or Iraq, often carried out later than they would have been legally permissible, because governments wanted to wait until they had publicly disclosable evidence to justify the strike.[149]

That practitioner mentioned North Korea as another example of how the politico-strategic and legal arguments for force may be misaligned.[150] North Korea has repeatedly carried out acts that could be construed as attacks on South Korea, thus legally justifying force in response by South Korea and its allies such as the United States in individual and collective self-defence. The practitioner argued even Japan and the United States might claim a right of anticipatory self-defence against North Korea's repeated threats to attack them, and in the past there might even have been an arguable case for intervention to alleviate humanitarian catastrophe in North Korea. But states had not exercised any of these potential rights to use force against North Korea for obvious politico-strategic reasons – North Korca's nuclear weapons.

Strikingly, even though a majority of seven participants saw no point in the humanitarian intervention scenario when force was legally justifiable, only two saw no political-strategically point to use force, and only one saw no ethically justifiable point. Eleven participants identified points in that

[148] Participant 10.
[149] Participant 18.
[150] Participant 18.

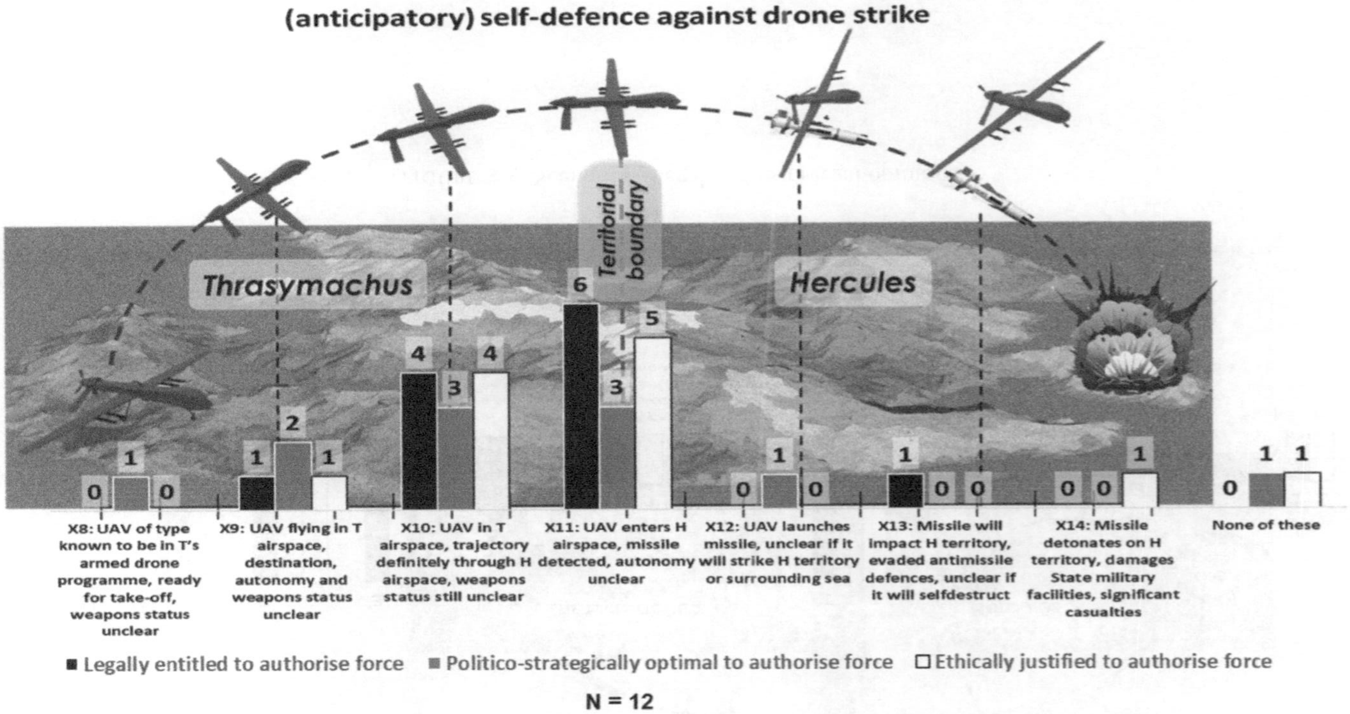

FIGURE 5.5 Scenarios – legal and extra-legal opinions

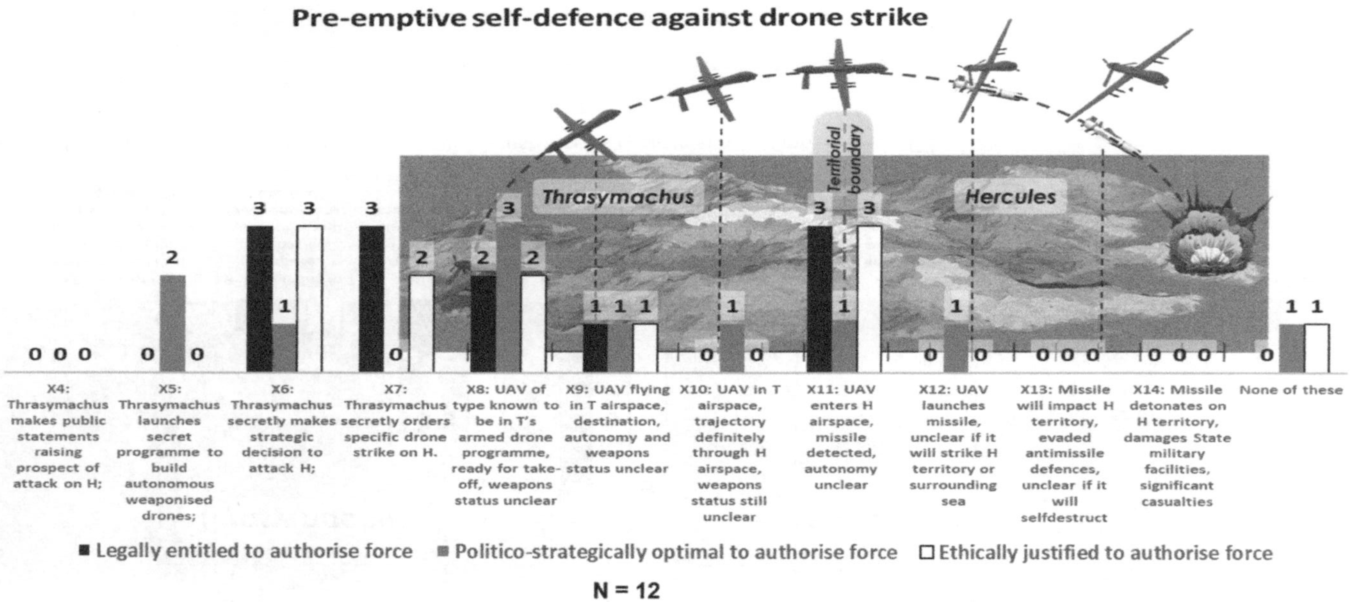

FIGURE 5.5 Scenarios – legal and extra-legal opinions

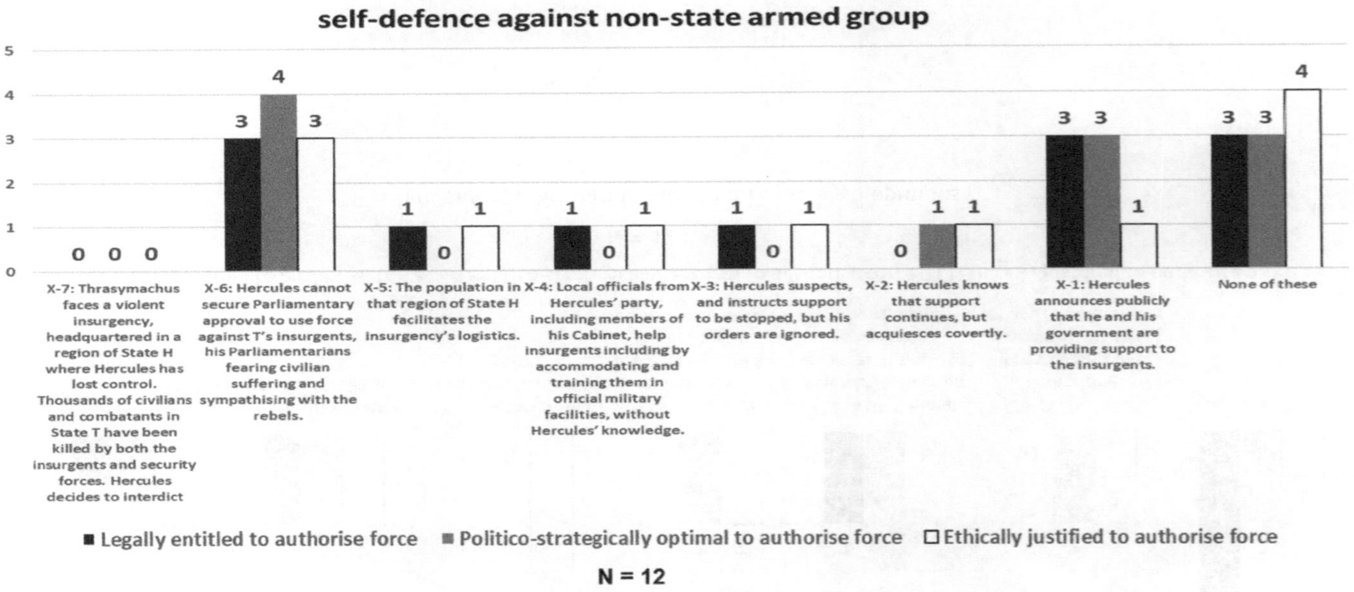

FIGURE 5.5 Scenarios – legal and extra-legal opinions

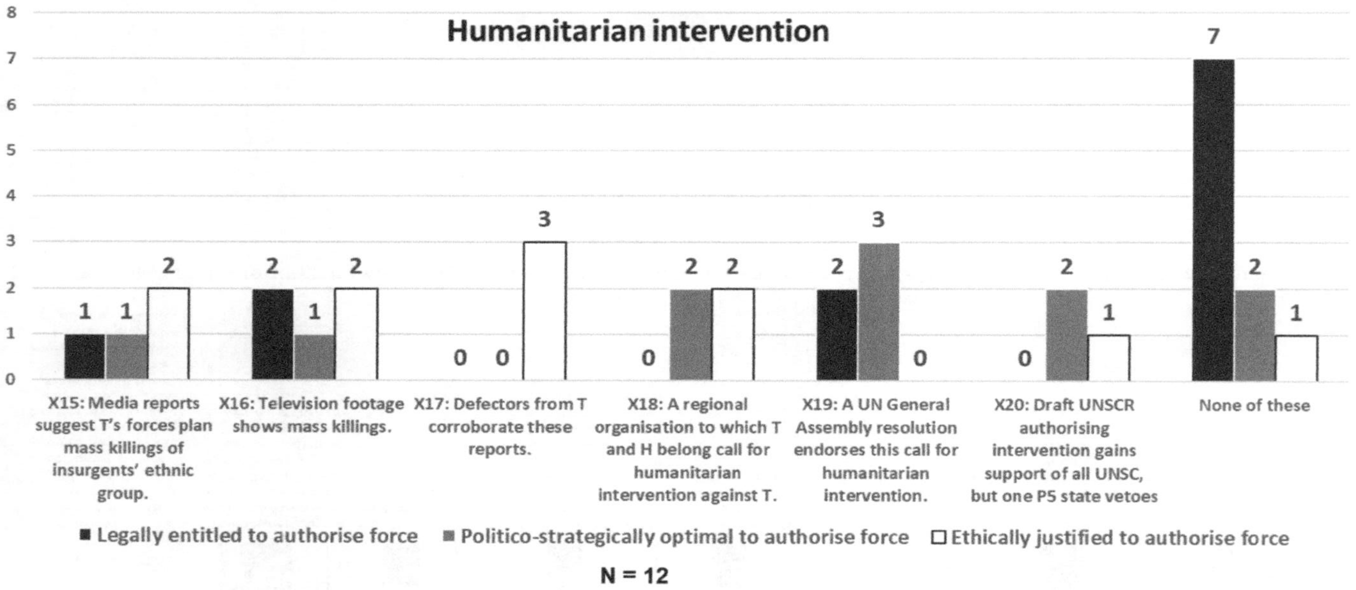

FIGURE 5.5 Scenarios – legal and extra-legal opinions

scenario where force was ethically justified, nine identified points where force was politico-strategically justified. This was consistent with many participants' interview comments that they wanted a legal norm of humanitarian intervention to emerge because they saw ethical and politico-strategic justifications for it, but they believed such a norm had not yet emerged in international law.[151]

Legal and extra-legal opinions correlated. Correlation analysis of participants' legal and extra-legal opinions relating to force produced the third key observation: for these lawyers, legal opinions on unilateral use of force broadly correlated with their politico-ethical opinions.[152] The scatterplot in Figure 5.6 illustrates the responses, with 'restrictive-expansionist' legal scores on the X axis, and 'pacificist-interventionist' extra-legal scores on the Y axis. There is a correlation coefficient of 0.687 between the lawyers' opinions on lawful justifications for force and their extra-legal assumptions about force. In social

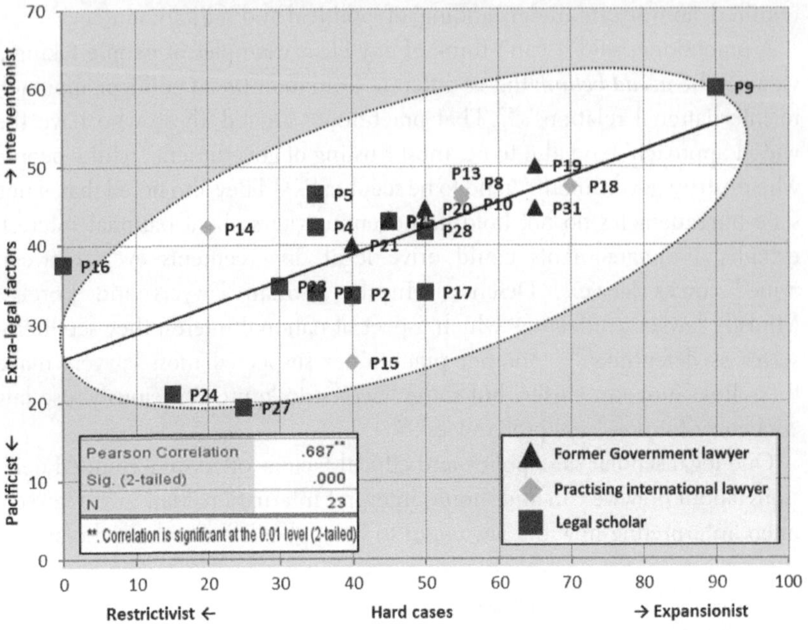

FIGURE 5.6 Correlating views on hard cases and 'extra-legal' assumptions

[151] Participants 1, 2, 4, 6, 7, 14, 15, 17, 20, 22, 23, 27, 29, 30.

[152] Analytical method similar to that in Chapter 4: answers to questions scored 0 to 100, averaged. For extra-legal opinions, score of zero described as most 'pacificist', 100 most 'interventionist'.

science terms, this is a strong correlation coefficient – changes in legal opinions and political-ethical justifiability of force are fairly closely aligned. The correlation is statistically significant at the 0.01 level, with 'a risk of only 1 in 100 that the results could have arisen by chance (that is, due to sampling error)' – strong significance for social science research.[153]

Twenty-two interviewees expected an association between lawyers' extra-legal and legal opinions about justifications for force.[154] One practising international lawyer said most lawyers start with what they feel is the right answer, based on principles such as the protection of individuals or the primacy of the security council, and use the available legal materials and interpretive techniques to justify that answer.[155] That lawyer said states were similar, the United Kingdom usually adopting formalist interpretation, yet asserting rapid emergence of custom on humanitarian intervention. One legal scholar said 'you cannot avoid politics or international relations' when considering force.[156] Another scholar noted that 'applying imminence, proportionality, necessity' required 'an intricate understanding' of 'political and military strategy'.[157]

A practitioner said 'I can't think of any clear examples of people taking a view on the *jus ad bellum* that is different from their broad political approach to international relations'.[158] That practitioner argued 'those who have the widest approach' tend also to be 'most trusting of government', while 'people who mistrust governments' 'tend to be sceptical'.[159] They also noted that, since state bureaucracies do not hold homogenous views about national interest, extra-legal disagreements could drive legal disagreements even between armed forces lawyers, Defence Ministry civilian lawyers and Foreign Ministry lawyers, reflecting 'which aspect of national interest they see themselves as defending'.[160] Another practitioner suspected most lawyers make these links 'unconsciously', but some lawyers do 'quite consciously' use law 'as a cover for non-legal preferences'.[161]

One legal scholar said 'policy and ethical factors' often underpinned decisions 'about how we can and should interpret international law', with lawyers often 'interpreting how the law *ought* to be applied'.[162] Another scholar said

153 Bryman and Teevan, *Social Research Methods*, 274.
154 Participants 1, 3, 4, 5, 6, 7, 9, 10, 13, 14, 15, 17, 18, 22, 23, 24, 25, 26, 27, 28, 29, 30, 31.
155 Participant 18.
156 Participant 9.
157 Participant 7.
158 Participant 13.
159 Participant 13.
160 Participant 13.
161 Participant 14.
162 Participant 5.

they had seen lawyers 'move between different theories' of legal interpretation, driven by 'competing world views', and lawyers are often 'more rigid' about their 'ideology and values' than about principles of legal interpretation.[163] A practitioner said even strong textualists may take a purposive approach when unhappy with the result of textual interpretation.[164]

But views differed about the strength of links between legal and extra-legal views on force, and when they occurred. One practising international lawyer thought ethics was most important, saying 'if it's unethical then it can't be the right answer legally', but 'law needs to be cautious' about reflecting politics and national interests, which can be changeable and destabilising.[165] One scholar argued in similarly Dworkian terms that 'non-legal considerations' are 'not always non-legal' and can legitimately be 'advanced within the legal framework' to make sense of the rules.[166] However, another legal scholar was 'very dubious' about ethics, 'not quite sure what it means' in such contexts, while accepting international law 'cannot be understood outside of the political context'.[167] A further scholar thought 'the strategic interests' of states affect the way they interpret law, for example while Russia was usually 'highly positivist and restrictive' it still found legal justifications for annexing Crimea.[168] Another scholar agreed the link could be seen in the five hard cases examined in this study, but said it was 'not obvious' if the link would hold for more minimal uses of force.[169] A former government lawyer observed one clear link between politics and law: new legal justifications under the *jus ad bellum* were less likely to be agreed when there was heightened geopolitical confrontation between powerful states.[170]

One legal scholar argued the relationship between legal and extra-legal views was 'on a spectrum', some lawyers 'won't fit that trend', and there was unlikely to be an 'exact correlation' in every case.[171] A practising international lawyer said while certain commentators' legal disagreements 'are attributable to non-legal differences', it was not possible to generalise.[172] Many may disapprove of force for humanitarian or other extra-legal reasons, but may 'be instructed to defend the use of force' in such situations, at which point 'I

163 Participant 6.
164 Participant 18.
165 Participant 10.
166 Participant 30.
167 Participant 24.
168 Participant 7.
169 Participant 30.
170 Participant 11.
171 Participant 4.
172 Participant 26.

would leave at the door my own views' and 'use whatever intellectual arguments I had to try to construct a defence'.[173]

A related finding of the survey responses was that, for a significant minority, commitment to legal interpretation principles appeared to be independent of extra-legal factors. For example, there was a relatively weak correlation coefficient of 0.464 between the participants' scores for their responses on legal interpretive principles and extra-legal presuppositions in principle. In other words, a relatively large minority – four of the twenty-three participants making up this sample – defied expectations and held relatively dynamist legal interpretive principles alongside pacifistic extra-legal views, or relatively less pacifistic extra-legal views alongside formalist interpretive principles. Once these outliers were removed, the correlation between the remaining nineteen lawyers' interpretive views and extra-legal views yielded a much stronger coefficient of 0.745. In line with the findings of the textual analyses of writings by legal scholars and ICJ judgments, these outliers may have found ways to justify expansionist legal opinions using formalist interpretation, or restrictivist legal opinions using dynamist interpretive techniques.

Conclusions

As with the assessment of legal interpretation techniques reported in Chapter 4, and the analyses of scholarly writings and ICJ opinions in this chapter, this analysis seems to show a relationship between these lawyers' attitudes to the legality of the unilateral use of force and their underlying politico-strategic and ethical assumptions. The lawyers seemed to express broadly consistent, mutually reinforcing political, strategic and ethical beliefs, intuitions, and factual assumptions about conflicts, broadly aligning with the competing 'pacificist' and 'interventionist' strategic cultures proposed in Chapter 3. Those lawyers most likely to reject many justifications for unilateral use of force tended to express 'pacificist' extra-legal opinions about conflicts in general and the specific fictional scenarios used in this study. Lawyers likely to support many justifications for unilateral force tended to express 'interventionist' extra-legal opinions about conflicts in general and the scenarios in this study.

There was however a fourth observation in this part of the study: for some lawyers, commitment to the law overrides their politico-strategic and ethical intuitions. The imperfect correlation between these lawyers' extra-legal opinions and their acceptance of justifications for unilateral force suggests such legal opinions remain partially although not completely autonomous of extra-legal

[173] Participant 26.

factors. For example, three participants acknowledged that states accepted the lawfulness of self-defence against non-state actors, but worried strong states could abuse this justification to unjustifiably attack weaker states.[174] One scholar said they would not 'go against the will' of the international community, and realised 'September 11 was a fundamental tipping point', but they were 'unhappy about it', 'terribly opposed to Afghanistan', and didn't think legal change 'was unequivocal', as the relevant UNSC resolutions were 'Afghanistan-specific'.[175] Another scholar sceptical of western interventions said self-defence against non-state actors was still 'law in the making', and not contemplated when the UN Charter was drafted, although anti-colonial struggles, self-determination and the additional protocols to the Geneva Conventions were 'a significant adjustment'.[176]

This effect was clear when participants were asked what legal advice they would provide on a potential use of force which they believed had strong politico-strategic and ethical justification, but weak legal basis. The example used was humanitarian intervention in a situation similar to Rwanda in 1993, with overwhelming evidence of an ongoing genocide, where a plan to intervene seemed likely to succeed, there was no great power likely to counter-attack, but the UNSC was deadlocked.[177]

Eight participants said they would advise the state to intervene without offering a legal justification.[178] Seven said in various ways in such situations the government should break the law – several arguing most states often tolerated such 'ethical' lawbreaking.[179] One former government lawyer said in such hard cases 'you're stuck with a legal position' which may be 'morally utterly wrong', that settled law at present would prevent action, but 'if that is the law, I'm not sure it's a law I want to have anything to do with'.[180] Another former government lawyer said governments had an imperative to obey the law – as the UK *Ministerial Code* and *Civil Service Code* imposed specific obligations on the UK government to obey the law.[181] But it was also 'conceivable and sometimes even proper that there may be an imperative not to obey the law', when 'a breach of the law' is at least 'a legitimate policy consideration' if not 'necessarily the lesser of two evils'.[182] For that former government lawyer,

174 Participants 24, 27, 3.
175 Participant 27.
176 Participant 24.
177 Participant 20.
178 Participants 1, 3, 4, 7, 19, 23, 30, 20.
179 Participants 20, 19, 23, 3, 4, 1, 7.
180 Participant 20.
181 Participant 19.
182 Participant 19.

this was not the kind of 'red line issue' such as torture that should prompt a legal adviser to resign.[183]

Several participants were glad the United States had not advanced a legal justification for the 2017 air strikes on Syria following chemical weapons use – one scholar described this as 'the best thing about Trump'.[184] Another scholar said they were 'happy that it occurred', but 'international law has technically been violated', and while US failure to justify the 2017 strikes was problematic, at least it 'protects the law because it hasn't tried to mangle it and distort it'.[185] Another scholar noted most states 'did nothing' after those strikes, because 'they thought the act of law-breaking was not that bad', but they 'didn't say it was lawful either'.[186] These comments fit with Hakimi's conception of the 'procedural and particularistic' rather than 'substantive or generalizable' informal regulation of the *jus ad bellum*, and her argument that the 2017 US air strikes on Syria may have received some legitimation after eleven states endorsed the operation (without declaring it lawful) and only four states condemned it in the UNSC.[187]

Six other participants said they would advance legal arguments for an ethically justified use of force, even if they were uncertain whether it was lawful.[188] One practising international lawyer said 'where clearly the ethical answer was intervention and the legal answer was uncertain' they would advise 'there's a reasonable enough case'.[189] Another practitioner said lawyers should not 'come up with some tricksy argument to justify the case' but 'try to articulate what it is' about the case 'that makes it exceptional and justifies action' on 'a moral level', hoping this would eventually 'become established as a rule of law'.[190] Another practitioner said they would advance 'what I thought the strongest arguments for legality were', advising 'they were morally strong but ultimately not legally', and that the facts were key.[191]

A former government lawyer said they would say 'to hell with the legality, this is the right thing to do', advise this was only *lex ferenda*, not the law as it currently is, but still 'put forward an arguable case'.[192] Another former government lawyer said there was understandable pressure to seek legal justifications

183 Participant 19.
184 Participant 7.
185 Participant 1.
186 Participant 23.
187 Hakimi, '*Jus ad bellum*', 180–1, 155.
188 Participants 6, 10, 13, 15, 20, 31.
189 Participant 10.
190 Participant 13.
191 Participant 15.
192 Participant 20.

because ministers in such crises often felt it was not 'legitimate just to sit back and say, "well its unlawful so we're not going to do anything"'.[193] A legal scholar said they would advise there was not a solid legal argument, but would do their best to provide legal arguments, and build on these to seek UNSC reform.[194]

Humanitarian intervention may thus mark a particular boundary for many international lawyers otherwise sympathetic to an expansionist *jus ad bellum*, their understandings about current international law limiting the effects of their policy preferences on their legal opinions. One scholar recalled a seminar in which several senior international lawyers argued humanitarian intervention was currently clearly unlawful, while expressing strong sympathy for its ethical and politico-strategic justifications.[195] It was notable that, in this group, many legal scholars were willing to contemplate breaking the law and not advancing legal justifications for what they would regard as a genuine humanitarian intervention. On the other hand, practitioners and former government lawyers were more likely to suggest governments should try to advance a legal justification for such actions that did not obviously fall within the generally accepted exceptions to the prohibition on resort to force in international law.

But four participants simply rejected unilateral humanitarian intervention.[196] One legal scholar admitted 'the law is moving', but states almost always had 'ulterior motives' for humanitarian interventions.[197] That scholar argued it was ultimately 'for the people of the countries concerned to sort things out', and 'from a prudential point of view' humanitarian intervention should be avoided, since they were rarely successful – UK intervention in Sierra Leone was the only successful example.[198] Another scholar said 'sometimes you're stuck with the rules' preventing you from doing something that most wanted to do, but such rules 'also prevent states from doing something that they shouldn't'.[199] A former government lawyer said 'what might seem a good idea for one state may not necessarily be accepted by others' with 'risk of fallout if it's not accepted by other states'.[200] Another former government lawyer said 'wanting to do something is not the same as being able to do

193 Participant 31.
194 Participant 6.
195 Participant 7.
196 Participants 2, 24, 29, 25.
197 Participant 24.
198 Participant 24.
199 Participant 2.
200 Participant 29.

something', and lawyers should not 'just make it up', relying on their 'own opinions' and their 'own politics'.[201]

Several said such cases highlighted that[202] 'lawyers have to be humble about how useful law really is in these circumstances'.[203] One legal scholar said with humanitarian intervention and many other hard cases, legality is an important consideration 'but not the only one', and it is valid to ask whether the law in such cases was 'useful, whether it can be obeyed or should be obeyed'.[204] Another scholar said there was no 'supernatural force of law', and while states believed law was important, it does not solve every problem: 'I don't think it ever has, and it's highly unlikely to in the future.'[205] A former government lawyer said international law provided 'a framework' but 'not the only framework'.[206] That lawyer said, since there is no world government, and international law 'deals with real world politics and realities' and the varying views of almost 200 countries and their jurists, there will never be 'absolutely cut and dried law on absolutely everything' – in fact, it was surprising how much agreement had been achieved over the last 100 years.[207]

Finally, most participants – nineteen – echoed H. L. A, Hart in saying law did not necessarily produce ethical or legitimate outcomes.[208] Only one participant, a practising international lawyer, clearly said law and ethics must 'be intertwined'; that it was 'bad law' to stop action that is 'plainly the ethical thing'.[209] One legal scholar said sometimes 'the law is patently not good, but that's what the law is'.[210] Another scholar argued 'positivism necessarily says something which is lawful is not necessarily therefore moral' and vice versa.[211] That scholar said 'no legal system in history has ever had perfect alignment' between 'law and justice'; the challenge was to create a system that 'aligned with justice yet also serves other purposes such as to prevent abuse'.[212] Another scholar said they were 'not expecting law to conform to my world view' and 'can't pretend that the law is something that it's not'.[213] A practising

201 Participant 25.
202 Participants 22, 24, 25, 30.
203 Participant 22.
204 Participant 30.
205 Participant 24.
206 Participant 25.
207 Participant 25.
208 Participants 1, 2, 3, 4, 6, 12, 13, 15, 19, 20, 21, 22, 23, 24, 25, 27, 28, 30, 31.
209 Participant 10.
210 Participant 4.
211 Participant 23.
212 Participant 23.
213 Participant 6.

international lawyer said 'there's a difference between identifying an evolution in law and pretending that an objective that is desired has been evolved'.[214] Another practitioner argued treaties and custom are 'relatively modest attempts to lay down a few basic rules', not 'a comprehensive moral code', so they obviously 'leave a lot unresolved'.[215]

A scholar said an intervention could be, like Kosovo, 'illegal but legitimate', yet set a precedent that created a real possibility of abuses.[216] A former government lawyer gave the example of Russia's 2015 annexation of Crimea and 2008 intervention in Georgia, justified using language about averting humanitarian catastrophe that the United Kingdom had used in Kosovo.[217] One scholar said in applying law, 'morality doesn't come into it', although they admitted action could be lawful but wrong.[218] Giving an example, the scholar said that if the UNSC had authorised the 2003 Iraq intervention, 'all the lefties', including themselves, would have said it was 'dreadful', but it would have 'had the mandate of the security council': 'I would have had to accept that it was lawful, but I would have still said that it was an extremely bad idea.'[219]

CONCLUSION

This chapter explored associations between disagreements about the law governing resort to force and disagreements about the politico-strategic and ethical evaluation of military crises. It tested whether and under what conditions the law might be described as only partially autonomous of extra-legal factors, as suggested in Chapter 3: that lawyers hold consistent, mutually reinforcing political, strategic and ethical intuitions about conflicts, and disagreements between lawyers about these 'extra-legal' intuitions are consistent with their disagreements about the law. Textual analysis of scholarly writings, UK government statements, and ICJ opinions examined in Chapter 4, and survey and interview research conducted with thirty-one UK-based international lawyers, broadly supported the relationship proposed in Chapter 3. What this research suggested is that uncertainty about the *jus ad bellum* as a system of prescriptive rules and principles, encourages these different groups of lawyers, to different degrees, to practise 'strategic behaviour

214 Participant 12.
215 Participant 13.
216 Participant 2.
217 Participant 25.
218 Participant 24.
219 Participant 24.

in interpretation', to use the *jus ad bellum* as a system of argumentative practices, to justify or criticise the lawfulness of behaviour using arguments which align with and rely on specific sets of extra-legal beliefs and intuitions.[220] This reliance on extra-legal intuitions seems likely to hold whether those legal arguments are advanced as sincerely held beliefs about the law as it is, or as more self-conscious action to manipulate or change the law.

Lawyers with a 'restrictivist' approach to the *jus ad bellum* when considering a 'hard case' of resort to force, tended to apply politico-strategic and ethical assumptions, intuitions and beliefs that could be grouped under the broad heading of a 'pacificist' strategic culture. When assessing a potential use of force in which the requirements of the law were contested, they tended to choose the interpretation of the law that minimises the potential for future legal uncertainty and abuse, which best protects weaker states rather than trusting militarily and economically dominant states, and which regards the prohibition on force as always the most important principle. When assessing different interpretations of complex, incomplete or contradictory factual evidence, and when constructing forecasts about the consequences of using or not using force, they tended to proceed on the basis that such force almost always causes more harm than it prevents for the state using force and for the international community, that only self-interested states use force unilaterally, and only a few political interests and ethical values are sufficiently widely shared to guide decisions about unilateral force. And thus, such 'pacificist' lawyers who tended to see little political, strategic and ethical justification for force in specific cases, also tended to see political, strategic and ethical reasons to support a restrictivist *jus contra bellum* in general.

Opposing them, lawyers with an 'expansionist' approach to the *jus ad bellum* when considering a 'hard case' of resort to force, tended to apply politico-strategic and ethical assumptions, intuitions and beliefs that could be grouped under the broad heading of an 'interventionist' strategic culture. When assessing a potential unilateral use of force in which the requirements of the law are contested, 'interventionists' tended to choose the interpretation of the law that best fits with changes in conflict since the adoption of the UN Charter, and which regards principles such as human rights, preventing genocide, fighting terrorism or countering WMD proliferation as often more important than the prohibition on force. When assessing different interpretations of complex, incomplete or contradictory factual evidence, and constructing forecasts about the consequences of using or not using force unilaterally, they tended to proceed on the basis that such force often prevents

[220] Kennedy, *Legal Reasoning*, 159; Koskenniemi, *From Apology to Utopia*, 67–9.

more harm than it causes for the state using force and for the international community, that states that use force unilaterally often advance common interests as well as self-interest, and that various political interests and ethical values are sufficiently widely shared to guide decisions about unilateral force. And thus 'interventionist' lawyers who tended to see more such extra-legal political, strategic and ethical justifications for force in specific cases, also tended to see political, strategic and ethical reasons to support an expansionist approach to the *jus ad bellum* in general.

What this research suggests is that, as Chapter 3 proposed, both interpretive and strategic cultures seem to represent groups of individuals who share broadly similar coherent patterns of 'cognitive biases', 'motivated biases' and 'heuristics'. Motivated biases include 'cultural bias, organizational bias', bias reflecting one's own self-interest and 'emotional or intellectual predisposition toward a certain judgment'.[221] Cognitive and other 'unmotivated' biases, include 'the tendency to see information confirming an already-held judgment more vividly than one sees "disconfirming" information'.[222] Such biases are inherent or learned intuitions, presuppositions and heuristics – rules of thumb – 'which reduce the complex tasks of assessing probabilities and predicting values to simpler judgmental operations'.[223] Such intuitive expertise is often economical and effective in making rapid decisions, particularly in situations that recur frequently and conclude rapidly, allowing decision-makers to practice and learn effective intuitive judgment and thus accurately predict consequences from observable cues.[224] But in situations that are complex, idiosyncratic and infrequently recurring, biases and heuristics can 'lead to severe and systematic errors'.[225] As one former CIA analyst puts it 'The mind is poorly "wired" to deal effectively with both inherent uncertainty (the natural fog surrounding complex, indeterminate intelligence issues) and induced uncertainty (the man-made fog fabricated by denial and deception operations).'[226]

As Kahnemann has noted, any 'learned associations between ideas' can become so deeply internalised that they become incorporated into instinctive cognitive processes, becoming 'motivated biases' skewing even expert

221 Heuer, *Psychology of Intelligence Analysis*, 111.
222 'Introduction: Improving Intelligence Analysis at CIA: Dick Heuer's Contribution to Intelligence Analysis', in Richards J Heuer, *Psychology of Intelligence Analysis*, (Washington, DC: CIA, 1999), xxi.
223 Tversky and Kahneman, 'Judgment under Uncertainty', 1124.
224 Kahneman and Klein, 'Conditions for Intuitive Expertise', 254.
225 Tversky and Kahneman, 'Judgment under Uncertainty', 1124.
226 Davis, 'Introduction', xx–xxi.

judgement on ideologically charged questions where decision-making principles and factual evidence are complex.[227] Thus lawyers' opinions about interpretive techniques, and the political, strategic and ethical intuitions that this book explores, may well function as cognitive and motivated biases. Legal interpretive techniques are 'learned associations between ideas', so may become motivated biases particularly for lawyers highly committed to particular interpretive methods.[228] Some interviewees in this study spoke of deeply internalised politico-strategic and ethical beliefs and intuitions, shaping lawyers' assumptions and assessments in ways they were not entirely conscious of, akin to cognitive biases.[229] And Tetlock has noted that multi-scenario forecasts and counterfactual judgements – which this book argues are crucial to key *jus ad bellum* tests such as necessity, proportionality and imminence – rely on deeply internalised intuitions 'about how events would have unfolded' with different 'key factors', grounded in specific 'assumptions about how the world works'.[230]

But, as with Chapter 4, there are important caveats to these conclusions. First, the lawyers did not form polarised, clearly defined strategic cultures. Instead, their views about the politics, strategy and ethics of force were distributed on a continuum between the two strategic cultures, as were their views on principles of legal interpretation and the restrictiveness of the *jus ad bellum*. In fact, lawyers' views on the politico-strategic and ethical evaluation of force displayed the forms of vagueness described in this book. These principles were vulnerable to epistemic vagueness, as politico-strategic and ethical evaluation often relied on information that was not available and required analysis of potential alternative outcomes or future outcomes. All the principles displayed the sorites paradox and fuzzy logic, prescribing no hard boundary between force that was clearly politico-strategically and ethically advisable and unacceptable. They displayed supervaluationism, as politico-strategic and ethical evaluation are essentially multi-part tests, composed of several distinct, overlapping but not necessarily co-extensive tests – situations may meet all the tests, or none, or only some. And they displayed social supervaluationism, since lawyers formed distinct groups that disagreed about politico-strategic and ethical reasoning.

Second, the correlation between 'extra-legal' views and restrictiveness of the *jus ad bellum* in the survey was not perfect, and in fact slightly weaker than the

[227] Kahneman, *Thinking Fast and Slow* (London: Penguin, 2011), 22.
[228] Ibid.
[229] E.g. Participants 15, 23.
[230] Tetlock, *Expert Political Judgment*, 145, 146.

correlation between principles of legal interpretation and restrictiveness. This suggests that any causal link between extra-legal views and willingness to assess force as lawful cannot explain all the variation seen. There were clear examples of lawyers who accepted an interpretation of the *jus ad bellum* that they believed politico-strategically and/or ethically unsound. Many said humanitarian intervention was unlawful but politico-strategically and ethically justified, several admitting they would advise a government to use force to prevent humanitarian catastrophe if the factual evidence was strong enough, while accepting it would be unlawful. Some accepted self-defence against non-state actors was lawful but politico-strategically and ethically worrying. This suggests the *jus ad bellum* does exert 'normative pull', causing at least some lawyers to reach legal conclusions contradicting their personal politico-strategic and ethical intuitions – *jus ad bellum* decisions remain partially if not wholly autonomous of extra-legal considerations.

Third, there was relatively weak correlation between lawyers' extra-legal views and interpretive principles. Interviews and textual analysis of scholarly writings and ICJ opinions suggested a possible explanation in that some lawyers were able to justify relatively 'pacificist' views with 'dynamist' interpretive techniques, or relatively 'interventionist' views with 'formalist' interpretive techniques. Lawyers did not always display the full set of interpretive preferences grouped under the broad headings of 'formalism' and 'dynamism', and these preferences did not always align with the extra-legal preferences of the 'pacificist' and 'interventionist' strategic cultures, or with opinions about the *jus ad bellum* that this book first proposed. For example, Greenwood and the UK government used a textual reading of UNSC Resolution 1441 (2002) to justify force in Iraq, while others looked to wider evidence about the UNSC meetings at that time to argue this was not the purpose of that resolution. Justifications for force in Afghanistan deployed textual arguments, that the text of the UN Charter did not confine self-defence only to attacks by states, as well as dynamist arguments that States' support for the intervention signalled rapid acceptance of this legal conclusion even though that contradicted the dominant view of the law before then. In the *Nicaragua* case, judges used textual arguments to argue for the lawfulness of self-defence against non-state actors, while in the *Wall* and *Congo* cases other judges used dynamist, purposive and textual arguments to argue both for the same position and against the earlier *Nicaragua* ruling. This suggested that, in some cases, lawyers' extra-legal intuitions about a case encouraged them to adopt interpretive principles that they would not have chosen in other cases.

Fourth, none of the textual analyses showed evidence of the scholars explicitly considering alternative counter-factual scenarios as several of the *jus ad bellum*'s tests seem to require. In fact, the legal assessments often displayed what Philip Bobbitt has described as 'Parmenides' Fallacy'.[231] They evaluated policy options by comparing potential *future* consequences of different policies with *present* conditions, or evaluating a past policy by comparing the *present* with the *past*, when they should in fact compare the alternative possible outcomes of different policies *after* they have been implemented. Nor did the texts specify factual thresholds for the *jus ad bellum*'s tests: how much force used in an attack, how many casualties caused and how much damage to satisfy the scale and effects test; how brief must be the advance warning of an attack to meet the imminence test; how high must the probability of force succeeding in averting or ending an attack be; how many casualties constitute an overwhelming humanitarian catastrophe?

Thus the overall conclusion of Part II of this book is that disagreements between lawyers about the lawfulness of resort to force are affected not only by disagreements about principles of legal interpretation, but also disagreements about politico-strategic and ethical assumptions and presuppositions about the resort to force. This suggests lawyers' extra-legal beliefs and intuitions, and their choices about legal interpretation, combine to create contestation and uncertainty only in cases where law is most unclear, where facts and forecasts of consequences are particularly contestable, or where the most obvious reading of the law creates results which appear politico-strategically or ethically unacceptable. Politico-strategic and ethical intuitions act as forms of cognitive biases that for most, although not all international lawyers, shape but do not entirely determine their opinions about legal interpretation, law formation and the *jus ad bellum*. This evidence for the existence of competing interpretive and strategic cultures, the uncertain future outcomes of specific cases of force and the uncertain future evolution of conflict more generally are all reasons why vagueness and uncertainty may be necessary features of the *jus ad bellum*, enabling it to flex and adapt to the complexities of both the conflicts it seeks to regulate and the international community that seeks to apply it.[232]

This analysis does not suggest what these findings might mean for how lawyers should seek to produce advice in complex cases engaging the *jus ad bellum*. Can and should lawyers seek to extinguish such extra-legal effects on their legal decision-making in hard cases or should they embrace such effects? Part III of this book seeks to address this question.

[231] Bobbitt, *Shield of Achilles*, 10.
[232] Hart, *Concept of Law*, 131; Kelsen, *Introduction*, 78–81.

PART III

MANAGING UNCERTAINTY: RECONCILING LEGAL AND EXTRA-LEGAL REASONING

6

Legal Risk, Strategic Assessment, Forecasting and the *Jus Ad Bellum*

Two roads diverged in a yellow wood,
And sorry I could not travel both
And be one traveler, long I stood
And looked down one as far as I could
To where it bent in the undergrowth;

Then took the other, as just as fair,
And having perhaps the better claim,
Because it was grassy and wanted wear;
Though as for that the passing there
Had worn them really about the same,
Robert Frost, *'The Road Not Taken'*[1]

INTRODUCTION

Parts I and II of this book sought to describe legal and factual uncertainty and the role of extra-legal intuitions in *jus ad bellum* decision-making. Those parts used theoretical and empirical evidence to argue that the nature of the *jus ad bellum* encourages contestation and uncertainty about what the law requires in cases significantly different from 'plain cases' of lawful and unlawful resort to force. Applying this law requires factual analysis and forecasts of alternative outcomes of different policy choices either using force or not, yet the law prescribes no techniques for such analysis. And the factual evidence needed for controversial *jus ad bellum* assessments is often chaotic, incomplete and contradictory.

[1] Robert Frost, 'The Road Not Taken'. *Mountain Interval* (New York: Henry Holt and Company, 1920).

Such 'hard cases' suggest the *jus ad bellum* is 'specifically' if not 'systemically' indeterminate. Uncertainty and contestation about hard cases engaging the *jus ad bellum* seem driven partly by lawyers' disagreements about legal interpretation, and partly by competing politico-strategic and ethical intuitions – 'background assumptions' about force which are 'extra-legal (in the sense of not-doctrine based)'.[2] Thus, in hard cases, *jus ad bellum* decisions are only partially autonomous of 'extra-legal' politico-strategic and ethical factors.

This final part of the book attempts to address the 'so what' question many legal practitioners, policy advisers and political decision-makers ask when confronted with theoretical and empirical analysis of the kinds this book has so far presented. Such analysis may be interesting, but what can practitioners do about these legal, factual and forecasting uncertainties, and extra-legal intuitions in hard cases engaging the *jus ad bellum*?

The dominant competing legal interpretation techniques, which this book groups under broad categories of formalism and dynamism, either ignore or accept lawyers' underpinning politico-strategic and ethical assumptions. 'Formalism' is often used synonymously with 'positivism', which specifically seeks to separate law from extra-legal imperatives. And yet, as Koskenniemi has argued, 'formalism can be critical too', which, '[i]n a fundamentally unfree and unequal world', 'carries the ideal of a free and self-determining humanity', enabling less powerful states to resist western hegemony using commonly accepted rules, principles and argumentative strategies to serve their own interests and ideologies.[3] Meanwhile, Dworkinian naturalism, policy process and related theories associated with dynamism assert their own underpinning political and ethical principles, expecting lawyers in hard cases to choose the interpretation which advances those 'principles and policies' providing 'the best political justification' for the law.[4]

Lawyers might choose an alternative to these families of interpretive techniques, simply accepting that law reflects political competition, and choosing the legal and factual assessments that support their own or their client's interests and intuitions. For example, many legal realists argue international law emerges from 'nations acting rationally to maximize their interests', after assessing other states' goals and the international distribution of power.[5] Thus 'nations have no moral obligation to comply with international law', and

[2] Marxsen, 'Indeterminacy', 80.

[3] Koskenniemi, 'Constitutionalism as Mindset', 35; Craven et al., 'Teachers of International Law', 371.

[4] Dworkin, *Matter of Principle*, 145, 129.

[5] Jack Goldsmith and Eric A. Posner, 'The New International Law Scholarship', *Georgia Journal of International and Comparative Law*, 34 (2006), 463–88, 463.

should find whatever legal argument best justifies those actions which advance their interests.[6] Meanwhile, critical legal theorists advocate an international law 'in which political considerations are integrated in an explicit manner', which 'should not and cannot be separated from politics'.[7] Thus critical lawyers should use indeterminacy in law deliberately to defend the interests of marginalised, less powerful countries from western hegemony.

Unlike such approaches, this chapter considers how international lawyers might assess hard cases engaging the *jus ad bellum* and their legal and factual uncertainties in ways which seek to mitigate the effects of extra-legal intuitions without ignoring or embracing them. The chapter draws on three fields that have dealt with such challenges. Legal risk management developed in commercial law to deal with situations where uncertainty about the law governing a transaction creates uncertainty about future legal disputes concerning that transaction. For decades military commanders have applied international humanitarian law to battlefield targeting decisions, facing legal and factual uncertainties similar to those posed by the *jus ad bellum*. Finally, and perhaps most relevant, strategic intelligence analysis techniques emerged from private sector and government efforts to deal with factual uncertainty in commercial, political and military assessment, developing particularly after the intelligence failures around the 11 September 2001 terrorist attacks and Iraq's alleged WMD programmes in 2003.

This chapter introduces the three fields, outlining their broad concepts and the uncertainties each seeks to address. The chapter builds on the argument in this book that the extra-legal intuitions which seem to affect controversial *jus ad bellum* decisions function effectively as cognitive or motivated biases – internalised instinctive or learned associations between ideas, skewing decision-making in predictable ways that may not align with the available evidence. Using insights from legal risk management, international humanitarian law, and strategic intelligence analysis, this chapter develops a framework international lawyers might use to assess the lawfulness of resort to force in cases facing significant legal and factual uncertainty, while seeking to identify and mitigate the distorting effects of their own biases and intuitions. This chapter briefly demonstrates how this framework might assess two cases examined earlier in the book: the 1999 Kosovo intervention and the 2001 Afghanistan intervention. Finally, the chapter considers how such methods might have affected the UK attorney general's legal advice on the 2003 Iraq intervention.

6 Ibid., 478.

7 Deborah Z. Cass, 'Navigating the Newstream: Recent Critical Scholarship in International Law', *Nordic Journal of International Law*, 65 (1996), 341–83, 377, 345.

THREE APPROACHES TO UNCERTAINTY

Legal Risk Management

Risk 'has long been a useful category to absorb and manage uncertainty'.[8] Legal risk management emerged in commercial law to manage legal and factual uncertainty by using both non-legal and legal assessment techniques. These approaches particularly developed in the financial services sector, where complex instruments operating in multiple markets created uncertainties about potential legal liabilities, partly causing the 2008 global financial crash.[9] Legal advisers to the UK government now assess risks of legal challenge when advising on foreign policy questions, using guidance issued by the UK Government Legal Department.[10] Indeed, the penultimate section of the UK attorney general's detailed, internal 2003 legal advice on the Iraq intervention was a brief legal risk analysis, setting out possible consequences of acting without a second UNSC resolution.[11]

The International Standardisation Organisation (ISO) defines risk as the 'effect of uncertainty on objectives', of 'deviation from the expected', defining uncertainty as 'deficiency of information related to, understanding or knowledge of, an event, its consequence, or likelihood'.[12] Although this definition can include unexpected positive effects, 'risk' usually refers to negative developments. There is no single authoritative definition of *legal* risk. The UK Government Legal Department defines it as 'any risk of court action occurring whether domestic, European or international, or the risk of any penalty resulting from non-compliance with legal requirements'.[13] One scholar describes it as 'the risk of being sued or being the subject of a claim or proceedings due to some infringement of laws or regulations'.[14] Two other scholars describe it as 'the risk of financial loss that can result from lack of awareness or misunderstanding of, ambiguity in, or reckless indifference to, the way law and regulation apply to your business, its relationships, processes, products and services'.[15] An

8 Ambrus, Rayfuse and Warner, 'Risk and International Law', 3.
9 Roger McCormick, *Legal Risk in the Financial Markets*, 2nd ed. (Oxford: Oxford University Press, 2010), 1–3.
10 Participant 21; HM Government Legal Department, *Guidance Note on Legal Risk* (April 2015).
11 Goldsmith, 'Iraq: Resolution 1441', paras. 32–5.
12 ISO/Guide 73:2009(en), 'Risk management – Vocabulary'.
13 HM Government Legal Department, *Guidance Note on Legal Risk*.
14 McCormick, *Legal Risk*, 21.
15 Matthew Whalley and Chris Guzelian, *The Legal Risk Management Handbook: An International Guide to Protect Your Business from Legal Loss* (London: Kogan Page, 2016), 23.

International Bar Association working party identified sources of financial legal risk as including financial institutions' behaviour, failure to follow legal advice, abiding by 'the Letter but not the Spirit of the Law', law framed in vague terms to cover many circumstances and thus unclear in specific cases, the potential for unexpected new legislation or enforcement, and 'Unpredictable Judicial Reasoning'.[16]

Common to these descriptions of legal risk is a focus on uncertainty about:

- whether, and subject to what requirements, behaviour is permitted by the law at present and as it may evolve in future
- how other actors might respond to that behaviour, creating unexpected legal disputes or forcing the decision-maker to behave differently to avoid such disputes
- how courts or other authorities may interpret the law in any dispute
- other current or future facts concerning the behaviour in question that may trigger or affect a legal dispute.

Legal risk methodology proposes 'risk management' principles, 'coordinated activities to direct and control an organization with regard to risk', by identifying and analysing risk, and evaluating 'whether the risk should be modified by risk treatment'.[17] Risk management is future-oriented, 'proactive and anticipatory', seeking to affect 'the present by anticipating – preventing or pre-empting – future dangers', so that 'prognosticated dangers' prompt 'immediate action to anticipate them'.[18]

Clearly, *jus ad bellum* decisions differ from commercial legal risk management decisions. Unlike companies, states are law-makers as well as law-takers, particularly in customary international law. Commercial decisions almost never carry risks of harm as serious as states' decisions about using military force. Commercial decisions are more likely to face legal challenge and are subject to more intrusive enforcement. And, as one scholar has noted, unlike financial risks, there is 'no broad aggregate data' about international security to guide risk calculations about use of force, which occurs within 'a broad and unstable environment with many variables – political, economic, religious, social', where 'evidence is imperfect, inconclusive, or fragmented'.[19]

[16] Dr Joanna Benjamin, 'Sources of Legal Risk for Financial Institutions', *Journal of International Banking & Financial Law*, 19:4 (2004) 30–40.

[17] ISO, 'Vocabulary'; ISO 31000:2009(en), 'Risk Management – Principles and Guidelines'.

[18] Nicholas Tsagourias, 'Risk and the Use of Force', in Mónika Ambrus, Rosemary Rayfuse and Wouter Werner, eds., *Risk and Uncertainty in International Law* (Oxford: Oxford University Press, 2017), 17.

[19] Ibid.

Nevertheless, the essentials of legal risk management may assist a *jus ad bellum* decision-maker, who must 'assess the probability and the potential of risks', decide which risks justify action, what action must be taken and when, and 'be held accountable to their people or to the international community' for their decisions.[20] The purpose of legal advice about use of force is at least partly to avoid legal challenges, and the likelihood of such challenge partly depends on what unwelcome developments may emerge in military crises, including 'false positives' if the factual justification for force turns out to be false, or if the chosen legal justification can be challenged successfully, harming the affected state's reputation, relationships, national security, and potentially wider international security.[21] Legal risk management techniques may help manage such risks. However, such techniques provide no guidance on how to make the actual assessments of fact and forecasting that the *jus ad bellum* requires.

International Humanitarian Law

For decades states have applied international humanitarian law (IHL) in combat-targeting decisions, grappling with legal and factual uncertainty, which partly requires extra-legal assessment. For example, NATO's 2011 Libya intervention is estimated to have involved almost 1,000 IHL assessments of air strikes over seven months.[22] The sheer volume of IHL jurisprudence from tribunals such as the ICTY provide legal materials far exceeding those covering the *jus ad bellum*, motivating particularly Western states to develop systematic processes for integrating IHL into military decision-making.

Although the *jus in bello* clearly differs from and is separate to the *jus ad bellum*, there are obvious parallels. Both areas of law regulate behaviour in military conflict, IHL at the tactical/operational level, the *jus ad bellum* at the strategic level. Both areas of law concern means, methods and timing of military action to achieve a desired effect whilst limiting unintended harm. Decisions about the two fields can affect each other, since 'the way in which governments decide to resort to military force exerts a strong pull on the kinds of force they decide to use and on the ways in which they want to use it', according to a former UK FCO legal adviser.[23]

20 Tsagourias, 'Risk and Use of Force', 17.
21 Lubell, 'Problem of Imminence', 19.
22 Luke A. Whittemore, 'Proportionality Decision Making in Targeting: Heuristics, Cognitive Biases, and the Law', *Harvard National Security Journal*, 7 (2016), 581.
23 Berman, 'Lawyers in Armed Conflict', 628.

Both areas of law use similar concepts, displaying similar forms of vagueness. They contend with often patchy, contradictory factual information, in fast moving, chaotic, unpredictable circumstances, with belligerents deliberately trying to mislead and conceal. The factual uncertainties affecting IHL are arguably more tactical, time-bound versions of the uncertainties affecting the *jus ad bellum*. And both areas of law regulate decisions where states can expect to face *post hoc* scrutiny for compliance with relevant rules, generating demands for action to address non-compliance.

There *are* important differences. Necessity in the *jus ad bellum* is usually understood as concerning whether resort to force is the only reasonable option to address an attack, while in IHL the concept concerns objects which are necessary targets to achieve a military goal.[24] Proportionality in IHL forbids attacks 'expected to cause incidental' civilian harm, 'excessive in relation to the concrete and direct military advantage anticipated', requiring commanders to balance anticipated military gain against anticipated collateral harm to civilians.[25] Proportionality in the *jus ad bellum* is often understood as requiring decision-makers to establish whether an attack 'as a whole' is of sufficient scale and effects to justify force in response, and to ensure any military response uses only as much force as is required to stop the attack.[26] These are all complex tests, subject to supervaluationism, fuzzy logic and epistemic vagueness, but they assess different values.

Despite these and other differences, the framework developed in this chapter draws on some insights from IHL. However, like legal risk management, IHL does not address all the uncertainties, and particularly the problems of factual assessment and forecasting, that *jus ad bellum* decision-makers face.

Strategic Intelligence Analysis and Forecasting

Finally, and perhaps most relevant for the *jus ad bellum*, strategic intelligence analysis and forecasting have developed 'structured analytic techniques', emerging from private sector and government efforts to assess and forecast

24 *Hostage* case (*USA* v. *List et al.*) (American Military Tribunal, Nuremberg, 1948), 11 NMT 1230, 1253.

25 International Committee of the Red Cross, 'Protocol Additional to the Geneva Conventions of 12 August 1949, and Relating to the Protection of Victims of International Armed Conflicts (Protocol I)', 8 June 1977, 1125 UNTS 17512, Laws of Armed Conflicts, 73; Yoram Dinstein, *The Conduct of Hostilities under the Law of International Armed Conflict*, 2nd ed. (Cambridge: Cambridge University Press, 2010), 130.

26 Wilmshurst, 'Chatham House Principles', 968.

commercial, political and military situations involving competing actors using incomplete information in unpredictable situations.[27] The field draws on cognitive psychology and political science studies of decision-making and judgement, analytical techniques developed in the private sector and a history of reflection within the intelligence community about analysis of unpredictable situations involving actors actively seeking to conceal, misdirect and deceive.[28] Western intelligence agencies further developed these techniques following the 'false negative' failure to disrupt the 11 September 2001 terrorist attacks, and the 'false positive' incorrect 2003 assessment that Iraq possessed WMDs.[29] Strategic intelligence analysis has thus often tackled crises relevant to *jus ad bellum* decision-making, proposing structured analytic techniques for developing the kinds of alternative scenarios and forecasts this law requires.

These techniques particularly seek to manage the kinds of extra-legal intuitions this book has identified – the human propensity when faced with uncertainty to rely on cognitive and motivated biases and 'heuristics', 'simplifying strategies and rules of thumb to ease the burden of mentally processing information to make judgments and decisions'.[30] This book has already suggested that extra-legal intuitions functioning as cognitive and motivated biases appear to underpin the factual and forecasting assessments lawyers rely on in hard cases engaging the *jus ad bellum*. Even intuitions and beliefs about legal interpretation may function as cognitive or motivated biases. Many psychologists refer to such biases, intuitions and heuristics as characteristics of 'system 1' cognition, operating 'automatically and quickly, with little or no effort and no sense of voluntary control'.[31] As this book has already noted, such intuitive judgement can be effective where situations recur frequently and conclude rapidly, allowing assessors to practice repeatedly, learn effective intuitive judgment and thus accurately predict consequences from observable cues.[32]

27 Randolph H. Pherson and Richards J. Heuer, Jr, *Structured Analytic Techniques for Intelligence Analysis*, 3rd ed. (Los Angeles: SAGE Publications, 2021), xvii.

28 Tetlock, *Expert Political Judgement*; Weber et al., 'God Gave Physics the Easy Problems', 43–76; Tetlock and Gardner, *Superforecasting*; Daniel Kahneman, *Thinking Fast and Slow*; Pierre Wack, 'Scenarios: Uncharted Waters Ahead', *Harvard Business Review* (September 1985); Courtney, *20/20 Foresight*; Sherman Kent, 'Words of Estimative Probability', *Sherman Kent and the Board of National Estimates: Collected Essays* (CIA: 19 March 2007); Heuer, *Psychology of Intelligence Analysis*.

29 Lubell, 'Problem of Imminence', 19; CIA, *A Tradecraft Primer: Structured Analytic Techniques for Improving Intelligence Analysis* (4 May 2009).

30 Heuer, *Psychology of Intelligence Analysis*, 111.

31 Kahneman, *Thinking Fast and Slow*, 20; Pherson and Heuer, *Structured Analytic Techniques*, 17.

32 Kahneman and Klein, 'Conditions for Intuitive Expertise', 524.

However, decisions about force rarely meet these conditions. In politico-military matters, 'it is impossible to lay down binding rules', 'two cases will never be exactly the same' and '[g]uidelines are the best we can do in a world where nothing is certain or exactly repeatable'.[33] Effective reasoning about such complex, idiosyncratic phenomena as military crises requires what psychologists refer to as 'system 2' cognition, which 'allocates attention to the effortful mental activities that demand it, including complex computations'.[34] As Kahneman puts it, '[u]ncertainty and doubt are the domain of System 2'.[35] A part of 'system 2' cognition known as 'reflective' reasoning is particularly important in the critical thinking needed to deal with the errors which intuitions and biases can cause.[36] Strategic intelligence analysis proposes a range of structured analytic techniques – systematically reviewing assumptions and quality of information, analysing competing hypotheses, performing multi-scenario analyses – to encourage analysts to switch from automatic, intuitive system 1 reasoning, to the more systematic, effortful reflective system 2 reasoning. Such insights may be relevant to those seeking to address the kinds of factual uncertainties and extra-legal intuitions that this book suggests can affect legal decision-making in difficult *jus ad bellum* cases.

A RISK MANAGEMENT FRAMEWORK FOR THE *JUS AD BELLUM*

This section uses insights from legal risk management, IHL and strategic intelligence analysis to outline a possible framework for legal decisions about resort to force in situations of legal and factual uncertainty, seeking to take account of legal, factual, political and other risks concerning a decision to use force. This book does not claim to have developed the ideal way of using such insights. In addition, since *jus ad bellum* decisions are rare and idiosyncratic, they are unlikely to benefit from a rigid, detailed decision-making framework. This book suggests one possible way of using insights from these fields to assist such decisions.

The fields of legal risk management, IHL and strategic intelligence analysis suggest five overarching common-sense practices for *jus ad bellum* decisions. First, legal risk management recommends inter-disciplinary analyses,

33 Tetlock and Gardner, *Superforecasting*, locs. 4190–3.

34 Kahneman, *Thinking Fast and Slow*, 21; Pherson and Heuer, *Structured Analytic Techniques*, 17.

35 Kahneman, *Thinking Fast and Slow*, 80.

36 Keith E. Stanovich, 'Distinguishing the Reflective, Algorithmic, and Autonomous Minds: Is It Time for a Tri-process Theory?', in Jonathan Evans and Keith Frankish, eds., *In Two Minds: Dual Processes and Beyond* (Oxford: Oxford University Press, 2009), 55–88, 60.

involving non-legal subject matter specialists alongside lawyers specialising in the area of law being examined, since such analyses require both assessments of law and (non-legal) assessment of fact.[37] Second, IHL recommends involving lawyers closely in politico-military decision-making. Additional Protocol I to the Geneva Conventions requires 'that legal advisers are available, when necessary, to advise military commanders', and many western forces involve legal advisers closely in targeting decisions.[38] The *jus ad bellum* has no equivalent formal requirement, but it would be logical to involve lawyers closely and early in strategic decisions about force, just as they are involved in tactical targeting decisions.

Third, strategic intelligence analysis recommends a technique known as 'analysis of competing hypotheses' (ACH), systematically evaluating against the available information all plausible alternative explanations, however unwelcome, of what is currently happening and/or of what might happen as a situation evolves.[39] Seeking to ensure all information and arguments are 'given equal treatment or weight when considering each hypothesis', ACH counteracts biases to privilege information confirming rather than questioning a preferred hypothesis and to ignore information supporting unwelcome alternative hypotheses.[40] Fourth, strategic intelligence analysis encourages analysts to apply 'Bayesian reasoning' – challenging intuitions and revising beliefs in line with new information, accepting that '[f]or every good policy argument, there is typically a counterargument that is at least worth acknowledging'.[41] Such structured analytic techniques require analysts to display intellectual humility, acknowledge mistakes, conduct 'unflinching post-mortems' to identify errors, while being careful not 'to learn too much', since previous erroneous assessments may have made relatively minor mistakes with major ramifications.[42]

Fifth, all three disciplines separate complex assessments into more tractable sub-tasks, allowing systematic analysis using flexible techniques. This combination of systematic and flexible analysis is potentially challenging for rule-oriented disciplines such as law. But it is an important way of encouraging decision-makers to switch from system 1's intuitive reasoning and potentially

37 Tobias Mahler, 'Tool-Supported Legal Risk Management: A Roadmap', *European Journal of Legal Studies*, 2:3 (2010), 153–7.

38 Additional Protocol I to the Geneva Conventions, Article 82; Leslie Green, *The Contemporary Law of Armed Conflict*, 3rd ed. (Manchester: Manchester University Press, 2008), 308–9.

39 Heuer, *Psychology of Intelligence Analysis*, 97; CIA, *Tradecraft*, 14; Pherson and Heuer, *Structured Analytic Techniques*, 131.

40 CIA, *Tradecraft*, 14.

41 Tetlock and Gardner, *Superforecasting*, loc. 4137.

42 Ibid., locs. 4171–5.

error-inducing cognitive and motivated biases, to system 2's more systematic reflective reasoning, while still accommodating the idiosyncratic nature of conflicts.[43] Figure 6.1 illustrates the ISO's recommended risk management process, and a suggested process for legal risk management developed by a legal scholar.[44] The figure also summarises a possible risk management process that this book proposes for the *jus ad bellum*, using insights from these fields of legal risk management, IHL and strategic intelligence analysis, incorporating understanding of legal and factual context, identifying potential legal, factual, political and other risks and ways of treating those risks, decision-making, monitoring and evaluation. The rest of this section explains these steps.

Legal and factual context. In a *jus ad bellum* case, this phase would set out the known facts about the military crisis that may justify resort to force, the available policy options involving force or not, the applicable law and key legal questions it poses about use of force in this situation.[45] This phase would identify a fairly stable body of law as Chapter 2 outlined, including the UN Charter, customary law including the *Caroline* criteria, UNGA resolutions, ICJ judgments, regional and other treaties such as the North Atlantic Treaty and ICC Statute, and national legal positions such as the United Kingdom's doctrine of humanitarian intervention.

This stage would also identify factual 'indicators of change', 'observable events or trends', 'critical variables', 'clashing causal forces' and 'tell-tale clues' that would be observed if a situation changes, or would differentiate factual hypotheses or forecasts, indicating which are likely to be true or false.[46] The process would identify indicators that have most impact on a situation and are most uncertain, and thus most likely to signal major changes. The 'most critical or compelling' information indicates uncertainties that distinguish different hypotheses or scenarios from each other.[47] Evidence about them should be gathered and reviewed frequently to identify critical changes. Highly impactful but stable features, such as a state's total population, or volatile indicators with little effect on major developments, such as junior staffing decisions, are often not worth reviewing frequently as they are unlikely to distinguish different scenarios relevant to this kind of analysis.[48] In *jus ad bellum* cases, important

43 Ibid., loc. 4095.

44 ISO, 'Risk Management – Principles and Guidelines'; Tobias Mahler, 'Assessing Legal Risks of Closed Generic Top-Level Domains', *European Journal of Law and Technology*, 5:3 (2014), 12.

45 Mahler, 'Roadmap', 153.

46 CIA, *Tradecraft*, 12; Tetlock and Gardner, *Superforecasting*, locs. 4138, 4124–5, 4140.

47 CIA, *Tradecraft*, 11, Weber et al., 'God Gave Physics the Easy Problems', 54.

48 Ibid., 54.

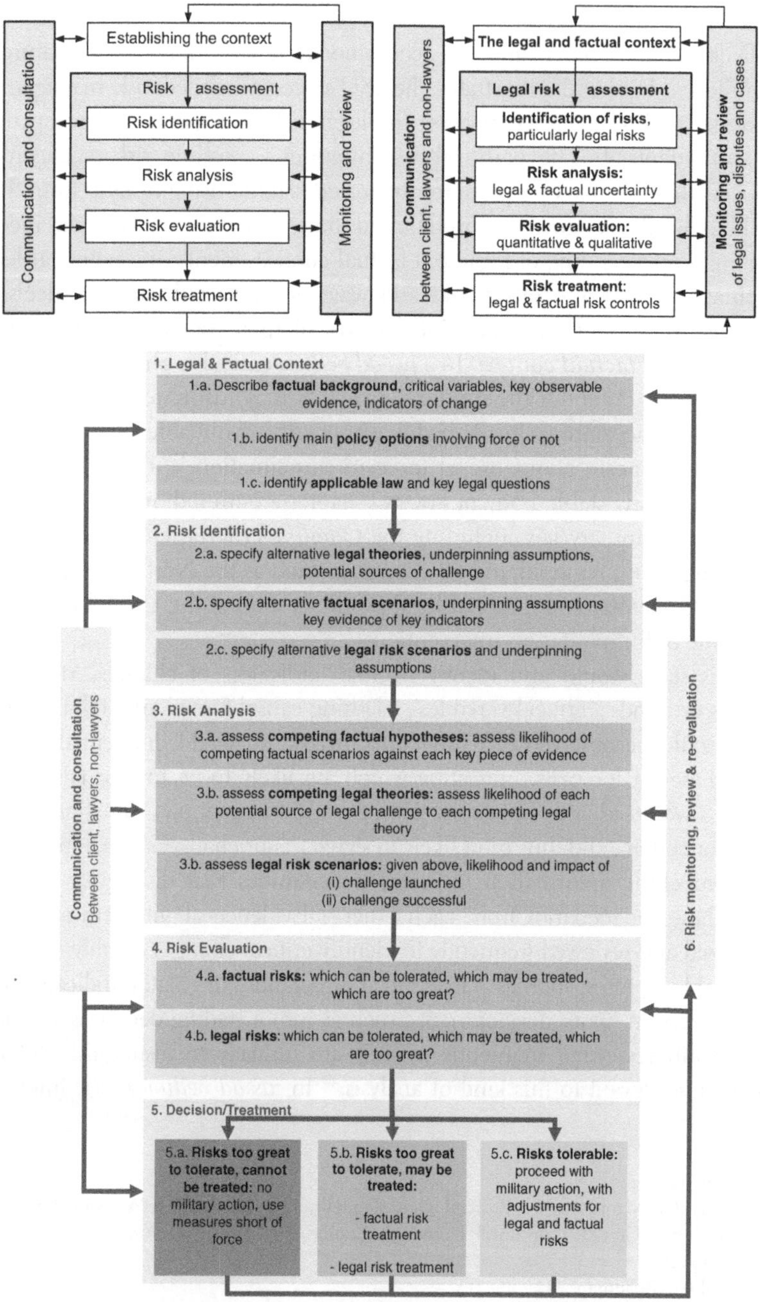

FIGURE 6.1 ISO risk management (top left), legal risk management (top right) and risk management in the *jus ad bellum*.[49]

49 ISO 31000:2009(en), 'Risk Management – Principles and Guidelines'; Mahler, 'Assessing Legal Risks', 12.

indicators could include public statements by an adversary's political leadership; parliamentary or media comment about a military dispute; movements of military forces; intensity of military clashes in a volatile area; relative influence of an adversary's policy makers advocating or opposing force; actions of other influential states. This phase should also include indicators and sources of various potential challenges to an action's lawfulness, such as commentary by influential jurists, statements about legality from other states, and attitudes of actors such as media, campaigning groups or parliamentarians.

Analysts should systematically review the *quality of available information*, ensuring 'ambiguous information has been interpreted and caveated properly', and 'indicating a level of confidence' in sources.[50] They should check evidence about critical indicators has 'sufficient and strong corroboration',[51] using tests such as the ICJ rules of evidence identified in Chapter 3 (Figure 3.3). Analysts should regularly review previously discarded evidence, in case new developments cast it in a different light.[52]

Perhaps most importantly, the process should review the 'stated and unstated assumptions' about 'how the world works', the presuppositions, intuitions and biases that underpin and potentially distort analysts' assessments.[53] This process does not necessarily seek to undermine or abandon such assumptions. Rather it seeks to make them explicit, amend any that are unreasonable, identify what new information might revise them, and identify reasonable alternative assumptions that generate alternative interpretations and assessments of the available evidence. This phase should also check assumptions about states, legal experts, civil society groups and media commentators who share or oppose the assumptions being relied on to justify a military action, and their willingness and ability to challenge that justification.

In a *jus ad bellum* case, these are likely to include the factual and legal assumptions identified in previous chapters as distinguishing competing interpretive and strategic cultures. Legal assumptions and intuitions could include what purposes can justify force, whether to privilege purposive or textual interpretation of legal texts, whether law is protean or static, how to identify and weigh *opinio juris* and state practice, the extent to which states can act without unambiguous UNSC authorisation. Factual and extra-legal assumptions could include what threats, interests and values justify unilateral force, whether states can be trusted to use force, the harm to civilians and friendly

50 CIA, *Tradecraft*, 11; Pherson and Heuer, *Structured Analytic Techniques*, 136, 171.

51 CIA, *Tradecraft*, 11.

52 Ibid.

53 CIA, *Tradecraft*, 7; Pherson and Heuer, *Structured Analytic Techniques*, 132.

forces that military action might cause, the effectiveness of friendly and adversary forces, the potential effects on international relations and international security, or the potential to set precedents that increase conflict and violations of the *jus ad bellum*.

Risk identification. This stage constructs 'risk scenarios', events that may trigger challenges to the lawfulness of the potential military action.[54] Strategic intelligence analysis would advise analysts to build *alternative hypotheses/ scenarios* describing situations both where the proposed military action succeeds and its lawfulness is unchallenged, and where the military action fails and faces legal challenge. To construct such scenarios, analysts are advised to use the most uncertain and important of the indicators and assumptions already identified – features most observably different under competing hypotheses, and varying the weight given to different critical pieces of information.[55] One technique converts 'the two most critical and uncertain forces' into axes, constructing alternative scenarios in different 'quadrants' of the resulting graph where assumptions about the values for each indicator clearly differ.[56]

Other techniques to build alternative scenarios include MECE trees, as illustrated in Chapter 3, using the 'mutually exclusive, collectively exhaustive' principle, mapping how different scenarios may emerge from different consequences from a single starting point.[57] 'Cone of plausibility' analysis helps analysts identify 'scenarios that are plausible – and fall inside the cone – and implausible – and fall outside the cone'.[58] 'Devil's advocacy' is a technique that builds 'the best possible case for an alternative explanation', challenging a strongly held or consensus view.[59] 'Team A/Team B' techniques task separate teams with developing competing factual hypotheses or forecasts based on the available evidence.[60] 'High-impact/low-probability' analysis develops scenarios that might otherwise be ignored as highly unlikely, but which could have major consequences if they materialised.[61] Similar techniques can be used to generate competing legal theories which support or oppose the legal position which could justify force in this situation, and which thus reach different assessments of the lawfulness of the action being considered.

54 McCormick, *Legal Risk*, 389.
55 CIA, *Tradecraft*, 12; Pherson and Heuer, *Structured Analytic Techniques*, 148–50.
56 Wack, 'Scenarios'.
57 Courtney, *20/20 Foresight*, 25, 120–1.
58 Pherson and Heuer, *Structured Analytic Techniques*, 268.
59 CIA, *Tradecraft*, 17, 19; Pherson and Heuer, *Structured Analytic Techniques*, 58–60.
60 CIA, *Tradecraft*, 17, 19; Pherson and Heuer, *Structured Analytic Techniques*, 58–60.
61 CIA, *Tradecraft*, 22; Pherson and Heuer, *Structured Analytic Techniques*, 189.

For a *jus ad bellum* assessment, the team could identify current and future alternative factual scenarios using different assumptions about the relevant politico-strategic factors, such as those identified in Figures 5.1 and 5.2 in Chapter 5. These scenarios would describe alternative interpretations of current military events and their consequences, consistent with available evidence. In some scenarios the initial threat assessment justifying force would be proven false – a 'false positive', in other scenarios the assessment would be proven correct, and in different scenarios force may or may not be effective and create more or less harm than non-forceful measures,[62] as the 'MECE tree' in Figure 3.1 illustrates.

The team would also identify alternative legal theories, justifying the use of force as lawful in this situation or assessing it to be unlawful. The team would finally outline risk scenarios in which the legal justification for force is challenged and a competing legal theory finding use of force unlawful prevails, perhaps using the different criteria for lawfulness and pre-suppositions about legal interpretation identified in Chapters 2 and 4 (e.g. Figures 4.1, 4.2 and 4.4). Such risks could include challenges to the lawfulness of the military action in parliaments, domestic courts, expert legal opinion, public opinion, other states, the UNSC, the UNGA or the ICJ. Many states would regard even the launch of such challenges as risks to be avoided, given the effort needed to respond to them, and the political and reputational damage even unsuccessful challenges can cause.

Risk analysis. The team should assess the likelihood and impact of each risk scenario – both of adverse factual situations arising and of adverse legal, political or other harmful outcomes flowing from challenges to an action's lawfulness.[63] Strategic intelligence analysis offers techniques to evaluate the relative likelihoods of alternative hypotheses/scenarios by assessing whether the available evidence supports the key assumptions about those scenarios, or whether it suggests critical indicators are changing.[64] This requires the analyst to make an initial assessment of the relative likelihood of each hypothesis based on their initial knowledge of the situation, and then to adjust that assessment by considering whether each piece of specific available evidence confirms, contradicts or casts no particular light on each hypothesis, evaluating the volume and reliability of evidence consistent and inconsistent with each, perhaps using an analytical grid such as in Figure 6.2.[65]

62 Lubell, 'Problem of Imminence', 19.
63 Mahler, 'Roadmap', 153.
64 CIA, *Tradecraft*, 12.
65 CIA, *Tradecraft*, 14–15; Heuer, *Psychology of Intelligence Analysis*, 95–7; Pherson and Heuer, *Structured Analytic Techniques*, 161–3.

	Competing Factual Hypotheses		
Evidence	**Hypothesis 1**	**Hypothesis 2**	**Hypothesis 3**
Evidence 1	✓✓×	✓✓	××
Evidence 2	×	✓✓	××
Evidence 3	×	✓	××
Evidence 4	-	×	✓
Evidence 5	✓	-	-
Result	3✓,2×	5✓,1×	1✓,6×

✓ = consistent with hypothesis
× = inconsistent with hypothesis
- = neither consistent nor inconsistent
Hypothesis 3 least plausible
Hypothesis 2 most plausible

	Competing Legal Theories		
Legal stakeholder	**Theory 1**	**Theory 2**	**Theory 3**
Stakeholder 1	✓✓×	✓×	××✓
Stakeholder 2	✓✓×	✓×	××✓
Stakeholder 3	××✓	✓✓×	✓✓×
Stakeholder 4	××✓	✓✓×	✓✓×
Stakeholder 5	××	×✓	✓✓×
Stakeholder 6	×✓	×✓	✓✓×
Stakeholder 7	××	×✓	✓✓
Result	7✓,11×	9✓,7×	12✓,8×

✓ = extent of likely support for theory; × = extent of likely opposition to theory; Theory 3 likely to attract most support on balance. Theory 1 likely to attract most opposition on balance.

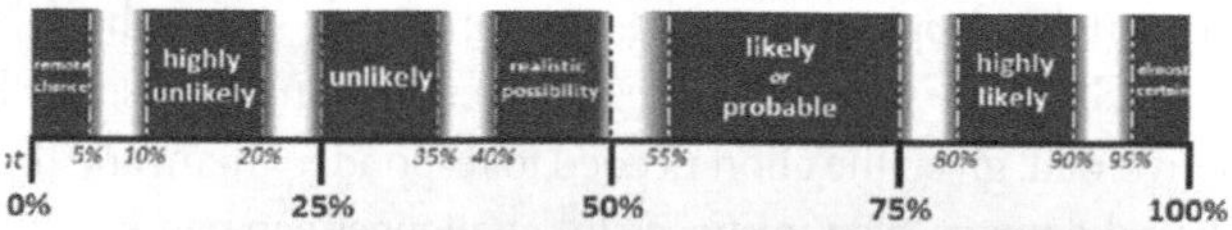

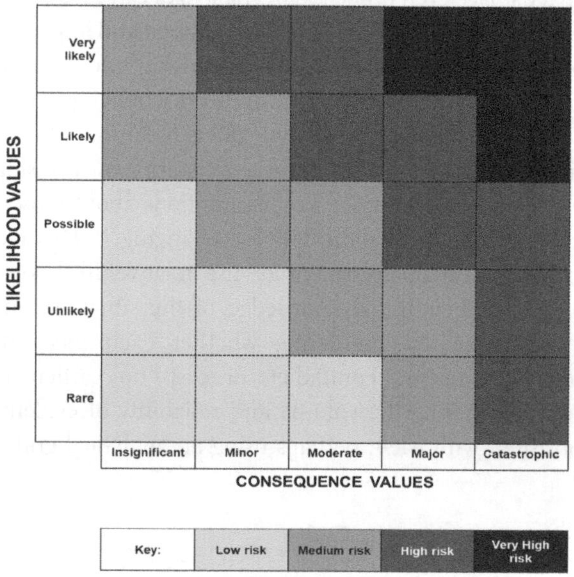

FIGURE 6.2 Analysing competing hypotheses and legal theories, the probability yardstick, a risk matrix (from top)[66]

66 Adapted from Marco Valtorta et al., 'Extending Heuer's Analysis of Competing Hypotheses Method to Support Complex Decision Analysis', 10 February 2005, Center for Information Technology, 5; UK Ministry of Justice, *Intelligence Collection, Analysis and Dissemination Policy Framework* (London: UK Ministry of Justice, 11 March 2019), 9.

The team can use a similar approach to assess competing legal theories relevant to this case. This could involve assessing what support or opposition each legal theory may receive from the different potential sources of legal challenge or legal stakeholders that have already been identified. In making this assessment, the team would need to assess the different legal and extra-legal opinions prevalent in each group. The team might use a further analytical grid for this assessment such as that in Figure 6.2.

Such analyses should balance 'inside and outside views', to envisage how an analyst operationalising different assumptions and intuitions may assess what is happening now or how events may develop on the basis of the evidence available about the current case and similar past cases.[67] Effective analysts acknowledge fuzzy logic without exaggerating it, ensuring that their 'uncertainty dial' has 'more than three settings', distinguishing 'as many degrees of doubt as the problem permits, but no more', and accepting that 'few things are either certain or impossible'.[68] Such analysts 'tend to be incremental belief updaters', making subtle shifts of probabilities and small modifications to the assumptions underpinning them as they consider the available evidence, unless they find evidence that strongly suggests a bigger shift is needed.[69] They balance 'prudence and decisiveness', incorporating new evidence without overreacting, understanding 'risks both of rushing to judgement and of dawdling too long near "maybe"'.[70] The analyst should thus establish which hypotheses are more or less likely, perhaps using probabilistic language such as the UK assessment community's 'Probability Yardstick' (Figure 6.2).[71] Finally, on the basis of these analyses of competing factual hypotheses and legal theories, the team should make an overall assessment of the likelihood and impact of the different scenarios occurring – including those scenarios that pose legal risks for the decision-maker.

In a *jus ad bellum* case, the inter-disciplinary team would assess the likelihood of alternative factual scenarios in which the threat assessment justifying force is shown to be true or false, and in which the outcome of the military campaign shows force was or was not necessary, proportionate and made the situation better or worse than if force had not been used. The team would assess how different legal theories either justifying or condemning the proposed use of force would be received by key legal stakeholders who may be sources of legal risk, such as Parliament, public opinion and media, international legal

67 Tetlock and Gardner, *Superforecasting*, locs. 4110–15.

68 Tetlock and Gardner, *Superforecasting*, locs. 4145–8.

69 Tetlock and Gardner, *Superforecasting*, locs. 4132–3.

70 Tetlock and Gardner, *Superforecasting*, locs. 4124–5, 4165–8.

71 *Understanding and Intelligence Support to Joint Operations*, Joint Doctrine Publication 2–00, 3rd ed. (Development, Concepts and Doctrine Centre, UK Ministry of Defence, 2011), 3–23.

commentators, other states in the UNGA or the UNSC, domestic courts or ultimately even the ICJ. The team would then assess the likelihood of legal risk scenarios – assessing what the combination of likely factual scenarios and distribution of legal opinion means for the likelihood of legal challenges being launched or succeeding. The team should assess the full range of impacts of risk scenarios – embarrassment and other damage to the state's standing, disruption to alliances, findings of illegality in the UNSC, UNGA, ICJ or other international bodies, sanctions, condemnation by international lawyers and media and so on. The team could thus assess the likelihood and impact of adverse factual scenarios transpiring, of legal challenges being launched, and of success for legal theories condemning the resort to force, 'scoring' scenarios for likelihood and impact and assigning each an overall risk rating between very high to low risk, perhaps using a matrix such as in Figure 6.2.[72]

Risk evaluation. The team would then *evaluate* the risks of various kinds of challenge, using decision criteria reflecting their government's objectives and the external and internal context, including relevant law. They would examine the legal and factual drivers underpinning those risks of challenge, and identify those that can be accepted with no further action, those that are to be accepted with appropriate contingency plans, and those to be 'treated' to try to reduce the risk of legal challenge.[73] Legal or factual drivers chosen for 'treatment' should be likely, of high impact for the government's objectives, and amenable to influence. Strategic intelligence analysts would distinguish between risk drivers that are unlikely to be influenced in the timescales of a military crisis, such as the global economy, from those that might be influenced more rapidly, such as tactical decisions of allies or adversaries.[74] 'Red team analysis' can help, by modelling how adversaries might respond to any proposed 'risk treatment'.[75] Risk management recommendations will depend on the decision-maker's risk appetite, and the inter-disciplinary team's assessment of the likely costs and harms to the policy-maker's interests of alternative courses of action or inaction. Logically, decision-makers should have greater legal risk appetite where alternative, less legally risky options pose greater threats, costs or harms for decision-makers' most valued interests.

In a *jus ad bellum* case, the team in this part of the process should apply a version of the 'principle of doubt' described by Additional Protocol I to the

72 Tobias Mahler, presentation at www.industrijuristgruppen.no/dokumenter/pres12/tobias_mahler.pptx.

73 Mahler, 'Roadmap', 153; ISO 31000:2009(en), 'Risk Management – Principles and Guidelines'.

74 CIA, *Tradecraft*, 30; Pherson and Heuer, *Structured Analytic Techniques*, 250–2.

75 CIA, *Tradecraft*, 31; Pherson and Heuer, *Structured Analytic Techniques*, 202–4.

Geneva Conventions: 'In case of doubt whether an object which is normally dedicated to civilian purposes' is being used for military action 'it shall be presumed not to be so used', 'unless and until the presumption is rebutted'.[76] How much doubt is required to prevent action is not clear, but the principle requires targeting to be based on well-evidenced facts, not hypothetical assessments of 'worst-case scenarios'.[77] Similarly, *jus ad bellum* assessments should presume against resort to force unless decision-makers have sufficiently few doubts about their factual basis for action. As the MECE tree in Chapter 3 shows, purely in terms of logical consequences, there are more scenarios in which military intervention may eventually be viewed as unlawful than lawful. However, scenarios in which intervention is judged lawful may be collectively more probable than scenarios where intervention is judged unlawful – a reason for carefully weighing case-specific evidence.

Decision/treatment. The policy-maker will then face three broad options: use force immediately because the legal and factual risks are assessed to be less undesirable than the risks of non-forceful responses; choose non-forceful responses, because force creates unacceptable risks that cannot be reduced to tolerable levels; or take measures to reduce risks to tolerable levels, because although the risks of force are currently unacceptable, the costs and risks of non-forceful responses are also assessed to be unacceptable. Risk treatments include actions to avoid or deal with risks, to increase the likelihood of desirable outcomes and reduce the likelihood of undesirable outcomes, contingency plans in case undesirable outcomes occur, and actions to maximise benefits if desired outcomes transpire.[78] Risk treatment effort should be allocated according to relative likelihoods and impacts of risk scenarios compared to the costs of treating them.[79]

In a *jus ad bellum* case, risk treatment could include redesigning action to reduce the likelihood of events that may trigger legal challenge. It could include sharing information about the situation, about the threat and about the law, encouraging media, academic or other independent sources to report on it. It could include engaging allied states, legal academics and others to generate more expressions of *opinio juris*, state practice and expert legal opinion supporting the favoured legal theory, and to gain support from those who doubt the favoured legal theory. Applying a doctrine of humanitarian

76 Additional Protocol I to the Geneva Conventions, Article 52(3); Dinstein, *Conduct of Hostilities*, 98.

77 Dinstein, *Conduct of Hostilities*, 89–99, 100.

78 McCormick, *Legal Risk*, 402.

79 Mahler, 'Roadmap', 153.

intervention requires a further assessment of whether force is likely to cause less harm than would occur without military action.

Both IHL and the *jus ad bellum* must grapple with similarly complex calculations of harm, and the vagueness of the law's thresholds in unpredictable military conflicts. US and NATO forces have developed a structured methodology for tackling IHL assessments; the published US version is named 'No Strike and Collateral Damage Estimation Methodology' (CDM), enabling decision-makers to adjust the means and methods of attack to reduce risks of harm to 'protected or collateral' objects or people, if necessary accepting a higher risk of failure for the attack.[80] Similarly, decision-makers in a *jus ad bellum* case should adjust their tactics and military means to what is needed and no more than is needed to stop an imminent or ongoing attack. They could also calibrate action according to their degree of factual confidence about the threat, adopting more limited reversible means if there is significant uncertainty – for example, limited special forces raids or highly targeted air strikes rather than large-scale, coordinated air, ground and maritime operations.

Risk monitoring. In conducting such assessments, analysts and decision-makers need to be clear about the limitations of forecasting, multi-scenario analysis and factual and legal risk management in situations as complex as military crises.[81] A warning about IHL assessments also applies to any *jus ad bellum* risk management: it 'is not an exact science', and can address but cannot eliminate uncertainty, since it relies on intelligence and assessments which have 'inherent error and uncertainty'.[82] The true facts of chaotic emerging conflicts that often motivate *jus ad bellum* decisions, or the outcomes of the military campaigns that such decisions may initiate, are not usually situations amenable to high confidence probability analysis, but are instead 'cloud-like'.[83] The same kind of uncertainty applies to assessments of whether stakeholders may challenge the lawfulness of a decision to use force, and whether such a challenge is likely to succeed legally or politically and significantly harm the decision-maker. Such situations accommodate many more potential interpretations of current facts and potential future outcomes of decisions than could be captured by any viable analytical framework or precise calculation of likelihood and impact.[84]

80 Chairman of The Joint Chiefs of Staff, Instruction 3160.01, *No-Strike And The Collateral Damage Estimation Methodology* (13 February 2009); *Joint Staff Targeting, Joint Targeting Cycle and Collateral Damage Estimation Methodology* (CDM), Slides (Nov. 10, 2009), at D-A-7.

81 Pherson and Heuer, *Structured Analytic Techniques*, 253.

82 CDM at D-2.

83 Tetlock and Gardner, *Superforecasting*, locs. 4082–4.

84 Mervyn King and John Kay, *Radical Uncertainty: Decision-Making for an Unknowable Future*, Kindle version (London: Little, Brown Book Group, 2020), loc. 238.

These caveats mean risk management cannot be viewed as a linear process with a definitive conclusion, rather an ongoing process, regularly reviewing evidence and reassessing analysis to reflect changes in fact, legal opinion and other relevant factors.[85] In a *jus ad bellum* case, the inter-disciplinary team should regularly review their analysis during the military crisis, repeatedly reviewing new evidence and, where necessary, updating/revising assumptions underpinning their analysis. They should regularly reassess the risks and costs of force compared to other courses of action, if necessary adjusting their view of the law in question, and of the need and viability of force in light of new information and as new legal opinions are advanced.

Using this kind of framework to assess the lawfulness of a decision to use force after it has been taken, lawyers could test whether such a decision could have been taken by a 'reasonable strategic decision-maker', adapting the IHL concept of the 'reasonable military commander'.[86] The ICTY *Galić* opinion described this test as 'whether a reasonably well-informed person in the circumstances of the actual perpetrator, making reasonable use of the information available to him or her' would have made that decision.[87] This is a difficult test to apply, since 'what might be unreasonable to one commander might be reasonable to another', and some military crises are so unpredictably dynamic they are 'not capable of optimization'.[88] But the test accepts that decision-makers are imperfect and constrained by 'environment, cognitive abilities, and lack of complete information'.[89] In a *jus ad bellum* decision, the 'circumstances of the actual perpetrator' would include time pressures, threat perceptions, resources and capabilities, socio-political and emotional pressure, and other distorting factors when the decision-maker made their choice.[90]

Finally, this kind of framework would recommend making public the legal and factual reasoning underpinning a decision to use force, as an important way of managing the risks of legal and political challenge. Doing so would also provide material enabling any court or legal commentator to assess a past resort to force decision, using this kind of framework and drawing on politico-military expertise to assess the factual and wider politico-military context.

85 McCormick, *Legal Risk*, 399–400.

86 Whittemore, 'Proportionality Decision Making', 578.

87 *Prosecutor* v. *Galić*, Case No. IT-98–29-T, Judgment (International Criminal Tribunal for the Former Yugoslavia (ICTY) Dec. 5, 2003), 58; ICTY, *Final Report to the Prosecutor by the Committee Established to Review the NATO Bombing Campaign Against the Federal Republic of Yugoslavia*, 50.

88 Whittemore, 'Proportionality Decision Making', 602–3, 631.

89 Whittemore, 'Proportionality Decision Making', 595.

90 *Prosecutor* v. *Galić*, Judgment, 58.

APPLYING THE FRAMEWORK: KOSOVO AND AFGHANISTAN

To assess the viability of the framework this chapter proposes, this section applies it to two of the 'hard cases' this book has considered: the US-led interventions in Kosovo and Afghanistan. The framework is applied from the point of view of international lawyers advising UK government decision-makers. It is applied in summary form only, using published sources, without weighing the factual and legal arguments in-depth, so the conclusions do not necessarily represent the author's definitive assessments. The section does however illustrate how the framework might be used by international lawyers assessing such cases, and the kinds of answers it might produce.

Kosovo 1999

The factual context for this potential intervention is escalating violence in the Kosovo province of the Federal Republic of Yugoslavia (FRY) between Serb-dominated FRY forces and ethnic Albanian Kosovar independence forces.[91] Unarmed monitors from the Organisation for Security and Co-operation in Europe (OSCE) deployed to monitor compliance with UNSC Resolution 1199 (1998) have not stopped tensions escalating.[92] The FRY (and Russia) have rejected NATO's proposed Rambouillet Agreement, which attempted to end violence by making Kosovo an autonomous part of FRY under temporary NATO administration.[93] The main policy options for the United Kingdom as a NATO member are:

- continue non-forceful measures, including OSCE monitoring and diplomacy, combined with political and economic pressure
- military action to expel Serb forces from Kosovo to stop ethnic cleansing and thus avert or end a humanitarian catastrophe.

The legal context for the option involving force includes treaty and customary law concerning the *jus ad bellum* already described, including the UN Charter, Caroline Criteria and UNGA resolutions. There are three competing legal theories concerning the legality of any NATO-led military action in this situation:

[91] IICK, *Kosovo Report*, 2.

[92] OSCE, 'OSCE Kosovo Verification Mission/OSCE Task Force for Kosovo (Closed)'.

[93] US State Department, 'Rambouillet Agreement -Interim Agreement for Peace and Self-Government in Kosovo' (March 1999).

Legal Theory A Humanitarian Intervention – use of force in another state to protect civilians from humanitarian catastrophe perpetrated by their government – is lawful under customary international law.[94] It evolved through use of force in Iraq after 1991 to protect civilians, alongside developments in international human rights law, international humanitarian law and international law prohibiting genocide. It has roots in 1970s interventions by India in East Pakistan/Bangladesh, and by Tanzania in Uganda, and in nineteenth-century interventions to protect civilian populations. Such use of force must be based on compelling evidence of an imminent overwhelming humanitarian catastrophe, be assessed as likely to do more good than harm, and be limited only to action necessary and proportionate to prevent that humanitarian catastrophe and not for unrelated purposes.[95]

Legal Theory B Humanitarian Intervention as described by Legal Theory A is only *lex ferenda* – a legal norm still emerging and not yet crystallised as customary international law.[96] Relying on this legal theory to justify force in Kosovo and gaining wide expressions of supportive *opinio juris* and state practice may provide more evidence that the norm is crystallising as *lex lata*.

Legal Theory C Humanitarian Intervention is only lawful if authorised by the UNSC. Cases of unilateral action since 1945 provide too little evidence for new custom.[97] It is arguably unlawful interference in matters essentially in the domestic jurisdiction of states, even with a UNSC resolution, unless intervention is necessary to address a genuine threat to international peace and security, such as conflict spreading into neighbouring states.[98]

94 Greenwood, 'NATO Intervention in Kosovo', 926.
95 Robertson, 'Kosovo'.
96 Lowe, 'Kosovo Crisis', 934.
97 Gray, *International Law*, 47–51.
98 Brownlie and Apperley, 'Kosovo Crisis Inquiry', 904.

Key differences in legal assumptions underpinning these theories include the effects of developments in other areas of *jus cogens* international law, such as human rights law and genocide law, the role of the UN Charter's wider objects and purposes such as human rights, and the time and amount of *opinio juris* and state practice needed to crystallise justifications for force not explicitly articulated in the UN Charter.

Evidence and assumptions about the following key factors are critical both for assessing the facts of the current situation in Kosovo, and for forecasting different ways in which that situation and the wider international system may evolve following different policy responses:

(a) *FRY capability and intent to commit massacres of Kosovars.* Multiple independent media and civil society groups, OSCE monitors, and intelligence report events such as the 15 January 1999 massacre of forty-five civilians in the village of Racak, other repressive actions by FRY forces, and Kosovar citizens' fearful reactions.[99]

(b) *Kosovar intent and capability to commit unlawful attacks against Serbs and misreport events.* Multiple media and other reports suggest pro-independence Kosovar armed groups are stoking violence against Serb civilians, arguably engaging in criminal activity, and misreporting events to encourage external military help.[100]

(c) *FRY reliability to report events in Kosovo.* The Milosevic regime's reporting of events previously in Bosnia-Herzegovina and now in Kosovo consistently contradicts independent media, civil society and OSCE monitors' reports.[101]

(d) NATO *reliability to report events in Kosovo, and to use force for humanitarian purposes not self-interest.* NATO's reporting broadly aligned with independent media, civil society and OSCE reporting. Intervention would only marginally increase NATO's existing economic and geopolitical dominance.

(e) *Potential for non-forceful means to prevent escalation.* OSCE monitors and diplomatic talks had failed to stop violence. Violence in Bosnia-Herzegovina only ended after NATO military action.[102]

(f) *FRY capability and intent to resist NATO.* The FRY has extensive military forces, although significantly less sophisticated than

99 Wheeler, *Saving Strangers*, 265.

100 Alan J. Kuperman, 'The Moral Hazard of Humanitarian Intervention: Lessons from the Balkans', *International Studies Quarterly*, 52 (2008), 49–80, 69–71; IICK, *Kosovo Report*, 52–3.

101 IICK, *Kosovo Report*, 134.

102 Wheeler, *Saving Strangers*, 256.

NATO.[103] The FRY views Kosovo as more integral to its territory than Bosnia-Herzegovina and other former Yugoslav republics.

(g) NATO *capability and intent to use force effectively to defeat FRY resistance without causing unacceptable harm.* Experience in Iraq, Bosnia-Herzegovina and Sierra Leone suggest NATO countries have the capability and will to conduct a successful military campaign. However, what is widely perceived as the failed US-led intervention in Somalia suggests success is not guaranteed.[104] In addition, US refusal to conduct ground operations or low-altitude air strikes reduces military effectiveness and increases risks of collateral damage.[105]

(h) *International community support for military action.* Many Arab states and most NATO Allies support military action against FRY forces in Kosovo. But there is opposition from the public even in some NATO states such as Greece. Russia, China and important Non-Aligned Movement states have repeatedly described such action as unjustifiable interference in internal affairs.[106]

(i) *Intervention sets precedent for unjustified future action.* It is unclear whether other states disagreeing with NATO might use the action as a precedent. Their opposition to any intervention in Kosovo might suggest it is unlikely.

By applying different interpretations of the evidence and assumptions about these facts, four broad alternative factual hypotheses can be developed, yielding different assessments of what is currently happening in Kosovo and how the situation may evolve following different policy responses:

Hypothesis 1	A FRY massacre of Kosovar civilians is imminent. Military action from NATO will prevent that massacre, without disrupting international peace and security, or setting precedents for future harmful military action undermining international law governing resort to force. Options not involving force would result in greater suffering in Kosovo and disruption to international peace and security, international society, and the wider rule of law.

103 IICK, *Kosovo Report*, 86.

104 Wheeler, *Saving Strangers*, 244.

105 IICK, *Kosovo Report*, 289; Wheeler, *Saving Strangers*, 272–3.

106 Wheeler, *Saving Strangers*, 268.

Hypothesis 2	A FRY massacre of Kosovar civilians is imminent. However, NATO military action will fail to prevent the massacre, or will prevent the massacre while disrupting international peace and security and setting precedents undermining future international security and international law. Options not involving force would cause less long-term harm.
Hypothesis 3	A FRY massacre of Kosovar civilians is not imminent. Military action from NATO will precipitate inter-ethnic violence, including by Serb forces. Options not involving force would cause less suffering.
Hypothesis 4	Reports of imminent FRY massacres are Kosovar terrorist fabrications. Military action from NATO will enable terrorists to cause more suffering, justifying FRY military responses. Options not involving force would cause less suffering.

Analysing these Competing Hypotheses against the available evidence, as illustrated in Figure 6.3, an inter-disciplinary team might find this situation finely balanced, as the key assessments are *forecasts* about whether FRY forces are about to commit atrocities, and whether intervention will prevent more harm than it causes. The team may assess Hypothesis 4 as least likely, as the FRY's claims have been consistently contradicted by multiple independent sources. But they might find only marginal evidence to favour Hypotheses 1 and 2 over Hypothesis 3, as there is evidence of Kosovar armed groups committing violence and exaggerating claims, and considerable uncertainty about future FRY actions and the outcome of NATO military action. The team might at this stage find Hypotheses 1 and 2 equally compelling: that it is a realistic possibility that atrocities are imminent, but that NATO action is no more likely to improve the situation than non-forceful responses.

There are broadly seven sets of stakeholders whose reactions to any legal justification for unilateral force are likely to be important to UK decision makers: Parliament, the public and media, influential international lawyers and commentators, domestic judiciary who may adjudicate any domestic legal challenge, states that make up the UNSC, states in the wider UN, judges of the ICJ and, for any use of force in Kosovo, the ICTY. Analysing the competing legal theories, as illustrated in Figure 6.3, the inter-disciplinary team might see significant challenges to persuading some although not all these stakeholders to accept Legal Theory A, which justifies resort to force in

	H1: Massacre imminent, NATO saves more than kills	H2: Massacre imminent, NATO kills more than saves	H3: Massacre not imminent, NATO makes it happen	H4: Massacre is terrorist lie, NATO helps terrorists
FRY intent to kill	✓	✓	✗	✗
K intent to misreport	✗	✗	✓	✓
FRY reliability	✓✓	✓✓	✗	✗✗
NATO reliability	✓	✓	✗	✗
Potential for non-force	✓	✓	✗	✗✗
FRY mil capability	✗	✗	✓	-
NATO mil capability	✓	✓	✓	✓
International support	✗	✗	✓	✓
Harmful precedent	✓	✓	✓	✓
Assessment	3✗, 7✓	3✗, 7✓	4✗, 5✓	6✗, 4✓

✓: consistent with hypothesis; ✗: inconsistent with hypothesis; - : neither consistent nor inconsistent

	LT(A): Humanitarian Intervention lawful	LT(B): Humanitarian Intervention *lex ferenda*	LT(C): Humanitarian Intervention unlawful
Parliament	✓✓✓✗	✓✗	✗✗✗✓
Public and Media	✓✓✓✗	✓✗	✗✗✗✓
UK Courts	✓✗✗✗	✓✓✗✗	✓✓✗✗
International lawyers	✓✗✗✗	✓✗	✓✓✓✗
UNSC	✓✗✗✗	✓✗	✓✓✓✗
UNGA / UN States	✓✗✗✗	✓✗	✓✓✓✗
ICJ or ICTY	✗✗✗✗	✓✗	✓✓✓✗
Assessment	18✗, 10✓	8✗, 8✓	12✗,16✓

✓: extent of support for legal theory; ✗: extent of opposition to legal theory;

FIGURE 6.3 Analysis of competing hypotheses and legal theories about Kosovo

Kosovo as lawful. Assessing the likely distribution of legal and extra-legal opinions and intuitions amongst these stakeholders (see Figures 4.1, 4.2, 5.1 representing textual analyses of Kosovo in Chapters 4 and 5), the team may assess that key international stakeholders – ICJ judges, most UNSC members, most UN states and international lawyers – are highly likely to support Legal Theory C – that humanitarian intervention is unlawful. The team might however assess it is at least likely that a majority of the UK Parliament, public and media could be persuaded of Legal Theory A – that humanitarian intervention is lawful. While the team might assess there is a realistic possibility of persuading a domestic court to accept Legal Theory B – humanitarian intervention is *lex ferenda* – they might also assess there is a realistic possibility that domestic judges would support Legal Theory C – humanitarian intervention is unlawful.

The team would identify seven broad 'risk scenarios' of legal or political challenge to the action's lawfulness from the key stakeholders identified as potential sources of legal risk:

(i) Parliament or parliamentary committees challenge and reject the lawfulness of the action, refusing to pass a vote supporting the military action before it begins, or declaring it unlawful afterwards.
(ii) A significant proportion of public and media reject the factual or legal justification for action, leading to persistent opposition, demonstrations, media criticism, public lobbying of parliamentarians and ministers.
(iii) A significant proportion of influential international lawyers and politico-military commentators reject the government's legal or factual arguments, declaring the intervention unlawful.
(iv) A domestic legal challenge is launched and rules the action unlawful, such as judicial review by a civil society organisation, or public and political pressure prompting judge-led or other public inquiry.
(v) A significant majority of states reject the legal and/or factual justification, declare the action unlawful, take other action, such as majority vote in the UNGA, sanctions against NATO countries, political, military or other support to FRY forces opposing NATO.
(vi) A majority of UNSC states reject the legal and/or factual justification by voting for a UNSC resolution declaring the action unlawful, demanding it end, and imposing sanctions and other measures, even if blocked by veto.
(vii) The ICJ or ICTY declares the action unlawful, after the UNGA refers the case to Court for an advisory opinion, or if the FRY or a neighbouring state launch a case in the ICJ or ICTY.

To assess the potential likelihood and impact of these risk scenarios, the team would combine the assessments they have already conducted of the competing factual hypotheses and competing legal theories in this case, to assess the capability and will of each source of legal risk to launch any challenge given this set of factual and legal circumstances. As illustrated in Figure 6.4, the team might conclude that:

– Scenarios (i), (ii) and (iv) are unlikely, because widespread parliament, media and public concern about past FRY violence in Bosnia-Herzegovina and Kosovo suggest the action's lawfulness is likely to be challenged only by a minority of politicians and campaigning groups, who are unlikely to gain sufficient support to overturn government decisions or launch domestic legal challenges.

- The team may assess the international legal community is too divided to suggest risk scenario (iii) is likely and high impact. Most international lawyers oppose a doctrine of humanitarian intervention, but most support human rights law and genocide law, and many are concerned about the Milosevic regime's violations of these laws.
- However, the team might assess risk scenarios (v), (vi) and (vii) as likely and relatively high impact, that the FRY, Russia and the Non-Aligned Movement are likely to press for the UNGA, UNSC, ICJ, and ICTY to declare NATO action unlawful. Although NATO states could probably prevent UNSC decisions condemning NATO without using vetoes, adverse UNGA votes are possible. It is questionable whether the FRY joined the ICJ in time to allow them to launch this case, and the United States and France have rejected ICJ compulsory jurisdiction, but it is not certain the ICJ would refuse to hear cases against the United Kingdom and other NATO states that have accepted compulsory jurisdiction. The UNGA may vote to refer the case to the ICJ for an advisory opinion. Since the United States, Germany and other NATO states refuse to assert a doctrine of humanitarian intervention, and most ICJ judges adopt a broadly formalist approach to legal interpretation, the ICJ would likely find any action unlawful if they consider its merits.

The analysis might thus conclude that use of force in this case faces considerable risks of challenges to its lawfulness, as Figure 6.4 shows. Several high-impact risks have moderate to high likelihood, suggesting significant risk treatment is advisable before considering force. The team might thus conclude there is currently a fine balance between options to use force now, or to continue armed vigilance and coercive diplomacy. On balance, and in line with the principle of doubt in the face of factual uncertainty, there may be a stronger case for deferring military action until and unless violence reaches levels making a more compelling factual case. The team could recommend risk treatment, including working with media and civil society to gather and share factual information about the humanitarian situation, and diplomacy and engagement with the legal community to generate support for a doctrine of humanitarian intervention from NATO and other sympathetic states. The team might also recommend carefully tailoring military plans to minimise collateral damage and humanitarian suffering, including low-altitude air

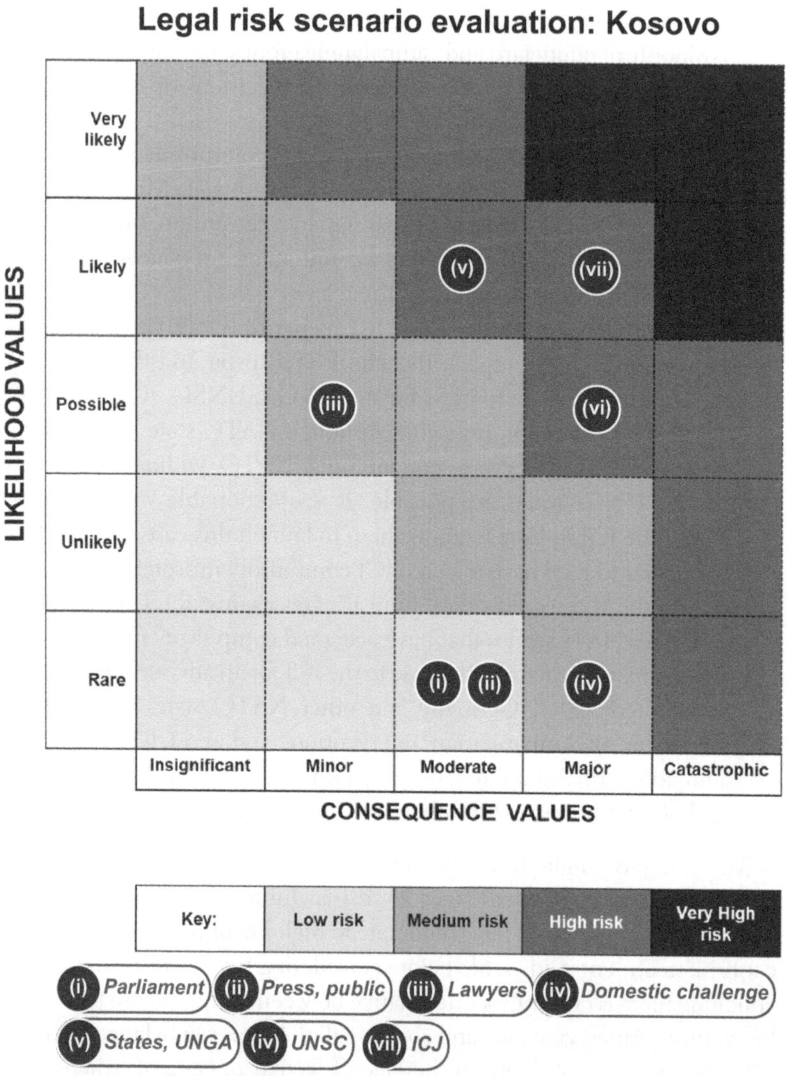

FIGURE 6.4 Kosovo – evaluating legal risk scenarios

strikes using only precision munitions and ground-based target spotters to maximise accuracy, even if that increases risks to NATO personnel.

A court or commentator using the framework to assess the intervention afterwards would note that NATO did launch military action. They may agree that the decision was reasonable from a strategic perspective, as it was a finely balanced assessment whether force or non-forceful options would more effectively avert a humanitarian catastrophe. Their assessment would note that NATO actively gathered and disseminated factual information about the humanitarian situation, and that independent media and civil society also reported information that contributed to relatively wide public support for the intervention in many NATO countries (polling showed a majority in the United Kingdom supported the action in 1999).[107]

But the assessment would also note little support from other states for the United Kingdom's doctrine of humanitarian intervention, with the United Kingdom and Belgium the only states participating in the action prominently claiming it lawful.[108] It would note that the United Kingdom made efforts to gain international support for its position, circulating in NATO a legal justification for force and issuing a justification as a parliamentary statement, with jurists such as Christopher Greenwood promoting the theory.[109] But as the United States, Germany and other NATO governments apparently believed the operation unlawful and should not set a precedent, it is arguable more could have been done to build support for it.[110] The assessment may note that a Russian draft UNSC resolution condemning the action was defeated by a majority (only Russia, China and Namibia voted for it).[111] When the FRY took NATO states to the ICJ for unlawful use of force, the Court declared it was 'profoundly concerned' with the intervention, while ruling it did not have jurisdiction to proceed.[112] And the Non-Aligned Movement declared its rejection of humanitarian intervention.[113]

Thus an assessment using this framework might, like the Kosovo Commission, conclude the action was 'illegal but illegitimate', or that the legal and factual case was not sufficiently strong to justify military action when NATO launched it.[114] And the assessment might regret that so many NATO states agreed to launch military action without advancing a clear legal justification, as the United Kingdom had done.

107 Mark Gillespie and Robert Manchin, 'Kosovo Air Strikes Receive Support in Britain, Hungary', *Gallup News Service* (30 March 1999).

108 *Legality of use of Force (Yugoslavia* v. *Belgium)*, Verbatim Record, 10 May 1999, ICJ CR99/15.

109 Roberts, 'So-Called "Right"', 24.

110 Simma, 'NATO', 1; Wood, 'Law on the Use of Force', 11.

111 UN Security Council, Press Release SC/6659, 'Security Council Rejects Demand for Cessation of Use of Force against Federal Republic of Yugoslavia', 26 March 1999, SC/6659.

112 *Yugoslavia* v. *United States*, Provisional Measures, para. 16.

113 UN, Press Release GA/SPD/164, '"Humanitarian Intervention", Slow Reimbursement Rates Assailed as Special Committee Reviews Peacekeeping Operations', 18 October 1999; Non-Aligned Movement, 'Final Communique', para. 171.

114 IICK, *Kosovo Report*, 4.

Afghanistan 2001

The factual context for the US-led intervention in Afghanistan in 2001 is the terrorist attack on the United States on 11 September 2001, resulting in over 3,000 mainly civilian deaths. The United States, United Kingdom and other allies allege Al-Qaeda based in Afghanistan planned and directed the attack, facilitated by the Taleban.[115] They demand that the Taleban hand over Osama Bin Laden and other Al-Qaeda leaders and end Al-Qaeda operations in Afghanistan. The Taleban has not yet complied. The main policy options available to the United Kingdom, supporting the United States and its allies, are:

- non-forceful diplomatic, legal and economic pressure on the Taleban
- military action against Al-Qaeda in Afghanistan and possibly also the Taleban.

The legal context remains that described in the previous section. The main competing legal theories are:

Legal Theory A States are permitted to use force in self-defence against armed non-state groups located in another state, without the consent of that latter state and without specific UNSC authorisation, subject to tests of necessity, imminence and proportionality and IHL constraints, if the state hosting the non-state group is unable or unwilling to stop the group committing attacks.[116] UN Charter Article 51 does not limit self-defence to armed attacks from states. Customary law (the *Caroline* criteria) permits self-defence against a non-state actor.

Legal Theory B States are permitted to use force in self-defence against armed non-state groups in another state without the consent of that latter state with the tests and constraints in Legal Theory A, only *with* specific UNSC authorisation, unless the host state exercised effective control over the armed group and so was legally responsible for the attack.[117] The context and purposes of the UN Charter, and materials

[115] Office of the UK Prime Minister, 'Responsibility for the Terrorist Atrocities in the United States, 11 September 2001 – An Updated Account' (14 November 2001).

[116] Gray, *International Law*, 156–60; Wilmshurst, 'Chatham House Principles'; Moir, *Reappraising the Resort to Force*, 41–71; Deeks, 'Unwilling or Unable'.

[117] Chinkin, 'Rethinking Legality/Legitimacy', 225; Gray, *International Law*, 203; Myjer and White, 'Twin Towers', 6.

such as the UNGA's 'Declaration on Friendly Relations' and the ICJ *Nicaragua* case make clear that self-defence applies only to attacks by states.

Legal Theory C States are not permitted to use force in self-defence against armed non-state groups in another state without the consent of that latter state even *with* specific UNSC authorisation, unless the host state was legally responsible for the attack as described in Legal Theory B.[118] Non-state attacks are crimes, to be addressed by law enforcement not military action.[119]

Key differences in assumptions about legal interpretation underpin these competing legal theories, including about the relative authority as sources of law of formal UNGA resolutions, academic writings, and ICJ jurisprudence, and the extent to which different kinds and quantities of state behaviour and statements count as state practice and *opinio juris*.

Evidence and assumptions about the following key factors are critical both for assessing who was responsible for the 11 September attacks, and for forecasting how the situation in Afghanistan and the wider international system may evolve following different policy responses either involving the use of force or not:

(a) *Al-Qaeda capability and intent to carry out attacks.* The United States and its allies share evidence shortly after the attack that Mohammed Atta and eighteen other citizens of Middle Eastern states hijacked four aeroplanes, deliberately flying three into buildings in New York and Washington, DC.[120] Evidence suggests the hijackers were members of Al-Qaeda, who travelled to Afghanistan, planned the attack in Hamburg and trained in the United States to take off and fly but not land airliners.[121] Al-Qaeda leaders had publicly called for attacks on US targets. Evidence suggests Al-Qaeda had previously attacked US targets, including USS *Cole* in 2000, US embassies in Kenya and Tanzania in 1998, and the World Trade Center itself in 1993.[122]

118 Moir, *Reappraising the Resort to Force*, 71.

119 Ibid.

120 UK Prime Minister, 'Responsibility for the Terrorist Atrocities'.

121 Julian Borger, Stuart Miller, 'How "Shy Foreigners" Learned to Pilot Flying-Bomb Boeings', *The Guardian* (14 September 2001).

122 UK Prime Minister, 'Responsibility for the Terrorist Atrocities'.

(b) *Taleban knowledge of and complicity with Al-Qaeda.* The Taleban had refused to comply with UNSC resolutions demanding they extradite Al-Qaeda leaders, even after Al-Qaeda leaders called for attacks on the United States.[123] Some Taleban statements seem to defend the 11 September attacks.[124] But no clear evidence shows the Taleban knew about the attacks in advance.

(c) *Taleban willingness to tackle Al-Qaeda threat.* The Taleban authorities appear to distance themselves from Al-Qaeda leaders, asking them to leave the country.[125] Some Taleban statements offer to extradite Al-Qaeda leaders to a Muslim country if further evidence of Al-Qaeda involvement was presented.[126]

(d) *Prospects of further attacks.* US/allied intelligence and Al-Qaeda actions before 11 September suggest Al-Qaeda is planning further attacks.[127] Reports of Islamists internationally praising the 11 September attacks suggest further attacks are more likely if Al-Qaeda is perceived to have attacked the United States with impunity.

(e) *Reliability and trustworthiness of US and allied assessments.* The United States sharing of evidence casting a poor light on its security agencies bolsters its plausibility. Almost all states and most non-governmental experts broadly endorse US and allied assessments that Al-Qaeda carried out the attack and the Taleban at least knew about Al-Qaeda's general intention to attack the United States.[128]

(f) *Taleban and Al-Qaeda military capability and popular support.* US, Allied and other state and non-state assessments suggest the Taleban and Al-Qaeda have significant loyal, committed Afghan and foreign fighters equipped to mount significant resistance to any military intervention.[129] Afghanistan is historically difficult for military operations, and its population hostile to foreign interventions.

(g) *US and Allied politico-military capability and reliability to remove Al-Qaeda and Taleban without causing unnecessary harm.* The United States and its allies have military capabilities significantly superior to Al-Qaeda and the Taleban. Earlier US-led interventions in the

123 UN Security Council, Document S/2001/946, 'Letter Dated 7 October 2001 from the Permanent Representative of the United States of America to the United Nations Addressed to the President of the Security Council', 7 October 2001, S/2001/946.

124 Voice of America, 'Mullah Omar – In His Own Words', *The Guardian* (26 September 2001).

125 Staff and Agencies, 'US Rejects Taliban Concession', *The Guardian* (20 September 2001).

126 Kathy Gannon, 'Bush Rejects Taliban Bin Laden Offer', *Washington Post* (14 October 2001).

127 S/2001/946.

128 Derek Brown, 'Timeline: Terror and Its Aftermath (Part 1)', *The Guardian* (5 October 2001).

129 BBC News, 'MoD Warns of Long Campaign' (11 October 2001).

Balkans and Iraq suggest the allies have the ability to defeat forces superior to Al-Qaeda and Taleban. However, what is widely perceived as the failure of US-led intervention in Somalia shows the risks. Al-Qaeda has established relatively conventional military bases making some targeting easier, but fighting is likely to cause significant collateral damage. Reporting suggests significant, potentially viable Afghan ground forces opposing the Taleban in the Northern Alliance, and discontent with Taleban from significant sections of the Afghan population.[130]

(h) *International willingness to support US-led action.* The United States receives almost immediate and universal expressions of political support even from traditionally hostile states such as Iran, and offers of facilitation from Russia and Central Asian states.[131] The Taleban has almost no allies internationally, and diplomatic relations only with Saudi Arabia, Pakistan and the United Arab Emirates, none of whom defend Taleban refusal to hand over Al-Qaeda.

(i) *Potential to set legal and politico-military precedent that other states will abuse.* Interventions in Iraq, Sierra Leone and Kosovo before 2001 seem not to have set such harmful precedents, although it is arguably too recent to judge reliably. The 11 September attacks themselves may suggest increased action against armed non-state groups is necessary. Wide international support for US-led action may set a precedent that future action must have similarly wide approval.

By applying different interpretations of the evidence and assumptions about these facts, four broad alternative factual hypotheses can be generated assessing responsibility for the 11 September 2001 attacks, and forecasting how the situation in Afghanistan and the wider international community may evolve following different policy responses involving use of force or not:

Hypothesis 1 — Al-Qaeda conducted the attacks and the Taleban were complicit. Military intervention led by the United States will stop future Al-Qaeda attacks on the United States and its allies more effectively and cause less damage to Afghanistan, international

130 International Institute for Strategic Studies, *The Military Balance 2000* (Oxford: Oxford University Press, 2000), 160, 166.

131 UN Security Council, Press Release SC/7143, 'Security Council Condemns, "In Strongest Terms", Terrorist Attacks on United States', 12 September 2001, SC/7143.

peace and security, international society and international law than non-forceful means.

Hypothesis 2 Al-Qaeda conducted the attacks, but the Taleban were not complicit. Military intervention led by the United States will stop future Al-Qaeda attacks more effectively and cause less immediate and long-term harm than non-forceful means.

Hypothesis 3 Al-Qaeda conducted the attacks. The Taleban may or may not have been complicit. But US-led intervention will fail to end Al-Qaeda attacks, or will be less effective and cause more immediate and long term harm than non-forceful means.

Hypothesis 4 Al-Qaeda did not conduct the attacks. The Taleban were not complicit. Military intervention led by the United States is unnecessary.

Analysing the competing hypotheses as illustrated in Figure 6.6, an interdisciplinary team might discard Hypothesis 4, assessing that the evidence suggests Al-Qaeda was almost certainly responsible for the attacks. They might find only marginal evidence to favour Hypotheses 1 and 2 over Hypothesis 3: that US-led military action *may* defeat Al-Qaeda and the Taleban, causing less immediate and long-term harm than non-forceful responses. The team might find Hypotheses 1 and 2 equally compelling, that the Taleban probably knew about Al-Qaeda intent to attack the United States, but no more than a realistic possibility that the Taleban were complicit in the specific attacks.

The seven sets of legal stakeholders identified in the previous section are again likely to be important to UK decision-makers considering whether to authorise force: Parliament, the public and media, influential international lawyers and commentators, domestic judiciary who may adjudicate any domestic legal challenge, states that make up the UNSC, the states that make up the wider UN membership, and judges of the ICJ. Analysing the competing legal theories, as illustrated in Figure 6.5, the team might see significant potential for gaining fairly wide support for a legal justification for resort to force in self-defence against Al-Qaeda. Taking into account the likely distribution of legal assumptions and intuitions amongst key stakeholders (see Figures 4.1, 4.2, 5.1 reflecting textual analyses of Afghanistan in Chapters 4 and 5), the team may conclude that Legal Theory C, that resort to force in self-defence against non-state actors not controlled by another state is in all circumstances unlawful, is unlikely to gain much support among those stakeholders. The team may assess that the UK Parliament, public, media,

	H1: Al-Qaeda responsible Taleban complicit, intervention works	H2: Al-Qaeda responsible, Taleban not complicit, intervention works	H3: Al-Qaeda responsible, Taleban complicit or not, intervention fails	H4: Al-Qaeda & Taleban innocent, intervention unnecessary
Al-Qaeda attack capability/intent	✓✓	✓✓	✓✓	✗✗
Taleban knowledge of Al-Qaeda	✓	✓	✓	✗
Taleban will to tackle Al-Qaeda	✗	✗	✗	✓
Prospect of more attacks	✓✓	✓✓	✓	✗✗
Reliability of US/allied assessments	✓✓	✓✓	✗	✗✗
Taleban/Al-Qaeda defensive capability	✗✗	✗✗	✓✓	-
US/Allied intervention capability	✓	✓	✓	-
International support for US	✓✓	✓✓	✗✗	-
Risk of unhelpful precedent	✓	✓	✓	-
Assessment	3✗, 11✓	3✗, 11✓	4✗, 8✓	7✗, 1✓

✓ : consistent with hypothesis; ✗ : inconsistent with hypothesis; - : neither consistent nor inconsistent

	LT(A): Force in Self-defence vs non-state actors is lawful	LT(B): Force in self-defence vs non-state actors needs UNSC resolution	LT(C): Force in self-defence vs non-state actors is unlawful
Parliament	✓✓✓✗	✗✗✗✓	✗✗✗✗
Public and Media	✓✓✓✗	✗✗✗✓	✗✗✗✓
UK Courts	✓✓✓✗	✗✗✗✓	✗✗✗✗
International lawyers	✗✗✗✓	✓✓✓✗	✗✗✗✓
UNSC	✓✓✓✓	✗✗✗✗	✗✗✗✗
UNGA / UN States	✓✓✓✗	✗✗✗✓	✗✗✗✗
ICJ	✗✗✗✓	✓✓✓✗	✗✗✗✓
Assessment	11✗, 18✓	18✗, 10✓	25✗, 3✓

✓ : extent of support for legal theory; ✗ : extent of opposition to legal theory;

FIGURE 6.5 Afghanistan – analyses of competing hypotheses and competing legal theories

courts, UNSC and other UN states are highly likely to support Legal Theory A – unilateral proportionate force in self-defence against armed attacks by non-state actors is lawful, where the non-state group's host country is unable or unwilling to stop those attacks. The team may however also conclude that the majority of international lawyers and ICJ judges are most likely to

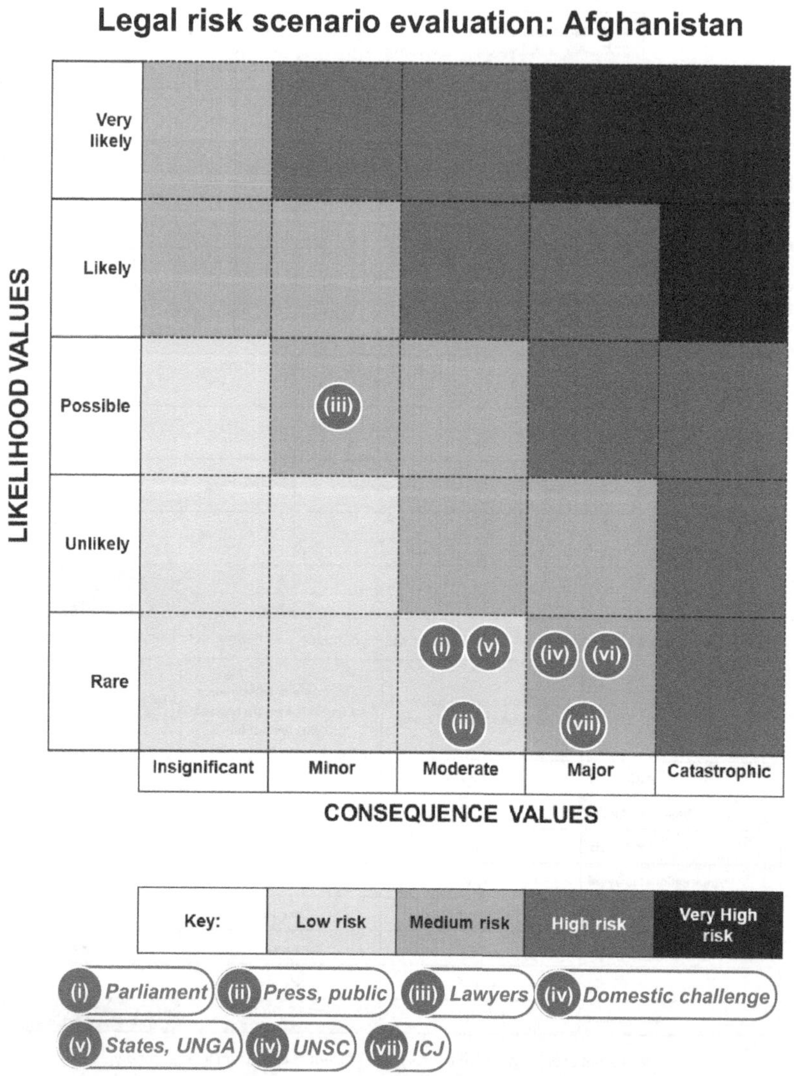

FIGURE 6.6 Afghanistan – evaluating legal risk scenarios

support Legal Theory B – that use of force in self-defence against non-state actors is lawful only if authorised by the UNSC.

The main alternative scenarios for legal challenge are the seven identified in the previous section, in which parliament, public, media and legal scholars find the action unlawful, or sufficient states do so leading to UNGA, UNSC or ICJ action. To assess the potential likelihood and impact of these risk scenarios, the team would combine the assessments already conducted of competing factual hypotheses and competing legal theories in this case, to assess the capability and will of each source of legal risk to launch any challenge given these factual and legal circumstances. As illustrated in Figure 6.6, the team might thus conclude that:

- Scenarios (i) and (ii) – parliamentary, media and public condemnation – are unlikely. It is probable that Parliament, public and media hold broadly textual, formalist views of the law, and a minority are likely to vocally oppose the action on factual and legal grounds. But the 11 September attacks cause such scale of harm and shock that a large majority are likely to accept the factual and legal arguments justifying military action, which polling suggests is supported by a large majority of the UK public.[132]
- Scenario (iii) – condemnation by a majority of international lawyers – is more likely. Although influential lawyers argue self-defence against non-state actors is lawful, the majority internationally and probably even in the United Kingdom view it as unlawful.[133] It is reasonable to suppose from the analysis in Chapters 4 and 5 of this book that significant numbers of international lawyers are generally sceptical of force by western powers, although most seem to accept Al-Qaeda conducted the attacks.
- Scenario (iv) is unlikely. A campaigning organisation opposed to force in Afghanistan may lobby for judicial review or inquiry into the action. But a lobbying organisation may not launch a judicial review without significant wider public and political pressure, and such pressure is even more necessary for any public inquiry to be launched. The strong public support for military action suggest such pressure is unlikely. Any domestic court or inquiry panel considering the legality of the action may well give as much weight to evidence that most states seem to endorse the action as to evidence that legal scholars oppose it.
- Scenarios (v), (vi) and (vii) – widespread condemnation by states leading to UNGA condemnation, adverse UNSC votes and action in the ICJ – may also be judged highly unlikely. Most states already support the action, offering practical and political support. The Taleban have not engaged with international institutions like the UN or ICJ, and the United States no longer accepts ICJ's compulsory jurisdiction. However, if the Court were to consider such a case, the generally formalist views of ICJ judges revealed in Chapter 4 suggest the ICJ may rule the military action unlawful unless

[132] Ipsos MORI, 'War in Afghanistan Poll', *Ipsos MORI* (4 November 2001).

[133] Kammerhofer, 'Self-Defence', 203.

there is clear formal evidence that states endorse the principle of self-defence against non-state actors.

Risk scenarios (iv), (vi) and (vii) would have the greatest impact. But since all risk scenarios apart from the relatively low-impact scenario (iii) are low likelihood, the risks of various challenges to the legality of military action in this case might be assessed as low. The team and decision-maker may thus conclude that none of the risks is sufficiently serious to prevent military action, but that some risk treatment is worthwhile, including:

(a) seeking a UNSC resolution authorising the action, or an UNGA expression of support for it
(b) making public evidence of Al-Qaeda responsibility and Taleban inaction or complicity, and continue gathering and sharing such information
(c) building a wide international coalition
(d) engaging the international legal community to promote Legal Theory A justifying military action
(e) in line with the principle of doubt, targeting only Al-Qaeda, and engaging the Taleban militarily only if/when they use force to obstruct US-led military action.

A court or commentator reviewing the decision after it was taken could examine how far US/UK decision-making diverged from the reasoning above, asking whether a reasonable strategic decision-maker would have reached a similar decision. Such an assessment would show the United States and United Kingdom did apply conclusions (a) to (c). UNSC resolutions of September and October 2001 recognised the inherent right of self-defence in the context of the fight against terrorism. Significant information was and continued to be made public about Al-Qaeda responsibility. Many states supported the action, including granting basing and overflight rights.

The United States and United Kingdom did not apply conclusion (d) – engaging the legal community – as extensively as this analysis suggested. And their military action did not apply conclusion (e), since they targeted the Taleban from the start of operations. This element of the military operation might be legally challenged. But there is an argument that uncertainty about Taleban complicity and deployment of Taleban and Al-Qaeda forces made it unreasonable for US/UK military action to distinguish between the two.

The analysis may thus conclude the action had sufficient factual justification – Al-Qaeda conducted the attacks, and there was too little chance of non-forceful measures effectively halting future attacks. The action could also be assessed as having low risk of legal challenge and sufficient legal justification – either because self-defence against non-state actors was never clearly prohibited, or because the near universal state support for the operation show state practice and *opinio juris* supporting its lawfulness.

Conclusion

These examples demonstrate that the framework this chapter proposes can be used to assess competing factual and legal hypotheses in difficult *jus ad bellum* cases, without simply choosing the assumptions associated with one of the competing legal and strategic cultures that often underpin disagreement in such cases. The framework still does not specify the factual thresholds for the *jus ad bellum*'s tests: how much force must be used in an attack, causing how many casualties and how much damage to satisfy the scale and effects test; how brief must the advance warning of an attack be to meet the imminence test; how high must be the probability of force succeeding; how many casualties constitute an overwhelming humanitarian catastrophe. However, this kind of inter-disciplinary process provides a structured method to assess the alternative thresholds that may be applied to these tests, the alternative choices and their possible outcomes, their relative merits and underpinning assumptions, against the available factual evidence about the situation and broadly similar past situations.

It is worth noting that the framework, at least as applied by this author, reaches conclusions on both cases which are more cautious than the decisions actually made by the UK government. This suggests a systematic, risk management approach to managing the legal and factual uncertainties associated with controversial decisions to use military force may produce more cautious outcomes than a less structured approach. It is also worth noting that the framework manages but does not eliminate the uncertainty caused by sources of vagueness identified by this book – paradigms, the sorites paradox and fuzzy logic, supervaluationism, and competing interpretive cultures. Finally, it should be observed that in neither example used here does the framework claim to identify which legal theory might be described as the 'objectively correct' interpretation of the law. Instead, the framework identifies which interpretation is likely to expose the decision-maker to the least legal risk.

IRAQ 2003: LEGAL RISK MANAGEMENT IN (IMPERFECT) ACTION?

More information has been released about the United Kingdom's strategic and legal decision-making around the 2003 Iraq intervention than for any other post-Cold War UK military intervention, particularly in the 2016 Chilcot report.[134] This section examines how that decision-making incorporated legal risk management, and how the framework developed in this chapter might have affected the judgments informing that decision.

The UK attorney general's 17 May 2003 legal advice contains many features of legal risk management. It outlines the legal context in similar terms to those recommended in this chapter, and specifies competing legal theories about the action, namely:

- 'that provided there is a Council discussion, if it does not reach a conclusion, there remains an authorisation to use force', because UNSC Resolution 1441 (2002) 'revived' the authorisation for force in UNSC Resolution 678 (1990) by finding Iraq in 'material breach' of ceasefire conditions imposed by UNSC Resolution 687 (1991)
- 'that nothing short of a further Council decision will be a legitimate basis for the use of force'.[135]

The attorney general's advice compares the legal theories systematically. It specifies factual requirements for the justification for force: 'strong factual grounds for concluding that Iraq has failed to take the final opportunity' to disarm, requiring 'hard evidence of non-compliance and non-cooperation', in which 'the views of UNMOVIC and the IAEA will be highly significant'.[136] And it outlines potential risks of the case being challenged in international or domestic courts or the UNGA, giving a sense of their possible likelihood. The Chilcot report shows there was legal involvement from early in the policy-making process around the intervention in Iraq, including before and during the negotiation of UNSC Resolution 1441 (2002).[137]

However both the 2003 advice and wider policy process depart from the method suggested in this chapter in crucial ways. First is the timing and use of

[134] Iraq Inquiry, 'Section 5: Advice on the Legal Basis for Military Action, November 2002 to March 2003' and 'Section 3.5: Development of UK Strategy and Options, September to November 2002 – The Negotiation of Resolution 1441', *The Report of the Iraq Inquiry* (London: Her Majesty's Stationery Office, 2016).

[135] Iraq Inquiry, 'Legal Basis for Military Action', para. 533.

[136] Goldsmith, 'Iraq: Resolution 1441', para. 29.

[137] Iraq Inquiry, 'Development of UK Strategy', paras. 1000–79.

legal advice. This chapter's proposed framework would recommend legal advice be delivered earlier in the decision-making process than occurred in the Iraq crisis. This could potentially have been as early as December 2001, when the prime minister, Tony Blair, suggested 'a strategy for regime change in Iraq' in a note to President Bush, and certainly from February 2002, when the prime minister and foreign secretary began publicly asserting that 'Iraq was a threat which had to be dealt with'.[138] Legal advice could thus have shaped preparations for the military intervention, including prompting action to reduce legal risks.

The Chilcot report demonstrates that key legal advisers – the attorney general, senior lawyer in the attorney general's office Cathy Adams, FCO legal adviser Sir Michael Wood, deputy legal advisers John Grainger and Elizabeth Wilmshurst, and legal adviser in the United Kingdom's UN Mission Iain MacLeod – were not fully aware of high-level policy discussions and factual analysis about Iraq and its suspected WMD programme.[139] On 18 October, during negotiation of UNSC Resolution 1441 (2002), Sir Michael Wood wrote to the attorney general that 'this resolution cannot be read as permitting the revival argument', and that day the attorney general told the foreign secretary the 'draft would not be sufficient to authorise the use of force without a second resolution'.[140] Sir Michael developed legal advice from November 2002, delivering it in December 2002, setting out the competing legal theories, and wanted to state his view that UNSC Resolution 1441 (2002) did not authorise force without a further resolution, but he did not do so, reportedly on the foreign secretary's instructions.[141] The attorney general was asked for legal advice in December 2002, but was told not to deliver it 'now'; he nevertheless provided a provisional view in January 2003 arguing a further UNSC decision – although not necessarily a Chapter VII resolution – was required to authorise force.[142]

Yet the legal concerns that Sir Michael and the attorney general expressed were not widely communicated. Neither the UK permanent representative to the UN nor UK legal adviser in the UN knew of Sir Michael's concerns until late November, after UNSC Resolution 1441 (2002) had been negotiated.[143] The attorney general delivered his full legal advice to the prime minister on

138 Iraq Inquiry, *Executive Summary*, paras. 57, 66.
139 Iraq Inquiry, 'Development of UK Strategy', paras 1000–2.
140 Ibid., 621, 632.
141 Iraq Inquiry, 'Legal Basis for Military Action', para. 131.
142 Ibid., para. 167.
143 Iraq Inquiry, 'Development of UK Strategy', para. 1029.

7 March, just thirteen days before military action, and the whole Cabinet only saw the summary legal advice that was eventually published on 17 March.[144]

The then attorney general told the Chilcot inquiry that the advice was delivered so late because the prime minister and other key government ministers already knew his legal opinion. But the UK legal adviser in the UN told the inquiry 'there seemed to be no definitive view from the AG's Office during the 1441 process', which he thought was 'a big mistake', contrasted with the process during negotiations around earlier use of force in 1997 and 1998.[145] Blair's explanation for the attorney general's delay was vague: '[T]his was a very tricky and difficult question. . . . the only concern, and I am speaking from memory here; generating bits of paper the entire time on it, but, I mean, it was obviously important that he was involved.'[146]

This chapter's proposed framework would have required a multi-agency process to assess competing factual hypotheses about the situation in Iraq against the available evidence. But, as the Chilcot report noted, 'At no stage was the hypothesis that Iraq might no longer have chemical, biological or nuclear weapons or programmes' considered by the assessment or policy community.[147] It was not among the 'possible scenarios' that the prime minister's special adviser outlined in December 2002.[148] The attorney general's assessment of evidence was confined to saying the legal basis for force 'will only be sustainable if there are strong factual grounds for concluding that Iraq has failed to take the final opportunity', which needed 'hard evidence of non-compliance and non-cooperation', with particular significance for UNMOVIC and IAEA views, and '[i]n the light of the latest reporting by UNMOVIC, you will need to consider extremely carefully whether the evidence of non-cooperation and non-compliance by Iraq is sufficiently compelling' to conclude Iraq had 'failed to take its final opportunity'.[149]

This chapter's proposed framework would also have recommended that the attorney general assess the competing legal theories, and the likelihood and impact of a wider range of negative reactions to the legal justification for resort to force in more detail, not only challenges in courts and the UNGA, but also challenges from states, legal opinion, the wider public and media. The attorney general's legal advice made a less detailed attempt to assess the risks, concluding that '[s]ome of these seem fairly remote possibilities, but given the strength of

144 Iraq Inquiry, 'Legal Basis for Military Action', para. 65.
145 Iraq Inquiry, 'Development of UK Strategy', paras. 1029, 1036.
146 Iraq Inquiry, 'Legal Basis for Military Action', para. 165.
147 Iraq Inquiry, *Executive Summary*, para. 290.
148 Iraq Inquiry, 'Legal Basis for Military Action', para. 147.
149 Goldsmith, 'Iraq: Resolution 1441', para. 29.

opposition to military action against Iraq, it would not be surprising if some attempts were made to get a case of some sort off the ground. We cannot be certain that they would not succeed. The GA [General Assembly] route may be the most likely.'[150] The attorney general left it to the government to assess whether enough UNGA states would be willing to vote for such action.

Under this chapter's proposed framework, the attorney general's advice would not have been revised to be more categorical, removing nuance and uncertainty. The chief of defence staff and treasury solicitor were unhappy with the attorney general's assessment, and pressed on behalf of the armed forces and civil service for 'a clear-cut answer on whether military action would be lawful'.[151] The attorney general then delivered his summary advice of 17 March circulated to the whole Cabinet, in which he assessed military intervention without a further UNSC resolution was lawful. The Cabinet never received 'written advice which set out, as the advice of 7 March had done, the conflicting arguments regarding the legal effect of resolution 1441'.[152] The Chilcot report notes that '[g]iven the gravity of this decision, Cabinet should have been made aware of the legal uncertainties'.[153] It might also be argued that it was unreasonable of the chief of defence staff and treasury solicitor to press the attorney general to give a 'clear cut answer', instead of accepting the reality of legal uncertainty, and informing the prime minister of any politico-strategic or ethical concerns they may have had.

This section does not criticise the work of the UK attorney general, other government lawyers or the civil servants and military officers involved in the policy and legal debates before the 2003 intervention in Iraq. They worked under difficult circumstances, with less experience than now of scrutiny of the legality of use of force decisions, and when legal risk management itself was less well-developed (the crisis took place a year before McCormick's major work on legal risk was published). In that context, it could be argued that the attorney general's use of legal risk management was innovative. But the framework proposed in this chapter would have made differences to the timing of the attorney general's advice, its dissemination, and the way it reflected and inputted to the wider factual analysis and policy-making process. The legal advice process before the 2003 Iraq intervention appears to have been fragmented, pressured to assert an unrealistic degree of legal certainty, and not integrated into the factual analysis and policy-making process in ways which might have enabled the legal and factual risks to

150 Goldsmith, 'Iraq: Resolution 1441', para. 35.
151 Iraq Inquiry, 'Legal Basis for Military Action', para. 930.
152 Ibid., para. 165.
153 Ibid., para. 954.

have been systematically identified, assessed and 'treated' by what this chapter describes as a 'reasonable strategic decision-maker'.

CONCLUSION

This chapter used insights from legal risk management, IHL and strategic intelligence analysis to devise a potential framework for dealing with legal and factual uncertainty and extra-legal intuitions in *jus ad bellum* decisions. The chapter briefly applied that framework to two interventions examined earlier in the book – the 1999 Kosovo intervention and the 2001 Afghanistan intervention. And it examined how the UK legal advice developed for the 2003 Iraq intervention might have differed if it had used such a framework.

The chapter shows that the proposed framework, at least as applied by this author, does not change the 'ordering' of assessment of the three interventions using more orthodox analysis. The intervention in Afghanistan remains the case with the highest confidence legal and factual justification for military action. For Kosovo the framework would have identified significant concerns about the legal basis and some factual concerns, arguing for a delay to develop a stronger legal and factual case. With Iraq, the framework would have integrated legal advisers more systematically, more widely and at an earlier stage in the policy process, would have assessed a wider range of legal and factual risks, including risks of media and political challenge and that Iraq had no WMDs, and would have insisted on describing the legal uncertainties. Such an assessment might have made a more compelling case against resort to force in 2003.

All this suggests the framework proposed in this chapter can be used to assess competing factual and legal hypotheses in difficult *jus ad bellum* cases, without simply choosing one set of assumptions from the competing legal and strategic cultures that often underpin those competing hypotheses. The proposed framework still does not specify factual thresholds for the *jus ad bellum*'s tests of necessity, imminence and proportionality. However, the inter-disciplinary process it describes provides a structured method for reaching robust conclusions, after assessing alternative thresholds that may be applied to these tests, the alternative choices and their possible outcomes, their relative merits and underpinning assumptions, against the available evidence about the situation and broadly similar past situations.

The framework does however raise some difficult questions. First, it requires a more complex, potentially time-consuming process drawing on wider skills and expertise than more orthodox approaches to legal evaluation. The reality of many *jus ad bellum* decisions would make thorough implementation of such a process difficult, given the need for secrecy, fast-moving political developments, and rapidly changing requirements. However, the framework is 'scaleable' – its thoroughness can be varied according to available resources, capabilities and time. A single person drawing on sources from various disciplines, or a small interdisciplinary team working virtually, drawing on online non-government and media sources, could rapidly pull together some version of the assessments the framework recommends.

There are however more fundamental objections. The framework does not eliminate the uncertainties caused by the forms of vagueness identified by this book – paradigms, fuzzy logic, supervaluationism and competing interpretive and strategic cultures. Indeed, the structured analytical techniques this framework is based on are themselves subject to vagueness and uncertainty.[154] The framework also requires lawyers and courts to accept that multiple legal theories may have comparable validity, rather than enabling them to give clear advice. Most importantly, the framework treats law in instrumental rather than normative terms – recommending ways of reducing risks of various forms of legal challenge to enable states to do what they want, rather than guiding states to adapt their behaviour to obey what the law prescribes they ought to do. The framework does not claim to identify which competing legal theory might be the 'objectively correct' interpretation of the law. Instead, the framework simply identifies the interpretation least likely to expose the decision-maker to legal risk. And those lawyers who argue that there can be an objectively correct interpretation of the law in hard cases such as these do not include legal risk amongst the considerations they rely on to identify objective law, such as 'structural integrity', 'relation with other rules', moral consensus, 'fit with the relevant legal materials', and 'best political justification for the statute at the time it was passed'.[155]

The framework further assumes that decision-makers care about the legal risks described here – formal or informal legal challenge, in national or international courts, parliaments and the media. Yet it is unlikely that all decision-makers at all times in all states care about or are exposed to all these legal risks. *In extremis*, the framework may even encourage a decision-maker to take military action that most well-informed, well-qualified international lawyers would assess as clearly unlawful, if political and strategic conditions mean the risks of legal challenge or other disbenefits to the decision-maker are very low. The next chapter explores such practical and normative objections in more detail.

154 Mandeep K. Dhami, Ian K. Belton, David R. Mandel, 'The "Analysis of Competing Hypotheses" in Intelligence Analysis', *Applied Cognitive Psychology*, 33(2019), 1080–90, 1080.

155 Fuller, 'Positivism', 670; Devlin 'Law, Morality and Democracy', 638; Dworkin 'Matter of Principle', 145, 129.

7

Uncertainty, Risk Management and Duty to the Law

The fear o' hell's a hangman's whip,
To haud the wretch in order;
But where ye feel your honour grip,
Let that aye be your border;
Its slightest touches, instant pause-
Debar a' side-pretences;
And resolutely keep its laws,
Uncaring consequences.

Robert Burns, *'Epistle to a Young Friend'*[1]

INTRODUCTION

The dilemmas this book has examined raise profound questions for the professional duties and responsibilities of international lawyers. What should international lawyers do if they cannot determine with confidence whether a potential justification for resort to force is permitted or prohibited in international law? What if their respected, highly qualified colleagues disagree about whether a justification for force is lawful? What if the facts underpinning such a justification are contested and unclear, and the consequences of using or not using force seem particularly uncertain? To what extent may lawyers rely on what many jurists would consider extra-legal political, strategic and ethical intuitions and reasoning, when legal rules alone appear not to resolve the legal and factual uncertainties concerning specific cases of resort to force?

[1] Robert Burns, 'Epistle to a Young Friend', *Poems and Songs* (Edinburgh: William P. Nimmo, 1868), 122–4, 124.

Chapter 6 proposed a framework that lawyers may use to address the *jus ad bellum*'s specific indeterminacy due to legal and factual uncertainty, and partial autonomy from extra-legal intuitions in difficult *jus ad bellum* cases. However, in seeking a systematic, pragmatic way of handling these challenges, the framework poses serious normative questions for how international lawyers discharge their duties in accordance with the ethics of their profession. This chapter draws on the interviews conducted for this book as well as scholarly writings about the professional duties of international lawyers to consider these questions.

The chapter first discusses the varied understandings about the duties of different categories of international lawyers – academics, private practitioners, government legal advisers and judges – and in different nations. The chapter then outlines potential normative concerns the framework developed in Chapter 6 creates for international lawyers' professional duties. Most importantly, by encouraging lawyers to suggest ways of reducing legal and other risks to a client considering using force, the proposed framework serves lawyers' instrumental role of 'counselor' enabling states to justify whatever they want, rather than their normative role of 'conscience', encouraging states to adapt their behaviour to obey the law.[2] The chapter looks back on analysis developed throughout this book, alongside scholarly writings and interviews, to advance pragmatic and empirical responses to many of these normative objections, supporting the viability of the kind of systematic approach developed in Chapter 6. This chapter however accepts that the framework raises genuine normative concerns, and draws on Rawls' concept of reflective equilibrium to outline one potential approach lawyers may adopt to tackle these dilemmas.[3]

VARYING DUTIES AND ROLES OF INTERNATIONAL LAWYERS

Before considering challenges to lawyers' professional ethics posed by uncertainty, extra-legal reasoning and the framework for handling uncertainty and biases proposed in Chapter 6, it is worth considering how those responsibilities and professional ethics vary for different categories of international lawyers and in different states. As Chapter 2 noted, it is likely that the interpretive cultures this book suggests reflect the interaction of structural factors and individuals' own agency. Key structural factors include the national legal system in which lawyers are educated, gain professional experience and internalise approaches to legal interpretation and substantive issues such as

2 Koh, 'Eight Decades in Peace and War', 1758.

3 John Rawls, *A Theory of Justice* (Cambridge, MA: Harvard University Press, 1999), 18.

the resort to force. Other structural factors could include institutional settings within which lawyers work – legal scholars, private practitioners, lawyers working for non-governmental campaign groups and government legal advisers all have different professional priorities and incentives. Individual interpretive cultures are themselves likely to evolve through interaction with other cultures and agents, including those outside law – clients and competitors, government, media and other aspects of wider culture including public attitudes. And individual lawyers' preferences and characteristics are likely to shape how each operationalises these structural factors in their own legal decision-making.

As this book has also already noted, different categories of lawyers inevitably advance different objectives when they assess the lawfulness of resort to force. As Raz notes, the concept of law that any set of actors operationalises will be shaped by 'the interests and the capacities' of that group and 'the questions which trouble it'.[4] Similarly, Benda-Beckmann has argued that different academic and professional groups need 'a different concept of law for different purposes'.[5] Hart's distinction between his 'general and descriptive' concept of law and Dworkin's 'evaluative and justificatory' concept points to different approaches to law that international lawyers apply when they fulfil different professional and academic roles.[6] Most obviously, international lawyers working for individual states, whether as government legal adviser or practitioner representing a state before an international court, fulfil the role of '*counselor*', constructing legal arguments to help their clients justify and defend actions they wish to take to achieve their objectives, including potentially the resort to military force.[7] Judges, on the other hand, are generally expected to make impartial, objective, 'authoritative determinations' of what the relevant legal rules are and whether those rules have been broken in cases they adjudicate – identifying and applying international law as it is.[8]

Finally, legal scholars and commentators can be expected to play some combination of these roles. The writings of such lawyers may indicate what society agrees the law actually is, since lawyers with high standing as academics or practitioners have 'some right to claim, on the basis of professional training and experience' an ability to predict 'what a judge would decide' on specific controversial issues.[9] Scholars can also play a more justificatory role,

4 Raz, 'Two Views', 10.
5 Benda-Beckmann, 'Who's Afraid of Legal Pluralism?', 40.
6 Hart, *Concept of Law*, 239, 240.
7 Koh, 'Eight Decades in Peace and War', 1758.
8 Hart, *Concept of Law*, 96–7.
9 D'Amato, 'Legal Uncertainty', 1.

advocating for 'some concept of what the law ought to be', whether as applied in a particular case at present, or as it ought to evolve in future.[10]

And many interviewees did observe that different categories of international lawyers had different duties, expectations, and outlooks when faced with legal and factual uncertainty and extra-legal considerations concerning the resort to force.[11] One academic noted that all 'may belong to the same community of international lawyers', but 'factionally' they have 'different allegiances', with legal scholars, practitioners and government lawyers each inhabiting 'their own little world'.[12] A practising international lawyer said 'a huge amount turns on the background of the lawyer', their 'political views', 'training and how they use the law', and these differ between government lawyers, academics and practitioners.[13]

Many interviewees observed that government lawyers and lawyers consulted by governments have different perspectives on use of force decisions compared to lawyers not directly advising on such decisions. Some former government lawyers said academics and private practitioners usually did not 'see the scale of the threat', nor face questions about how to respond to apparently compelling information about threats, and so often 'discount the pressures that Ministers and others can come under, as they did with Kosovo'.[14] A practitioner praised academics' intellectual skills, but said 'life in the ivory tower is very different from life on the street', and since most scholars were not consulted by governments, they 'don't actually know what they're talking about' when writing about *jus ad bellum* decisions, instead 'speculating about something they've heard or were involved in peripherally'.[15] In other words, many interviewees argued that access to government information and assessments about military crises, and direct experience of decision-making about force, affect lawyers' views about the legality, strategy and morality of such decisions.

Many interviewees also had different expectations about the duties and responsibilities of different categories of government lawyers – internal government legal advisers and external counsel.[16] One practising international lawyer said when governments approach external lawyers, 'there is a greater expectation that they're going to get "counsel"', advising governments how to

[10] Hart, 'Positivism', 608.
[11] Participants 7, 9, 19, 26, 31.
[12] Participant 9.
[13] Participant 26.
[14] Participants 19, 31.
[15] Participant 12.
[16] Participants 10, 14, 18, 23, 24, 26.

get what they want, whereas in-house government legal advisers are expected 'to be "counsel" and "conscience" wrapped up in one' – justifying governments' actions, but also urging governments to adjust their behaviour to obey the law.[17] Several participants accepted that barristers can be 'creative' in 'thinking about how to make a case', as Christopher Greenwood had when he outlined a potential justification for the 2003 Iraq intervention for the UK government.[18] But internal government legal advisers should 'be very conservative and cautious', 'do legal analysis' as objectively as possible 'as if you were a judge', using the UN Charter, ICJ judgments and authoritative sources such as the Chatham House principles on use of force.[19] Several said private lawyers, academics and government lawyers all had more freedom than judges to interpret the law and even to declare the law was unclear.[20]

International lawyers in different countries will also approach international law in different ways, shaped by their national legal cultures. Oscar Schachter famously described 'the professional community of international lawyers', which, 'though dispersed throughout the world and engaged in diverse occupations, constitutes a kind of invisible college dedicated to a common intellectual enterprise'.[21] More recent scholars of transnational law argue globalisation and private transnational legal mechanisms are driving legal convergence, 'a universal code of legality' emerging from 'transnational networks of public and private actors'.[22]

However, Anthea Roberts in her recent wide-ranging study suggests 'international lawyers may be better understood as constituting a "divisible college"'.[23] International lawyers from different states, regions or geopolitical groupings likely form 'separate, though sometimes overlapping, communities with their own understandings and approaches', 'influences and spheres of influence' and 'socializing forces', approaching international law in different ways.[24] Other scholars have noted distinct national legal cultures persisting even between law-governed democracies such as the United States, Germany,

17 Participant 26.
18 Participants 24, 29.
19 Participants 24, 29.
20 Participants 18, 23.
21 Oscar Schachter, 'Invisible College of International Lawyers', *Northwestern University Law Review*, 72:2 (1977–8), 217–26, 217.
22 Klaus Gunther, 'Legal Pluralism or Uniform Concept of Law? Globalisation as a Problem of Legal Theory', *No Foundations*, 5 (2008), 5–21, 7.
23 Roberts, *Is International Law International?*, 2.
24 Ibid., 2, 6, 8.

the Netherlands and Japan, helping to explain differences in numbers of lawyers and courts, and litigation rates.[25]

There are many possible causes for different national approaches to international law, including 'different incentive structures, such as the level of academic freedom', or 'more subtle processes of socialization, such as divergent facts that are reported, or narratives that are developed' in the media.[26] This book has already argued that legal evaluation of any specific hard case of resort to force relies on 'one's understanding of the facts', and yet 'international lawyers in different states often rely on different media, which present different representations of reality'.[27] As Roberts argues, while it is not possible to prove these various external factors *cause* national differences in legal approach, 'as international lawyers are shaped in different national environments, it is not unreasonable to surmise that differences in their national contexts might influence the way in which they understand and approach international law'.[28]

Kammerhofer notes the effects of what he describes as international lawyers' national 'cultural prejudice' and 'preconceptions of how a legal system works' – 'every international lawyer a national lawyer first'.[29] Prosper Weil described international law's 'inherent polynormativity', that principles 'of self-interpretation and self-appreciation' enable different states to interpret the law in different ways, so '[i]nternational law as understood by one country is not necessarily the same as that understood by another'.[30] Jouannet argued 'cultural' differences may mirror differences between common law and civil law systems, with US, UK and other common law jurists more comfortable with the evolutionary features of international law than continental European lawyers, acculturated to interpretation-constraining legal codes.[31] Roberts describes UK and French international lawyers 'competing to establish the influence of the common law and civil law traditions on international tribunals like the ICJ', through 'continuous "selling"' of their national legal models to influence 'establishment of international norms and institutions' reflecting the Anglo-Saxon or continental tradition.[32]

25 David Nelken, 'Rethinking Legal Culture', in Michael Freeman, ed., *Law and Sociology* (Oxford: Oxford University Press, 2005), 200–24, 203–5.
26 Roberts, *Is International Law International?* 231.
27 Ibid. 236.
28 Ibid. 231.
29 Kammerhofer, 'Self-Defence', 552.
30 Weil, 'Non Liquet Revisited', 118, 119.
31 Jouannet, 'French and American Perspectives', 292–337.
32 Roberts, *Is International Law International?* 128.

Writing about interpretive technique, Koskenniemi has contrasted opposing cultures of largely European, rule-focused 'formalism' or 'Constitutionalism', compared to largely US rule-sceptical 'dynamism' or 'managerialism'.[33] Verdirame has noted differences between US and UK international lawyers' 'fundamental assumptions and methodological choices', how they 'understand, describe and characterize' international law.[34] He noted that US lawyers are more ambivalent than Europeans about supra-national rules, more willing to use 'scientific and empirical methods', more influenced by international relations scholarship, and giving higher priority to the 'is' in international law while Europeans are more committed to the 'ought'.[35]

Roberts similarly describes German 'legal science' treating 'the materials of law', such as legislation, executive actions and court decisions, as 'naturally occurring phenomena', expecting 'the legal scientist' to 'use inductive reasoning to determine the natural laws that explain these phenomena', while seeking 'to exclude non-legal data, insights, and theories from social science and moral philosophy'.[36] Legal academics in the United Kingdom are also unlikely to have 'non-legal' training, and are 'traditionally renowned for their black-letter-law approach'.[37] Legal academics in the United States, however, often have postgraduate degrees 'in a non-legal subject such as history, economics, international relations, and sociology', which alongside wider acceptance of legal realism generate 'interdisciplinary legal scholarship, including in international law'.[38] Meanwhile, Russian international law books describe '"principles" of international law', drawing from Article 2 of the UN Charter, underpinning 'the typical Russian approach of arguing deductively' from principles rather than 'inductively from state practice and case law'.[39]

Different national legal cultures also have different approaches to legal uncertainty. Since Prussia's General Law of 1794, Germany's legal system has operated an extensive legal code, constraining interpretive discretion for lawyers and even judges.[40] Yet even Germany has 'abandoned the ideal of a gap-free' law, its Federal Supreme Court and Federal Constitutional Court acknowledging in the 1960s that 'law in practice' always combined 'statutory

33 Koskenniemi, *Gentle Civiliser of Nations*, 500–7; Koskenniemi, 'Constitutionalism as Mindset', 18–23.
34 Verdirame, 'Divided West', 554, 555.
35 Ibid., 555–6, 558, 562.
36 Roberts, *Is International Law International?* 218.
37 Ibid. 223.
38 Ibid. 222.
39 Ibid. 186.
40 Maxeiner, 'Legal Certainty', 570.

and case law' and 'creative law finding'.[41] Other national legal systems actively *require* judges to practise 'interstitial law-making'.[42] In countries with common law systems, 'common law rules are not made by legislatures' but 'created by courts simultaneously with the application of those rules to concrete cases'.[43] In Switzerland, the Civil Code requires that, 'in the absence of a provision' of law relevant to a case, 'the court shall decide in accordance with customary law and, in the absence of customary law, in accordance with *the rule that it would make as legislator*' (emphasis added), finding a rule appropriate to present and future cases that fits with precedent and existing laws.[44]

The interviewees also remarked on the relevance of national differences around the roles of government legal advisers' in different countries,[45] making it difficult to 'be prescriptive across systems'.[46] Nationally specific factors that interviewees mentioned included contractual obligations, whether the Foreign Ministry institutionalised 'autonomous legal thinking' or a 'more service orientation', and if such legal advisers were 'part of the broader political discourse'.[47] Legal cultures also differed between equivalent organisations in different nations. For instance, one practising international lawyer described US State Department lawyers as traditionally justifying their government's positions, while UK legal advisers tended to state the 'better view' regardless of policy preferences, setting out risks of different options, and letting ministers decide.[48]

Several interviewees said all lawyers inevitably operationalise a theory of law, which can vary according to national legal cultures.[49] One former government lawyer said few English lawyers thought much about legal theory, unlike 'lawyers from the continent'.[50] Another former government lawyer thought German lawyers 'might follow Kelsen and look for a grundnorm', and adopt a 'very positivist' and 'rules based' approach, while lawyers from different traditions would take other things into account.[51] A scholar referred

41 Maxeiner, 'Legal Certainty', 575.

42 Frederick Schauer, 'Is Common Law Law?', *California Law Review*, 77:2 (1989), 455–71, 457.

43 Schauer, 'Is Common Law Law?', 455.

44 The Federal Council of Switzerland, *Swiss Civil Code of 10 December 1907 (Status as of 1 July 2020)*; Alfred E. von Overbeck, 'Some Observations on the Role of the Judge in the Swiss Civil Code', *Louisiana Law Review*, 37:3 (1977), 681–700, 690.

45 Participants 3, 18, 30.

46 Participant 3.

47 Participant 30.

48 Participant 18.

49 Participant 4.

50 Participant 21.

51 Participant 25.

to their 'doctrinal upbringing' in Germany as encouraging them to work within the existing canons of interpretation.[52] Another said they had observed divisions across 'national and regional boundaries', with some German and Swiss scholars taking 'a more value based approach' and thus arguing for the lawfulness of humanitarian intervention.[53]

A former government lawyer argued African international lawyers tended to accept only justifications of force under 'classic self-defence' and with unambiguous UNSC authorisation, while government lawyers for Arab states saw the *jus ad bellum* through the prism of conflict with Israel, although all would, if needed, seek to 'justify their government doing something that wasn't obviously covered'.[54] Another former government lawyer said the United States had got themselves into difficulty by adopting 'a very originalist approach to treaty interpretation', yet customary processes could change even the application of treaties.[55] For example the UN Charter does not mention peacekeeping, yet it is now generally accepted that the UN may establish peacekeeping operations.[56]

Roberts notes important differences between how international law books in different countries deal with humanitarian intervention, the 1999 intervention in Kosovo, and the 2003 intervention in Iraq. The US textbook she assessed 'devotes almost twenty pages to humanitarian intervention, the Kosovo conflict, and its legal aftermath', presenting the issue 'as a pressing matter of international law', 'in a state of flux but moving toward greater protection of individual rights and more exceptions to sovereignty and non-interference'.[57] Meanwhile, Chinese scholars 'often refer to humanitarian intervention in quotation marks or with a dismissive qualification, such as "so-called humanitarian intervention," implying that it is not an accepted doctrine' and can instead be a 'pretextual justification' for force.[58] And the Russian books Roberts analysed did not discuss 'whether a right of unilateral humanitarian intervention is emerging' or might be 'illegal but legitimate', instead contrasting a Western view that only '"dictatorial" intervention' is illegal, with Russian doctrine that 'any intervention is forbidden', including 'attempts to interfere in the internal affairs of a state'.[59]

52 Participant 30.
53 Participant 4.
54 Participant 31.
55 Participant 19.
56 Participant 19.
57 Roberts, *Is International Law International?* 195.
58 Ibid.
59 Ibid. 198.

On the 2003 Iraq intervention, French textbooks deal with it 'as a clear violation of international law, typically meriting little in-depth analysis'.[60] However, the US book implies it was neither 'a clearly lawful use of force' nor 'an obviously aggressive violation of the UN Charter' but 'was an arguable case on which reasonable minds could differ', while the UK book detailed the arguments of states that supported and opposed the intervention, giving readers 'two fleshed-out sides in order to make their own determination'.[61] Overall, Roberts found the legal conclusions of all the scholars she assessed 'tended to broadly align with the positions of their states or geopolitical regional groupings'.[62]

It can be argued that such differences between nations are critical to understanding the particular value of law in wider politico-military decision-making by states. Any decision-maker who says they want peace, who would normally condemn acts of deliberate violence, and who operates in a political system that holds them accountable for their actions, will need some justification for any decision to resort to the organised violence that is the use of military force. The analysis in this book suggests debates around the *jus ad bellum* are a distillation and reflection of the kinds of political, strategic and ethical rationalisations that any such decision-maker needs to undertake to justify taking action they would otherwise condemn. International law governing resort to force can be seen as providing a specific, transnational normative framework, language and set of argumentative practices within which to make such rationalisations and justifications.

Even so, legal decision-makers in different countries and different forms of government are likely to face different pressures and incentives around whether and how to articulate a legal justification for resort to force. For example, it is reasonable to expect decision-makers in democracies to be more vulnerable to public pressures to advance a legal justification for resort to military force than leaders in non-democratic governments. It is also a fact that the Permanent Five members of the UNSC, states that they protect, states rejecting ICJ compulsory jurisdiction and leaders lacking independent domestic political, judicial or media scrutiny, will face fewer constraints and potential challenges to decisions to use force than states lacking these characteristics. Even democracies appear to hold different attitudes to the legal justification of force – and indeed different attitudes as to the necessity for states to articulate a legal justification for force at all. Former FCO legal

60 Roberts, *Is International Law International?* 199.
61 Ibid. 203, 205.
62 Ibid. 237.

adviser Franklin Berman has written of a 'dangerous' gap between US lawyers, who tend to believe the law 'should allow the United States to use force whenever it feels it must', and European lawyers, who tend to believe law should 'outlaw force altogether except in the most extreme circumstances', and require all disputes to be resolved in the UNSC.[63]

The UK government seems to have been among those Western states most consistently willing to use military force, while at the same time more concerned about articulating a legal justification for its decisions to use force than other Western countries. Examples include the difficult evolution of NATO decision-making to intervene in Kosovo in 1999, and the failure to persuade a similarly extensive coalition of nations to intervene in Iraq in 2003.[64] The United Kingdom appears to have been more concerned than some of its allies about explaining the lawfulness of its action in Kosovo, declaring the intervention legal.[65] But the United States and Germany privately believed the operation was unlawful and should not set a precedent, and France too advanced no legal justification.[66] Meanwhile the United Kingdom adopted a narrower, less ambitiously expansionist legal justification for its intervention in Iraq than the United States.[67] As one former government lawyer interviewee noted, there seems to be more interest in the legality of military intervention in the United Kingdom than other countries, recalling an FCO lawyer asking French colleagues if their government had taken a view on the legality of the Iraq intervention, and being told that Paris thought the action 'unwise, but the question of whether it was lawful just doesn't feature': 'nobody's terribly interested'.[68]

This difference between the United Kingdom and its allies may be partly a result of the UK *Ministerial Code*, prescribing an 'overarching duty on Ministers to comply with the law'.[69] Even the UK statement concerning the controversial 2020 UK Internal Market Bill, which provided that certain powers 'may be exercised in a way that is incompatible with provisions of the Withdrawal Agreement' – an international treaty – still reaffirmed that the 'established principle of international law that a state is obliged to discharge its

63 Berman, 'Lawyers in Armed Conflict', 628–9.
64 Simma, 'NATO', 1; Cassese, '*Ex Inuria Ius Oritur*', 29; Wood, 'Law on the Use of Force', 11.
65 Symons, 'Kosovo'; Roberts, 'So-Called "Right"', 24.
66 Simma, 'NATO', 1; Wood, 'Law on the Use of Force', 11.
67 UN Security Council, Document S/2003/351 (United States); S/2003/350 (United Kingdom); S/2003/352 (Australia); Goldsmith, 'Use of Force against Iraq'; Australian Attorney-General, 'Use of Force against Iraq', 415; Taft and Buchwald, 'Preemption', 553; Gray, *International Law*, 355; Craven et al., 'Teachers of International Law', 363–74.
68 Participant 31.
69 HM Government Cabinet Office, *Ministerial Code* (January 2018), 1.

treaty obligations in good faith' was 'and will remain, the key principle in informing the UK's approach to international relations'.[70]

It would be going too far to argue that the extent to which any state is bound by international law governing resort to force entirely depends upon the personal attitudes of its leaders, the socialising forces of its national legal and political culture, and the constraints and incentives within its domestic political and legal system. The UN Charter, UNSC and UNGA, whatever the criticism directed at them, provide international mechanisms to discuss controversial instances of resort to force that even the most powerful, least domestically accountable decision-maker cannot entirely evade. So it seems reasonable to conclude that international law in this as in other areas of international politics does impose 'real constraints and influences on State behaviour'.[71] Even if those constraints and influences seem to shape behaviour between states in less determinative ways than domestic law shapes the behaviour of individuals within states.

UNCERTAINTY AND CHALLENGES TO LAWYERS' DUTY TO THE LAW

Whatever variations there may be in the duties and responsibilities of different categories of international lawyer in different countries, there are good reasons to argue that all share a common core set of responsibilities, duties and professional ethical norms. The framework developed in Chapter 6 creates significant potential practical and normative problems for those professional responsibilities and norms as described by a range of scholarly writings. The interviews and survey research conducted for this book also uncovered a range of views about the appropriateness for *jus ad bellum* decisions of extra-legal reasoning and some of the techniques proposed in Chapter 6.

First, *the framework potentially challenges lawyers' normative responsibility to encourage clients to obey the law, and to maintain the integrity of international law itself.* For example, the International Law Association *Hague Principles on Ethical Standards for Counsel appearing before International Courts and Tribunals* specifies a principle of 'integrity' whereby '[c]ounsel shall not engage in any activity for a client', nor 'advise or assist a client to engage in conduct that he or she knows or ought to know is criminal or

[70] HM Government Cabinet Office, 'HMG Legal Position: UKIM Bill and Northern Ireland Protocol' (10 September 2020).

[71] Chanaka Wickremasinghe, 'Preface', in Chanaka Wickremasinghe, ed., *The International Lawyer as Practitioner* (London: British Institute of International and Comparative Law, 2000), xix.

fraudulent or otherwise in conflict with these Principles'.[72] Harold Koh describes US State Department legal advisers balancing their role as '*counselor*', giving legal advice to help clients achieve their objectives, and '*conscience*', encouraging governments to obey the law even where that constrains their objectives.[73] Another former US government lawyer argues 'there are limits to the legal arguments that government lawyers can ethically offer'. Where government lawyers exceed the bounds of honest and responsible argument – functioning purely as apologists or 'hired guns', they 'betray not only their responsibilities but their vocation'.[74]

Many international lawyers recognise this tension 'between duties to the client and responsibilities to the integrity of the international legal system'.[75] The framework developed in Chapter 6 recommends that lawyers identify ways of reducing legal and other risks a state may face if advancing a legal justification for force. It thus recommends an instrumental approach to law, suited to the role of 'counsellor', helping a client address obstacles that law may present, rather than the normative, prescriptive duty of 'conscience'.

But many lawyers agree with former FCO legal adviser Sir Michael Wood, that 'all lawyers, especially all government lawyers, have a duty to the law going beyond a duty merely to advise on what the law is', and should also regard 'support for the international legal system' as integral to their functions.[76] Former FCO legal adviser Sir Franklin Berman argues that a government lawyer's 'main role' is to '"make" his Government comply with international law', not 'to *compel*' Governments, but also not 'simply to ascertain what the law is' and 'explain it'.[77] Former FCO lawyer Philip Allott describes international lawyers as 'servants not of power but of justice' and of 'international

72 International Law Association, *Hague Principles on Ethical Standards for Counsel Appearing before International Courts and Tribunals* (27 September 2010).

73 Koh, 'Eight Decades in Peace and War', 1758.

74 Bilder, 'On Being an International Lawyer', *Loyola University of Chicago International Law Review*, 3 (2006), 135–47, 145.

75 Andraž Zidar, 'Legal Advisers and Professional Ethics' in Andraz Zidar and Jean-Pierre Gauci, eds., *The Role of Legal Advisers in International Law* (Leiden: BrillNijhoff, 2016), 322; Arthur Watts, 'International Law and International Relations: United Kingdom Practice', *European Journal of International Law*, 2 (1991), 164.

76 Sir Michael Wood, 'Legal Advisers', *Max Planck Encyclopedia of Public International Law* (May 2013); Jean-Pierre Gauci and Kate Jones, 'Conference Report: The Role of Legal Advisers in International Law', in Zidar and Gauci, *The Role of Legal Advisers in International Law* (Leiden: Brill Nijhoff, 2016), 374.

77 Berman, 'Role of the International Lawyer', 3–4.

society', with a duty to consider not only the interests of their state but also 'the long-term interest of international society'.[78]

Jennings noted how, during the Suez crisis, FCO legal adviser Sir Gerald Fitzmaurice made 'every effort to assist the Government in its claims against Colonel Nasser', but remained so 'firmly of the opinion that the use of force against Colonel Nasser's Government was unlawful' that Prime Minister Eden said, 'The lawyers are always against our doing anything. For God's sake keep them out of it. This is a political affair.'[79] Most interviewees also wanted international lawyers to fulfil their 'duty to the law' when advising governments on the *jus ad bellum*.[80] A former government lawyer said any international lawyer should 'steer your policy clients' towards the 'legally correct' option.[81] Another former government lawyer said legal advisers should 'argue forcefully where we think the government should adopt a particular policy to comply with the law'.[82]

For many, the absence of international courts with compulsory jurisdiction made that duty particularly important.[83] A former US government lawyer has warned that the lack of a court may tempt governments 'to stretch the law in what they see as essential national interests' in cases concerning use of force.[84] As Wood told the Chilcot inquiry, in domestic cases a lawyer proposing creative arguments knows 'a judge, will decide in the end', but in international law, 'because there is no court, the Legal Adviser and those taking decisions based on legal advice have to be all the more scrupulous in adhering to the law'.[85] Another former FCO legal adviser, Elizabeth Wilmshurst, who resigned from the FCO over the intervention in Iraq, similarly told the inquiry that the lack of international courts with compulsory jurisdiction over use of force decisions means, in such cases, lawyers should be 'more cautious about trying to keep within the law, not less'.[86]

78 Philip Allott, 'State Responsibility and the Unmaking of International Law', *Harvard International Law Journal*, 29 (1988), 1–26, 24.
79 Jennings, 'Introduction', xxiv.
80 Participants 3, 6, 7, 8, 9, 10, 11, 12, 13, 15, 17, 18, 20, 21, 22, 23, 24, 25, 26, 27, 29, 30, 31.
81 Participant 25.
82 Participant 21.
83 Richard B. Bilder, 'International Lawyer', 145.
84 Teresa A. Bailey, 'Presidential Plenary Panel: An Exchange with Former Legal Advisors of the US Department of State', *Proceedings of the American Society of International Law*, 98(2004), 131–4, 133.
85 Iraq Inquiry, 'Legal Basis for Military Action', 71; see also Public Hearing (26 January 2010), 33–4.
86 Iraq Inquiry, 'Legal Basis for Military Action', 71; see also Public Hearing (26 January 2010), 9.

Several interviewees agreed.[87] A former government lawyer said in use of force cases, 'in effect we are the court' so have a 'duty to obey or to shape the law in a way which is responsible'.[88] A legal scholar said with such decisions, government lawyers have 'a greater obligation to the law'.[89] A practitioner said it was important to assert clear 'limits and constraints' on government behaviour.[90] Many interviewees said legal justifications for resort-to-force decisions need 'a high degree of certainty' for their legal and factual basis.[91] A legal scholar argued for a higher 'threshold' than 'reasonable rational argument' or 'plausible that it is lawful' in such cases.[92] A practitioner said a lower threshold may be appropriate only in situations where lawyers can be confident courts will eventually rule, with 'no enormous harm done if you're wrong'.[93] One former government lawyer described the danger of ministers seeing the absence of international courts as a sign that states 'can get away with' violating the *jus ad bellum*, even though the UK *Ministerial Code* obliges ministers to comply with law, including international law.[94]

Second, *the framework encourages lawyers to consider multiple alternative interpretations of the lawfulness of proposed military action and about relevant facts, making it harder to provide determinate legal advice*. Many international lawyers argue the existence of multiple interpretations, disagreement and uncertainty on hard cases does not imply there is 'vagueness' in the law that needs to be accepted and managed.[95] The unacceptability of *non liquet* in adjudication is one sign of this, which many lawyers argue 'is a consequence of the completeness of the international legal system'.[96]

Shaw supports Oppenheim's assertion that 'while there may not always be an immediate and obvious rule applicable to every international situation, "every international situation is capable of being determined as a matter of law"'.[97] Many lawyers hold that gaps can be resolved by 'closing rules' or principles such as the 'Lotus principle', 'namely, that anything not prohibited by international law is permitted', either as a logical consequence of the

87 Participants 7, 8, 21.
88 Participant 21.
89 Participant 7.
90 Participant 8.
91 Participants 17, 24, 3, 26.
92 Participant 17.
93 Participant 10.
94 Participant 25.
95 *Legality of the Threat or Use of Nuclear Weapons*, Judge Higgins, dissenting opinion, ICJ Reports 1996, para. 40.
96 Weil, 'Non Liquet Revisited', 110.
97 Shaw, *International Law*, 99.

principle of completeness, or flowing from the principle of sovereignty.[98] Kelsen argued that international law applies even in cases where treaties or custom require no specific behaviour, since then 'the subject is under international law legally free to behave as it pleases'.[99] Higgins has argued that norms frequently 'pull in different directions – for example, States may not use force/states may use force in self-defence', but judges can and should determine why one of those competing norms should apply in specific cases, 'in context, and on grounds that should be articulated'.[100] Legal advisers can rely on similar principles and methods to provide determinate legal opinions.

In addition, policymakers and military commanders usually *want* clear, determinate legal advice. Before the Iraq intervention, the UK attorney general's detailed legal advice of 7 March 2003 found a 'reasonable case' that intervention without a further UNSC resolution would be lawful.[101] However, as Chapter 6 reported, the United Kingdom's chief of defence staff and treasury solicitor insisted that the attorney general 'give a clear-cut answer on whether the "reasonable case" was lawful'.[102] On 13 March 2003, the attorney general concluded 'on balance the "better view" was that there *was* a legal basis for the use of force without a further resolution'.[103] Both senior public servants wanted legal certainty from the attorney general.

And almost all interviewees said legal advisers must always try to articulate what they considered to be 'the better view' in cases they advised on, even if the answer was not obvious.[104] As one former government lawyer said, it was 'all very well for legal advisers to say there are arguments on one side and on the other side', but 'at the end of the day, they and the AG may need to express a view as to whether an act is legal or not', even if they say 'on the balance of probabilities' or 'there is a respectable case, but if challenged in court it is not likely to win'.[105] Several interviewees said if they were advising on a prospective use of force, they 'would feel uncomfortable' 'merely setting out good or best arguments' without also 'expressing a view as to whether it was lawful'.[106]

98 Bodansky, 'Non Liquet'.
99 Hans Kelsen, *Principles of International Law*, 2nd ed. (New York: Holt Rinehart and Winston, 1966), 438–9.
100 *Nuclear Weapons*, Higgins, para. 40.
101 Iraq Inquiry, 'Legal Basis for Military Action', 101.
102 Ibid., 123.
103 Ibid., 123.
104 Participants 11, 15, 21, 29.
105 Participant 21.
106 Participant 15.

Third, *the framework asks lawyers in hard cases to identify and reflect extra-legal considerations and risks, potentially conflating legal and policy assessment.* Many international lawyers agree with Wilmshurst that government lawyers must 'distinguish between policy and law', and 'not dress up as law what is really advocacy'.[107] Allott has noted that if a lawyer 'behaves as if there were no distinction between political purposes and legal purposes, political values and legal values, political judgment and legal judgment, then public decision-making is deprived of a dimension that is otherwise liable to improve its quality, efficiency and even its effectiveness'.[108] Koh has similarly emphasised the State Department's separation and 'creative tension' between career lawyers and political appointees.[109] All interviewees argued lawyers should advance what they in their professional opinion assessed was the best interpretation of the law as it is, not the law as they wanted it to be.[110] As one practising international lawyer said, a 'legal adviser acting ethically for her client', was obliged to say 'what is the law and how that affects what the client wants to do or should do or could do'.[111]

The surveys and interviews also revealed reluctance to allow extra-legal factors to shape legal advice. Figure 7.1 illustrates participants' survey responses when asked what role extra-legal intuitions *should* play and *actually do* play when different categories of lawyers evaluate resort to force where there is factual and legal uncertainty. Around 40 per cent of participants said government lawyers took insufficient account of law, allowing politics and strategy to play *too great* a role when dealing with legal and factual uncertainty.[112] Around 25 per cent said judges and commentators take insufficient account of law, while around 40 per cent said judges and commentators allowed politics and strategy to play the appropriate role when dealing with factual uncertainty. Only 7 per cent said politics and strategy played *too little* role when addressing legal uncertainty. Nine interviewees argued lawyers should provide legal advice on use of force decisions based only on their

107 Elizabeth Wilmshurst, 'Disciplining the Discipline: Roles and Responsibilities of International Lawyers: Remarks', *Proceedings of the Annual Meeting (American Society of International Law)*, 100 (2006), 449–50, 449; Gauci and Jones, 'Conference Report', 374.

108 Philip Allott, 'The International Lawyer in Government Service: Ontology and Deontology', *Wisconsin International Law Journal*, 23:1 (2005), 13–23, 18.

109 Koh, 'Eight Decades in Peace and War', 1752.

110 Participants 22, 12, 6, 15.

111 Participant 12.

112 Differences between percentages of participants saying law *actually was* very or fairly significant and saying law *ought to be* very or fairly significant when dealing with factual and legal uncertainty.

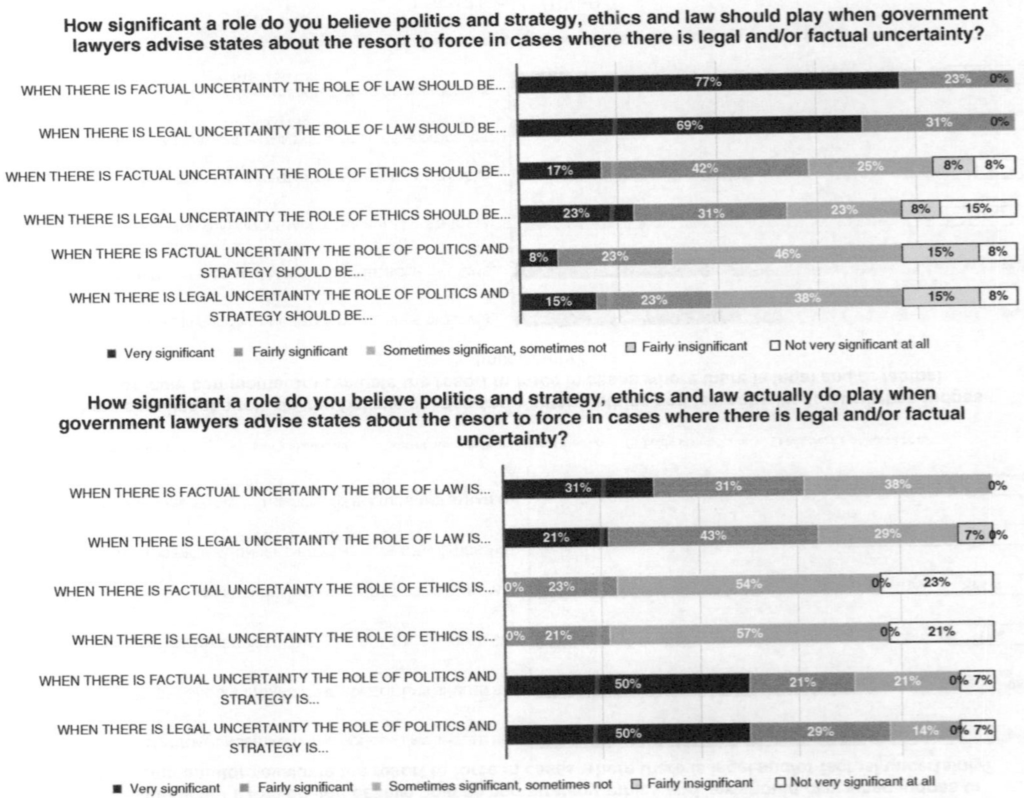

FIGURE 7.1 Extra-legal factors in hard cases – is and ought

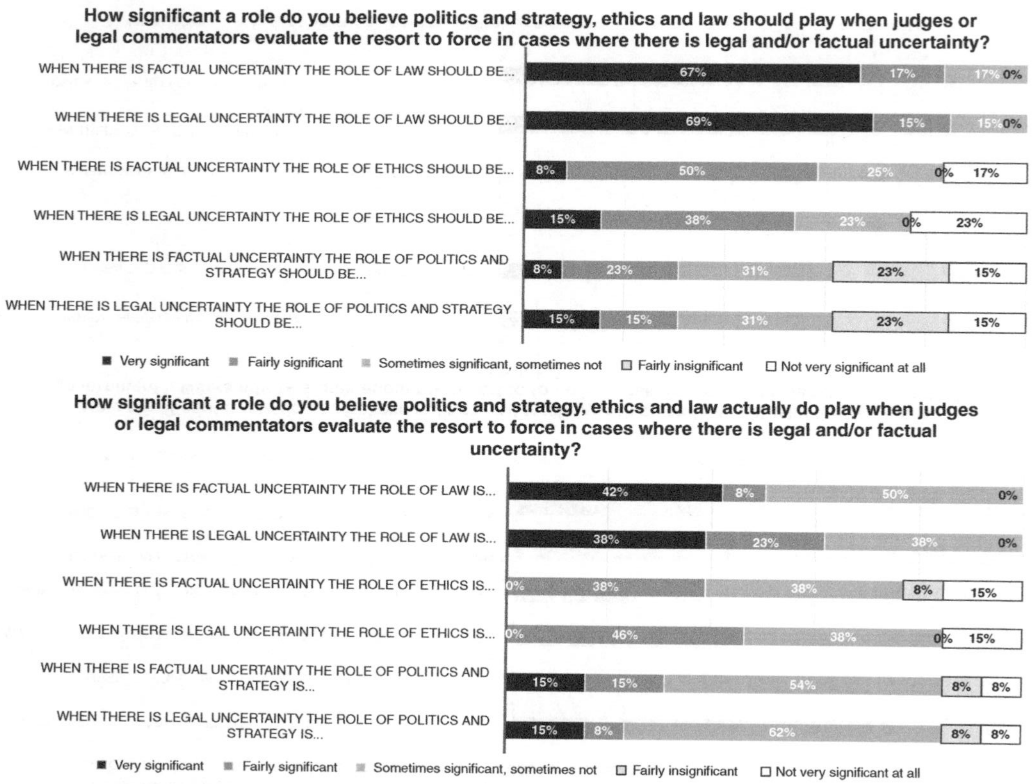

FIGURE 7.1 (Cont.)

professional opinion of the law as it is,[113] leaving political decision-makers to evaluate extra-legal implications.[114] One practising international lawyer said it was 'irresponsible' for lawyers to apply 'their own ethical and personal convictions' because 'then everyone's being a politician'.[115] Instead, the lawyer's role 'is to try and work out what the rules are' and apply those rules to determine the legality of actions.[116]

Most survey participants said *ethics* ought not to and actually did not shape decisions by government lawyers, judges and commentators when dealing with such uncertainty. One legal scholar said 'sometimes I may have world views that don't necessarily conform with black letter law', but in such cases their role was 'to urge a change to the black letters', not to pretend their views *were* the law.[117] Another scholar argued it was possible to make an entirely legal argument for humanitarian intervention without resorting to 'non-legal' factors such as ethics, for example drawing on human rights law, IHL, genocide law and international criminal law.[118] A further scholar said 'I've often given legal advice that's contrary to my ethical views', and lawyers should never tailor legal advice 'to suit the political regime'.[119]

Fourth, *many argue that lawyers who get too involved in policy undermine their own credibility*, their 'distinctive character, role and authority' and their 'potential contribution to public decision-making'.[120] Berman argues government lawyers 'whose role is strictly limited to advice may acquire greater influence', and separating legal and policy advice in the FCO meant legal advisers have 'important control over the way in which the law is applied', while lawyers who get too involved in policy risk 'downgrading' their contribution 'to the same level as expendable policy advice'.[121] Among interviewees, one former government lawyer said some lawyers tend 'to work out what the client wants' and 'go about producing precisely that', but effective legal advisers had 'strength of character', to 'do your research', 'satisfy yourself' of

113 Participants 4, 12, 15, 22, 26, 27, 28, 29, 31.
114 Participants 22, 25, 27, 29.
115 Participant 22.
116 Participant 22.
117 Participant 6.
118 Participant 7.
119 Participant 27.
120 Gauci and Jones, 'Conference Report', 374; Allott, 'International Lawyer', 17; Participants 25, 31.
121 Berman, 'Role of the International Lawyer', 12, 13; Franklin D. Berman, 'The International Lawyer, inside and outside Foreign Ministries', in Christopher Hill and Pamela Beshoff, eds., *Two Worlds of International Relations – Academics, Practitioners and the Trade in Ideas* (London: Routledge, 1994), 85.

the answer, and 'stick to it' even under political pressure.[122] A legal scholar said states that view themselves as law-abiding should value independent legal officers below the level of attorney general, even if politics re-entered 'higher up', to eventually overrule advice 'on political grounds'.[123]

Fifth, and closely related, *lawyers who emphasise uncertainty, get too involved in policy, and enable action stretching the law, may encourage law to evolve in harmful ways.* As former FCO legal adviser Sir Michael Wood told the Chilcot inquiry, legal advisers and foreign policy-makers 'have to be all the more scrupulous in adhering to the law' because they 'are setting precedents by the very fact of saying and doing things'.[124] Wood has separately noted that international lawyers for governments have a responsibility for 'the development of international law' in 'the common interest' as well as the interest of their state.[125] Allott warns that for a lawyer '[t]o trim one's sails to every change of political direction, and to say only what one presumes that those one advises want to hear', only serves to undermine their 'capacity to identify and to present different horizons of national interest, including long-term horizons' in which 'an immediately convenient course of action may be a bad course of action in the long run'.[126]

Several interviewees highlighted the potential for harmful customary change as a reason for international lawyers' duty to the law.[127] Former government lawyers described how internal legal advisers should start their analysis from their government's established legal position on similar cases, 'understand those previous positions and stick to them unless there are good reasons to change',[128] rather than applying 'your own opinions and politics'.[129] One former government lawyer described a 'risk of exponential deviation from the mean', where justifying one operation deviating only 'five percent' from a current legal interpretation creates a new 'starting point for the next operation'.[130] This potentially creates a 'legality trajectory' in which operations progressively deviate further, so that after multiple operations, thresholds for force are 'orders of magnitude' dangerously divergent from the original *jus ad bellum* boundaries.[131] One practitioner condemned lawyers who wrote legal

122 Participant 11.
123 Participant 3.
124 Iraq Inquiry, 'Legal Basis for Military Action', 71.
125 Wood, 'Legal Advisers'.
126 Allott, 'International Lawyer', 17.
127 Participants 7, 19, 27.
128 Participant 21.
129 Participants 25, 21, 31.
130 Participant 19.
131 Participant 19.

opinions claiming the law had already changed, to 'evangelise' for law to evolve in ways they believed ethically or politically desirable, hoping 'enough policymakers will believe it and then it will have happened'; such lawyers were guilty of 'intellectual fraud' and a 'disservice to public international law'.[132]

It might also be argued that the methods proposed in Chapter 6 are better suited to dealing with factual uncertainty than legal uncertainty. For cases where there is little legal uncertainty – where there is general acceptance of the validity of a legal justification for resort to force – but where factual uncertainty is the most likely source of controversy – which this study suggests is the case for the use of force in anticipatory self-defence or self-defence against armed attacks by non-state actors, the factual analysis and structured analytic techniques proposed in Chapter 6 can obviously add value. However, where controversy is generated by disagreement about what the law itself prohibits or permits rather than about the facts – which this study suggests is the case for the use of force for pre-emptive self-defence, to stop an overwhelming humanitarian catastrophe, or to enforce a WMD prohibition – the assessment of competing legal theories proposed in Chapter 6 is more likely to play a role. Yet those assessment techniques do not try to identify which competing legal theory accurately represents the law as it is. Rather they seek to assess how key stakeholders might react to those legal theories when justifying a specific instance of resort to force. The techniques Chapter 6 proposes do not help lawyers identify the 'ground truth' of international law governing resort to force in any specific situation. Indeed, the techniques do not even presuppose there is such a legal 'ground truth' to be discovered.

Sixth, *for normative and practical reasons, several interviewees were uncomfortable with government lawyers advising on use of force using some of the structured analytic techniques proposed in* Chapter 6.[133] Some said legal risk management might be appropriate for litigation or policy submissions, but should not 'colour the normativity' of a government lawyer's legal assessment.[134] One practitioner derided such methods as 'neither risk nor management', creating a 'danger of painting a normal exercise in giving legal advice in some sort of American jargon', which looks like 'trying to help your client in a bad way as opposed to just giving good legal advice', 'identifying the possible lines of argument', 'their potential as well as their actual strengths', then providing 'your view as to which is the stronger argument'.[135]

132 Participant 12.
133 Participants 6, 15, 17, 24, 26, 29.
134 Participant 29.
135 Participant 15.

Several participants expressed doubts about multi-hypothesis factual analysis and forecasting. One former government lawyer noted that time is more constrained in military crises than court cases, 'you can't just sit back and say sorry I'll need another three weeks', so while using scenarios was advisable, analysts needed to pick one as most likely with limited time for reflection.[136] And such analysis may not affect the final decision – for example, if analysts in 2003 had concluded on balance Iraq probably did not have WMDs, ministers may still have regarded inaction as unacceptably risky, given memories of 11 September 2001 and Iraq's confirmed past possession of chemical weapons.[137] Another former government lawyer argued forecasting was not needed in many cases of self-defence where the facts were clear, for example after an invasion, since 'armed attack triggers the legal right to use force' whatever the potential consequences, and does not require states to consider responses not involving force.[138] A practising international lawyer criticised forecasts about resort to force as 'like predicting the price of oil in a year or what's going to happen on Brexit'; there were 'so many unknowns', and a danger that 'some sort of fancy percentage' might encourage decision-makers 'to put undue weight on it'.[139] Such methods also have limitations in post hoc evaluations since, as a former government lawyer noted, one '[c]annot use hindsight to evaluate legality', but must only evaluate actions 'in light of the knowledge they had or should have had at the time'.[140]

And, as has already been noted, there are real limitations to forecasting, multi-scenario analysis and other structured analytic techniques in situations as complex as military crises.[141] The true facts of chaotic conflicts prompting *jus ad bellum* decisions, and the outcomes of the military campaigns that such decisions initiate, are not usually amenable to high confidence probabilistic analysis and forecasting, but are instead 'cloud-like'.[142] Similar uncertainty applies to assessments of whether different actors may challenge the lawfulness of a decision to use military force, whether such challenges may succeed, and what harm that may cause for a decision-maker. In such situations, there are many more potential interpretations of current facts and potential future outcomes than could be captured by any viable analytical framework. To believe that multi-scenario analyses, risk assessments or other structured

136 Participant 31.
137 Participant 31.
138 Participant 21.
139 Participant 15.
140 Participant 21.
141 Pherson and Heuer, *Structured Analytic Techniques*, 253.
142 Tetlock and Gardner, *Superforecasting*, locs. 4082–4.

analytic techniques can capture all potential outcomes and precisely calculate their relative likelihood and impact is 'at best unhelpful and at worst actively misleading'.[143]

Mervyn King, former governor of the Bank of England, and fellow economist John Kay have recently argued that probabilistic analytic techniques are particularly unsuitable in situations like military crises, which are affected by 'radical uncertainty', and 'cannot be described in the probabilistic terms applicable to a game of chance. It is not just that we do not know what will happen. We often do not even know the kinds of things that might happen.'[144] The US military operation in Pakistan that resulted in the death of Osama Bin Laden is one example. President Barack Obama reportedly described the intelligence assessments about whether Bin Laden was in the compound in Abbottabad, using the kinds of structured analytic techniques described in Chapter 6 as 'probabilities that disguised uncertainty as opposed to actually providing you with useful information'.[145] And a recent study of structured analytic techniques in intelligence assessment, particularly the analysis of competing hypotheses technique, found it was vague about 'how hypotheses should be selected; what criteria should be used to rate evidence as being consistent or inconsistent with a hypothesis; or what criteria should be used to judge evidence diagnosticity' (reliability and relevance for comparing hypotheses).[146] The study also found most analysts trained to use the technique deviated from the prescribed steps, and 'were no more likely than their untrained counterparts to identify the four alternative hypotheses' or even 'to choose the correct hypothesis' in the experiment.[147]

Koskenniemi sees particular dangers in what he describes as legal 'managerialism', using extra-legal analytical methodologies, tables and grids.[148] He condemns 'these new realists', who, 'in their hubris, believe in the power of their predictive and explanatory matrices and think that words such as "power," "bargain," "costs and benefits," or "legitimacy" mark out entities in the empirical world that would automatically guide policy'.[149] He notes that such extra-legal reasoning is no more determinate than law, simply institutionalising 'an anti-political, technical mindset that, under the cover of

143 King and Kay, *Radical Uncertainty*, loc. 238.
144 Ibid., locs. 308–15.
145 Mark Bowden, *The Finish: The Killing of Osama Bin Laden* (New York: Atlantic Monthly Press, 2012), 160.
146 Dhami et al., 'Analysis of Competing Hypotheses', 1080–1.
147 Ibid., 1085–6.
148 Koskenniemi, 'Constitutionalism as Mindset', 35.
149 Ibid., 35.

seeking effectiveness, looks no further than the next internal audit', 'the next promotion: my success as the criterion of the world's happiness'.[150]

Seventh, *lawyers who accept legal uncertainty and allow too close a relationship between legal and political assessment potentially encourage law-breaking even in cases where there is little legal uncertainty*, by encouraging governments to circumvent obstacles that law properly poses. When leaders of states believe their interests are best served by behaviour whose legality is controversial, they face incentives to emphasise uncertainty and gaps in the law, to increase their room for manoeuvre. One legal scholar worried that legal and factual uncertainty might tempt decision-makers to make 'strategic use of the law' to justify military action that might otherwise be clearly unlawful, as they believed Tony Blair had done before the Iraq war.[151] In hard cases, the framework proposed in Chapter 6 will only encourage compliance with the law where government decision-makers are vulnerable to and care about risks of legal challenge to their actions. But, as this chapter has already noted, the Permanent Five members of the UNSC, states they protect, states rejecting ICJ compulsory jurisdiction and leaders lacking independent domestic political, judicial or media scrutiny, will have less reason to fear such risks. A legal adviser for a militarily powerful autocratic government that has accepted the jurisdiction of no international courts, is protected by a UNSC veto, and is considering using force purely for economic gain against a militarily weaker state with no powerful friends, might apply the framework proposed in Chapter 6 and identify no significant legal or other risks to such a clearly unlawful act.

In addition, psychological research suggests creativity by decision-makers and ambiguity in the principles governing their decisions can facilitate dishonest behaviour. Gino and Ariely suggest 'greater creativity can lead to greater dishonesty by increasing individuals' ability to justify their immoral actions'.[152] Hsee suggests that, in decision-making processes, when the 'justifiable factors' that 'decision makers believe they should take into consideration' are ambiguous or open to multiple interpretations, decision-makers feel greater leeway and less guilt about considering factors they want to consider but would otherwise believe were 'unjustifiable'.[153] One legal scholar interviewee highlighted the risk that highly creative government legal advice

150 Ibid., 30.

151 Participant 7.

152 F. Gino and D. Ariely, 'The Dark Side of Creativity: Original Thinkers Can Be More Dishonest', *Journal of Personality and Social Psychology*, 102:3 (2012), 445–59, 455.

153 Christopher K. Hsee, 'Elastic Justification: How Unjustifiable Factors Influence Judgments', *Organizational Behavior and Human Decision Processes*, 66:1 (1996), 122–9, 122.

becomes 'a violation because it's not a reasonable interpretation of the law', the US attorney general's 2002 torture memo being an example.[154]

Finally, *the framework recommends governments make public their detailed legal and factual reasoning about resort to force, potentially threatening the client confidentiality necessary for lawyers to give, and policy-makers to seek, frank advice.* Client confidentiality is generally regarded as 'indispensable to the lawyer's function as advocate', because lawyers can only provide effective legal advice 'if the client is free to disclose everything, bad as well as good', which is considered 'impossible without discretion'.[155] *Erskine May*, a guide to UK parliamentary practice, explains that the purpose of client confidentiality 'is to enable the government to obtain frank and full legal advice in confidence'.[156] Confidentiality enables honest advice in a policy-making process that may need to consider unpalatable policy options – very likely the case when governments consider using military force. As Berman has noted, it is 'fundamental' to Legal Advisers' 'ability to advise properly and effectively that their advice should be given, and received, in confidence', making it possible for them 'to encourage as well as to warn, to canvass the risks and benefits of alternative courses, to depict potentially adverse precedential consequences, and to advise on tactics', without 'compromising their own integrity or causing the client to lose face or tactical advantage'.[157]

To require such advice to be published may harm both policy-making and law, potentially discouraging decision-makers from keeping records of legal advice, fearing criticism for having considered actions later discarded as unacceptable. Fear of disclosure may encourage decision-makers to exclude legal advisers from policy discussions, delay seeking formal legal advice or avoid weighing all options thoroughly, potentially enabling legally or factually erroneous policy decisions. Such fears may even discourage governments from providing guidance for policy-making in such situations of military crises, such as described in Figure 6.1 in Chapter 6, for fear of legal challenge should a particular decision deviate even slightly from recommended policy procedures under time and other pressures in a crisis.

154 Participant 7.

155 Geoffrey C. Hazard, Jr, 'An Historical Perspective on the Attorney-Client Privilege', *California Law Review*, 66:5 (1978), 1061–91, 1061; Arman Sarvarian, *Professional Ethics at the International Bar* (Oxford: Oxford University Press, 2013), 97.

156 Sir Malcolm Jack, ed., *Erskine May's Treatise on The Law, Privileges, Proceedings and Usage of Parliament* (London: LexisNexis, 2011), 447; Nicola Newson and Sarah Tudor, *Publishing Government Legal Advice: House of Lords Library Briefing* (London: UK Parliament, 7 November 2018), 2.

157 Sir Franklin Berman, 'Conclusion', in Zidar et al., *Legal Advisers*, 382.

Some of these effects may have been seen in the UK legal advice process before the 2003 intervention in Iraq. UK government ministers in December 2002 asked the UK attorney general to provide legal advice on the potential operation, but asked the attorney general not to provide that advice 'now'.[158] This may have been because ministers feared legal advice would constrain military options they were using as leverage in negotiations over Iraq's alleged WMD programme. Ministers may have wanted to avoid creating written records of unhelpful advice, as hinted by Tony Blair's reply at the Chilcot inquiry when asked why he had not requested legal advice earlier, that 'the only concern' had been 'generating bits of paper the entire time on it'.[159]

Fourteen interviewees – the majority expressing a view – opposed publishing more internal legal advice,[160] 'warts and all'.[161] One practising international lawyer said only a government's 'considered legal position' mattered for developing customary law, not the internal debate preceding it. So Tony Blair's Chicago speech on humanitarian intervention, 'the considered position taken by the United Kingdom as a state', was 'of infinitely greater value as a generator of law than whatever legal advice he was given if he had any'.[162] A former government lawyer noted that, if lawyers think 'everything is going to be published' then they would hesitate 'to put things down on paper', and when they do so it would be 'very safe and very uncontroversial and even try not to address issues', and 'might even inhibit a government from asking for legal advice'.[163]

Several said it was unreasonable to expect government lawyers to publish advice that accurately identified weaknesses in their position, and thus assist potential legal challenges,[164] putting 'your client in the dock'.[165] Not only was legal challenge time consuming, but in *jus ad bellum* cases, security classification may prevent sharing of relevant information with courts.[166] A practising international lawyer said, for this reason, published legal opinions whether from NGOs or governments often 'have the interesting stuff taken out', and are often 'totally unconvincing'.[167] All who expressed a view agreed 'legal advisers

[158] Iraq Inquiry, 'Legal Basis for Military Action', 21.
[159] Ibid., para. 165.
[160] Participants 9, 10, 11, 13, 14, 18, 19, 20, 21, 23, 24, 25, 29, 31.
[161] Participant 18.
[162] Participant 13.
[163] Participant 25.
[164] Participants 10, 18, 29, 31.
[165] Participant 31.
[166] Participant 29.
[167] Participant 18.

should not talk publicly about their advice while they are in office' without authorisation, and sensitive information may need to remain confidential for national security reasons long after a decision has been taken.[168]

JUSTIFYING A RISK MANAGEMENT APPROACH

These are powerful normative and practical reasons to question whether international lawyers can use the kind of structured analytic techniques Chapter 6 proposed for handling uncertainty and extra-legal factors while acting according to their professional responsibilities and ethics. However, there are also pragmatic, empirical and normative responses to these objections, supporting the viability of the kind of framework Chapter 6 proposed.

First, *this book has presented evidence suggesting specific indeterminacy – uncertainty, disagreement and vagueness in law and fact in hard cases – exists in the* jus ad bellum. As Weil put it, 'international law is not complete. No legal order is, because there is not, cannot be, and should not be a rule at hand for every concrete or new situation. . . . To a certain extent every legal system is "open-textured." This "fuzziness" of the law, however, is by far more pronounced in the international legal system.'[169] And as 'long as no clear rule has emerged from the norm-creating process, there is simply no legal truth. One state may interpret the law one way and another state may interpret it in another way.'[170] Legal advice that underplays such uncertainty potentially misleads a client about the policy options open to them, and the contestation they are likely to face.

Causes of uncertainty this book has identified include the structure of the *jus ad bellum*'s rules, the factual complexity of hard cases of resort to force, and the diverse normative and factual assumptions and worldviews of the actors whose actions and beliefs constitute the law. The law is subject to *supervaluationism*, since it is based on *paradigms* of lawful and unlawful force, defined by multiple 'family resemblances', which constitute overlapping but not always co-extensive multi-part tests distinguishing 'lawful' from 'unlawful' activity.[171] Both the law and the activity it regulates operate according to fuzzy rather than bivalent logic: conflicts can be located along 'a line of continuity' 'from invasions by tanks and divisions through training, arming, sheltering and

[168] E.g. Participant 1.
[169] Weil, 'Non Liquet Revisited', 118.
[170] Weil, 'Non Liquet Revisited', 119.
[171] Deeks 'Multi-Part Tests', 1037.

infiltrating neighboring insurgents, all the way down to hostile radio propaganda calling for revolution'.[172]

The tests that the law prescribes, such as proportionality, necessity and imminence, are vulnerable to *epistemic vagueness* or ignorance, requiring lawyers to assess facts that are often contested and may not be discoverable in the fog of an emerging or past military crisis. These tests also require lawyers to compare multiple counter-factual or future scenarios flowing from decisions either to use force or not. Those tests are subject to *social supervaluationism*: different, knowledgeable, well-qualified lawyers will interpret the law and facts in different ways, applying different standards, reflecting different intuitions and understandings about how law and war *actually* work and *ought* to work. As already noted, the reality of competing views about law and fact, and the uncertain future of specific cases of force and of conflict more generally, are reasons why vagueness and uncertainty may be necessary features of the *jus ad bellum* as with all law, enabling it to accommodate the complexities of the conflicts it regulates and the international community that applies it.[173]

Many interviewees – and in particular practising international lawyers – said legal advisers should not hide such uncertainties.[174] One practising international lawyer said legal advisers must not 'make out the law to be clearer than it is'.[175] Another practitioner said legal advisers should give advice 'which isn't simply one way' and should convey 'the complexities of the situation'.[176] Lawyers 'should certainly say' where a case 'is obviously unlawful', but in many hard cases 'there will not be one obvious answer', and it is 'hard for the legal adviser to play God'.[177] A fourth practitioner said sometimes in law it is possible to be '99.9% certain' that one view is correct, but with use of force it is often 'notoriously difficult to predict the outcome, you can really only deal with a range of probabilities', and nobody 'can say this is what the answer is going to be'.[178]

Second, *this book has also presented evidence suggesting extra-legal intuitions seem to be associated with assessment of law and fact in hard cases engaging the* jus ad bellum – that the law is only partially autonomous of extra-legal considerations. In hard cases, lawyers inevitably have to apply 'some concept of what the law ought to be' to reach a determinate

[172] Franck, 'Who Killed Article 2(4)?', 813–14.
[173] Hart, *Concept of Law*, 131; Kelsen, *Introduction*, 80, 81, 78.
[174] Participants 8, 13, 17, 18, 22, 29.
[175] Participant 22.
[176] Participant 18.
[177] Participant 8.
[178] Participant 13.

conclusion.[179] The reality of legal and factual uncertainty creates 'room for cognitive activity beyond discovering the frame', so that legal opinions in such cases are often 'motivated by political choices', and 'extra-legal' 'background assumptions'.[180] The evidence in Part II suggested that in hard cases, lawyers tend to conform to different 'interpretive cultures' and 'strategic cultures', displaying consistent beliefs about legal interpretation, politico-strategic assessment and ethical evaluation of war. These legal and extra-legal intuitions, biases and beliefs appeared to encourage lawyers to take clear positions on hard cases of the *jus ad bellum*, opposing the opinions of other lawyers whose legal and extra-legal intuitions and biases conformed to different interpretive/strategic cultures. Legal advice that ignores those extra-legal dimensions again risks underestimating the controversy a client may face, particularly if their client's own extra-legal assumptions prove incorrect.

And some international lawyers argue that, when giving advice on a difficult course of action, lawyers can and *should* follow their own extra-legal reasoning. In important cases, lawyers 'ought to also ask whether it is wise', and 'speak frankly when a proposed course of action is "lawful but awful"'.[181] Koh has written that, as well as advising on law, legal advisers may provide their 'assessment of the wisdom of lawful' actions, especially 'in the complex, delicate, and contentious realm of international law, where legal issues may bleed into moral and policy issues'.[182] He argues there is a 'perpetual feedback loop' between policy and law, which 'helps explain how government lawyers help their nations obey international law'.[183]

Wilmshurst argues that, where law may be developing or changing, where there are 'gaps in the law', conflicts of laws, or 'problems of interpretation that cannot be solved by reference to standard interpretative techniques', government lawyers 'can call in aid principles of some kind', 'fundamental values of the international system which include order, justice, and the welfare of the individual'.[184] Berman also writes that when advising governments on issues where 'the law is indefinite, or still unformed, or in an evident state of development or change', lawyers might go beyond pure legal advice to highlight 'the likely shaping effect on the development of the law'.[185] Indeed, 'the

179 Hart, 'Positivism', 608.
180 Kelsen, *Introduction*, 83; Marxsen 'Indeterminacy', 80.
181 Gauci and Jones, 'Conference Report'.
182 Koh, 'Eight Decades in Peace and War', 1759, 1758.
183 Harold Hongju Koh, 'The Legal Adviser's Duty to Explain', in Zidar et al., *Legal Advisers*, 312.
184 Wilmshurst, 'Disciplining the Discipline', 450.
185 Berman, 'Lawyers in Armed Conflict', 631.

good lawyer' must have a view of 'the desirable direction for the law to develop, and be prepared to explain and defend it', and advise on which 'possible legal developments the Government ought to favour from a policy point of view'.[186] As another scholar has noted, '(t)he only extraordinary feature of the way we appeal to normative considerations' when justifying 'propositions, not just in law but in every instance of practical reasoning, is that these considerations are often too obvious to require spelling out'.[187]

Most research participants who answered the relevant survey questions also believed lawyers ought to and actually do draw on extra-legal factors in reaching decisions in contested *jus ad bellum* cases. This was true for participants with restrictive and permissive views of the *jus ad bellum*. As Figure 7.1 shows, significant minorities of those who answered the relevant questions said ethics *should* play a greater role in legal advice than at present: over 30 per cent said government lawyers do not allow ethics a sufficient role in situations of factual or legal uncertainty, while around 10 per cent thought the same of judges and commentators.

Many interviewees broadly accepted the role of extra-legal factors, while maintaining that law was a separate mode of reasoning.[188] One legal scholar said 'your underlying political view' had 'an inescapable influence' in 'difficult cases' which had not been authoritatively determined.[189] A practising international lawyer said many people's attitudes to use of force 'are very heavily coloured by ethical and political perspectives', and it was 'very hard to say which comes first'.[190] Another practitioner said ethics should play a stronger role than politics, that 'if it's unethical then it can't be the right answer legally', admitting that this kind of approach may be more acceptable to lawyers from common law systems, where there was greater expectation of dynamic interpretation of the law to advance the public good than in civil law systems.[191] But other interviewees said 'political considerations' are relevant because 'we provide advice in a political context and that needs to be taken into account', for example through assessments of 'how other states are going to react', and 'implications for international and world order'.[192]

One legal scholar argued it was 'inevitable' that lawyers 'have a sense as to what they think the right answer should be', but people only 'change their

[186] Berman, 'Conclusion', 384.
[187] Voyiakis, 'Customary International Law', 199.
[188] Participants 3, 5, 7, 9, 10, 13, 18, 28, 29.
[189] Participant 3.
[190] Participant 13.
[191] Participant 10.
[192] Participants 21, 24, 29.

minds' about legal advice 'to suit their policy preferences' if there is significant doubt about what the law prescribes.[193] A former government lawyer said that, as a lawyer, their role was to provide a legal opinion, but as an academic in hard cases they may prefer 'the more honest approach' of admitting 'the law does not provide an answer here', and instead 'look to morality, ethics', because at times 'we're asking the law to do too much', since it is not 'the be all and end all' of foreign policy decision-making.[194] A scholar said that 'every judge and every lawyer has the right to apply their own personal theory' if it 'falls within the bounds' of professional acceptability, although that does not mean judges should say, 'I don't like America, so whenever America is before the ICJ, I should rule against them.'[195] Two legal scholars noted there was no 'completely objective way of interpreting' law, since even the VCLT rules are not 'clear and unambiguous',[196] only providing 'parameters for making arguments' or 'fairly vague guidelines as opposed to delivering the one true and right outcome', leaving 'room for flexibility, pragmatism, or bias'.[197]

Several said it was right for lawyers to prompt policy-makers to reflect on potential political, ethical or other extra-legal consequences.[198] One legal scholar said most lawyers 'use the same variables' but give each different 'weight, priority, intensity' based on their extra-legal views.[199] They argued those with a more expansionist view do not discount legal values, but see 'the universality of values' outside law, while restrictivists regard 'peace as a kind of universal value' while dismissing as subjective the morality underpinning for example humanitarian intervention.[200] A practising international lawyer said legal advisers naturally consider 'ethical and political dimensions', because they wish to justify their advice, particularly since 'resort to force is about killing people', which has clear moral dimensions.[201] One scholar went so far as to dispute whether what the research conducted for this book described as 'non-legal considerations' are always non-legal, since they can often 'legitimately' be 'advanced within the legal framework for making sense of the rules'.[202]

193 Participant 17.
194 Participant 20.
195 Participant 23.
196 Participant 1.
197 Participant 30.
198 Participants 1, 22, 25, 31.
199 Participant 9.
200 Participant 9.
201 Participant 18.
202 Participant 30.

Third, *this book has presented evidence to suggest the* jus ad bellum's *factual tests cannot be applied effectively without some extra-legal evaluation of facts.* As former FCO lawyer, Judge David Anderson writes, it is 'possible to fall into the trap of applying legal techniques (weight of evidence; burden of proof; punish the guilty) beyond their true courtroom context', and lawyers should be 'non-fanatical', 'apply a bit of common sense, the reasonable humane sceptic, alongside his or her non-lawyer colleagues'.[203] Weisburd has noted that assessing *jus ad bellum* cases requires lawyers to evaluate difficult factual information requiring 'specialized knowledge of some subject other than law', including knowledge of military analysis.[204] And as this book has argued, legal rules and principles alone do not prescribe how to sort and weigh the kinds of evidence available in military crises, nor how to conduct the assessments which the tests of necessity, imminence and proportionality seem to require.

Almost all interviewees said lawyers needed to work with non-legal specialists for effective factual analysis.[205] Lawyers experienced in cases involving use of force can develop their own expertise on such issues.[206] However, as one legal scholar noted, in military crises 'there's only so much that you as an international lawyer can say about the matter, so you will depend on experts'.[207] A former government lawyer said, on matters of fact, they would 'expect a dialogue between lawyer and administrator'.[208] One legal scholar said lawyers could not apply the tests of 'imminence, proportionality, necessity' without 'an intricate understanding of the political and military strategy'.[209] Another scholar said politico-strategic analysis 'has got to be there', as it is 'massively complicated trying to work out what states actually want'.[210] A former government lawyer said factual analyses needed to draw on knowledge outside law, including 'historical knowledge', 'social knowledge', 'religious knowledge', 'the history of the region' and 'the history of your own decision making', 'where it's gone right and where it's gone wrong', to learn from and avoid repeating 'your own mistakes'.[211]

203 Judge David Anderson, CMG, 'The Role of the International Lawyer in the Negotiation of Treaties', in Wickremasinghe, *International Lawyer*, 37.
204 A Mark Weisburd, 'Use of Force: Justiciability and Admissibility', 331–2, in Weller, *Use of Force in International Law*.
205 Participants 1, 2, 7, 8, 11, 17, 20, 23, 24, 25, 26, 27, 28, 29, 30, 31.
206 Participant 10.
207 Participant 30.
208 Participant 25.
209 Participant 7.
210 Participant 24.
211 Participant 11.

Fourth, *most interviewees saw value in the kinds of structured analytic techniques recommended in* Chapter 6. Most interviewees agreed comparing multiple hypotheses appeared useful for assessing facts.[212] A practising international lawyer said 'that's the way any practical lawyer would approach the same kinds of analyses'.[213] A legal scholar said that 'there's no other way to process this stuff'.[214] Several interviewees said lawyers usually did not apply such techniques consciously,[215] but they did usually engage implicitly with the various alternative options in a case, 'applying implicit probabilities to them', as one scholar put it.[216] Another scholar thought lawyers' use of such practices 'needs to be more open and transparent'.[217] One practising international lawyer said it would be 'a very positive development' to apply such techniques more systematically, 'provided it's done well by people who are interrogating what's going on properly'.[218] A former government lawyer said the 'more one maintains an open mind' and takes account of information 'that disagrees with one's previous hypothesis', then 'the less likelihood there is for screwing up'.[219] Another former government lawyer said it was often useful to have 'a red team arguing the other side' to reduce risks of 'reading what you want' in the available evidence.[220] One practitioner observed that lawyers advising on cases involving military action were often given only one scenario to assess, when multiple scenarios would better reflect the dynamics of a military crisis. That practitioner thought even NGOs were too quick to reach conclusions about the lawfulness of force without considering alternative explanations.[221]

Several interviewees said multiple hypotheses and forecasting were particularly needed when considering necessity, proportionality, anticipatory self-defence and humanitarian intervention.[222] A scholar said assessing 'all that is necessary and no more', 'obviously' required 'forward thinking assessment based on prospective effects'.[223] A former government lawyer said forecasting was also needed when considering humanitarian intervention, to assess 'whether a humanitarian catastrophe would be averted or made worse using

212 Participants 1, 2, 4, 8, 11, 12, 14, 18, 19, 20, 22, 23, 24, 28, 29, 30.
213 Participant 12.
214 Participant 23.
215 Participant 4.
216 Participant 1.
217 Participant 23.
218 Participant 14.
219 Participant 11.
220 Participant 20.
221 Participant 29.
222 Participants 4, 8, 18, 21, 28.
223 Participant 4.

force'.[224] A scholar said such analyses needed 'the greatest application of wisdom to extremely imprecise evidence', since different people can interpret the same facts differently, 'knowledge is never perfect', 'you cannot predict the outcome' of ICJ cases and 'international politics is like the weather', where predictions were often wrong.[225]

Several interviewees thought such techniques could assist with the 'balancing test' of the impact, gravity, likelihood and imminence of the threat that should determine the degree of factual certainty required for a decision to use force.[226] One legal scholar said 'there's no such thing as 100% certainty', and if considering 'anticipatory action to prevent a nuclear strike on London', they might accept only '65% certainty' before advising a military response was lawful, but for lower impact threats such as 'a torpedo at a small naval ship', they might want '95% certainty'.[227] A former government lawyer said 'the higher the risk' and 'the higher the value of the target', the 'lower the percentage certainty you require, because if you wait for 100% certainty you'll never get it'.[228]

It is also the case that critics of structured analytic techniques still recommend that decision-makers compare competing interpretations of evidence or forecasts. Recent research identifying flaws in the analysis of competing hypotheses technique recommended other techniques, such as '"consider-the-opposite" strategy', computer-based methods such as 'serious games', and more explicit application of Bayesian statistical reasoning.[229] Mervyn King and John Kay, who criticised the use of probabilities in intelligence assessments, also argue that decision-makers 'confronted by radical uncertainty' should not pretend they can predict the future, but should 'organise action around a reference narrative' while accepting that their narrative might be incorrect. And so decision-makers should 'visualise alternative future scenarios', have some sense of their relative likelihood, 'and ensure that plans are robust and resilient to a range of plausible alternatives', without assigning those alternatives misleadingly precise numerical probabilities.[230]

As Chapter 6 noted, such techniques help to avoid 'Parmenides' Fallacy', the mistake of evaluating policy options by comparing potential *future* consequences of different policies with *present* conditions, or evaluating a past

224 Participant 21.
225 Participant 24.
226 Participants 6, 12, 20.
227 Participant 6.
228 Participant 20.
229 Dhami et al., 'Analysis of Competing Hypotheses', 1087.
230 King and Kay, *Radical Uncertainty*, locs. 4282, 6235.

policy by comparing the *present* with the *past*. In such cases, decision-makers should in fact compare the alternative possible outcomes of different policies *after* they have been implemented.[231] Such techniques help to avoid decisions that fail to consider that current or future events may not be what we believe or want. And, as this book has argued, key tests of the *jus ad bellum* – necessity, imminence and proportionality – appear to *require* decision-makers to construct and compare alternative forecasts of the consequences of decisions either to use force or not to use force.

And most interviewees agreed that legal risk management could assist in difficult *jus ad bellum* cases,[232] so that 'the government decides being fully aware of what the risks are' and informed 'of all the possible scenarios' as one scholar put it.[233] One former government lawyer familiar with risk management argued it was right to 'point out controversy and indicate the possible policy and legal repercussions', including assessing how current ICJ judges might rule if they considered the case, based on past record – an analytical method the UK government sometimes used.[234] Another former government lawyer said legal risk is not part of the assessment of legality, but must be part of the decision-maker's assessment, because it could cover litigation risk and 'reputational harm' – both of which may of themselves persuade a government not to act, even if the lawyer assesses action is 'demonstrably legal', particularly if the assessment relies on classified information that could not be disclosed in court.[235] A practising international lawyer said risk management was particularly useful in cases such as anticipatory self-defence where, rather than make assumptions or 'jump to factual conclusions', lawyers must 'work with a degree of probabilities', based on the threat's imminence, how concrete and reliable is the evidence, using intelligence and political assessment.[236]

And, as one former government lawyer noted, government lawyers can use risk management to encourage states to obey the law by setting out 'consequences of unlawful behaviour – public opinion, international opinion, perhaps the international court'.[237] For example, assessing in greater detail the legal risks of the 2003 intervention in Iraq earlier in the process might have affected the UK government's calculus about joining the operation, at least making that decision more uncomfortable for more government ministers.

231 Bobbitt, *Shield of Achilles*, 10.
232 Participants 1, 2, 5, 7, 8, 9, 10, 14, 18, 19, 21, 22, 25, 27, 31.
233 Participant 2.
234 Participant 21.
235 Participant 19.
236 Participant 8.
237 Participant 21.

That process does not seem to have shown legal advisers deeply engaged 'at the takeoff of a new foreign policy episode to help establish the legal and political legitimacy of the actions that follow', as Koh advises and as Chapter 6 recommends.[238]

Fifth, *the greater transparency about a state's legal decision-making around force that* Chapter 6 *recommends could enhance a state's justification for its actions in law and encourage compliance with law.* As one writer puts it, the principle of client confidentiality is often 'invoked to conceal legally dubious or dirty business', and can be 'a device for cover-ups'.[239] There are already exceptions to the principle of confidentiality in national jurisdictions, including 'for evidence of future crimes or frauds or in the advocate's own defence'.[240] Sarvarian argues sometimes confidentiality may 'be detrimental to the interests of justice by preventing advocates who know of abusive misconduct by parties from informing the Court', and on balance the need for counsel 'to disclose grave and potential threats to procedural integrity . . . outweighs the potential erosion of trust between counsel and client'.[241] More positively, most international lawyers agree governments have a 'duty to explain' decisions to use force, 'to set forth the position of the government, the reasons behind it and the facts on which it was based, and when appropriate its limits'.[242] Koh has argued attorney-client privilege 'is only an argument for keeping government legal opinions temporarily, not permanently, secret'.[243]

All interviewees agreed governments should articulate a legal justification when they used force, at least through a letter to the UNSC after using force or a statement summarising their legal justification, since 'parliament and public have a right to know' as one former government lawyer put it.[244] Some interviewees also supported more publication of internal legal advice.[245] One legal scholar said more such transparency would encourage better compliance with law, since if a legal adviser clearly concluded that military action would be unlawful, governments would be less likely to act if that advice was published.[246] Another scholar said publication 'supports the democratic process, it supports transparency in the decision-making' of governments, showing

238 Koh, 'Eight Decades in Peace and War', 1756–7.
239 Hazard, 'Historical Perspective', 1062.
240 Sarvarian, *Professional Ethics*, 97.
241 Ibid., 97, 102.
242 Berman, 'Conclusion', 382.
243 Koh, 'Legal Adviser's Duty to Explain', 310.
244 Participant 19.
245 Participants 1, 2, 3, 6, 7, 27, 30.
246 Participant 1.

that they had thought about legality 'and didn't jump the gun', and the ICJ could later use such documents if assessing the legality of action.[247] One practising international lawyer said it was unfortunate more advice was not published, because many 'would be surprised by how carefully things are thought through'.[248] A legal scholar thought more transparency might drive better legal advice, as they believed the thoroughness of advice described by the Chilcot inquiry was not typical of how international law usually affects government policy.[249] Most interviewees accepted it was justified to disclose internal legal advice in 'cases of extreme controversy such as the Iraq war',[250] which justify holding a public inquiry,[251] especially where there are suggestions of 'skulduggery', as one former government lawyer put it.[252]

Koh has argued that, in international law, 'the need to establish *opinio juris* cuts in favour of legal advisers explaining their clients' international legal positions' widely, to 'Congress, the public, foreign governments, intergovernmental organisations, and non-governmental organisations'.[253] Several interviewees hoped publishing more legal advice would provide evidence of state practice and *opinio juris*, to 'fill in the principles' and drive greater legal certainty, as a legal scholar put it.[254] Another scholar said more transparency and publication would produce 'greater density of security council debates, greater rigour to diplomatic exchanges', including 'one state calling another out' or justifying 'proportionality or necessity judgements'.[255] Several interviewees welcomed detailed government statements articulating a state's understanding of the law, such as recent speeches on self-defence by the US State Department legal adviser and UK attorney general, as expressions of *opinio juris* that could increase legal certainty and encourage 'better understanding of the development of the law' as a scholar put it.[256]

And finally, *over-emphasising lawyers' role as 'conscience' risks legal advice overstepping its proper advisory role, becoming so detached from political decision-makers that it is ignored, or causing lawyers' collective conceptions of international law to diverge fatally from state behaviour.* One example of the potential for harm when legal institutions detach from state consent is US

247 Participant 2.
248 Participant 10.
249 Participant 3.
250 Participant 29.
251 Participants 29, 21, 19, 11.
252 Participant 11.
253 Koh, 'Legal Adviser's Duty to Explain', 310.
254 Participant 7.
255 Participant 30.
256 Participant 9.

withdrawal from the ICJ's compulsory jurisdiction when the *Nicaragua* case proceeded without US consent.[257] Another is the trend within the African Union to threaten withdrawal from the International Criminal Court, fuelled by indictments of heads of state, which some African states claim disrupt ongoing peace processes.[258] The potential for divergence between opinions within the community of international lawyers and among states is shown by the continued belief by many European international lawyers and ICJ judges that self-defence against non-state actors is unlawful.[259] This is in spite of most states explicitly supporting or taking part in the Afghanistan operation, and acquiescing to instances of force against non-state actors overseas since then, including the 2011 US raid on Abbottabad Pakistan resulting in the death of Osama Bin Laden.[260]

Several interviewees were uncomfortable with government legal advisers acting as 'conscience', particularly in cases where the law was contested or unclear.[261] One legal scholar said for lawyers to press governments to take a view on hard cases simply moves 'the decision-making power to the legal adviser'.[262] A former government lawyer said legal advisers would be 'crossing the line' if they 'say there is a legal argument here but politically I'm against it, so I advise you not to do it', although that may be acceptable for political appointees.[263] Some interviewees said it was right for legal advisers to 'ask the tough questions' and remind governments 'of the value of the rule of law', but it would in all but the most extreme cases be 'departing too far' from lawyers' proper role to say, 'I believe that you should not use force in this situation because it's against the law.'[264] One scholar said lawyers ultimately must accept that law is just one of the frameworks that guides government decisions 'about how best to protect the national interest'.[265] A former government lawyer said 'ultimately it is part of the job that your view is not always going

257 UN, Declaration Recognizing as Compulsory the Jurisdiction of the Court, in Conformity with Article 36, Paragraph 2, of the Statute of the International Court of Justice Washington, 14 August 1946: Termination', 7 October 1985, 1408 UNTS 270.

258 Samuel Okpe Okpe, 'Anti-Impunity Norm of the International Criminal Court: A Curse or Blessing for Africa?', *Journal of Asian and African Studies*, 55:7 (2020), 1077–90.

259 Kammerhofer, 'Self-Defence', 203; Myjer and White, 'Twin Towers Attack', 7–8; *Wall*, Opinion, paras. 139, 194.

260 Kress, 'Post-Westphalian Shifts', 53; Ashley S. Deeks, 'Pakistan's Sovereignty and the Killing of Osama Bin Laden', *ASIL Insights*, 15:11 (2011).

261 Participants 1, 2, 5, 14, 19, 29.

262 Participant 2.

263 Participant 25.

264 Participant 14, 19.

265 Participant 5.

to be accepted'.[266] A scholar argued that, if legal advisers disagree very strongly with a government's action following their legal advice, they could resign, as Elisabeth Wilmshurst did in 2003 over the military intervention in Iraq.[267]

And most interviewees[268] said it was legitimate for legal advisers to help their governments 'get what they want within the law'.[269] One practising international lawyer said 'a legal adviser acting ethically' is obliged 'to try to find ways for the client to achieve what they want' and try to justify 'something that the client has done, to the best of their ability under the law'.[270] Another practitioner said they routinely chose principles of interpretation 'that best suits my client's case', 'within the bounds of what is properly arguable, and properly available' in law.[271] A former government lawyer said a legal adviser's initial legal assessment may find against a proposed policy, but they should be 'pragmatic within reason', without 'being overly creative' to explore 'ways to be helpful' and put their client's case 'as strongly as possible within the law'.[272] And indeed, several interviewees[273] distinguished between a lawyer's duties before a decision is made, when the legal adviser should give 'fearless advice' on the lawfulness of options, and after a decision is taken, when they become 'your attorney', and 'if conscience allows' they should work for 'loyal implementation' of that decision, and 'zealously promote that argument to its fullest'.[274]

CONCLUSION: REFLECTIVE EQUILIBRIUM AND HARD CASES

So there are pragmatic, empirical and normative responses to this chapter's critiques of the framework proposed in Chapter 6. This book maintains that the kinds of structured analytic techniques in the framework proposed in Chapter 6 can provide valid assistance to lawyers developing legal assessments of resort to force, to deal with legal and factual uncertainty and forecasting, and the role of extra-legal intuitions and biases. But this chapter raised a valid core normative objection: by focusing on identifying and reducing risks of challenge to the lawfulness of a decision to use force, the techniques Chapter 6 proposes do not necessarily assist lawyers in their normative role

266 Participant 29.
267 Participant 1.
268 Participants 8, 12, 13, 25, 26, 29.
269 Participant 8.
270 Participant 12.
271 Participant 26.
272 Participant 29.
273 Participants 13, 23, 29, 31.
274 Participant 23; Koh, 'Legal Adviser's Duty to Explain', 312.

of identifying lawful and unlawful behaviour. Such techniques could even advise decision-makers to proceed with clearly unlawful military action, if they assess the risks of challenge are minimal due to political and other circumstances. This section outlines an approach lawyers may adopt, drawing on Rawls' concept of reflective equilibrium, to deal with the valid critiques this chapter describes and the wider analysis of uncertainty and extra-legal reasoning in *jus ad bellum* decisions that this book presents.

Throughout this book, an impulse towards equilibrium, moderation and balance between countervailing imperatives has been explicit or implicit in the scholarly writings examined and interviews conducted. Many legal advisers argue they should strive to 'maintain a balance between law and policy', neither 'insisting on only following the law' nor 'imagining themselves a political wizard', rather seeking both to advance a government's political goals and to 'uphold the law in the face of political pressure'.[275] Berman has argued that 'if we can't engage, with a combination of realism and principle', in working out 'what can reasonably be expected of law, then we become either yes-men or no-men, either apologists or prophets of doom' and then 'law's place in world affairs' will suffer.[276] Koh has argued that 'competing commitments' require legal advisers 'to balance the concerns of politics and the law', 'not just to interpret but more fundamentally to shape international law'.[277] Wilmshurst has noted that legal advisers have a duty both 'to assist their client to implement its policies' and 'to persuade' government 'to give international law proper weight' and 'to comply with international law'.[278] A former senior UN lawyer argues 'the lawyer who has no concern with policy whatsoever and the lawyer whose function is to find a legal justification for every policy are equally inconsistent with his essential responsibilities'.[279]

The concept of equilibrium occurs throughout law more generally. Customary law is an equilibrium of state practice and *opinio juris*, as Allott described, 'the product of a *dialectic of practice*'.[280] The text of legal documents including UNSC resolutions, the UN Charter, VCLT and all treaties, embody equilibria produced by the negotiations and other interactions of the states involved; like almost all forms of legislation, they are 'the product of

275 Gauci and Jones, 'Conference Report', 378–9.
276 Berman, 'Lawyers in Armed Conflict', 629.
277 Koh, 'Eight Decades in Peace and War', 1756–7.
278 Wilmshurst, 'Disciplining the Discipline', 449.
279 Dr Ralph Zacklin, 'The Role of the International Lawyer in an International Organisation', in Wickremasinghe, *International Lawyer*, 60.
280 Philip Allott, 'The Concept of International Law', *European Journal of International Law*, 10:1 (1999), 39, 40.

a *dialectic of ideas*'.[281] 'A treaty is a disagreement reduced to writing', in which 'compromises are enacted in formulas that are known to be, and may be intended to be, ambiguous or even meaningless'.[282] ICJ judgments also represent equilibria between the judges' opinions, based on the competing arguments and evidence advanced by the opposing parties.[283] And clients want balance from legal advisers. Fitzmaurice was clear governments did not want 'impartial advice' from their lawyers, rather 'sympathetic but accurate advice', sympathetic because 'duty to the client' is 'of primary importance', but also accurate because of 'the overriding duty of honesty and objectivity', for the lawyer to 'tell it like it is, not as the client might like it to be'.[284]

The interviews and surveys conducted for this research showed moderate positions were often most popular responses to questions about legal interpretation and extra-legal factors. All interviewees agreed legal advisers needed to balance the roles of counsellor and conscience, even if they disagreed about what the right balance was. Many interviewees pointed to balance between legal and extra-legal reasoning when advising on force.[285] Balance was also evident in interviewees' views about publishing legal advice,[286] which required balancing considerations of confidentiality and public interest, whether 'the government is under a duty of candour because it's party to litigation' or whether legal advice could be 'adduced as part of evidence'.[287] And the framework proposed in Chapter 6 recommends weighing and balancing arguments for and against competing interpretations of fact and law which create uncertainty in hard cases engaging the *jus ad bellum*.

So it fits with this more general imperative for balance in the law to consider Rawls' concept of reflective equilibrium as one approach lawyers might use to balance the pragmatic and normative benefits and risks of using a framework such as that proposed in Chapter 6, while abiding by their professional ethics and responsibilities.[288] Aristotle's 'doctrine of the mean' suggests the roots of reflective equilibrium.[289] For Aristotle, 'virtue is concerned with passions and actions, in which excess is a form of failure, and so is defect, while the

281 Allott, 'Concept of International Law', 39, 40.
282 Allott, 'Concept of International Law', 43; Allott, 'International Lawyer', 15.
283 Green, *Self-Defence*, 177–8.
284 Berman, 'Lawyers in Armed Conflict', 630–1.
285 Participants 1, 6, 14, 17, 20, 21, 22, 23, 24, 25, 30, 31.
286 Participant 19.
287 Participant 26.
288 Rawls, *Theory of Justice*, 18.
289 Fisher, *Morality and War*, 112.

intermediate is praised and is a form of success'.[290] This equilibrium was not absolute and universal nor 'equidistant from each of the extremes', but context-specific, 'neither too much nor too little' and 'not one, nor the same for all'.[291] And this equilibrium was not instinctive or accidental, but the product of deliberate 'choice', through the exercise of 'reason by which the man of practical wisdom would determine it'.[292]

The contemporary concept of reflective equilibrium most clearly advocated by Rawls articulates a similar concept, directly incorporating the 'belief revising' that is central to the Bayesian reasoning that leading political analysis scholars recommend.[293] As Daniels describes, the underlying idea of reflective equilibrium is that 'we "test" various parts of our system of moral beliefs against other beliefs we hold, seeking coherence amongst the widest set of moral and non-moral beliefs by revising and refining them at all levels', 'aiming for the system of strongest mutual support among them'.[294] Rawls accepted that in reasoning about justice, decision-makers must accept that even 'considered judgments' may be 'subject to certain irregularities and distortions' and may need revision.[295] An individual, faced with a situation where their intuitive assessment conflicts with more considered principles, can modify their judgment either of the situation or of those considered principles, since 'even the judgments we take provisionally as fixed points are liable to revision'.[296] By 'going back and forth, sometimes altering the conditions of the contractual circumstances, at others withdrawing our judgments and conforming them to principle' the evaluator can achieve a 'reflective equilibrium' where 'principles and judgments coincide'.[297]

Thus reflective equilibrium proposes that 'the best account of a person's sense of justice is not the one which fits his judgments prior to his examining any conception of justice, but rather the one which matches his judgments in reflective equilibrium', after having 'weighed various proposed conceptions' and 'either revised his judgments to accord with one of them or held fast to his initial convictions'.[298] This reflective equilibrium is therefore the product of

290 Aristotle, *The Nicomachean Ethics*, ed. D. Ross (Oxford: Oxford University Press, 2009), 30, 31.
291 Ibid., 30.
292 Ibid., 31.
293 Tetlock and Gardner, *Superforecasting*, locs. 4095, 4184–5.
294 Norman Daniels, *Justice and justification: Reflective Equilibrium in Theory and Practice* (Cambridge: Cambridge University Press, 1996), 4, 10.
295 Rawls, *Theory of Justice*, 42.
296 Ibid., 18.
297 Ibid.
298 Ibid., 43.

an iterative process by which decision-makers find coherence between multiple countervailing principles of decision-making and their own intuitions of what is right.

It is an individual decision-maker's reasoning that generates either the virtuous mean or the reflective equilibrium described in this section. However, this book emphasises law as the product of social interactions rather than solitary reflection. And Chapter 6 proposes ways of addressing uncertainty and vagueness in law through collective processes of analysis and reasoning. So any attempt to use reflective equilibrium to help reconcile lawyers' professional requirements to provide clear, determinate, autonomous legal advice with the reality of legal and factual uncertainty and extra-legal reasoning must include this social element.

An approach that sought to apply the methods of reflective equilibrium to the dilemmas set out in this chapter might operate as follows. It would accept that international lawyers asked to advise on the lawfulness of a controversial use of force should start with their own assessment of the lawfulness of the case, based on their knowledge and intuitions about what is lawful in the *jus ad bellum* and about the facts of the case. The lawyer would accept that these intuitions reflect wider intuitions and biases about methods of interpreting law and facts, and so would test those intuitions and their conclusions against plausible alternatives. They would involve other lawyers and non-legal experts in that process of testing, using techniques such as those outlined in Chapter 6, with reference to the state's previous positions.

Reflective equilibrium's 'belief revising' would then suggest the lawyer reflect on and, where necessary, revise their own preferred legal opinion, and their underlying legal and extra-legal assumptions, in light of their evaluation of alternative explanations of fact and law produced by the framework proposed in Chapter 6. This is likely to be an iterative process. The legal adviser should be ready to adjust their own legal conclusions and the alternatives as policy analysts report new, compelling facts, and as discussion with other lawyers reveals further legal complexities. However, at the end of the process, when a conclusion is delivered, the legal adviser must once again refer to their own – possibly revised – intuitions, knowledge and judgments, to deliver as clear a legal opinion as they can, while also being clear about the legal principles and factual assumptions being applied, and being open about their uncertainties and level of confidence. Figure 7.2 illustrates how reflective equilibrium might be incorporated into the framework proposed in Chapter 6.

Transparency is key in such a process. Many government legal advisers argue they 'should make very clear when they are giving legal advice and when they are participating in policy discussions', acknowledging that legal advisers

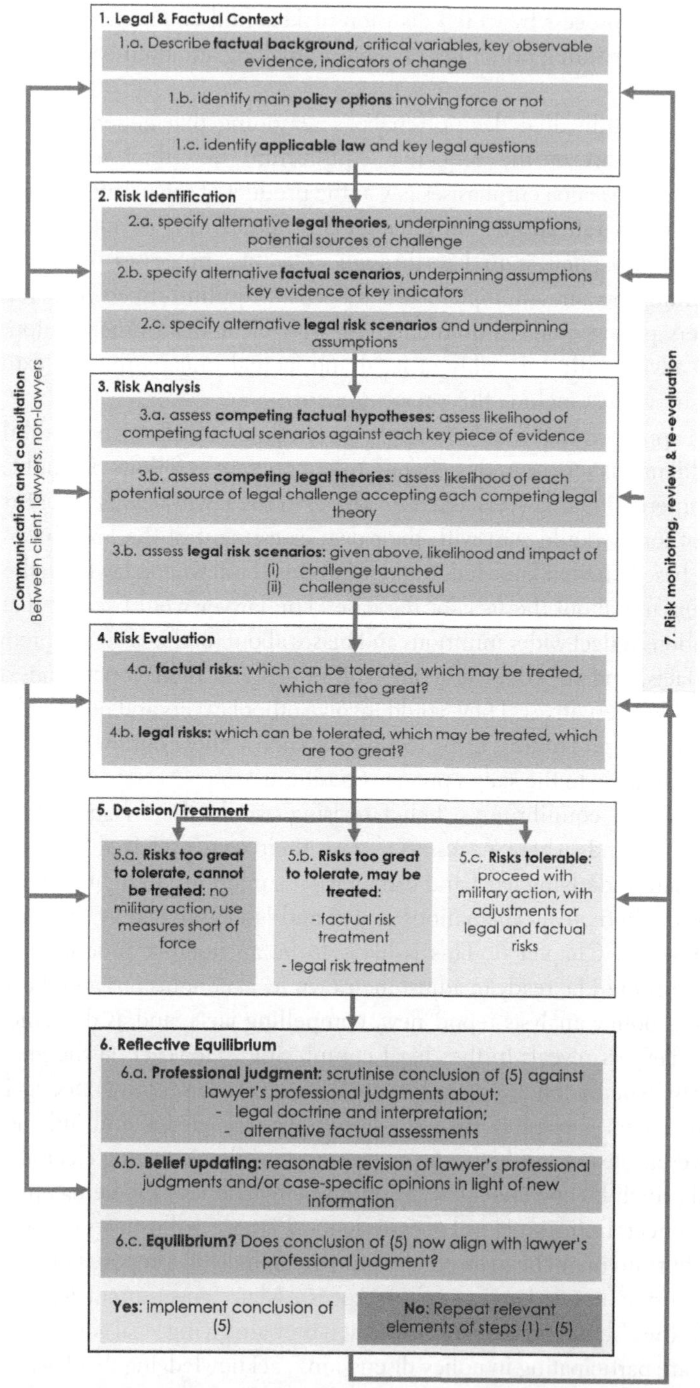

FIGURE 7.2 Reflective equilibrium and risk management

cannot avoid engaging in policy as well as law, and, '(t)o the extent that the Legal Adviser has a political role, that should be recognised and care should be taken not to disguise political advice as legal advice'.[299] Many interviewees said lawyers need to be transparent about the capacity in which they comment on legal or extra-legal issues.[300] A legal scholar said lawyers must make sure their extra-legal considerations do not 'skew their legal advice'.[301]A practising international lawyer said legal advisers need to be clear where their role as legal adviser ends and where 'good sense, morality and ethics begins'.[302] Another scholar said lawyers 'shouldn't be pretending' to offer such considerations as lawyers, but 'as moral beings', 'reflecting on the usefulness of the law in a given setting'.[303] A further scholar said lawyers should explain their 'underlying values and positions', and 'their background values and theories', recognising these are often not 'black and white questions'.[304] Another practising international lawyer argued lawyers should be more 'explicit' about 'our own biases and our own backgrounds' when writing.[305]

Ultimately, lawyers need to exercise their own legal and factual judgement, and provide advice that they believe best reflects their own professional view, aligning with their professional ethics, responsibilities and duties as international lawyers. This requires lawyers to understand the underlying legal and extra-legal intuitions they themselves hold and how they apply them in specific cases engaging the *jus ad bellum*. Feedback from interviewees and survey participants suggests answering the survey and qualitative questions used in this book's research, alongside the kinds of techniques discussed in Chapter 6, may help some international lawyers identify and reflect on their underlying legal and extra-legal intuitions.[306] But ultimately, how lawyers handle legal and factual uncertainty, and their own extra-legal intuitions in assessing hard cases of resort to force, is a question about personal professional ethics. How lawyers choose to balance the complex, countervailing imperatives at play cannot be determined solely by 'adherence to and membership in the community of international legal professionals', but must also be driven by their personal 'ethical stance', the qualities of 'personal integrity, reputation, prestige and respect for ethical standards'.[307]

299 Gauci and Jones, 'Conference Report', 379.
300 Participants 1, 9, 14, 15, 22, 30.
301 Participant 1.
302 Participant 22.
303 Participant 30.
304 Participant 9.
305 Participant 14.
306 Participants 1, 2, 4, 10, 14, 17, 18, 20, 23, 24, 27, 28.
307 Zidar, 'Professional Ethics', 322.

8

Conclusion: Competing Normative Cultures of War

One man's hand brushed its trunk – he said, 'This creature
Is like a pipe.' He based this on one feature.
Another could feel just its ears – that man
Believed the elephant was like a fan.
Another felt one of its legs alone:
'Its shape is like those columns made of stone.'
Another touched its back and then cried out:
'It's similar to a throne without a doubt.'
When they heard 'elephant' each one conceived
Only the part that they themselves perceived
Different perspectives meant discrepancies:
One called it straight like I's, one bent like c's.
For arguments there would have been no space
If each had held a candle in that place;
The sensual eye's no better than the hand –
The whole of it the hand can't understand.

Rumi, '*The Elephant in the Dark*'[1]

INTRODUCTION

When I began the research that eventually produced this book, I had a set of propositions in mind. The law is unclear about the legality of many contemporary forms of military intervention. Lawyers nevertheless express opinions with confidence – although not reaching consensus – about the lawfulness of those interventions. Those lawyers' legal opinions seem to align neatly with their political and ethical opinions about those interventions. Therefore, in

[1] Jalal al-Din Rumi, 'The Elephant in the Dark', *The Masnavi, Book Three* (Oxford: Oxford University Press, 2013), 79.

hard cases of resort to force, lawyers are simply giving you their political/strategic/ethical opinion when they say they are assessing those interventions' legality. In the background to this line of thought was the reality that I, a UK foreign policy official, supported the military interventions my government participated in, and believed they were legal, even if not all international lawyers shared that belief.

My studies and research revealed a more complex, nuanced picture. I found most lawyers agree on most aspects of the *jus ad bellum*. I discovered that many lawyers accepted legal positions they believed were unethical or unwise. And I learned that many disagreements about the *jus ad bellum* were not disagreements about the law at all. Instead, they were disagreements about the facts of the chaotic crises that may (or may not) justify resort to force, and about at least implicit forecasts and counter-factual conjectures about what might happen, or what might have happened, if force was or was not used. My studies and wider international developments led me to modify what was a relatively uncomplicated support for liberal interventionism, and to review my own intuitions. I believed UK interventions were lawful in part because I wanted to believe they were lawful, based on my particular view of how the world worked and how it ought to work.

This chapter reflects on some of the basic implications of this research. It might be easy to take the analysis of this book as a call to abandon any role for international law in decision-making about resort to force in international relations. That is not my intention, and in this chapter I explain why. I consider the fact that the *jus ad bellum* is in most cases determinate and clear, and so adds value to foreign and defence policy and international peace and security in important ways. Before that, I review the research methods used for this book, their shortcomings, possible improvements and other potential opportunities to use those methods in future. But first, I recapitulate this book's main arguments, findings and conclusions.

RECAPITULATION: ARGUMENT, FINDINGS AND CONCLUSIONS

This book investigated the nature and practical implications of legal and factual uncertainty and the role of extra-legal intuitions in the *jus ad bellum*, building on several long established, interconnected, but still contentious propositions about the law governing resort to force. First, *the* jus ad bellum, *like many areas of international and domestic law, might be described as 'specifically indeterminate'*: what the law governing resort to force prescribes in at least some cases is vague, and the law displays specific forms of vagueness described by the philosophy of knowledge. The concept of 'paradigms' argues that the *jus ad bellum* is based around ideal examples or 'plain cases' of lawful and unlawful force.[2] 'Supervaluationism' observes that these paradigms are determined not by one test and set of values, but by 'multi-part tests' composed of sub-tests, often incommensurable, overlapping but not entirely co-extensive – cases may meet all tests or only some.[3]

The sorites paradox and fuzzy logic observe that there is no sharp, binary distinction between lawful and unlawful force, either in general or according to the law's individual tests.[4] Instead, clearly lawful and unlawful cases are end-points of a continuum of cases, separated by a 'penumbra of uncertainty'.[5] Finally, competing cultures of legal interpretation are sociological sources of uncertainty, since lawyers at least unconsciously conform to interpretive cultures holding different views about valid legal tests, how they should be interpreted, and what boundaries distinguish lawful and unlawful force.[6] Interviewees and survey participants displayed significant if varying levels of disagreement about the lawfulness of several 'hard cases' of resort to force: anticipatory self-defence, pre-emptive self-defence, self-defence against non-state actors, humanitarian intervention, and use of force to prevent proliferation of WMDs. Their responses collectively displayed the forms of vagueness already identified.

Second, *factual uncertainty exacerbates uncertainty about what the law requires in specific cases.* The forms of vagueness and uncertainty described in this book can affect the factual assessments necessary to assess cases engaging the *jus ad bellum*. Such military crises are often chaotic and fast moving, involving competing actors deliberately attempting to deceive and mislead, where factual evidence is thus patchy and open to multiple interpretations. Key *jus ad bellum* tests, such as necessity, imminence and proportionality, require decision-makers to construct and compare multiple forecasts or counter-factual scenarios of the harms potentially caused or permitted if force is or is not used. The research showed how survey participants evaluated the lawfulness of force in four fictional scenarios, demonstrating that even hypothetical 'facts' elicited varying opinions about anticipatory self-defence, pre-emptive self-defence, self-defence against non-state actors, and humanitarian intervention.

Third, *the* jus ad bellum, *like other law, appears to be 'partially autonomous'.* Uncertainty about law and facts in specific cases encourages lawyers to draw

2 Hart, *Concept of Law*, 127.
3 Williamson, 'Vagueness In Reality', 690; Deeks 'Multi-Part Tests', 1038.
4 Williamson, 'Vagueness in Reality', 693.
5 Hart, *Concept of Law*, 131, 134; Endicott, *Vagueness in Law*, 35.
6 Friedman, 'Legal Culture', 189; Waibel, 'Interpretive Communities', 148.

on consistent, mutually reinforcing 'extra-legal' 'political and ideological viewpoints' and intuitions '*as to the principle(s) of law underlying the system*', including about strategy and ethics, to choose between competing interpretations of law and fact and reach conflicting legal conclusions in hard cases.[7] The ICJ has sought to deal with factual uncertainties through rules of evidence, but this book argued such rules only reduce rather than resolve factual uncertainty, and offer no advice for the forecasts or counter-factuals the *jus ad bellum* requires. So, when dealing with factual uncertainties, making inferences about facts for which evidence is patchy, and particularly when making the forecasts or counter-factual analyses of alternative consequences that the necessity, proportionality and imminence tests require, lawyers must rely at least in part on extra-legal assessments of how and why actors behave in conflicts. In addition, uncertainty about the *jus ad bellum* as a system of prescriptive rules and principles encourages lawyers to practise 'strategic behaviour in interpretation', using the *jus ad bellum* as a system of argumentative practices to justify or criticise the lawfulness of specific behaviour using arguments aligning with their extra-legal beliefs and intuitions.[8] This reliance on specific extra-legal intuitions seems to hold whether those legal arguments are advanced as sincerely held beliefs about the law, or as more self-conscious action to manipulate the law or to change it. In effect, lawyers are compelled to draw on at least implicit politico-strategic and ethical theories of how the world works and how it ought to work to reach determinate legal decisions in hard cases.

Fourth, *faced with factual and legal uncertainties, lawyers tended to conform to competing interpretive and strategic cultures*. This conclusion was suggested by this book's textual analyses of UK legal statements and writings by legal scholars on US-led military interventions in Kosovo, Afghanistan and Iraq, of judgments and separate opinions in ICJ cases concerning *Nicaragua* (1986), *Wall* (2004) and *Congo* (2005), and by interviews and survey research with thirty-one UK-based international lawyers. These strands of research suggested lawyers inhabited separate normative cultures, in which lawyers share similar, mutually reinforcing intuitions about legal interpretation and extra-legal factors, such as strategy and ethics, thus reaching similar conclusions about the legality and facts of specific military interventions. The research suggested these cultures were not clearly distinct and separate. Instead, lawyers were distributed along a continuum from 'restrictivists', likely to see few legal and

7 Green, *Self-Defence*, 184.

8 Kennedy, *Legal Reasoning*, 159; Koskenniemi, *From Apology to Utopia*, 67–9.

extra-legal justifications for force, to 'expansionists', likely to see more such justifications.

This book suggested membership of interpretive and strategic cultures seem to reflect what psychologists term 'cognitive biases', 'motivated biases' and 'heuristics'. These are inherent or learned intuitions, presuppositions and rules of thumb 'which reduce the complex tasks of assessing probabilities and predicting values to simpler judgmental operations', which are usually economical and effective, but sometimes 'lead to severe and systematic errors'.[9] The book does not suggest lawyers necessarily conform to these cultures consciously. Rather, they are likely to reflect deeply held intuitions and preferences either reflecting individual lawyers' inherent characteristics, or learned and internalised through national, professional or institutional experiences.

In terms of legal interpretation, 'restrictivist' lawyers who in effect regard the law as a *jus contra bellum*, tended to adopt a set of interpretive approaches that might be grouped into a culture of 'formalism'. When assessing the lawfulness of resort to force, formalists emphasised the ordinary meaning of the text of the UN Charter and other formal sources of law. They held that the law has evolved little since 1945, preferred to accept explicitly legal statements as evidence of *opinio juris*, and required clarity and overwhelming quantity of state practice as evidence that new customary international law had crystallised. They tended to regard only the UNSC as permitted to authorise force when the law is unclear. Opposing them, 'expansionist' lawyers tended to adopt approaches to legal interpretation that could be grouped into a culture of 'dynamism'. In assessing the lawfulness of force, dynamists were more willing to take account of the UN Charter's wider purposes and other law. They more readily argued that law had evolved since 1945, and were willing to accept a wider variety and smaller volume of expressions of *opinio juris* and state practice as evidence that new customary international law had crystallised. And they tended to see more discretion for states and bodies outside the UNSC to interpret the *jus ad bellum* when the law is unclear. The survey data showed a strong correlation coefficient of 0.718 between responses to questions assessing whether participants made 'formalist' or 'dynamist' interpretive choices, and whether they made restrictivist or expansionist choices about the *jus ad bellum*.

In terms of extra-legal reasoning, lawyers with a 'restrictivist' approach when considering a 'hard case' of resort to force, tended to apply a set of politico-strategic and ethical assumptions, intuitions and beliefs that could be grouped

9 Tversky and Kahneman, 'Judgment under Uncertainty', 1124.

under a 'pacificist' strategic culture. When assessing a case in which the requirements of the law were contested, pacificists tended to choose the interpretation of the law that minimised the potential for future legal uncertainty and abuse, which best protected less powerful states rather than trusting militarily and economically dominant states, and which held that the prohibition on force is always the most important principle. When assessing different interpretations of complex, incomplete or contradictory factual evidence, and when constructing forecasts about the consequences of using or not using force unilaterally, pacificists tended to proceed on the basis that such force almost always caused more harm than it prevents for the state using force and for the international community, that only self-interested states use force unilaterally, and only a narrow range of political interests and ethical values are sufficiently widely shared to guide decisions about force.

Opposing them, lawyers with an 'expansionist' approach when considering 'hard cases' of resort to force tended to apply a set of politico-strategic and ethical assumptions, intuitions and beliefs which could be grouped under an 'interventionist' strategic culture. When assessing a case in which the requirements of the law were contested, 'interventionists' tended to choose the interpretation of the law that best fitted with changes in conflict since the adoption of the UN Charter, and which held that principles such as human rights, preventing genocide, fighting terrorism or countering WMD proliferation were often more important than the prohibition on force. When assessing different interpretations of complex, incomplete or contradictory evidence, and when constructing forecasts about the consequences of using or not using force unilaterally, interventionists tended to proceed on the basis that such force often prevented more harm than it caused for the state using force and for the international community, that states that use force unilaterally could often advance common interests as well as self-interest, and a range of political interests and ethical values were often sufficiently widely shared to guide decisions about force. The survey data again showed a strong correlation of 0.687 between responses to questions assessing whether participants made 'interventionist' or 'pacificist' choices about the extra-legal implications of force and whether they made restrictivist or expansionist choices about the *jus ad bellum*.

And the research suggested that lawyers' 'pacifism' or 'interventionism' on specific cases also seemed to affect their wider approach to the *jus ad bellum* in general. 'Pacificist' lawyers who tended to see little political, strategic and ethical justification for force in specific cases also tended to apply a more restrictivist *jus contra bellum* in general as well. 'Interventionist' lawyers who tended to see more such extra-legal political, strategic and ethical justifications for force in specific cases, also tended to apply a more expansionist *jus ad bellum* more generally. In other words, lawyers' beliefs about the political, strategic and moral benefits or harms of the use of force in individual cases seemed to encourage them to generally prefer interpretations of the *jus ad bellum* which reflected those extra-legal intuitions.

The research did however identify important caveats to these conclusions, as suggested by the correlation coefficients which were strong, but not perfect. These suggest limits to the relationships between legal interpretation, extra-legal intuitions, and overall opinions on the restrictiveness or expansiveness of the *jus ad bellum*.

First, lawyers did not always display all the interpretive preferences grouped under the headings of 'formalism' and 'dynamism', and these preferences did not always align with opinions about the *jus ad bellum* which this book initially proposed. Expansionists deployed textual arguments to support a more expansionist *jus ad bellum* in Afghanistan, *Congo*, *Wall* and Iraq. They argued that the words of the UN Charter did not limit self-defence only to attacks by states, and the words of UNSC Resolution 1441 (2002) could be interpreted as reviving UNSC Resolution 687 (1991)'s authorisation to use force in Iraq. Restrictivists deployed dynamist arguments to argue for a restrictive *jus contra bellum* in those and the *Nicaragua* case, arguing the law had evolved to include UNGA declarations implying self-defence only justified force against non-state actors which were controlled by states, and using contextual arguments to argue UNSC states did not intend UNSC Resolution 1441 (2002) to authorise force.

Second, there appeared to be boundaries on how extra-legal factors affected legal opinions. Many relatively 'interventionist' lawyers accepted that law prohibits humanitarian intervention and more assertive military action against non-state actors, even though they saw politico-strategic and/or ethical reasons to support such actions. Other relatively 'pacificist' lawyers accepted the lawfulness of anticipatory self-defence and self-defence against non-state actors, even though they had serious politico-strategic and ethical misgivings about such actions. These findings suggested that, for many lawyers, extra-legal beliefs and intuitions, and choices about legal interpretation techniques, combined to create contestation and uncertainty only in cases where the law was most unclear and contested, and where facts were particularly uncertain. Politico-strategic and ethical intuitions seemed to act as forms of cognitive or motivated biases, shaping but not entirely overriding beliefs about legal interpretation and thus the *jus ad bellum*.

Fifth, *the book argued fields outside the* jus ad bellum *offered insights which might help lawyers manage these uncertainties and subjectivities.* Legal risk management, IHL and strategic intelligence analysis suggest techniques to identify uncertainties and legal and extra-legal assumptions, and to systematically evaluate multiple interpretations of fact and law. The book developed a potential framework drawing on techniques the three fields developed for assessing multiple interpretations of current facts, and multiple forecasts of the factual and other risks different course of action may create. Such risks included legal, political and media challenges to the lawfulness of military action, new evidence emerging showing information justifying force is incorrect, and force failing to achieve its goals or doing so only by causing unacceptable harms.

The proposed framework suggested a systematic, interdisciplinary approach to *jus ad bellum* assessments, involving legal and politico-strategic expertise to consider both factual and legal issues. The framework recommended such a process should describe the legal and factual context, including the main legal theories justifying or prohibiting force and the relevant factual tests they set. It should develop and systematically assess against the available evidence multiple scenarios describing possible interpretations of current facts and possible future consequences of either using or not using force, to decide whether the most likely assessment of current facts and future consequences meets the tests in the legal theory justifying force. It should assess how key legal stakeholders – from the public and media, to Parliament, courts and other states – might respond to the competing legal theories. It would then evaluate the likelihood and severity of potential risks that the chosen legal theory is challenged or disproven, to decide whether to accept these risks and use force, whether to take steps to reduce the risks, or if such risks are so severe that force should not be used. Throughout the process the team would review and revise its assessments as new factual and legal information emerges.

The book applied this framework to two cases examined in the book: the interventions in Kosovo in 1999 and Afghanistan in 2001. These showed how the framework systematically compared multiple legal theories, interpretations of facts and forecasts of consequences for both cases, producing recommendations somewhat more cautious about force than the decisions actually taken, at least as applied by this author. The book also considered how such a framework might have affected UK legal advice on the 2003 intervention in Iraq, which included a section on legal risks, suggesting the framework would have recommended legal advice earlier in the policy-making process, and raising a wider range of risks than the advice developed in 2003.

However, the interviews, scholarly writings about the responsibilities of international lawyers, and my own analysis identified that this book's proposed framework challenged lawyers' and especially government legal advisers' professional responsibilities. By focusing on managing risks of legal challenge to a decision to use force, the framework potentially encouraged lawyers to act only as 'counselor' – apologists enabling governments to navigate the law to achieve whatever they want, rather than fulfilling their normative role of 'conscience', encouraging governments to adjust their behaviour to obey the law. Such a framework might even advise decision-makers to proceed with clearly unlawful military action if political and other circumstances meant there was minimal risk of its lawfulness being challenged. In response to these concerns, the book suggested how lawyers could use the proposed framework alongside their own professional judgement through a form of Rawlsian 'reflective equilibrium', to evaluate hard cases in the *jus ad bellum* in accordance with their professional responsibilities. A framework of this sort could thus provide a reasonable tool for legal advisers and policy-makers to help find that 'reflective equilibrium', without allowing 'non-normative managerialism' to displace genuine good faith efforts to establish whether force is lawful. However, this framework, even applied using reflective equilibrium, could not eliminate legal and factual uncertainty and disagreement driven by incompatible legal and extra-legal intuitions in hard cases engaging the *jus ad bellum*. To some extent, vagueness and uncertainty are probably necessary features of the *jus ad bellum*, as with all law, enabling it to accommodate the complexities of the conflicts it regulates and the international community that applies it.

METHODOLOGICAL LIMITATIONS, FUTURE OPPORTUNITIES

A novel feature of this book is the mix of research methods used. These included analysis of writings about the law, politics and ethics of the *jus ad bellum*; textual analysis of writings of eight UK-based legal scholars and UK legal statements about US-led interventions in Kosovo in 1999, Afghanistan in 2001 and Iraq in 2003; textual analysis of ICJ judgments and separate opinions about the 1986 *Nicaragua*, 2004 *Wall*, and 2005 *Congo* cases; and interview and/or survey research with a total of thirty-one UK-based legal scholars, practising international lawyers, and former UK government lawyers. This book appears to be the first investigation of the *jus ad bellum* using this combination of methods. Given this methodological novelty, it is unsurprising that the research process revealed limitations, lessons and potential improvements, as well as ways of potentially applying such methods to different projects.

Most interviewees and survey participants gave positive feedback about their participation. One described it as 'almost social anthropology or an ethnography of what international lawyers do', which is 'very important in an area where there's actually not very much law'.[10] Twelve of the sixteen participants who completed the survey themselves commented favourably on it.[11] One former government lawyer described it as 'excellent – and not easy'.[12] Several said the survey made them think in new ways about their interpretive, strategic and ethical choices.[13] A legal scholar said it showed 'uncertainty not only on the hard cases' but 'even some of the medium cases' dealing with 'fundamental issues of international law'.[14] Another scholar hoped a further study could run the survey with more participants.[15] Eight of the twelve participants who completed the section of the survey concerning the fictional scenario praised it.[16] One scholar asked if they could include it in future exams they set.[17]

However, some participants questioned aspects of the research. One practising international lawyer said it was 'depressing' because the 'underlying thesis appears to be there is huge uncertainty' in the *jus ad bellum*, due to 'the happenstance of the makeup of the particular individual who is advising', which was 'probably correct' but simply 'leaves one in a position of dreary uncertainty'.[18] Another practitioner questioned whether people had the capacity for the 'internal self-evaluation' the study seemed to advocate, to identify whether they really were providing 'objective analysis of the law'.[19] One individual who eventually did *not* take part in the research argued that, while opinion surveys had some uses, they had nothing to do with the law. One practising international lawyer said most of the survey questions were too complex and 'fact-dependent' for their answers to be 'reduced to a red shape on a spectrum', a view echoed by others who also preferred to take part only in interviews.[20] One former government lawyer who completed the survey was 'sceptical of quantitative techniques', which were 'not a good tool' for 'deciding what the law is', although may 'have some value in helping to investigate how lawyers think about the law'.[21]

10 Participant 18.
11 Participants 1, 2, 4, 10, 14, 17, 18, 20, 23, 24, 27, 28.
12 Participant 20.
13 Participants 27, 14, 18.
14 Participant 27.
15 Participant 2.
16 Participants 2, 4, 10, 17, 18, 24, 27, 28.
17 Participant 17.
18 Participant 15.
19 Participant 26.
20 Participant 22.
21 Participant 21.

Several thought the survey was 'too long, especially the last scenario', which led me to amend the survey to identify its more and less important parts.[22] One former government lawyer thought the survey included too many ideas.[23] A scholar thought 'certain questions were loaded in the way that they were shaped'.[24] A practising international lawyer said it was 'difficult not to anticipate the answer', because questions were often worded to suggest 'a particular angle' and preconceptions about the 'categories that people fall into and were more or less likely to agree with'.[25] Another scholar felt some questions were 'premised on the selection of these five' hard cases, and that different cases involving 'minimal uses of force', where it was uncertain whether there had been a use of force at all, might have implied different disagreements about interpretation and extra-legal issues.[26] Six of the fifteen participants who completed the questions on lawyers' professional responsibilities felt they were hard to understand, capable of more than one response, or required participants to speculate on issues they could not know, such as how other lawyers made decisions.[27] Two of the twelve participants who completed the questions on the fictional scenarios found them too lacking in factual detail to be useful.[28]

One practising international lawyer questioned the assumed universality of the *jus ad bellum*, saying 'the concepts of *jus ad bellum* and *jus in bello* are peculiarly western European', only 'grudgingly accepted' but 'not completely implemented' elsewhere in the world.[29] One former government lawyer thought the study was 'too stressful on the law'.[30] Another thought 'international law is only ever part' of the decision, and 'not the only framework' for such decisions.[31] A further former government lawyer suggested the research should include 'recipients of legal advice', such as senior officials and decision-makers, to provide a more complete picture of how legal advice is implemented.[32]

One practising international lawyer noted that the research method encouraged lawyers to answer in ways which did not reflect normal professional

22 Participants 16, 21, 25.
23 Participant 25.
24 Participant 16.
25 Participant 14.
26 Participant 30.
27 Participants 9, 4, 14, 17, 23, 28.
28 Participants 21, 23.
29 Participant 12.
30 Participant 20.
31 Participant 25.
32 Participant 19.

practice.[33] When asked for legal advice, most lawyers research the relevant legal texts, judicial proceedings, scholarly writings and materials on relevant past cases. But the interviews and survey invited participants to provide opinions without conducting such research, potentially encouraging lawyers lacking contemporary, specialised knowledge of the *jus ad bellum* to provide intuitive opinions which may differ significantly from advice they would provide after more considered research. This weakness in the research design is partially mitigated by choosing participants with specialised knowledge of the *jus ad bellum*, by follow-up interviews, and by allowing participants to amend transcripts, giving time to reflect further on their answers.

This feedback suggests the following overall conclusions. First, it underlined the need for caution in drawing inferences from the survey and interviews. Both the questionnaire and interview questions were amended in response to ongoing feedback, but some criticisms are probably inevitable weaknesses with using a survey to research a complex topic such as the *jus ad bellum*, and are only partially mitigated with follow-up interviews. There are weaknesses in how far this research reliably reveals participants' 'true' views about the *jus ad bellum*, particularly for those not deeply familiar with this law. However, the positive feedback also suggests this research may reveal at least some useful information about participants' views on the *jus ad bellum*, particularly for those with specialised knowledge. The data thus may yield some more generalisable inferences about how experienced international lawyers deal with the legal and extra-legal questions raised by hard cases engaging the *jus ad bellum*, with appropriate caveats and caution.

Other important limitations to this research flow from resource, time and capacity constraints. Since I conducted this research for a PhD, there was a limit on the scope of written materials examined and number of lawyers interviewed. This research examined only three ICJ cases, involving textual analysis of twenty-seven judgments and alternative opinions, only fifteen legal assessments written by a total of eight UK-based legal scholars considering the legality of three military interventions, and interviewed or surveyed only thirty-one international lawyers. The research takes no account of wider psychological factors, such as whether participants displayed the thinking styles of 'hedgehogs' or 'foxes' – hedgehogs being more stubborn than foxes in practising cognitive consistency when faced with contrary information.[34] This sample size is too small to claim that it represents the spread of legal and extra-legal opinion concerning the *jus ad bellum* across the wider population of UK-based

33 Participant 22.
34 Tetlock, *Expert Political Judgement*, 2.

international lawyers. It is however, probably a large enough sample to suggest that the general relationships it detected – the associations between expansionism/dynamism/interventionism and restrictivism/formalism/pacificism – are likely to reflect the thinking of similar lawyers in the wider population.

Restricting the interviews and analysis of scholarly legal writings to UK-based international lawyers is another limitation, again driven largely by resource and time constraints, and by my lack of linguistic skills necessary to engage with non-English language writings and lawyers. This limitation had some methodological advantages, minimising variations in national legal culture and wider political and media environment that might have influenced participants to reach different assessments of resort to force, and increased the likelihood that the research focused on how individual lawyers' worldview affected their legal opinions. In addition, the issues that the UK-based scholars and interviewees discussed, and the legal and factual arguments they deployed or commented on, were not specific to the United Kingdom or to any regional jurisdiction, but instead relate to justification of resort to force under international law in general, including in the UNSC and ICJ. Several of the UK-based scholars analysed and interviewed are influential in international law across the world, as is UK international legal discourse more generally, as Roberts has noted.[35] And the book's reporting of systematic textual analysis of twenty-seven majority, separate or dissenting judicial opinions on three pivotal ICJ cases adds a more explicitly international perspective to this book, further underpinning the potential international applicability of its findings.

The research for this book did not examine much material reporting the internal legal deliberations of the UK or other governments, which was a further constraint. The research was able to examine the United Kingdom's public legal justifications for the interventions in Kosovo in 1999 and Afghanistan in 2001, which were relatively succinct assertions of lawfulness. For the 2003 intervention in Iraq, the research was able to draw on the report and papers published by the Iraq Inquiry to examine the full legal advice developed by the UK attorney general and wider testimony about the development of that advice. But, as a serving UK government official, I had agreed not to interview serving UK government lawyers or other officials, and not to seek access to internal government papers not already in the public domain.

The national focus on the United Kingdom meant this research was unable to examine whether some legal systems are better able to handle uncertainty in

35 Roberts, *Is International Law International?* 8–10.

international law than others. It may be that lawyers trained in the common law system are better able to handle such uncertainty than those trained in civil law systems. Aspects of the common law system that suggest this include its willingness to assess cases as 'arguable', or as presenting 'the better argument', its more developed rules of evidence and standards of proof, which allow judgments on the 'balance of probabilities' rather than requiring the judge or lawyer to rule an argument as clearly lawful or unlawful as in civil law systems, and the practice in common law systems of judges being tasked with first review of their own judgments on appeal, to decide if the alternative opinion has sufficient merit for an appeal to proceed.[36] The role of customary international law might also mean international law functions in a manner more understandable to common law than civil law systems, since common law systems rely less on detailed legal codes and more on evidence of implementation of law, including precedents, practice in enforcing and prosecuting breaches, and wider social attitudes to lawfulness.

Finally, I lacked the time and resources to more thoroughly test and develop the framework proposed in Chapter 6. The structured interviews included questions about some techniques the framework used, such as risk management and multi-hypothesis analysis. But with additional time and resources, participants might have been invited to provide more in-depth feedback about the framework and suggestions to improve it.

Obvious ways of addressing such shortcomings would be to conduct additional research, including textual analysis of more ICJ cases and more legal writings, and interviewing or surveying more international lawyers, including in different countries and in different languages. More research could be conducted to test and refine the methodology outlined in Chapter 6, including through focus groups with international lawyers and experts in the politics and strategy of conflict. There is also potential for these research methods to be applied to other areas of international law, particularly those where decisions rely on multi-part tests and factual evidence from contested, uncertain sources. The *jus in bello*, international criminal law, human rights law, and other areas of international law related to conflict and international security, are among potential areas where these research methods might be applied. All these additional research ideas would require more financial and staff resource, linguistic skills and knowledge of different areas of law.

36 Riddell and Plant, *Evidence*, 124.

CONCLUSION: DETERMINACY AND EFFICACY IN THE *JUS AD BELLUM*

This book has devoted considerable effort to conceptualising and demonstrating uncertainty, disagreement and the often distorting effects of extra-legal reasoning in the *jus ad bellum*. I have argued that uncertainty about hard cases of resort to force can be unavoidable. It flows from the structure and content of the *jus ad bellum*'s rules, the chaotic, deceit-filled factual nature of military crises, the intrinsic unknowability of the future outcomes of action or inaction, and the competing intuitions, biases and worldviews of different international lawyers. My attempt at developing a framework to tackle legal and factual uncertainty and extra-legal intuitions ultimately relied on lawyers exercising their own normative, practical and professional judgment.

It might be tempting to conclude from all this analysis that indeterminacy is a 'structural property' of the *jus ad bellum*, rendering the law '"weak" or manipulable', using Koskenniemi's words, and thus 'useless' for evaluating international behaviour, since 'professionally impeccable legal arguments' can defend any action.[37] Kammerhofer concludes that the law on self-defence provides 'little clarity as to what, exactly, the law demands'.[38] After all, the ICJ could not 'conclude definitively' whether use of nuclear weapons 'would be lawful or unlawful' self-defence when a state's survival was threatened – effectively a finding of indeterminacy.[39] And, as this book has noted, even established democracies such as the United States, Germany and France have been willing to use force without justifying their action in international law. Such analyses might support John Bolton's claim that 'international law is not law' but 'a series of political and moral arrangements', 'an untried system' based on 'assumptions' not 'reality', 'theology and superstition masquerading as law'.[40] It might thus be tempting to see this book as an extended call for lawyers to abandon any hope of law playing a determining or even shaping role in decisions about force in international relations.

Such a conclusion would be a mistake, and far from the intention of this book. The reality of paradigms, fuzzy logic and supervaluationism does not render the *jus ad bellum* 'radically indeterminate'.[41] 'Preoccupation with the penumbra', as Hart put it, is an unreasonable generalisation from abnormal

37 Koskenniemi, *From Apology to Utopia*, 66, 62, 67, 594.
38 Kammerhofer, 'Self-Defence', 202.
39 *Legality of the Threat or Use of Nuclear Weapons*, Advisory Opinion, ICJ Reports 1996, para. 266.
40 Bolton, '"Law" in International Affairs', 1, 7, 48.
41 Solum, 'Indeterminacy Crisis', 473.

cases.[42] All rules 'have exceptions incapable of exhaustive statement', but that does not mean states have complete discretion 'and are never bound to keep a promise'.[43] As Dinstein put it, 'the penumbra of uncertainty, which is characteristic of some segments of the contemporary *jus ad bellum*, should not be exaggerated'.[44] Most potential instances of use of force are similar to the paradigms of lawful and unlawful force when judged against *all* accepted criteria. Legal texts, their tests and criteria, and the interpretive and strategic cultures that lawyers inhabit clearly overlap and converge on 'plain cases' most closely resembling the paradigms of lawful and unlawful force. There is usually enough evidence of facts, sufficiently reliable and corroborated to enable a large majority of lawyers and policy-makers to agree that specific cases align with those paradigms.

This book thus rejects Koskenniemi's concept of the law as a constant see-saw between 'non-normative apology' and idealistic utopia as far as the *jus ad bellum* is concerned.[45] International law governing resort to force, just as international law more generally, adds considerable value to international peace and security. As Wickramasinghe notes, most senior international lawyers 'do not see international law as either infinitely malleable, to be regarded or disregarded at will, or as a perfected system capable of providing clear answers to every problem'.[46] They 'identify in international law real constraints and influences on State behaviour, and at the same time sufficient dynamism to ensure that, by means of legal creativity and imagination, the law remains responsive to the changing requirements of international society'.[47]

The value of international law has often been described and is worth repeating here. As a standard UK public international law textbook puts it, 'what distinguishes the rules and principles of international law from "mere morality" is that they are accepted in practice as legally binding by states in their intercourse because they are useful to reduce complexity and uncertainty in international relations'.[48] International law provides a framework of more or less accepted rules, processes and institutions providing states and those who lead them with a baseline of expectations about each other's behaviour. That contributes to predictability and stability in international relations, including in matters of war and peace. The *jus ad bellum* is a vital component of that

42 Hart, 'Positivism', 593, 615.
43 Hart, *Concept of Law*, 139.
44 Dinstein, *War, Aggression and Self-Defence*, 139.
45 Koskenniemi, *From Apology to Utopia*, 17.
46 Chanaka Wickremasinghe, 'Preface', in Wickremasinghe, *International Lawyer*, xix.
47 Ibid., xix.
48 Malanczuk, *Akehurst's*, loc. 1146.

network of expectations, rules and institutions, also including the UNSC, UNGA and ICJ, which together function as channels for states to manage and actively pursue competing objectives and disagreements *without* resorting to war. As Allot notes, international law gives states the 'capacity to identify and to present different horizons of national interest, including long-term horizons' in which 'an immediately convenient course of action may be a bad course of action in the long run'.[49] In effect, international law in general, and the *jus ad bellum* in particular, add additional rungs to what strategic theorist Herman Kahn called the 'escalation ladder' separating peace from war.[50]

One measure of the value of the *jus ad bellum* is the extent of contemporary international agreement about this area of international law. Many justifications for resort to force once regarded as lawful are now clearly prohibited – for recovery of debt, to enforce trade agreements, for imperial territorial gain or to replace a peaceful competing state's domestic political system or leaders.[51] The right of collective self-defence and use of force under UNSC authorisation, including through twelve UN peace-keeping operations in 2021, deploying around 90,000 personnel, are accepted as clearly lawful even where states feel such operations infringe on their spheres of influence.[52] As one interviewed former government lawyer put it 'the amazing thing is we have so much clarity worldwide on so much, which we certainly wouldn't have got a hundred years ago'.[53] A practising international lawyer noted that lawyers being 'driven by underlying motives political, legal, personal' is 'not specific to international law or *jus ad bellum*', and other areas of domestic and international law saw similar issues when dealing with hard cases.[54]

And as one legal scholar said, lawyers should not 'obsess about indeterminacy', which has always been 'part of the legal experience', was often exaggerated in international law, but was not a 'problem that needs to be solved', rather 'a feature of the system rather than a bug in the system', which 'needs to be managed' and 'is being managed'.[55] It might even be argued that competing interpretive and strategic cultures, and uncertainties about the future outcome

49 Allott, 'International Lawyer', 17.

50 Herman Kahn, *On Escalation: Metaphors and Scenarios; with a New Introduction by Thomas Schelling* (Abingdon: Routledge, 2017), 37–41.

51 Dinstein, *War, Aggression and Self-Defence*, 139.

52 'United Nations Peacekeeping', UN Website (https://peacekeeping.un.org/en).

53 Participant 25.

54 Participant 26.

55 Participant 23.

of specific cases of force and about the future evolution of conflict more generally, are reasons why vagueness in the *jus ad bellum*, like in all law, is both essential and inevitable. When activities regulated by law vary significantly in socially important ways, 'uniform rules' applied 'without further official direction cannot usefully be framed'.[56] In such contexts, law-makers must adopt general standards, delegating authority to a body such as the UNSC to apply those standards in specific cases.

And there are sound reasons for believing the *jus ad bellum* and its development in the post-World War II era has made a real contribution to international peace and security. As major studies of global conflict have noted, conflict between states has much reduced since 1945 – while conflict within states has increased.[57] That 'peace' between states is 'over-determined' and can be attributed to many causes.[58] The spread of increasingly destructive military technologies has dramatically increased the costs and risks of inter-state war for policy-makers. The growth in mutually beneficial global economic links has reduced states' and leaders' material incentives for conflict. And international law and its institutions also seem to have played their part – offering alternative channels for inter-state competition and dispute resolution, and helping change 'public and elite attitudes towards the legitimacy of war as an instrument of statecraft'.[59]

All this serves to emphasise an important final conclusion of this research. The law governing resort to force is only *specifically* indeterminate and *partially* autonomous. Most cases will score consistently 'high' or consistently 'low' against the multi-part tests prescribed by the *jus ad bellum*, and so will be clearly lawful or clearly unlawful. Lawrence Solum's general conclusion about legal indeterminacy almost certainly applies to the *jus ad bellum*: most potential cases of resort to force will be clearly lawful or unlawful, even considering the sources of uncertainty discussed in this book.[60] Most lawyers and states can agree about the lawfulness of most potential and actual uses of force, even where that contradicts their extra-legal intuitions. It is therefore not surprising that attention focuses on controversial cases of use of force. Nor is it surprising that in practice states tend to use force in their international relations in situations where it is either clearly lawful or where its lawfulness is at

56 Hart, *Concept of Law*, 131.

57 Therese Pettersson and Magnus Oberg, 'Organized violence, 1989–2019', *Journal of Peace Research*, 57:4 (2020), 2, 4.

58 HSRP, *Human Security Report*, 32.

59 Ibid.

60 Solum, 'Indeterminacy', 462, 478.

least arguable. It is in part because states understand and accept the law that they so rarely take actions clearly contravening it.

One of the central concepts used throughout this book is the sorites paradox and fuzzy logic. Important phenomena in human relationships do not operate according to simple binary logic, neatly fitting into different categories separated by clear boundaries. A 'line of continuity' runs between peace and war, legality and criminality, and the boundary between these categories is rarely a bright, sharp line, but is more often a fuzzy 'penumbra of uncertainty'.[61] It makes sense to apply similar nuance and humility to any assessment of international law in general and the *jus ad bellum* in particular. Acknowledging that the law is imperfect, has grey areas and gaps, is not the same as claiming the law is useless, or worse that the law does not exist. In the vast majority of potential cases of resort to force, the law is determinate, autonomous and effective, and so is worth defending and preserving. This book's examination of legal and factual uncertainty and extra-legal intuitions in the *jus ad bellum* seeks to support and assist lawyers and states in their mission to uphold and apply this crucial area of international law, not to encourage lawyers or states to undermine or abandon it.

At the same time, the *jus ad bellum*, like all law, is a social construction, emerging from the thoughts, communications and other interactions of human beings with varying perceptions and values, engaging in the complex, multi-dimensional, fuzzy activities of war.[62] Even Dworkin accepted that law is not metaphysically objective, embedded in a 'moral field', 'part of the fabric of the universe'.[63] When people talk about the law, 'no one thinks they report the declarations of some ghostly figure: they are not about what Law whispered to the planets'.[64] Vagueness and uncertainty are probably even necessary features of the *jus ad bellum*, enabling it to flex and adapt to the complexities of both the conflicts it seeks to regulate and the international community which seeks to apply it. And since law is a social construction, the sorites paradox, fuzzy logic and supervaluationism will be both necessary and inevitable in at least some cases: what the law requires may display only *degrees* of truth/falsity, and a penumbra of uncertainty that, as one scholar puts it, cannot 'be denied or removed by any legal analysis, no matter how exhaustive and competent'.[65]

61 Franck, 'Who Killed Article 2(4)', 813–14; Hart, *Concept of Law*, 131.
62 Leslie Green, 'Introduction' in Hart, *Concept of Law*, xvii.
63 Ronald Dworkin, 'Objectivity and Truth: You'd Better Believe It', *Philosophy and Public Affairs*, 25:2 (1996), 87–139, 97.
64 Dworkin, *Law's Empire*, 4.
65 Marko Milanovic, 'Self-Defense and Non-State Actors: Indeterminacy and the *Jus ad Bellum*', *EJIL: Talk!* (21 February 2010).

The methods this book suggests for lawyers to try to address the uncertainties and subjectivities in their assessments of *jus ad bellum* cases cannot eliminate all that uncertainty, nor dispense with the need for politico-strategic and ethical judgement about past or future wars. Would the 2003 intervention in Iraq have produced a less chaotic, more peaceful outcome if it had received unambiguous authorisation through a unanimously adopted UNSC resolution? Was peace and stability in Kosovo and Europe impaired by the lack of a UNSC resolution authorising NATO's 1999 intervention in Kosovo? Would the 2011 intervention in Libya have created more instability without the UNSC resolution providing authorisation for at least the initial intervention? Has Russia's intervention in Syria with the Assad government's consent created more stability than if a US-led coalition had intervened in 2013 without that consent? Did the almost universal state approval for the 2001 intervention in Afghanistan produce an outcome which was politico-strategically and ethically more successful than if more states had disapproved? Law alone cannot answer these questions.

This book is scholarship *about* the law, but not a piece of orthodox legal scholarship. It does not seek to determine the legality of specific wars, nor reveal 'the' 'correct' method of legal interpretation. This book and the framework it proposes do not tell legal advisers or their political leaders what the law ought to be. Nor does it tell them what their military actions ought to be – whether authorising or refraining from using force in any particular case will help or harm national interests or be ethically right. But, as several interviewees said, that would be 'asking the law to do too much'.[66] Sometimes, it is right to take 'the more honest approach', and admit 'the law does not provide an answer here', and instead 'look to morality, ethics', since law is not 'the be all and end all' of foreign policy.[67] There can be no 'completely objective way of interpreting' law, since even accepted canons of legal interpretation such as the VCLT are not 'clear and unambiguous', providing only 'parameters for making arguments' or 'fairly vague guidelines as opposed to delivering the one true and right outcome', leaving 'room for flexibility, pragmatism, or bias'.[68] And so legal advisers naturally should and do consider 'ethical and political dimensions', because they wish to justify their advice about the *jus ad bellum*, particularly since 'resort to force is about killing people', which has obvious moral dimensions.[69]

66 Participant 20.
67 Participant 20.
68 Participants 1, 30.
69 Participant 18.

Applying Hart's more general insight, there will be times with the *jus ad bellum*, as with all law, when we will find that '[w]ithin the framework of relatively well-settled law there jostle too many alternatives too nearly equal in attraction between which judge and lawyer must uncertainly pick'.[70] In such situations, to argue that there is no distinction between the law as it is and the law as it ought to be 'will serve (like earlier stories that judges only find, never make, law) only to conceal the facts, that here if anywhere we live among uncertainties between which we have to choose, and that the existing law imposes only limits on our choice and not the choice itself'.[71]

It is thus difficult always to obey the Utopians' rule that 'the plainest and most obvious sense of the words is that which ought to be put upon them', particularly 'when life forces us to choose between the lesser of two evils'.[72] Sometimes, highly qualified, trusted lawyers advise states to stand aside while unspeakable atrocities unfold. Are they counselling pragmatic, virtuous compliance with that essential legal principle, *pacta sunt servanda*? Or are they displaying what Bentham described as 'that spirit of obsequious *quietism*', seeing scarcely any difference between the law as it is and the law as it ought to be?[73] These dilemmas compel lawyers to develop increasingly 'refined expositions' of the law, usually reaching mutual understanding, sometimes talking past each other, stumbling through the shadows of Babel.[74]

70 Hart, 'Positivism', 629.
71 Ibid.
72 More, *Utopia*, 85; Hart, 'Positivism', 620.
73 Bentham 'Fragment on Government', 498.
74 More, *Utopia*, 85.

Bibliography

PRIMARY MATERIALS

Anonymised List of Interview and Survey Participants

Interview and survey inputs are attributed to an individual of a certain profession, such as 'legal scholar', 'former government lawyer' or 'practising international lawyer'. Some interviewees were willing to have their participation in the study recorded, although specific quotes are not attributed to them. To maintain anonymity for those that asked for it, all participants were assigned an identifying number at random between one and thirty-one (the researcher maintains a master list identifying the participants). Dates of interview or survey are not mentioned, and this form of identification was used in all footnotes citing participants' contribution and in the bibliography below.

Participant 1: Legal scholar – interview, survey
Participant 2: Legal scholar – interview (telephone), survey
Participant 3: Legal scholar – interview, survey (indirect)
Participant 4: Senior legal scholar – interview, survey
Participant 5: Legal scholar – interview, survey (indirect)
Participant 6: Legal scholar – interview
Participant 7: Legal scholar – interview
Participant 8: Practising international lawyer – interview, survey (indirect)
Participant 9: Legal scholar – interview, survey
Participant 10: Practising international lawyer – interview, survey
Participant 11: Retired armed forces lawyer – interview
Participant 12: Practising international lawyer – interview
Participant 13: International lawyer – interview, survey (indirect)
Participant 14: Practising international lawyer – interview, survey
Participant 15: Practising international lawyer – interview, survey (indirect)
Participant 16: Legal scholar – survey
Participant 17: Legal scholar – interview, survey
Participant 18: Practising international lawyer – interview, survey
Participant 19: Senior former government lawyer – interview, survey (indirect)
Participant 20: Retired armed forces lawyer – interview, survey

Participant 21: Senior former government lawyer – interview, survey
Participant 22: International lawyer – interview
Participant 23: Legal scholar – interview, survey
Participant 24: Legal scholar – interview, survey
Participant 25: Former government international lawyer – interview, survey
Participant 26: Practising international lawyer – interview
Participant 27: Legal scholar – interview, survey
Participant 28: Legal scholar – interview, survey
Participant 29: Former government lawyer – interview
Participant 30: Legal scholar – interview
Participant 31: Former government lawyer – interview, survey (indirect)

Official Government and Parliamentary Documents

Brownlie, Ian, 'Memorandum from Professor Ian Brownlie QC', Minutes of Evidence Taken Before the Foreign Affairs Committee, 24 October 2002, in Foreign Affairs Committee, *Foreign Policy Aspects of the War on Terrorism*, HC196, Session 2002–2003 (19 Dec. 2002).

Lord Butler of Brockwell, Review of Intelligence on Weapons of Mass Destruction (HC898) (London: The Stationery Office, 2004).

Cameron, David, 'Syria: Refugees and Counter-terrorism' (7 September 2015), *Hansard*, House of Commons, 6th ser., vol. 599, cols. 23–7.

Cameron, David, 'Syria' (26 November 2015), *Hansard*, House of Commons, 6th ser., vol. 602, cols. 1489–94.

Director of Public Prosecutions, 'Policy for Prosecutors in Respect of Cases of Encouraging or Assisting Suicide' (London: The Crown Prosecution Service, 2010).

The Federal Council of Switzerland, Swiss Civil Code of 10 December 1907 (Status as of 1 July 2020) (Bern: Official Publications Centre, 2020).

HM Government, 'Chemical Weapon Use by Syrian Regime: UK Government Legal Position' (London: HM Government, 2013).

HM Government, Criminal Justice and Immigration Act 2008 (London: HM Government, 2008).

HM Government, 'Policy Paper: Syria Action – UK Government Legal Position' (London: HM Government, 14 April 2018).

HM Government Cabinet Office, 'HMG Legal Position: UKIM Bill and Northern Ireland Protocol' (London: HM Government, 10 September 2020).

HM Government Cabinet Office, *Ministerial Code* (London: HM Government, May 2010).

HM Government Cabinet Office, *Ministerial Code* (London: HM Government, January 2018).

HM Government Legal Department, *Guidance Note on Legal Risk* (London: HM Government, April 2015).

Iraq Inquiry, *The Report of the Iraq Inquiry: Executive Summary* (London: HM Stationery Office, 2016).

Iraq Inquiry, 'Section 5: Advice on the Legal Basis for Military Action, November 2002 to March 2003', *The Report of the Iraq Inquiry*, vol. 5 (London: HM Stationery Office, 2016), 1–169.

Iraq Inquiry, 'Section 3.5: Development of UK Strategy and Options, September to November 2002 – The Negotiation of Resolution 1441', *The Report of the Iraq Inquiry*, vol. 2 (London: HM Stationery Office, 2016), 197–390.

May, Theresa, 'A Statement to the House of Commons by Prime Minister Theresa May Following the Salisbury Incident' (14 March 2018), *Hansard*, House of Commons, 6th ser., vol. 637, cols. 855–7.

Ministère des Armées, International Law Applied to Operations in Cyberspace (Paris: Ministère des Armées, 2019).

Newson, Nicola, and Sarah Tudor, *Publishing Government Legal Advice: House of Lords Library Briefing* (London: UK Parliament, 7 November 2018).

Office of the UK Prime Minister, 'Responsibility for the Terrorist Atrocities in the United States, 11 September 2001 – An Updated Account' (14 November 2001), https://fas.org/irp/news/2001/11/ukreport.html.

Robertson, George 'Kosovo' (25 March 1999), *Hansard*, House of Commons, 6th ser., vol. 328, cols. 616–8.

Baroness Symons, 'Kosovo: Use of Military Force' (16 November 1998), *Hansard*, House of Lords, 5th ser., vol. 594, col. WA 140.

UK Attorney General Goldsmith, 'The Use of Force Against Iraq', *International and Comparative Law Quarterly*, 52:3 (2003), 811–2.

UK Attorney General Goldsmith, 'Iraq: Resolution 1441', *International and Comparative Law Quarterly*, 54:3 (2005), 767–78.

UK Attorney General Wright, 'The Modern Law of Self-Defence', Speech, The International Institute for Strategic Studies (11 January 2017), https://assets.publishing.service.gov.uk/government/uploads/system/uploads/attachment_data/file/583171/170111_Imminence_Speech.pdf.

UK Ministry of Defence, *Understanding and Intelligence Support to Joint Operations*, Joint Doctrine Publication 2–00, 3rd ed. (London: Development, Concepts and Doctrine Centre, UK Ministry of Defence, 2011).

UK Ministry of Justice, *Intelligence Collection, Analysis and Dissemination Policy Framework* (London: UK Ministry of Justice, 11 March 2019).

US Department of Defense, Chairman of The Joint Chiefs of Staff, Instruction 3160.01, *No-Strike and the Collateral Damage Estimation Methodology* (Washington, DC: US Department of Defense, 13 February 2009).

US Department of Defense, Joint Chiefs of Staff, 'Joint Publication 3–60, Joint Targeting', II-1 (Washington, DC: US Department of Defense, 31 January 2013).

US Department of Defense, *Joint Staff Targeting, Joint Targeting Cycle and Collateral Damage Estimation Methodology* (CDM), Slides (Washington, DC: US Department of Defense, 10 November 2009).

US State Department, 'Rambouillet Agreement – Interim Agreement for Peace and Self-Government in Kosovo' (US State Department, March 1999), https://1997-2001.state.gov/www/regions/eur/ksvo_rambouillet_text.html.

The White House, *National Security Strategy September 2002* (Washington, DC: The White House, 2002).

Treaties and UN Documents

International Committee of the Red Cross, 'Protocol Additional to the Geneva Conventions of 12 August 1949, and Relating to the Protection of Victims of International Armed Conflicts (Protocol I)', 8 June 1977, 1125 UNTS 17512.

International Committee of the Red Cross, 'Protocol Additional to the Geneva Conventions of 12 August 1949, and Relating to the Protection of Victims of Non-international Armed Conflicts (Protocol II)', 8 June 1977, 1125 UNTS 17513.

International Court of Justice, Statute of the International Court of Justice (ICJ Statute) (18 April 1946).

International Criminal Court, 'Activation of the Jurisdiction of the Court over the Crime of Aggression', 14 December 2017, ICC-ASP/16/Res.5.

International Criminal Court, 'The Crime of Aggression', 11 June 2010, ICC-RC/Res.6.

International Criminal Court, Rome Statute of the International Criminal Court (17 July 1998).

International Law Association, Committee on Use of Force, *Draft Report on Aggression and the Use of Force* (May 2016).

International Law Association, *Hague Principles on Ethical Standards for Counsel Appearing before International Courts and Tribunals* (27 September 2010).

International Law Association, Study Group on Due Diligence in International Law, *Second Report* (July 2016).

International Law Commission, *Second Report on State Responsibility, Addendum*, 30 April 1999, A/CN.4/498/Add.2.

International Law Commission, 'State Responsibility', *Report of the International Law Commission on the Work of Its Fifty-Third Session, 23 April–1 June and 2 July–10 August 2001*, A/56/10, 20–143.

Organisation of African Unity, 'Constitutive Act of the African Union', 1 July 2000, 2158 UNTS 37733.

UN, *Charter of the United Nations*, 24 October 1945, 1 UNTS XVI.

UN, 'Declaration Recognizing as Compulsory the Jurisdiction of the Court, in Conformity with Article 36, Paragraph 2, of the Statute of the International Court Of Justice Washington, 14 August 1946: Termination', 7 October 1985, 1408 UNTS 270.

UN, 'Declaratory Statement by the Republic of South Africa on the Decision to Withdraw from the Rome Statute of the International Criminal Court', 19 October 2016, C.N.786.2016.TREATIESXVIII.10 (Depositary Notification).

UN, Press Release GA/SPD/164, '"Humanitarian Intervention", Slow Reimbursement Rates Assailed as Special Committee Reviews Peacekeeping Operations', 18 October 1999, GA/SPD/164.

UN, Vienna Convention on the Law of Treaties (VCLT), 23 May 1969, 1155 UNTS 18232.

UN General Assembly, *A More Secure World: Our Shared Responsibility: Report of the Secretary General's High-level Panel on Threats, Challenges and Change*, 2 December 2004, A/59/565.

UN General Assembly, Resolution 377, 'Uniting for Peace', A/RES/377 (3 November 1950).

UN General Assembly, Resolution 2625 (xxv), 'Declaration on Principles of International Law concerning Friendly Relations and Co-operation among States in Accordance with the Charter of the United Nations', 24 October 1970, A/RES/2625 (xxv).

UN General Assembly, Resolution 3314, 'Definition of Aggression', 14 December 1974, A/RES/3314 (xxix).

UN Security Council, Document S/2001/946, 'Letter Dated 7 October 2001 from the Permanent Representative of the United States of America to the United Nations Addressed to the President of the Security Council', 7 October 2001, S/2001/946.

UN Security Council, Document S/2001/947, 'Letter Dated 7 October 2001 from the Chargé d'affaires a.i. of the Permanent Mission of the United Kingdom of Great Britain and Northern Ireland to the United Nations Addressed to the President of the Security Council', 7 October 2001, S/2001/947.

UN Security Council, Document S/2003/350 (United Kingdom), 'Letter Dated 20 March 2003 from the Permanent Representative of the United Kingdom of Great Britain and Northern Ireland to the United Nations Addressed to the President of the Security Council', 20 March 2003, S/2003/350.

UN Security Council, Document S/2003/351 (United States), 'Letter Dated 20 March 2003 from the Permanent Representative of the United States of America to the United Nations Addressed to the President of the Security Council', 20 March 2003, S/2003/351.

UN Security Council, Document S/2003/352 (Australia), 'Letter Dated 20 March 2003 from the Permanent Representative of Australia to the United Nations Addressed to the President of the Security Council', 20 March 2003, S/2003/352.

UN Security Council, Document S/2015/946, 'Letter dated 10 December 2015 from the Chargé d'affaires a.i. of the Permanent Mission of Germany to the United Nations addressed to the President of the Security Council', 10 December 2015, S/2015/946.

UN Security Council, Document S/2016/523, 'Letter Dated 7 June 2016 from the Permanent Representative of Belgium to the United Nations Addressed to the President of the Security Council', 9 June 2017, S/2016/523.

UN Security Council, 'Note by the President of the Security Council', 31 January 1992, S/23500.

UN Security Council, Press Release SC/6659, 'Security Council Rejects Demand for Cessation of Use of Force against Federal Republic of Yugoslavia', 26 March 1999, SC/6659.

UN Security Council, Press Release SC/7143, 'Security Council Condemns, "In Strongest Terms", Terrorist Attacks on United States', 12 September 2001, SC/7143.

UN Security Council, Resolution 678, 29 November 1990, S/RES/678 (1990).

UN Security Council, Resolution 686, 2 March 1991, S/RES/686 (1991).

UN Security Council, Resolution 687, 8 April 1991, S/RES/687 (1991).

UN Security Council, Resolution 1199, 'The Situation in Kosovo (FRY)', 23 September 1998, S/RES/1199 (1998).

UN Security Council, Resolution 1291, 'The Situation concerning the Democratic Republic of the Congo', 24 February 2000, S/RES/1291 (2000).

UN Security Council, Resolution 1368, 'Condemnation of 11 September Attacks Against United States', 12 September 2001, S/RES/1368 (2001).

UN Security Council, Resolution 1373, 'Creation of Counter-Terrorism Committee', 28 September 2001, S/RES/1373 (2001).
UN Security Council, Resolution 1386, 'The Situation in Afghanistan', 20 December 2001, S/RES/1386 (2001).
UN Security Council, Resolution 1441, 8 November 2002, S/RES/1441 (2002).
UN Security Council, Resolution 1846, 'On Repressing Acts of Piracy and Armed Robbery at Sea off the Coast of Somalia', 2 December 2009, S/RES/1846 (2008).
UN Security Council, Resolution 1973, 'On the Situation in the Libyan Arab Jamahiriya', 17 March 2011, S/RES/1973 (2011).

Court Judgments and Opinions

Accordance with International Law of the Unilateral Declaration of Independence in Respect of Kosovo, Advisory Opinion, ICJ Reports 2010, 403.
Application of the Convention on the Prevention and Punishment of the Crime of Genocide (Bosnia and Herzegovina v. *Serbia and Montenegro)*, Judgment, ICJ Reports 2007, 43 [*Genocide*, Judgment].
Armed Activities on the Territory of the Congo (Democratic Republic of the Congo v. *Uganda)*, Judgment, ICJ Reports 2005, 168 [*Congo*, Judgment].
Separate Opinion of Judge Elaraby, ICJ Reports 2005, 327 [*Congo*, Elaraby].
Dissenting Opinion of Judge *Ad Hoc* Kateka, ICJ Reports 2005, 361 [*Congo*, Kateka].
Dissenting Opinion of Judge Kooijmans, ICJ Reports 2005, 306 [*Congo*, Kooijmans].
Declaration of Judge Koroma, ICJ Reports 2005, 284 [*Congo*, Koroma].
Separate Opinion of Judge Parra-Aranguren, ICJ Reports 2005, 292 [*Congo*, Parra-Aranguren].
Separate Opinion of Judge Simma, ICJ Reports 2005, 334 [*Congo*, Simma].
Declaration of Judge Tomka, ICJ Reports 2005, 351 [*Congo*, Tomka].
Declaration of Judge *Ad Hoc* Verhoeven, ICJ Reports 2005, 355 [*Congo*, Verhoeven].
Case Concerning the Barcelona Traction, Light and Power Company, Limited, Judgment, ICJ Reports 1970, 6.
The Corfu Channel Case, Merits, Judgment, ICJ Reports (1949), 4 [*Corfu*, Merits].
Dissenting Opinion of Judge Azevedo, ICJ Reports (1949), 78.
Dissenting Opinion of Judge Krylov, ICJ Reports (1949), 68.
Jacobellis v. *Ohio*, 378 US 184 No. 11 (Supreme Court of United States, 22 June 1964).
Judgment and Sentences, International Military Tribunal (Nuremberg), *American Journal of International Law* 41(1946).
Hostage case (*USA* v. *List et al.*) (American Military Tribunal, Nuremberg, 1948), 11 NMT 1230, 1253.
ICTY, *Final Report to the Prosecutor by the Committee Established to Review the NATO Bombing Campaign Against the Federal Republic of Yugoslavia*.
ICTY Appeals Chamber, 'Press Release: Convictions for Kosovo crimes upheld for four senior Serbian officials', MS/CS/1594e (The Hague: ICTY, 2014).
Legal Consequences of the Construction of a Wall in the Occupied Palestinian Territory, Advisory Opinion, ICJ Reports 2004, 136 [*Wall*, Opinion].
Separate Opinion of Judge Al-Khasawneh, ICJ Reports 2004, 235 [*Wall*, Al-Khasawneh].

Declaration of Judge Buergenthal, ICJ Reports 2004, 240 [*Wall*, Buergenthal].
Separate Opinion of Judge Elaraby, ICJ Reports 2004, 246 [*Wall*, Elaraby].
Separate Opinion of Judge Higgins, ICJ Reports 2004, 207 [*Wall*, Higgins].
Separate Opinion of Judge Kooijmans, ICJ Reports 2004, 219 [*Wall*, Kooijmans].
Separate Opinion of Judge Koroma, ICJ Reports 2004, 204 [*Wall*, Koroma].
Separate Opinion of Judge Owada, ICJ Reports 2004, 260 [*Wall*, Owada].

Legal Consequences for States of the Continued Presence of South Africa in Namibia (South West Africa) notwithstanding Security Council Resolution 276 (1970), Advisory Opinion, ICJ Reports 1971, 12 [*South West Africa*, Advisory Opinion].

Legality of the Threat or Use of Nuclear Weapons, Advisory Opinion, ICJ Reports 1996, 226.
Judge Higgins, Dissenting Opinion, ICJ Reports 1996, 583 [*Nuclear Weapons*, Higgins].

Legality of Use of Force (Yugoslavia v. *Belgium)*, Verbatim Record, 10 May 1999, ICJ CR99/15.
Order, 2 June 1999, ICJ Reports (1999) 916 [*Yugoslavia* v. *United States*, Provisional Measures].

Maritime Delimitation and Territorial Questions between Qatar and Bahrain, Joint Dissenting Opinion of Judges Bedjaoui, Ranjeva, and Koroma, ICJ Reports 2001, 145.

Military and Paramilitary Activities in and against Nicaragua, (Nicaragua v. *United States of America)*, Merits, Judgment, ICJ Reports 1986, 14 [*Nicaragua*, Merits].
Separate Opinion of Judge Ago, ICJ Reports 1986, 181 [*Nicaragua*, Ago].
Separate Opinion of Judge Elias, ICJ Reports 1986, 178 [*Nicaragua*, Elias].
Dissenting Opinion of Judge Sir Robert Jennings, ICJ Reports 1986, 528 [*Nicaragua*, Jennings].
Separate Opinion of Judge Lachs, ICJ Reports 1986, 158 [*Nicaragua*, Lachs].
Separate Opinion of Judge Ni, ICJ Reports 1986, 201 [*Nicaragua*, Ni].
Dissenting Opinion of Judge Oda, ICJ Reports 1986, 212 [*Nicaragua*, Oda].
Separate Opinion of Judge Ruda, ICJ Reports 1986, 174 [*Nicaragua*, Ruda].
Dissenting Opinion of Judge Schwebel, ICJ Reports 1986, 259 [*Nicaragua*, Schwebel].
Separate Opinion of Judge Sette-Camara, ICJ Reports 1986, 192 [*Nicaragua*, Sette-Camara].
Separate Opinion of President Nagendra Singh, ICJ Reports 1986, 151 [*Nicaragua*, Singh].

Prosecutor v. *Galić*, Case No. IT-98–29-T, Judgment (International Criminal Tribunal for the Former Yugoslavia (ICTY), 5 December 2003), 58; [*Prosecutor* v. *Galić*, Judgment].

Prosecutor v. *Tadic*, Judgment, ICTY Case No. IT-94–1-A, Appeals Chamber, *International Legal Materials* 38 (1999) [*Prosecutor* v. *Tadic*, Judgment].

R *(on the application of Purdy)* v. *Director of* Public Prosecutions, [2009] UKHL 45 (Lords of Appeal 30 July 2009).

The Supreme Court Sitting as the High Court of Justice (Israel) HCJ769/02, *The Public Committee against Torture in Israel et al – vs – the Government of Israel et al*, 11 December 2005 [Israel Supreme Court (2005)].

LATER WORKS

Academic Articles

Akande, Dapo, and Thomas Liefländer, 'Clarifying Necessity, Imminence, and Proportionality in the Law of Self-Defense', *The American Journal of International Law*, 107:3 (2013), 563–70.

Allott, Philip, 'The Concept of International Law', *European Journal of International Law*, 10:1 (1999), 31–50.

Allott, Philip, 'The International Lawyer in Government Service: Ontology and Deontology', *Wisconsin International Law Journal*, 23:1 (2005), 13–23.

Allott, Philip, 'State Responsibility and the Unmaking of International Law', *Harvard International Law Journal*, 29 (1988), 1–26.

Australian Attorney-General, 'Memorandum of Advice on the Use of Force against Iraq', *Australian Year Book of International Law*, 24 (2003), 415–18.

Bailey, Sydney D., 'New Light on Abstentions in the UN Security Council', *International Affairs*, 50:4 (October 1974), 554–73.

Bailey, Teresa A., 'Presidential Plenary Panel: An Exchange with Former Legal Advisors of the US Department of State', *Proceedings of the American Society of International Law*, 98 (2004), 131–4.

Bellamy, Alex J., and Paul D. Williams, 'The New Politics of Protection? Côte d'Ivoire, Libya and the Responsibility to Protect', *International Affairs*, 87:4 (2011), 825-50.

Benda-Beckmann, Frances von, 'Who's Afraid of Legal Pluralism?', *Journal of Legal Pluralism and Unofficial Law*, 47 (2002), 37–82.

Dr Joanna Benjamin, 'Sources of Legal Risk for Financial Institutions', *Journal of International Banking & Financial Law*, 19:4 (2004), 25–42.

Berman, Sir Franklin, QC, 'What Do We Expect of Lawyers in Armed Conflict?', *George Washington International Law Review*, 38 (2006), 627–33.

Bethlehem, Daniel, 'Self-Defense against an Imminent or Actual Armed Attack by Nonstate Actors', *The American Journal of International Law*, 106:4 (2012), 770–77.

Bieler, Andreas, and Adam David Morton, 'A Critical Theory Route to Hegemony, World Order and Historical Change: Neo-Gramscian Perspectives in International Relations', *Capital and Class*, 82 (2004), 85–113.

Bilder, Richard B., 'On Being an International Lawyer', *Loyola University of Chicago International Law Review*, 3 (2006), 135–47.

Boer, Lianne, '"Echoes of Times Past": On the Paradoxical Nature of Article 2(4)', *Journal of Conflict and Security Law*, 20 (2015), 5–26.

Bolton, John R., 'Is There Really "Law" in International Affairs?', *Transnational Law and Contemporary Problems*, 10:1 (2000), 1–48.

Bourdieu, Pierre, 'The Force of Law: Toward a Sociology of the Juridical Field', *Hastings Law Journal*, 38 (July 1987), 805–53.

Brownlie, Ian, and Brian Apperley, 'Kosovo Crisis Inquiry: Memorandum on the International Law Aspects', *The International and Comparative Law Quarterly*, 49 (2000), 878–905.

Byers, Michael, 'Agreeing to Disagree: Security Council Resolution 1441 and Intentional Ambiguity', *Global Governance*, 10 (2004), 165–86.

Byers, Michael, 'Custom, Power, and the Power of Rules', *Michigan Journal of International Law*, 17 (1995), 109–80.

Cass, Deborah Z. 'Navigating the Newstream: Recent Critical Scholarship in International Law', *Nordic Journal of International Law*, 65 (1996), 341–83.

Cassese, Antonio, '*Ex Inuria Ius Oritur*: Are We Moving towards International Legitimation of Forcible Humanitarian Countermeasures in the World Community?' *European Journal of International Law*, 10 (1999), 23–30.

Cassese, Antonio, 'Terrorism Is Also Disrupting Some Crucial Legal Categories in International Law', *European Journal of International Law*, 12 (2001), 993–1001.

Charney, Jonathan, 'The Use of Force Against Terrorism and International Law', *American Journal of International Law*, 95 (2001), 835–9.

Chinkin, Christine, 'The Legality of NATO's Action in the FRY', *The International and Comparative Law Quarterly*, 49 (2000), 910–25.

Cotterrell, Roger, 'Why Must Legal Ideas Be Interpreted Sociologically?', *Journal of Law and Society*, 25:2 (June 1998), 171–92.

Craven, Matthew, Susan Marks, Gerry Simpson and Ralph Wilde, 'We are Teachers of International Law', *Leiden Journal of International Law*, 17 (2004), 363–74.

D'Amato, Anthony, 'Legal Uncertainty', *California Law Review* 71 (1983), 1–55.

Deeks, Ashley, 'Multi-Part Tests in the *Jus Ad Bellum*', *Houston Law Review*, 53:4 (April 2016), 1035–64.

Deeks, Ashley, 'Unwilling or Unable: Toward a Normative Framework for Extraterritorial Self-Defense', *Virginia Journal of International Law*, 52 (2012), 483–550.

De Smet, Simon, 'Book Review', *The Cambridge Law Journal*, 68:3 (2009), 664–7.

Lord Devlin, 'Law, Morality and Democracy', *University of Pennsylvania Law Review*, 110:5 (1962), 635–49.

Dhami, Mandeep K., Ian K. Belton and David R. Mandel, 'The "Analysis of Competing Hypotheses" in Intelligence Analysis', *Applied Cognitive Psychology*, 33 (2019), 1080–90.

Dworkin, Ronald, 'Hard Cases', *Harvard Law Review*, 88:6 (1975), 1057–109.

Dworkin, Ronald, 'No Right Answer?', *New York University Law Review*, 53 (1978), 1–32.

Dworkin, Ronald, 'Objectivity and Truth: You'd Better Believe It', *Philosophy and Public Affairs*, 25:2 (1996), 87–139.

Ehrlich, Eugene and Nathan Isaacs, 'The Sociology of Law', *Harvard Law Review*, 36:2, (December 1922), 130–45.

Farrell, Theo, 'World Culture and Military Power', *Security Studies*, 14:3 (2005), 448–88.

Franck, Thomas M., 'Legitimacy in the International System', *American Journal of International Law*, 82:4 (1988), 705–59.

Franck, Thomas M., 'Who Killed Article 2 (4)?', *American Journal of International Law*, 64 (1970), 809–37.

Fuller, Lon L., 'Positivism and Fidelity to Law – a Reply to Professor Hart', *Harvard Law Review*, 71:4 (1958), 630–72.

Gewirtz, Paul, 'On "I Know It When I See It"', *Yale Law Journal*, 105 (1996), 1023–47.

Gino, Francesca and Dan Ariely, 'The Dark Side of Creativity: Original Thinkers Can Be More Dishonest', *Journal of Personality and Social Psychology*, 102:3 (2012), 445–59.

Glueck, Sheldon, 'The Nuremberg Trial and Aggressive War', *Harvard Law Review*, 59:3 (1946), 396–456.

Goldsmith, Jack, and Eric A. Posner, 'The New International Law Scholarship', *Georgia Journal of International and Comparative Law*, 34 (2006), 463–88.

Gray, Colin, 'National Style in Strategy: The American Example', *International Security*, 6:2 (1981), 21–47.

Gray, Colin, 'Out of the Wilderness: Prime Time for Strategic Culture', *Comparative Strategy*, 26:1 (2007), 1–20.

Greenwood, Christopher, 'Humanitarian Intervention: The Case of Kosovo', *Finnish Yearbook of International Law* (2002), 141–75.

Greenwood, Christopher, 'International Law and the NATO Intervention in Kosovo', *The International and Comparative Law Quarterly*, 49 (2000), 926–34.

Greenwood, Christopher, 'International Law and the "War against Terrorism"', *International Affairs*, 78 (2002), 301–17.

Greenwood, Christopher, 'International Law and the Pre-emptive Use of Force: Afghanistan, Al-Qaida, and Iraq', *San Diego International Law Journal*, 4 (2003), 7–38.

Griffiths, John, 'What Is Legal Pluralism?', *Journal of Legal Pluralism and Unofficial Law*, 18 (1986), 1–55.

Gunther, Klaus, 'Legal Pluralism or Uniform Concept of Law? Globalisation as a Problem of Legal Theory', *No Foundations*, 5 (2008), 5–21.

Haas, Peter, 'Introduction: Epistemic Communities and International Policy Coordination', *International Organization*, 46 (1992), 1–35.

Hakimi, Monica, 'The *Jus ad bellum's* Regulatory Form', *American Journal of International Law*, 112:2 (2018), 151–90.

Halink, Simone, 'All Things Considered: How the International Court of Justice Delegated Its Fact-Assessment to the United Nations in the Armed Activities Case', *International Law and Politics*, 40 (2008), 13–52.

Hart, H. L. A., 'Positivism and the Separation of Law and Morals', *Harvard Law Review*, 71 (1958), 593–629.

Hazard, Jr, Geoffrey C. 'An Historical Perspective on the Attorney-Client Privilege', *California Law Review*, 66:5 (1978), 1061–91.

Head, Namoi, 'Critical Theory and Its Practices: Habermas, Kosovo and International Relations', *Politics*, 28:3 (2008), 150–9.

Henkin, Louis, 'Kosovo and the Law of "Humanitarian Intervention"', *American Journal of International Law*, 3 (1999), 824–8.

Henriksen, Anders, and Marc Schack, 'The Crisis in Syria and Humanitarian Intervention', *Journal on the Use of Force and International Law*, 1 (2014), 127–47.

Hensley, Thomas R., 'National Bias and the International Court of Justice', *Midwest Journal of Political Science*, 12 (1968), 568–86.

Hsee, Christopher K., 'Elastic Justification: How Unjustifiable Factors Influence Judgments', *Organizational Behavior and Human Decision Processes*, 66:1 (1996), 122–9.

Jackson, Robert H., 'Martin Wight, International Theory and the Good Life', *Millennium – Journal of International Studies*, 19:2 (1990), 261–72.

Johnston, Alastair Iain, 'Thinking About Strategic Culture', *International Security*, 19:4 (1995), 32–64.

Jouannet, Emmanuelle, 'French and American Perspectives on International Law: Legal Cultures and International Law', *Maine Law Review*, 58:2 (2006), 292–337.

Kahneman, Daniel and Gary Klein, 'Conditions for Intuitive expertise: A Failure to Disagree', *American Psychologist*, 64:6 (2009), 515–26.

Kammerhofer, Jorg, 'Uncertainties of the Law on Self-Defence in the United Nations Charter', *Netherlands Yearbook of International Law*, 35 (2004), 143–204.

Kammerhofer, Jorg, 'Uncertainty in the Formal Sources of International Law: Customary International Law and Some of Its Problems', *European Journal of International Law*, 15 (2004), 523–53.

Keohane, Robert O. and Joseph S. Nye, Jr, 'Power and Interdependence Revisited', *International Organization*, 41:4 (1987), 725–53.

Kirgis, Frederic, 'Custom on a Sliding Scale', *American Journal of International Law*, 81 (1987), 146–51.

Koh, Harold H., 'Is There a "New" New Haven School of International Law?', *Yale Journal of International Law*, 32 (2007), 559–74.

Koh, Harold H., 'The State Department Legal Adviser's Office: Eight Decades in Peace and War', *Georgetown Law Journal*, 110 (2012), 1747–81.

Koskenniemi, Martti, 'Constitutionalism as Mindset: Reflections on Kantian Themes About International Law and Globalization', *Theoretical Inquiries in Law*, 8:1 (2007), 9–36.

Koskenniemi, Martti, '"The Lady Doth Protest Too Much" Kosovo, and the Turn to Ethics in International Law', *The Modern Law Review*, 65:2 (2002), 159–75.

Kress, Claus, 'Major Post-Westphalian Shifts and Some Important Neo-Westphalian Hesitations in the State Practice on the International Law on the Use of Force', *Journal on the Use of Force and International Law*, 1 (2014), 11–54.

Kuperman, Alan, 'A Model Humanitarian Intervention? Reassessing NATO's Libya Campaign', *International Security*, 38:1 (2013), 105–136.

Kuperman, Alan, 'The Moral Hazard of Humanitarian Intervention: Lessons from the Balkans', *International Studies Quarterly*, 52 (2008), 49–80.

Lauterpacht, Hersch, 'The Problem of the Revision of the Law of War', *British Year Book of International Law*, 29 (1952), 360–82.

Lowe, Vaughan, 'International Legal Issues Arising in the Kosovo Crisis', *The International and Comparative Law Quarterly*, 49 (2000), 934–43.

Lowe, Vaughan, 'The Iraq Crisis: What Now', *The International and Comparative Law Quarterly*, 52:4 (2003), 859–71.

Mahler, Tobias, 'Assessing Legal Risks of Closed Generic Top-Level Domains', *European Journal of Law and Technology*, 5:3 (2014), 1–25.

Mahler, Tobias, 'Tool-Supported Legal Risk Management: A Roadmap', *European Journal of Legal Studies*, 2:3 (2010), http://hdl.handle.net/1814/15122.

Maxeiner, James R., 'Legal Certainty: A European Alternative to American Legal Indeterminacy?', *Tulane Journal of International and Comparative Law*, 15 (2007), 541–607.

McCleery, Alistair, 'The Return of the Publisher to Book History: The Case of Allen Lane', *Book History*, 5 (2002), 161–85.

Murphy, Sean D., 'Protean Jus ad Bellum', *Berkeley Journal of International Law*, 27 (2009), 22–53.

Myjer, Eric, and Nigel White, 'The Twin Towers Attack: an Unlimited Right to Self-Defence?', *Journal of Conflict and Security Law*, 7 (2002), 5–17.

Neeleman, Jan, 'Suicide as a Crime: Legal History, International Comparisons and Present Implications', *Acta Psychiatrica Scandinavica*, 94 (1996), 252–7.

Okpe, Samuel, 'Anti-Impunity Norm of the International Criminal Court: A Curse or Blessing for Africa?', *Journal of Asian and African Studies*, 55:7 (2020), 1077–90.

Overbeck, Alfred. E. von, 'Some Observations on the Role of the Judge in the Swiss Civil Code', *Louisiana Law Review*, 37:3 (1977), 681–700.

Paulus, Andreas, 'Second Thoughts on the Crime of Aggression', *European Journal of International Law*, 20 (2009), 1117–28.

Pietrowski, Robert, 'Evidence in International Arbitration', *Arbitration International*, 22:3 (2006), 373–410.

Seuren, Pieter, 'Eubulides as a 20th-Century Semanticist', *Language Sciences*, 27 (2005), 75–95.

Roberts, Adam, 'The So-Called "Right" of Humanitarian Intervention', *Yearbook of International Humanitarian Law*, 3 (2000), 3–51.

Russell, Bertrand, 'The Ethics of War', *International Journal of Ethics*, 25:2 (1915), 127–42.

Schachter, Oscar, 'Invisible College of International Lawyers', *Northwestern University Law Review*, 72:2 (1977–8), 217–26.

Schachter, Oscar, 'The Right of States to Use Armed Force', *Michigan Law Review*, 82 (1984), 1620–46.

Schauer, Frederick, 'Is Common Law Law?', *California Law Review*, 77:2 (1989), 455–71.

Sellars, Kirsten, 'Imperfect Justice at Nuremberg and Tokyo', *The European Journal of International Law*, 21:4 (2011), 1085–102.

Shaffer, Gregory and Ginsburg, Tom, 'The Empirical Turn in International Legal Scholarship', *American Journal of International Law*, 106:1 (2012), 1–47.

Simma, Bruno, 'NATO, the UN and the Use of Force: Legal Aspects', *European Journal of International Law*, 10 (1999), 1–22.

Smith, Adam M., 'Judicial Nationalism in International Law: National Identity and Judicial Autonomy at the ICJ', *Texas International Law Journal*, 40 (2004), 197–232.

Smith, M. L. R. and John Stone, 'Explaining Strategic Theory', *Infinity Journal*, 4 (2011), 27–30.

Solum, Lawrence B., 'On the Indeterminacy Crisis: Critiquing Critical Dogma', *The University of Chicago Law Review*, 54:2 (1987), 462–503.

Steenbergen, Marco R. and Marks, Gary, 'Evaluating Expert Judgments', *European Journal of Political Research*, 46 (2007), 347–66.

Stern, Brigitte, 'Custom at the Heart of International Law', *Duke Journal of Comparative and International Law*, 11 (2001), 89–108.

Stroble, James A., 'Justification of War in Ancient China', *Asian Philosophy*, 8:3 (1998), 165–90.

Suh, Il Ro, 'Voting Behaviour of National Judges in International Courts', *American Journal of International Law*, 63 (1969), 224–36.

Taft, William H., IV, 'Self-Defense and the Oil Platforms Decision', *The Yale Journal of International Law*, 29 (2004), 295–306.

Taft, William H. and Todd F. Buchwald, 'Preemption, Iraq, and International Law', *The American Journal of International Law*, 97 (2003), 557–63.

Talmon, Stefan, 'Determining Customary International Law: The ICJ's Methodology between Induction, Deduction and Assertion', *European Journal of International Law*, 26 (2015), 417–43.

Tansey, Oisín, 'Process Tracing and Elite Interviewing: A Case for Non-probability Sampling', *PS: Political Science and Politics*, 40:3 (October 2007), 765–72.

Thirlway, Hugh, 'Reflections on Lex Ferenda', *Netherlands Yearbook of International Law* 32 (2001), 3–26.

Topik, Steven C., 'When Mexico Had the Blues: A Transatlantic Tale of Bonds, Bankers, and Nationalists, 1862–1910', *American Historical Review*, 105:3 (June 2000), 714–40.

Tropman, Elizabeth, 'Non-inferential Moral Knowledge', *Acta Analytica*, 26 (2011), 355–66.

Tversky, Amos and Daniel Kahneman, 'Judgment under Uncertainty: Heuristics and Biases', *Science*, 185:4157 (1974), 1124–31.

Varzi, Achille, 'Supervaluationism and Its Logics', *Mind*, 116 (2007), 633–75.

Verdirame, Guglielmo, '"The Divided West": International Lawyers in Europe and America', *European Journal of International Law*, 18:3 (2007), 553–80.

Verdirame, Guglielmo, 'The "Sinews of Peace": International Law, Strategy, and the Prevention of War', *British Yearbook of International Law*, 77:1 (2006), 83–162.

Voyiakis, Emmanuel, 'Customary International Law and the Place of Normative Considerations', *The American Journal of Jurisprudence*, 55 (2010), 163–200.

Pierre Wack, 'Scenarios: Uncharted Waters Ahead', *Harvard Business Review*, 85516 (September 1985), 73–89.

Waltz, Kenneth N., 'The Politics of Peace', *International Studies Quarterly*, 11:3 (1967), 199–211.

Watts, Arthur, 'International Law and International Relations: United Kingdom Practice', *European Journal of International Law*, 2 (1991), 157–65.

Weber, Steven, Steven Bernstein, Richard Ned Lebow and Janice Gross Stein, 'God Gave Physics the Easy Problems: Adapting Social Science to an Unpredictable World', *European Journal of International Relations*, 6:1 (2000), 43–76.

Weil, Prosper, '"The Court Cannot Conclude Definitively . . . " Non Liquet Revisited', *Columbia Journal of Transnational Law*, 36 (1998), 109–19.

Wendt, Alexander, 'Anarchy Is What States Make of It: The Social Construction of Power Politics', *International Organization*, 46:2 (1992), 391–425.

White, Nigel D. and Eric P. J. Myjer, 'Editorial: The Use of Force against Iraq', *Journal of Conflict and Security Law*, 8:1 (2003), 1–14.

Whittemore, Luke A., 'Proportionality Decision Making in Targeting: Heuristics, Cognitive Biases, and the Law', *Harvard National Security Journal*, 7:2 (2016), 577–636.

Wilmshurst, Elizabeth, 'The Chatham House Principles of International Law on the Use of Force in Self-Defence', *International and Comparative Law Quarterly*, 55 (2006), 963–72.

Wilmshurst, Elizabeth, 'Disciplining the Discipline: Roles and Responsibilities of International Lawyers: Remarks', *Proceedings of the Annual Meeting (American Society of International Law)*, 100 (2006), 449–50.

Wood, Michael, 'The Law on the Use of Force: Current Challenges', *Singapore Yearbook of International Law*, 11 (2007), 1–14.

Wright, Daniel B., Amina Memon, Elin M. Skagerberg and Fiona Gabbert, 'When Eyewitnesses Talk', *Current Directions In Psychological Science*, 18:3 (2009), 174–8.

Yablon, Charles M., 'The Indeterminacy of the Law: Critical Legal Studies and the Problem of Legal Explanation', *Cardozo Law Review*, 6 (1985), 917–45.

Books

Akande, Dapo and Antonios Tzanakopoulos, 'The International Court of Justice and the Concept of Aggression', in Claus Kreß and Stefan Barriga, eds., *The Crime of Aggression: A Commentary* (Cambridge: Cambridge University Press, 2015), 214–32.

Ambrus, Mónika, Rosemary Rayfuse and Wouter Werner, 'Risk and International Law', in Mónika Ambrus, Rosemary Rayfuse, Wouter Werner, eds., *Risk and the Regulation of Uncertainty in International Law* (Oxford: Oxford University Press, 2017), 3–9.

Anderson, David, CMG, 'The Role of the International Lawyer in the Negotiation of Treaties', in Chanaka Wickremasinghe, ed., *The International Lawyer as Practitioner* (London: British Institute of International and Comparative Law, 2000), 21–40.

Aristotle (D. Ross, ed.), *The Nicomachean Ethics* (Oxford: Oxford University Press, 2009).

Armstrong, David, Theo Farrell and Helene Lambert, *International Law and International Relations*, 2nd ed. (Cambridge: Cambridge University Press, 2012).

Jeremy Bentham, 'A Fragment on Government', in J. H. Burns and H. L. A. Hart, eds., *A Comment on the Commentaries and A Fragment on Government* (Oxford: Clarendon Press, 2008).

Bentham, Jeremy and Etienne Dumont, *Treatise on Judicial Evidence* (London: JW Paget, 1825).

Berman, Franklin, 'Conclusion', in Andraz Zidar and Jean-Pierre Gauci, eds., *The Role of Legal Advisers in International Law* (Leiden: BRILL Nijhoff, 2016), 380–6.

Berman, Franklin, 'The International Lawyer, inside and outside Foreign Ministries', in C. Hill and P. Beshoff, eds., *Two Worlds of International Relations – Academics, Practitioners and the Trade in Ideas* (London: Routledge, 1994).

Berman, Franklin, 'The Role of the International Lawyer in the Making of Foreign Policy', in Chanaka Wickremasinghe, ed., *The International Lawyer as Practitioner* (London: British Institute of International and Comparative Law, 2000).

Besson, Samantha, 'Theorizing the Sources of International Law', in Samantha Besson and John Tasioulas, eds., *The Philosophy of International Law* (Oxford: Oxford University Press, 2010).

Bobbitt, Philip, *The Shield of Achilles: War, Peace and the Course of History* (London: Penguin, 2003).

Bowden, Mark, *The Finish: The Killing of Osama Bin Laden* (New York: Atlantic Monthly Press, 2012).

Bryman, Alan and James J Teevan, *Social Research Methods* (Oxford: Oxford University Press, 2005).

Buchanan, Allen, *Justice, Legitimacy, and Self-Determination: Moral Foundations for International Law* (Oxford: Oxford University Press, 2003).

Bull, Hedley, *The Anarchical Society* (London: MacMillan, 1977).

Burns, Robert, 'Epistle to a Young Friend', *Poems and Songs* (Edinburgh: William P Nimmo, 1868), 122–4.

Byers, Michael, *War Law: Understanding International Law and Armed Conflict*, Kindle ed. (New York: Grove Press, 2005).

'The Caroline Case', in Martin Dixon and Robert McCorquodale, eds., *Cases and Materials on International Law, 4th ed.* (Oxford: Oxford University Press, 2003).

Cassese, Antonio, *International Law* (Oxford: Oxford University Press, 2005).

Ceadel, Martin, *The Origins of War Prevention: The British Peace Movement and International Relations 1730–1854* (Oxford: Oxford University Press, 1996).

Chinkin, Christine, 'Rethinking Legality/Legitimacy after the Iraq War', in Richard Falk, Mark Juergensmeyer and Vesselin Popovski, *Legality and Legitimacy in Global Affairs* (Oxford: Oxford University Press, 2012), 219–47.

Cicero, Marcus Tullius, 'Pro Milone', in Albert Curtis Clark, ed., *Oxford Classical Texts: M. Tulli Ciceronis: Orationes, Vol. 2: Pro Milone; Pro Marcello; Pro Ligario; Pro Rege Deiotaro; Philippicae I–XIV* (Oxford: Oxford University Press, 1918).

von Clausewitz, Carl, *On War*, trans. and ed. Michael Howard, Peter Paret and Beatrice Heuser (Oxford: Oxford University Press, 2007).

Connelly, James and Don Carrick, 'Ethical and Legal Reasoning About War in a Time of Terror', in Aidan Hehir, Natasha Kuhrt and Andew Mumford, *International Law, Security and Ethics* (Abingdon: Routledge, 2011), 44–57.

Corten, Olivier, *The Law Against War: The Prohibition on the Use of Force in Contemporary International Law* (London: Hart Publishing, 2010).

Courtney, Hugh, *20/20 Foresight: Crafting Strategy in an Uncertain World* (Boston: Harvard Business School Press, 2001).

D'Amato, Anthony A., *The Concept of Custom in International Law* (Ithaca, NY: Cornell University Press, 1971).

Daniels, Norman, *Justice and Justification: Reflective Equilibrium in Theory and Practice* (Cambridge: Cambridge University Press, 1996).

Jack Davis, 'Introduction: Improving Intelligence Analysis at CIA: Dick Heuer's Contribution to Intelligence Analysis', in Richards J. Heuer, *Psychology of Intelligence Analysis* (Washington, DC: CIA, 1999), xx–xxi.

Dinstein, Yoram, *The Conduct of Hostilities under the Law of International Armed Conflict*, 2nd ed. (Cambridge: Cambridge University Press, 2010).

Dinstein, Yoram, *War, Aggression and Self-Defence* (Cambridge: Cambridge University Press, 2005).

Dorr, Oliver and Kirsten Schmalenbach, eds., *Vienna Convention on the Law of Treaties: A Commentary* (Heidelberg: Springer, 2012), 533–6.

Dworkin, Ronald, *Law's Empire* (Oxford: Hart Publishing, 1998).

Dworkin, Ronald, *A Matter of Principle* (Oxford: Oxford University Press, 1985).
Easton, David, *The Political System* (New York: Knopf, 1953).
Endicott, Timothy A., *Vagueness in Law* (Oxford: Oxford University Press, 2000).
Falk, Richard, 'Introduction: Legality and Legitimacy', in Richard Falk, Mark Juergensmeyer and Vesselin Popovski, eds., *Legality and Legitimacy in Global Affairs* (Oxford: Oxford University Press, 2012), 4–39.
Fazal, Tanisha M., *Wars of Law: Unintended Consequences in the Regulation of Armed Conflict* (Ithaca, NY: Cornell University Press, 2018).
Fisher, David, *Morality and War* (Oxford: Oxford University Press, 2011).
Franck, Thomas M., *Fairness in International Law and Institutions* (Oxford: Oxford University Press, 1998).
Freedman, Lawrence, *Strategy: A History* (Oxford: Oxford University Press, 2013).
Friedman, Lawrence, 'The Place of Legal Culture in the Sociology of Law', in Michael Freeman, ed., *Law and Sociology* (Oxford: Oxford University Press, 2006), 185–99.
Galligan, Denis J., 'Legal Theory and Empirical Research', in Peter Cane and Herbert Kritzer, eds., *The Oxford Handbook of Empirical Legal Research* (Oxford: Oxford University Press, 2010), 976–1001.
Gauci, Jean-Pierre and Kate Jones, 'Conference Report: The Role of Legal Advisers in International Law', in Andraz Zidar and Jean-Pierre Gauci, eds., *The Role of Legal Advisers in International Law* (Leiden: BRILL Nijhoff, 2016), 371–79.
Gow, James, *Defending the West* (Cambridge: Polity Press, 2005).
Gray, Christine, *International Law and the Use of Force* (Oxford: Oxford University Press, 2008).
Green, James A., *The International Court of Justice and Self-Defence in International Law* (Oxford and Portland: Hart Publishing, 2009).
Green, Leslie, *The Contemporary Law of Armed Conflict*, 3rd ed. (Manchester: Manchester University Press, 2008).
Green, Leslie, 'Introduction to the Third Edition', in H. L. A. Hart, *The Concept of Law*, 3rd ed. (Oxford: Oxford University Press, 2012), xv–lv.
Green, Leslie, 'Notes to the Third Edition', in H. L. A. Hart, *The Concept of Law*, 3rd ed. (Oxford: Oxford University Press, 2012), 309–27.
Harman, Gilbert and Judith J. Thomson, *Moral Relativism and Moral Objectivity* (Oxford: Blackwell, 1996).
Hart, H. L. A., *The Concept of Law*, 3rd ed. (Oxford: Oxford University Press, 2012).
Heuer, Richards J., *Psychology of Intelligence Analysis* (Washington, DC: CIA, 1999).
Higgins, Rosalyn, *Problems and Process: International Law and How We Use It* (Oxford: Clarendon Press, 1994).
Hoffmann-Lange, Ursula, 'Methods of Elite Research', in Russell J. Dalton and Hans-Dieter Klingemann, eds., *The Oxford Handbook of Political Behavior* (Oxford: Oxford University Press, 2007), 910–29.
Hoffmann-Lange, Ursula, 'Studying Elite versus Mass Opinion', in Wolfgang Donsbach and Michael W. Traugott, eds., *The SAGE Handbook of Public Opinion Research* (London: SAGE Publications Ltd, 2008), 53–63.
Howard, Michael, *War and the Liberal Conscience* (London: Hurst, 2008).
Human Security Report Project, *Human Security Report 2009/2010* (Oxford: Oxford University Press, 2011).

IICK, *Independent International Commission on Kosovo: The Kosovo Report* (Oxford: Oxford University Press, 2000).

International Commission on Intervention and State Sovereignty, *The Responsibility to Protect: Report of the International Commission on Intervention and State Sovereignty* (Ottawa: International Development Research Centre, 2001).

International Institute for Strategic Studies, *The Military Balance 2000* (Oxford: Oxford University Press, 2000).

Jack, Malcolm, ed., *Erskine May's Treatise on The Law, Privileges, Proceedings and Usage of Parliament* (London: LexisNexis, 2011).

Jennings, Robert, 'Introduction', in Chanaka Wickremasinghe, ed., *The International Lawyer as Practitioner* (London: British Institute of International and Comparative Law, 2000).

Jessop, Bob, *State Theory: Putting the Capitalist State in Its Place* (Cambridge: Polity Press, 1990).

Kahn, Herman, *On Escalation: Metaphors and Scenarios; with a New Introduction by Thomas Schelling* (Abingdon: Routledge, 2017).

Kahneman, Daniel, *Thinking Fast and Slow* (London: Penguin, 2011).

Kelsen, Hans, *Introduction to the Problems of Legal Theory* (Oxford: Clarendon Press, 1992).

Kelsen, Hans, *Principles of International Law*, 2nd ed., ed. R. W. Tucker (New York: Holt Rinehart and Winston, 1966).

Kennedy, Duncan, *Legal Reasoning: Collected Essays* (Aurora, CO: The Davies Group Publishers, 2008).

Keohane, Robert O., 'Political Authority after Intervention: Gradations in Sovereignty', in J. L. Holzgrefe and Robert O. Keohane, eds., *Humanitarian Intervention: Ethical, Legal and Political Dilemmas* (Cambridge: Cambridge University Press, 2003), 275–98.

King, Mervyn and John Kay, *Radical Uncertainty: Decision-Making for an Unknowable Future* (London: Little, Brown Book Group, 2020).

Koh, Harold Hongju, 'The Legal Adviser's Duty to Explain', in Andraz Zidar and Jean-Pierre Gauci, eds., *The Role of Legal Advisers in International Law* (Leiden: BRILL Nijhoff, 2016), 290–312.

Koskenniemi, Martti, *From Apology to Utopia* (Cambridge: Cambridge University Press, 2005).

Koskenniemi, Martti, *The Gentle Civiliser of Nations: The Rise and Fall of International Law, 1870–1960* (Cambridge: Cambridge University Press, 2001).

Krosnick, Jon A. and Stanley Presser, 'Question and Questionnaire Design', in *Handbook of Survey Research*, 2nd ed. (Bingley: Emerald Group, 2010), 263–314.

Lovell, Julia, *The Opium War: Drugs, Dreams and the Making of China* (London: Picador, 2012).

Lubell, Noam, 'The Problem of Imminence in an Uncertain World' in Marc Weller, ed., *The Oxford Handbook of the Use of Force in International Law* (Oxford: Oxford University Press, 2014).

McCormick, Roger, *Legal Risk in the Financial Markets*, 2nd ed. (Oxford: Oxford University Press, 2010).

McLaughlin, Rob, 'The Legal Regime Applicable to Use of Lethal Force When Operating under a United Nations Security Council Chapter VII Mandate

Authorising "All Necessary Means"', *Journal of Conflict & Security Law*, 12:3 (2008), 389–417.

Madison, James, 'Concerning the Difficulties of the Convention in Devising a Proper Form of Government', in *The Federalist*, ed. George W. Carey and James McClellan (Indianapolis: Liberty Fund, 2001), 179–85.

Malanczuk, Peter, *Akehurst's Modern Introduction to International Law*, Kindle ed. (New York: Routledge, 1997).

Marxsen, Christian, 'A Note on Indeterminacy of the Law on Self-Defence Against Non-State Actors', *Self-Defence Against Non-State Actors: Impulses from the Max Planck Trialogues on the Law of Peace and War*, MPIL Research Paper Series No. 2017–07 (Heidelberg: Max Planck Institute, 2017), 79–81.

Merrills, Gerald, *Judge Sir Gerald Fitzmaurice and the Discipline of International Law: Opinions on the International Court of Justice, 1961–1973* (The Hague: Kluwer Law International, 1998).

Milanovic, Marko, 'Accounting for the Complexity of the Law Applicable to Modern Armed Conflicts', in Michael N. Schmitt, Shane R. Reeves, Christopher M. Ford, Winston S. Williams, eds., *Complex Battlespaces: The Law of Armed Conflict and the Dynamics of Modern Warfare* (Oxford: Oxford University Press, 2019), 33–59.

Milton, John, *Paradise Lost* (Oxford: Oxford University Press, 2005), bk 2., 329–35.

Moir, Lindsay, *Reappraising the Resort to Force: International law, Jus ad Bellum and the War on Terror* (London: Bloomsbury Publishing, 2010).

More, Thomas, *Utopia*, eBook ed., H. Morley, ed. (The Project Gutenberg, 2005).

Morgenthau, Hans J., *Politics among Nations: The Struggle for Power and Peace* (New York: McGraw-Hill, 2006).

Mullerson, Rein, *Ordering Anarchy: International Law in International Society* (Dordrecht: Martinus Nijhoff, 2000).

Nelken, David, 'Rethinking Legal Culture', in Michael Freeman, ed., *Law and Sociology* (Oxford: Oxford University Press, 2005), 200–24.

Norman, Richard, *Ethics, Killing and War* (Cambridge: Cambridge University Press, 1995).

Orend, Brian, *The Morality of War* (Peterborough, Ontario: Broadview Press, 2006).

Peters, Anne and Christian Marxsen, 'Editors' Introduction: Self-Defence in Times of Transition', *Self-Defence Against Non-State Actors: Impulses from the Max Planck Trialogues on the Law of Peace and War*, MPIL Research Paper Series No. 2017–07 (Heidelberg: Max Planck Institute, 2017), 3–13.

Pherson, Randolph H. and Richards J. Heuer, Jr, *Structured Analytic Techniques for Intelligence Analysis*, 3rd ed. (Los Angeles: SAGE Publications, 2021).

Plato, *The Republic*, 2nd ed., trans. A. Bloom (New York: Basic Books, 1991).

Rawls, John, *The Law of Peoples* (Cambridge, MA: Harvard University Press, 2001).

Rawls, John, *A Theory of Justice* (Cambridge, MA: Harvard University Press, 1999).

Raz, Joseph, 'Legal Principles and the Limits of Law', in Marshall Cohen, ed., *Ronald Dworkin and Contemporary Jurisprudence* (London: Duckworth, 1983).

Raz, Joseph, 'Two Views of the Nature of the Theory of Law A Partial Comparison', in Jules L. Coleman, ed., *Hart's Postscript: Essays on the Postscript to 'The Concept of Law'* (Oxford: Oxford University Press, 2001), 1–37.

Riddell, Anna and Brendan Plant, *Evidence before the International Court of Justice*, (London: British Institute of International and Comparative Law, 2009).

Roberts, Anthea, *Is International Law International?* (Oxford: Oxford University Press, 2017).

Rothstein, Bo, 'Political Institutions: An Overview', in Robert E. Goodin and Hans-Dieter Klingemann, eds., *A New Handbook of Political Science* (Oxford: Oxford University Press, 1998), 133–61.

Rumi, Jalal al-Din, *The Masnavi, Book Three* (Oxford: Oxford University Press, 2013).

Ruys, Tom, *Armed Attack and Article 51 of the UN Charter* (Cambridge: Cambridge University Press, 2010).

Sarvarian, Arman, *Professional Ethics at the International Bar* (Oxford: Oxford University Press, 2013).

Schachter, Oscar, *International Law in Theory and Practice* (Dordrecht: Martinus Nijhoff, 1991).

Shaw, Malcolm, *International Law*, 6th ed. (Cambridge: Cambridge University Press, 2008).

Soames, Scott, 'What Vagueness and Inconsistency Tell Us about Interpretation', in Andrei Marmor and Scott Soames, eds., *Philosophical Foundations of Language in the Law* (Oxford: Oxford University Press, 2011), 31–57.

Shapiro, Scott, 'What Is the Rule of Recognition (And Does It Exist)', in Matthew Adler and Keneth E. Himma, eds., *The Rule of Recognition and the U.S. Constitution* (Oxford: Oxford University Press, 2009), 235–68.

Smartt, Ursula, *Media and Entertainment Law* (Abingdon: Routledge, 2011).

Tebbit, Mark, *Philosophy of Law: An Introduction*, 2nd ed. (London: Routledge, 2005).

Tetlock, Philip, *Expert Political Judgement* (Princeton: Princeton University Press, 2005).

Tetlock, Philip and Dan Gardner, *Superforecasting: The Art and Science of Prediction*, Kindle ed. (London: Random House, 2015).

Tsagourias, Nicholas, 'Risk and the Use of Force', in Mónika Ambrus, Rosemary Rayfuse and Wouter Werner, eds., *Risk and Uncertainty in International Law* (Oxford: Oxford University Press, 2017).

Waibel, Michael, 'Interpretive Communities in International Law', in Andrea Bianchi, Daniel Peat, Matthew Windsor, eds., *Interpretation in International Law* (Oxford: Oxford University Press, 2015).

Waltz, Kenneth N., *Theory of International Politics* (New York: Random House, 1979).

Walzer, Michael, *Arguing about War* (New Haven, CT: Yale University Press, 2004).

Walzer, Michael, *Just and Unjust Wars: A Moral Argument with Historical Illustrations*, 3rd ed. (New York: Basic Books, 2000).

Weingast, Barry R., 'Political Institutions: Rational Choice Perspectives', in Robert E. Goodin and Hans-Dieter Klingemann, eds., *A New Handbook of Political Science* (Oxford: Oxford University Press, 1998), 167–85.

Weisburd, Mark, 'Use of Force: Justiciability and Admissibility', in Marc Weller, ed., *The Oxford Handbook of the Use of Force in International Law* (Oxford: Oxford University Press, 2014), 329–46.

Whalley, Matthew and Chris Guzelian, *The Legal Risk Management Handbook: An International Guide to Protect Your Business from Legal Loss* (London: Kogan Page, 2016).

Wheeler, Nicholas, *Saving Strangers* (Oxford: Oxford University Press, 2002).

Wickremasinghe, Chanaka, 'Preface', in Chanaka Wickremasinghe, ed., *The International Lawyer as Practitioner* (London: British Institute of International and Comparative Law, 2000), xvii–xx.

Williamson, Timothy, 'Vagueness in Reality', in Michael J. Loux and Dean W. Zimmermann, eds., *The Oxford Handbook of Metaphysics* (Oxford: Oxford University Press, 2009).

Zacklin, Ralph, 'The Role of the International Lawyer in an International Organisation', in Chanaka Wickremasinghe, ed., *The International Lawyer as Practitioner* (London: British Institute of International and Comparative Law, 2000).

Zidar, Andraž, 'Legal Advisers and Professional Ethics' in Andraz Zidar and Jean-Pierre Gauci, eds., *The Role of Legal Advisers in International Law* (Leiden: BRILL Nijhoff, 2016).

Internet Resources

Akande, Dapo, 'The International Criminal Court Gets Jurisdiction over the Crime of Aggression', *EJIL: Talk!* (15 December 2017), www.ejiltalk.org/the-international-criminal-court-gets-jurisdiction-over-the-crime-of-aggression.

Akande, Dapo, 'The Use of Nerve Agents in Salisbury: Why Does It Matter Whether It Amounts to a Use of Force in International Law?', *EJIL: Talk!* (17 March 2018), www.ejiltalk.org/the-use-of-nerve-agents-in-salisbury-why-does-it-matter-whether-it-amounts-to-a-use-of-force-in-international-law/.

Bodansky, Daniel, 'Non Liquet', *Max Planck Encyclopedia of Public International Law* (Oxford: Oxford University Press, 2006), http://opil.ouplaw.com/view/10.1093/law:epil/9780199231690/law-9780199231690-e1669?prd=EPIL.

Borger, Julian and Stuart Miller, 'How "Shy Foreigners" Learned to Pilot Flying-Bomb Boeings', *The Guardian* (14 September 2001), www.theguardian.com/world/2001/sep/14/september11.usa18.

Brandewinder, Mathias, PowerScatterPlot, Copyright © 2009, Clear Lines Consulting, LLC, www.clear-lines.com/blog/post/Excel-ScatterPlot-with-labels-colors-and-markers.aspx.

Brown, Derek, 'Timeline: Terror and Its Aftermath (Part 1)', *The Guardian* (5 October 2001), www.theguardian.com/world/2001/sep/11/september11.usa24.

Chambers and Partners, 'Public International Law Firms in London', www.chambersandpartners.com/11814/96/editorial/1/1.

CIA, *A Tradecraft Primer: Structured Analytic Techniques for Improving Intelligence Analysis* (4 May 2009), www.cia.gov/library/center-for-the-study-of-intelligence/csi-publications/books-and-monographs/Tradecraft%20Primer-apr09.pdf.

Deeks, Ashley S., 'Pakistan's Sovereignty and the Killing of Osama Bin Laden', *ASIL Insights*, 15:11 (2011), www.asil.org/insights/volume/15/issue/11/pakistans-sovereignty-land-killing-osama-bin-laden.

Edelstein, D. M., 'Why Realists Don't Go for Bombs and Bullets', *ForeignPolicy.Com* (21 July 2010), http://walt.foreignpolicy.com/posts/2010/07/20/why_realists_don_t_go_for_bombs_and_bullets.

Egan, Brian, US State Department Legal Adviser, 'International Law, Legal Diplomacy, and the Counter-ISIL Campaign', *American Society of International Law* (4 April 2016), www.justsecurity.org/wp-content/uploads/2016/04/Egan-ASIL-speech.pdf.

France24, 'France Stands Firm on Syria despite Shock UK Vote', *France 24* (30 August 2013), www.france24.com/en/20130830-france-hollande-syria-usa-uk-vote-francois.

Gannon, Kathy, 'Bush Rejects Taliban Bin Laden Offer', *Washington Post* (14 October 2001), www.washingtonpost.com/wp-srv/aponline/20011014/aponline135016_000.htm.

Gillespie, Mark and Robert Manchin, 'Kosovo Air Strikes Receive Support in Britain, Hungary', *Gallup News Service* (30 March 1999), https://news.gallup.com/poll/3967/kosovo-air-strikes-receive-support-britain-hungary.aspx.

Koh, Harold, 'Syria and the Law of Humanitarian Intervention (Part II: International Law and the Way Forward)', *JustSecurity* (2 October 2013), http://justsecurity.org/2013/10/02/koh-syria-part2/.

Ipsos MORI, 'War in Afghanistan Poll', *Ipsos MORI* (4 November 2001), www.ipsos.com/ipsos-mori/en-uk/war-afghanistan-poll-1

ISO 31000:2009(en), 'Risk Management – Principles and Guidelines', www.iso.org/obp/ui/#iso:std:iso:31000:ed-1:v1:en.

ISO/Guide 73:2009(en), 'Risk Management – Vocabulary', www.iso.org/obp/ui/#iso:std:iso:guide:73:ed-1:v1:en.

Journal of Conflict and Security Law, https://academic.oup.com/jcsl/pages/Editorial_Board.

Journal on the Use of Force and International Law, www.tandfonline.com/action/journalInformation?show=editorialBoard&journalCode=rjuf20.

Kent, Sherman, 'Words of Estimative Probability', *Sherman Kent and the Board of National Estimates: Collected Essays*, CIA (19 March 2007), www.cia.gov/library/center-for-the-study-of-intelligence/csi-publications/books-and-monographs/sherman-kent-and-the-board-of-national-estimates-collected-essays/6words.html.

Laville, Sandra, 'Mercy Killing Mother Cleared of Murder after Helping Seriously Ill Daughter Die', *The Guardian* (25 January 2010), www.guardian.co.uk/uk/2010/jan/25/mercy-killing-kay-gilderdale-cleared.

Mahler, Tobias, Presentation, www.industrijuristgruppen.no/dokumenter/pres12/tobias_mahler.pptx.

Milanovic, Marko, 'Self-Defense and Non-State Actors: Indeterminacy and the Jus ad Bellum', *EJIL: Talk!* (21 February 2010), www.ejiltalk.org/self-defense-and-non-state-actors-indeterminacy-and-the-jus-ad-bellum/.

Nessa, Jasmin Johurun, 'Self-Defense in International Law: What Level of Evidence?', *Just Security* (8 July 2019), www.justsecurity.org/64796/self-defense-in-international-law-what-level-of-evidence.

Non-Aligned Movement, 'Final Communique of the Meeting of Ministers for Foreign Affairs and Heads of Delegation of the Non-Aligned Movement, held in New York on 23 September 1999', www.nam.gov.za/minmeet/newyorkcom.htm.

Organisation for Security and Cooperation in Europe, 'OSCE Kosovo Verification Mission/OSCE Task Force for Kosovo (Closed)', www.osce.org/kvm-closed

Russell Group Universities, http://russellgroup.ac.uk/about/our-universities/.

Savage, Charlie, 'Obama Tests Limits of Power in Syria Conflict', *The New York Times* (8 September 2013), www.nytimes.com/2013/09/09/world/middleeast/obama-tests-limits-of-power-in-syrian-conflict.html?pagewanted=all&_r=0.

Urban, Mark, 'A Fork in the Road for UK Foreign Policy', *BBC News* (29 August 2013), www.bbc.co.uk/news/uk-23885524.

Stop the War Coalition, 'Constitution', www.stopwar.org.uk/constitution.

UN, 'United Nations Peacekeeping', UN Website (https://peacekeeping.un.org/en).

'US Rejects Taliban Concession', *The Guardian* (20 September 2001), www.theguardian.com/world/2001/sep/20/september11.usa11.

Valtorta, Marco, et al., 'Extending Heuer's Analysis of Competing Hypotheses Method to Support Complex Decision Analysis' (February 10, 2005), Center for Information Technology, http://citeseerx.ist.psu.edu/viewdoc/download?doi=10.1.1.122.3422&rep=rep1&type=pdf.

Verdirame, Guglielmo, 'The Law and Strategy of Humanitarian Intervention', *EJIL: Talk!* (30 August 2013), www.ejiltalk.org/the-law-and-strategy-of-humanitarian-intervention/.

Voice of America, 'Mullah Omar – In His Own Words', *The Guardian* (26 September 2001), www.theguardian.com/world/2001/sep/26/afghanistan.features11.

Wisehart, Daniel, 'The Crisis in Ukraine and the Prohibition of the Use of Force: A Legal Basis for Russia's Intervention?', *EJIL: Talk!* (4 March 2014), www.ejiltalk.org/the-crisis-in-ukraine-and-the-prohibition-of-the-use-of-force-a-legal-basis-for-russias-intervention/.

Wood, Michael, 'Legal Advisers', Max Planck Encyclopedia of Public International Law (May 2013), http://opil.ouplaw.com/view/10.1093/law:epil/9780199231690/law-9780199231690-e1064?prd=EPIL.

Images

Explosion Image by Oceloti, from Vectorstock.

Island generated using *Polygon Map Generator* by Amit Patel, Red Blob Games, www.redblobgames.com/maps/mapgen2/.

Predator Type Drone image by boscorelli3D, from 3DExport.com.

Sea Dart Missile image by Hristov, from 3DExport.com.

Index